D0875980

A Commentary on the Complete Poems of
GERARD MANLEY HOPKINS

DISCARDED

A Commentary on the Complete Poems of

GERARD MANLEY HOPKINS

∽

PAUL L. MARIANI

Cornell University Press ∽ *Ithaca and London*

Standard Book Number 8014-0553-x
Library of Congress Catalog Card Number 74-105909

PRINTED IN THE UNITED STATES OF AMERICA
BY KINGSPORT PRESS, INC.

To my parents,
  for "Those years and years,"

to Eileen,
  "wife / To my creating thought,"

and to Allen,
  "Of realty the rarest-veinèd unraveller."

✌ Acknowledgments

I am indebted to many people, to those I have spoken with and to those I know only through correspondence and by their articles and books; many of these latter are acknowledged in the notes. There are, especially, the late W. H. Gardner and Norman H. MacKenzie, the editors of the Fourth Edition of *The Poems of Gerard Manley Hopkins* (1967). Among the critics to whom I owe a note of special gratitude are John Pick for his 1942 classic on Hopkins as poet and priest, Elizabeth Schneider for her *PMLA* articles (her fine *The Dragon in the Gate* arrived too late to do more for this commentary than simply supply me with a footnote), J. Hillis Miller for his brilliant phenomenological reading of Hopkins (even though I question some of his emphases), and David Downes for the first half of his chapter on "Temper and Inscape" tucked away in *Victorian Portraits*. With Downes and Schneider I had that rare sensation that I was myself writing what I was reading, so fully did I agree with much of what they said.

I owe special thanks to Professor Pick for publishing my first article on Hopkins and for reading a second, and to Professor MacKenzie for his kind answers to certain queries; to the Reverend Charles J. Horan, P.P., a parish priest at Bedford Leigh, who painstakingly checked the local records for the name Felix Randal; to the Reverend Anthony Bischoff, S.J., for answering queries about Hopkins' life; and to the Reverend Peter Hebblethwaite, S.J., editor of *The*

Month, for help on a number of Hopkins matters. I also owe a note of thanks to several Jesuits of the Irish and English provinces for their kindness and hospitality when I was doing research in Dublin and Oxford in the summer of 1968: Fr. Fitzgibbon, S.J., Librarian at Campion Hall, Oxford; Fr. Diviney, S.J., of Clongowes Wood College; Fr. Troddyn, S.J., at Lower Leeson Street, Dublin; and Mr. Brendon Duddy, S.J., at Miltown, Dublin. Thanks are also due to the librarians at the Bodleian Library, Oxford; to a number of my students for their perceptive comments on some of Hopkins' poems; and to Mrs. Victor Bert and Mrs. John Weston for their patient typing of the manuscript at various stages of revision.

I owe a particular note of gratitude to three teachers of mine who read an earlier version of the manuscript: Marvin Magalaner, Wendell Stacy Johnson, and Allen Mandelbaum, my adviser and friend, to whom this book is dedicated. Finally, it is also dedicated to my parents and to my wife, Eileen, who, while taking care of one, two, and then three small boys, has read, typed, checked, and retyped this manuscript more times than either of us wishes to remember.

My readings, in largely different versions now, of *Felix Randal, The shepherd's brow,* and *Harry Ploughman* were originally published in, respectively, *Renascence, Victorian Poetry,* and *The Month,* and are here reprinted with permission. All quotations from Hopkins' poems are from the Fourth Edition of the *Poems* (Oxford University Press), edited by W. H. Gardner and Norman H. MacKenzie.

The City University of New York generously afforded me a research fellowship for study abroad; the University of Massachusetts kindly awarded me a grant-in-aid to cover the costs of retyping the manuscript.

P. M.

The University of Massachusetts
January 1970

∽ Contents

∽ A Hopkins Chronology

1844   July 28: Born at Stratford, Essex, to Manley Hopkins, marine insurance adjustor, author, and sometime poet, and the former Catherine Smith. Baptized into the Church of England. Oldest of nine children.

1852   Family moves to Hampstead.

1854–1863   Attends Cholmondeley Grammar School, Highgate.

1857   Tours Germany.

1860   Easter: Writes *The Escorial.*
Tours Southern Germany.

1862   Christmas: Writes *A Vision of the Mermaids.*

1863   April: Goes up to Balliol College, Oxford, having won an exhibition scholarship. Tutors include Walter Pater.

1864–1865   Writes most of his early poems.

1866   July 17: After a spiritual struggle, decides to become a Roman Catholic. Poetry trickles to a halt.
September 20: Talks with John Henry Newman at the Oratory in Birmingham about converting.
October 21: Received by Newman into the Catholic Church.

1867   June: Considered by Jowett to be the "Star of Balliol" for his classical scholarship, Hopkins graduates from Oxford with a double-first in "Greats."
September to following Easter: Teaches classics at Newman's Oratory.

1868   May 2: Resolves to become a priest, but doubtful whether as a Benedictine or Jesuit.

May 11: Burns finished copies of all his poems in his possession—his "innocents"—as interfering with his new vocation.

July: Vacations in Switzerland.

September 7: Enters the Jesuit Novitiate at Manresa House, Roehampton.

1870   September: Begins philosophy studies at St. Mary's Hall, Stonyhurst, Lancashire.

1871   August: Writes "Red Letter" to Robert Bridges, his Oxford classmate and closest friend, and is answered by a thirty-month silence in their correspondence.

1872   August: Discovers the writings of Duns Scotus, whose work influences him and in fact alters his future.

1873   September: Teaches rhetoric at Roehampton for one year; writes extensive notes on prosody.

1874   January: Correspondence with Bridges renewed, tenuously.

August: Begins three years of study in theology at St. Beuno's, North Wales.

1875   December: Begins *The Wreck of the Deutschland* after a seven-year silence.

1876   June: *The Deutschland* is sent to the Jesuit periodical *The Month,* but is eventually rejected.

1877   February–September: Composes ten sonnets, including *The Windhover.*

September 23: Ordained a Jesuit priest.

October: Sent as parish assistant and teacher to Mount St. Mary's College, Chesterfield.

1878   April: Composes *The Loss of the Eurydice,* which is also rejected by *The Month.* Gives up ideas of publishing.

April–July: Tutors classics to students at Stonyhurst College.

June: Begins correspondence with Canon Richard Watson Dixon, poet and historian.

July–November: Serves as curate at Mount Street, London.

December: Begins duties as curate at St. Aloysius' Church, Oxford.

1879   February–October: Composes nine poems at Oxford; sees little of the University except for Walter Pater. Interest in music begins.

October–December: Curate at St. Joseph's, Bedford Leigh.

December 30: Sent as select preacher to St. Francis Xavier's, Liverpool, where he works largely among Irish immigrants for twenty months. Composes only three lyrics during this period.

1881   September: Leaves Liverpool to fill in as assistant in Glasgow parish.

October: Begins tertianship (the long retreat) at Roehampton. Composes no poetry by choice during these ten months, channeling energies into writing his spiritual commentary on the *Exercises*.

1882   September: Begins duties as teacher of classics at Stonyhurst College.

October: Writes *The Leaden Echo and the Golden Echo.*

1883   July: Meets the sixty-year-old Coventry Patmore, then England's renowned Catholic poet, at Stonyhurst College; begins correspondence, which deals largely with Hopkins' readings of Patmore's poetry.

August: Goes to Holland to meet sister.

1884   February: Appointed Fellow of University College, Dublin; begins duties as lecturer in Latin and examiner in Greek, which last until his death.

March: Patmore reads Hopkins' poetry; reaction is unsympathetic.

July: Travels over Ireland on holiday.

1885   Writes the desolate sonnets; undergoes an experience similar to a "dark night of the soul."

August: On holiday in England.

1886   March–April: Heavy correspondence with A. W. M. Baillie—his close friend at Balliol, lawyer, and student of Egyptian language—on Greek-Egyptian cultural contacts.

May: On holiday in England; sees Bridges.

September: On holiday in North Wales; works on *St. Winefred's Well.*

November: Meets Kate Tynan, Irish poetess, John Yeats, and young William Butler Yeats; dislikes Yeats' *Mosada.*

1887   August: On holiday to England and to parents' new home at Haslemere.

September: *Harry Ploughman* and *Tom's Garland.*

1888   April [?]: *Epithalamion* fragment.

July: *That Nature is a Heraclitean Fire.*

August: On holiday to Scotland; health begins to deteriorate.

1889   January: Final retreat at Tullabeg.

March 17–April 22: last sonnets.

June 8: Dies at forty-four of typhoid fever, complicated by enteric fever; buried in the Jesuit plot at Glasnevin, Dublin. Bridges assumes custodianship of Hopkins' poetry.

1918   January: *The Poems of Gerard Manley Hopkins* published twenty-nine years after his death, with introduction and notes by Robert Bridges.

ᴄᴏ Abbreviations

Journals   *The Journals and Papers of Gerard Manley Hopkins.* Ed. Humphry House, completed by Graham Storey. London: Oxford University Press, 1959.

Letters I   *The Letters of Gerard Manley Hopkins to Robert Bridges.* Ed. Claude Colleer Abbott. Second edition. London: Oxford University Press, 1955.

Letters II   *The Correspondence of Gerard Manley Hopkins and Richard Watson Dixon.* Ed. Claude Colleer Abbott. Second edition. London: Oxford University Press, 1955.

Letters III   *Further Letters of Gerard Manley Hopkins: Including His Correspondence with Coventry Patmore.* Ed. Claude Colleer Abbott. Second edition. London: Oxford University Press, 1956.

Sermons   *The Sermons and Devotional Writings of Gerard Manley Hopkins.* Ed. Christopher Devlin, S.J. London: Oxford University Press, 1959.

Poems   *The Poems of Gerard Manley Hopkins.* Ed. W. H. Gardner and N. H. MacKenzie. Fourth edition. London: Oxford University Press, 1967. Numbers in parentheses in the *Commentary* refer to the numbering of the poems in this edition.

Boyle   Robert Boyle, S.J. *Metaphor in Hopkins.* Chapel Hill: University of North Carolina Press, 1961.

Gardner   W. H. Gardner. *Gerard Manley Hopkins (1844–1889) : A Study of Poetic Idiosyncrasy in Relation to Poetic Tradition.* 2 vols. Second edition. London and New York: Oxford University Press, 1958.

Ritz   Jean-Georges Ritz. *Le Poète Gérard Manley Hopkins, S.J.: L'homme et l'œuvre.* Paris: Didier, 1963.

᪥ Introduction

This commentary began, as most things do, modestly enough. It grew out of a single fine delight, an insight into the play on the name "Felix Randal" which John Fandel dropped like a seed during a creative writing class at Manhattan College back in the spring of 1962. That seed remained dormant for nearly five years, until, in the late fall of 1966, I wrote an article on *Felix Randal,* which was based in part on that insight and which John Pick accepted for publication in *Renascence.* I spent most of the following year writing my dissertation on Hopkins' sonnets and preparing two more articles on Hopkins for publication. When I began teaching modern poetry, and having ideas of publishing a book on Hopkins, it came home to me that what I had all along been working toward was, really, a commentary on the entire body of Hopkins' poetry.

This book, therefore, has come to include every complete poem and nearly every fragment that we know Hopkins to have written in English. True, there are a number of discarded lines and a few very short fragments, suspended like grubs in amber among some of Hopkins' manuscripts, that I have not mentioned. The Latin, Greek, and Welsh pieces have been given adequate glosses in the notes to the *Poems* and are only casually mentioned here. But it is fair to say that my commentary treats the complete poems.

While, certainly, I have attended to matters of scholarship, I have endeavored to keep the commentary interesting by remembering always that this is also in part a dramatic record of a man (and a priest) caught up in a dialogue with God about the things of God. I have, of course, read nearly everything in the corpus of Hopkins criticism, and my notes acknowledge my debt to the leads and interpretations of others. But in a number of places, as in my readings of *Felix Randal, Duns Scotus's Oxford, Andromeda,* and *The shepherd's brow,* for example, I have had to follow my own leads and present what to some may seem idiosyncratic readings. But this is because these are idiosyncratic poems, and, as Hopkins himself admitted, one sometimes has to squint a little if he is to see the poems from Hopkins' perspective.

Readers who have been unable to squint properly and who have thus encountered difficulty in understanding Hopkins' poetry are in good company, for the charges of obscurity are old. In the months after he met Hopkins, Coventry Patmore wrestled with a number of the Jesuit's poems. But, as much as Patmore admired the man, he could not reconcile himself to his poetry. What he says has since been echoed by many:

> It seems to me that the thought and feeling of these poems, if expressed without any obscuring novelty of mode, are such as often to require the whole attention to apprehend and digest them; and are therefore of a kind to appeal only to a few. But to the already sufficiently arduous character of such poetry you seem to me to have added the difficulty of following *several* entirely novel and simultaneous experiments in versification and construction, together with an altogether unprecedented system of alliteration and compound words—any one of which novelties would be startling and productive of distraction from the poetic matter to be expressed.[1]

Patmore covered nearly everything in his critique: Hopkins' ideas were difficult enough to understand without adding to them novelties of rhythm, compound rhyming, tor-

---

[1] *Letters III,* p. 355.

tuous syntax, complex alliteration, and multiple epithets. This is surprising criticism from a poet as skilled as Patmore; it commits the fallacy of separating matter and form, as if Hopkins could have made the same statements in prose. Hopkins, of course, knew better. But Patmore's emphasis on his obscurity of thought is interesting, for Hopkins always chafed at this accusation.

In November 1887, for example, after learning that Bridges had found one of his poems incomprehensible (*Harry Ploughman*), Hopkins told Bridges that he thought surely the poem was intelligible by itself. But he added that he had decided to prefix "short prose *arguments*" to some of his pieces. Some genres—epic, drama, the ballad—demand, he felt, immediate intelligibility. But the lyric does not. And, in fact, given certain priorities, there would be times when a lyric could not be intelligible on first reading. "Plainly," he insisted, "if it is possible to express a sub[t]le and recondite subject in a subtle and recondite way and with great felicity and perfection, in the end, something must be sacrificed, with so trying a task, . . . and this may be the being at once, nay perhaps even the being without explanation at all, intelligible." Furthermore, the prose argument could very well be longer than the poem itself, since economy, "terseness," is a poetic good. A good poem is constructed along the lines of a masterful chess play: "It is like a mate which may be given, one way only, in three moves; otherwise, various ways, in many." [2]

In one sense, what this commentary has set out to do is to provide prose arguments—and most of them are longer than the poems themselves—for the corpus of Hopkins' English poems. This means that every complete poem and nearly every fragment, including the large body of poems and fragments which Hopkins wrote before he became a Jesuit (and which every commentator has insufficiently attended to), is

[2] *Letters I,* p. 266.

here placed in its chronological context, insofar as this can be determined, and treated in a manner commensurate with its importance to the canon. And *explication de texte* still seems to offer the greatest yield in understanding that canon. As brilliant as J. Hillis Miller's phenomenological approach is [3]—and he has brought us closer to some aspects of the mind of Hopkins than critics using more conventional formal analyses—there are nevertheless certain inherent shortcomings in a method which atomizes the poems for their paraphrasable content and then fuses them together into a new whole. What Miller gives us is a dramatic analogue for Hopkins' thought. His method creates a good imitation of Hopkins in terms of psychic drama, and it is largely a convincing one, but it has one major flaw: Hopkins is made to fit a preconceived pantheon of nineteenth-century writers who all experienced a crisis of faith. And the missing fragments in a psychogenetic mosaic of a poet and thinker as active and as complex as Hopkins are all supplied by pieces stamped by Miller.

Since all of Hopkins' prose remains do not add up to anything like a complete portrait of the man, this study focuses on the poems not primarily as documents, but as works of art. My own assumption is that such a distinction is substantive and not accidental. Of course, I am interested in the genie in the urn, as Fr. Walter Ong, S.J., puts it, but first of all because the genie has made the urn. I should, however, like to stress early one point which explains a great deal about this particular genius in the poems. For all of his anguish in feeling himself "idle a being but by where wars are rife," Hopkins was very much still in the act of making himself, of becoming, more Christlike. Twenty-five years ago, Robert Lowell expressed the thought this way:

When we examine Pope, Wordsworth, Coleridge, Arnold, or Browning, I think we realize that after a certain point all these

[3] "Gerard Manley Hopkins," in *The Disappearance of God: Five Nineteenth-Century Writers* (Cambridge, Mass., 1965).

men—all of them great writers at times and highly religious in
their fashion—stopped living; they began to reflect, to imagine,
to moralize: some single faculty kept on moving and fanning the
air, but the whole-man had stopped. Consequently, in their writings they mused, they fabled, they preached, they schemed and
they damned. Hopkins is substantially dramatic (*in act* according to the language of scholastic philosophy) .

Now to be thoroughly *in act* is human perfection, in other
words, it is to be *thoroughly made*. According to Catholic theology perfection demands a substantial transformation which is
called first sanctifying grace and then beatitude, it involves the
mysterious co-working of grace and free-will. . . . [For] Hopkins,
life was a continuous substantial progress toward perfection. He
believed this, he lived this, this is what he wrote.[4]

Whatever desolation and isolation Hopkins experienced
at the end of his short life (he died at forty-four) , one thing
is clear: he was growing steadily closer to the condition of
sainthood. In the long view, *that* is the most important fact
about the man Hopkins beside which every other fact about
him becomes ancillary, including his poetry. Hopkins himself
put the emphasis in exactly the same place in a letter to
Bridges. Speaking about manners in a "gentleman," Hopkins moved toward the basic question of virtue. There is, he
insisted, a

chastity of mind which seems to lie at the very heart and be the
parent of all other good, the seeing at once what is best, the holding to that, and the not allowing anything else whatever to be
even heard pleading to the contrary. Christ's life and character
are such as appeal to all the world's admiration, but there is one
insight St. Paul gives us of it which is very secret and seems to
me more touching and constraining than everything else is: . . .
[Christ] finding, as in the first instant of his incarnation he did,
his human nature informed by the godhead . . . thought it nevertheless no snatching-matter . . . to be equal with God, but an-

---

[4] "Hopkins' Sanctity," in *Gerard Manley Hopkins*, by the Kenyon
Critics (Norfolk, Conn., 1945) , pp. 89–93.

nihilated himself, taking the form of servant; . . . he emptied or exhausted himself[,] so far as that was possible, of godhead and behaved only as God's slave, as his creature . . . and . . . humbled himself to death, the death of the cross. It is this holding of himself back, and not snatching at the truest and highest good, the good that was his right, . . . his own being and self, which seems to me the root of all his holiness and the imitation of this the root of all moral good in other men.[5]

It is this holding back on Hopkins' part, this attempt to forcefully empty himself of himself in imitation of Christ, this constant struggle to *become* more like Christ, that explains Hopkins' actions, including the creation of his poetry.

Much of Hopkins' development is not charted in his poetry, but a careful reading of the poems reveals changes in style and in tone which have their counterpart in the man himself. So, while the readings in this commentary are in one sense independent of each other, the book as a whole endeavors to unfold and reveal, in a real sense, part of a man's life. Living with his poetry convinces me that, wherever Hopkins was at the end of his life, he was not, as Miller says, "in a situation strangely like that recorded in his early poems—a situation of abandonment and impotent suffering." [6] That is not what a close analytical reading of the last sonnets tells us.

Of course I have used all of what we have of Hopkins' prose as an aid in understanding the poetry, and I have focused on relevant passages which seem to reflect his concerns in the poems themselves. In commenting on the poetry, I have made every attempt to let Hopkins speak for himself, to let him, at least in part, append prose arguments to his poems. The primary justification for this commentary, then, has been to unravel Hopkins' meaning. A number of things become clear in a reading of the poetry. Hopkins' poems often assume the tripartite structure of the *Spiritual Exer-*

[5] Letter of February 3, 1883, *Letters I,* pp. 174–175.
[6] Miller, *op. cit.,* p. 352.

cises of St. Ignatius Loyola: the evocation of a mental image of a physical place, a meditation on the spiritual significance of that image, and a colloquy or personal prayer to God asking for the spiritual good that has been meditated on. Hopkins sometimes reverses or telescopes the last two, but the tripartite structure is clear enough in *The Windhover* as in *Thou art indeed just, Lord,* in *Felix Randal* as in *Spelt from Sibyl's Leaves.* At the same time, the thought and phrasing are dependent upon the Bible, and especially St. Paul. And so, while Hopkins' manner of speech and the precise effect he wishes to achieve are highly idiosyncratic and personal, while it is the special pitch of his utterance, the startling degree of sensitivity and intelligence which make us wrestle with his poems, Hopkins' meaning is rooted deep in the English Catholic literary tradition. But studying a man's thought to understand his poetry is like trying to understand a man's heart by examining his skeleton. Poetic utterance is of an order altogether different from prose.

"You speak of writing the sonnet in prose first . . . ," he once wrote Bridges.

Do you often do so? Is it a good plan? If it is I will try it. . . . Years ago . . . a pupil of mine . . . was to write some English verses for me, to be recited: he had a real vein. He said he had no thoughts, but that if I would furnish some he would versify them. I did so and the effect was very surprising to me to find my own thoughts, with no variation to speak of, expressed in good verses quite unlike mine.[7]

This is *not* how Hopkins composed. In the final analysis, poetic utterance is not a matter of a man's logical meaning, as important as that is. What *is* essential is a man's rhythm, the way he fleshes out the idea; it is the pulse of a poem. Discussing Whitman's possible influence on him, Hopkins said that he had read only snatches, but they were "quite enough to give a strong impression of his marked and original manner and way of thought and in particular of his

[7] Letter of January 4, 1883, *Letters I*, p. 170.

rhythm." [8] That last is what one poet looks for in another—the rhythm in another's soul.

In Hopkins there are three essential rhythms. The first is that heard most frequently in the Oxford juvenilia, a conventional strain which often captures the wavelike tensions of Hopkins' conversion; these tensions are caught in the various poems which, like his diction, alternate between languor and crispness. These rhythms are moving toward a counterpointed alignment, but the mounting of thought onto feeling is not achieved until after Hopkins' seven-year silence. In the period from 1876 to 1883 what predominates are the excited rhythms and ecstatic climaxes of the poetry of the Incarnation, with its evidences of Christ's presence active in, instressed upon, nature and man. It is a poetry of double vision, of the spiritual inhering in the physical. And finally, there are the often harsh, weary, or quiet rhythms of the poems of 1885–1889, poems which for the most part turn on the struggle within and the activity of Christ in the self. In the second period, Hopkins may fairly be called a poet of sacramental vision, finding Christ in the selves of nature and men around him. In the third, he is more narrowly and more deeply concerned with finding Christ in his own "Jackself." This schema, of course, has a suspect tidiness, since such a carefree piece as the *Epithalamion* was written in the spring of 1888, but its outlines are valid.

There is in the last period a corresponding shift in Hopkins' rhythm which owes as much to his spiritual transformation as it does to Bridges' insistence that Hopkins become less singular and less odd. Hopkins' ebullient baroque style is an outgrowth of his Welsh experience primarily, and it gave rise to poems like *The Wreck of the Deutschland* and *The Windhover. Andromeda* (1879) is his first attempt at a "Miltonic plainness," but it is hardly plain. One has only to place the opening of this sonnet,

---

[8] Letter of October 18, 1882, *ibid.,* p. 154.

Now Time's Andromeda on this rock rude,
With not her either beauty's equal or
Her injury's, . . .

with the opening of *The shepherd's brow* (1889) :

The shepherd's brow, fronting forked lightning, owns
The horror and the havoc and the glory
Of it. . . .

This second has achieved what the first has not. "My style tends always more towards Dryden . . . ," Hopkins told Bridges in 1887. "He is the most masculine of our poets; his style and his rhythms lay the strongest stress of all our literature on the naked thew and sinew of the English language." [9] Even such late "baroque" pieces as *Spelt from Sibyl's Leaves* (1884–85) and *That Nature is a Heraclitean Fire* (1888) are starker, more controlled in their language, more percussive and insistent in their rhythms, than the poems of the late seventies.

Throughout this commentary attention has also been paid to the rhetoric of Hopkins' poetry, that is, as he himself explained, "the common and teachable element in literature, what grammar is to speech, what thoroughbass is to music, what theatrical experience gives to playwrights." [10] But since my remarks on technique are addressed to particular poems, it may be helpful to mention some of those rhetorical devices most central to Hopkins' poetic practice. He himself early stressed the figure or inscape of sound a poem makes:

Poetry is speech framed for contemplation of the mind by the way of hearing or speech framed to be heard for its own sake and interest even over and above its interest of meaning [i.e., its logical, grammatical, or etymological significance]. Some matter

---

[9] Letter of November 6, 1887, *ibid.*, pp. 267–268.
[10] Letter to Dixon of August 7, 1886, *Letters II*, p. 141.

and meaning is essential to it but only as an element necessary
to support and employ the shape which is contemplated for its
own sake. (Poetry is in fact speech only employed to carry the
inscape of speech for the inscape's sake—and therefore the inscape
[the particularity of the sound itself] must be dwelt on.) [11]

Hopkins believed that his style, as individual as it was,
was, like his meaning, rooted in the English tradition, in the
real soil of English poetry. And he never tired of telling
Bridges that he was not really odd, that, in fact, he was less
singular in many ways than Bridges himself. He was, he
insisted, closer to the ground of English poetry; what he had
done was simply to cultivate that ground. His rhythms were
the rhythms of prose, only more marked and more musical;
his language was an outgrowth of the original English language, the language as it was spoken, the idiom of the dia-
lects, of Milton and Shakespeare and Dryden—but heightened. There was not a poetic "excess" of his own which
Hopkins could not have defended by recourse to previous
poetic practice. What he did was to compress many older
forms—a native English rhythm and diction, an often elliptical, sometimes un-English, syntax taken in part from the
practice of Greek and Roman poets, a Welsh tradition of
baroque poetry which emphasized sound echoes—and create
out of these a new poetry: a highly individual idiom and a
new music.

That new music reinforces another fact about Hopkins:
he is a verb-centered poet, perhaps the most continually
dynamic poet in the English language. For the poetry, like
the man, is constantly in a state of becoming. It is never
restful or meditative. Rather, there is always in Hopkins a
sense of tremendous nervous tension, nearly always mastered, nearly always achieved in language, a tension which
explodes in a deeply felt release at the end of the lyric. (It is
no accident that many of Hopkins' images are sexual and

[11] *Journals*, p. 289.

gestatory, which is quite different from saying that they are erotic.) What Hopkins said of God's grandeur holds true of his own poems: they both "flame out," revealing themselves as a flash, and yield themselves slowly, gathering "to a greatness, like the ooze of oil / Crushed."

Thinking of his readers, Bridges remarked in his notes to the *Poems* of Hopkins that *The Wreck of the Deutschland* was a dragon in the gate which readers would be wise to circumvent. Others have seen other dragons. Thinking of modern readers of Hopkins, I have offered them a commentary with which to arm themselves, so they will be able not to tame whatever dragon they see, but rather to realize that in wrestling with it, they can be charmed by its labyrinthine coils of gold.

A Commentary on the Complete Poems of
GERARD MANLEY HOPKINS

1 ∽ Early Poetry and
Elected Silence: 1860–1875

Hopkins' extant early poems and poetic fragments, most of which were written between 1860 and 1866, take up about one hundred pages in the Fourth Edition. The entire body of his mature poetry and fragments, that composed between 1876 and 1889, covers only eighty pages. Yet if we look at three representative anthologies of Hopkins' poetry, we find less than a handful of the early poems included. John Pick's *A Hopkins Reader* (Garden City, N.Y., 1966) and James Reeves' *Selected Poems* (London, 1953) print only two, and those the same: *Heaven-Haven* and *The Habit of Perfection.* Gardner's Penguin paperback also prints these and adds *The Alchemist in the City* and the sonnet *Let me be to Thee as the circling bird.* And yet such a meager selection is really not uneven or unrepresentative, for Hopkins' greatness would not be challenged (*pace* Yvor Winters) if Hopkins had in fact destroyed all of his early poetry. Readers of Hopkins are glad for some of these pieces, for the jewellike precision and wistfulness of *Heaven-Haven* or for the charged blend of sensuousness and asceticism of *The Habit of Perfection,* but Hopkins' poetic reputation does not rest on these. Many would, without too much haggling, trade several pages of his carefully edited apprentice work for one more finished sonnet, say, from the Liverpool or Dublin period.

What is of critical value in these early poems is the versatility of stanzaic patterns which Hopkins played with, exploited, rejected, and sometimes returned to. And two things

1

call attention to themselves here: the Pre-Raphaelite tone
and diction, and the Anglican piety. Whatever the specific
influence of a particular poem, whether it be the Spenserian
stanzas of *The Escorial* in the Keatsian mode, the *terza rima*
form of *Winter with the Gulf Stream*, the heroic couplets of
A Vision of the Mermaids (after Keats's *Endymion*), or even
the sonnets which make up *The Beginning of the End*,
which in theme owe something to George Meredith, still the
informing spirit of the lyrical Tennyson and, even more, of
Christina Rossetti and the Pre-Raphaelite painters, hovers
above, diffusing a sweetness and honeyed tone which finally
cloys.

George Herbert is the most noticeable religious influence,
strong enough to break through Christina Rossetti's suffusing ambience. Father Lahey quotes a remark by William E.
Addis, Hopkins' closest friend at Oxford, that "George Herbert was his strongest tie to the English Church."[1] *Barnfloor
and Winepress, New Readings, Heaven-Haven, Easter,* all
owe something to Herbert (that "ah my dear" of the mature
Windhover is from Herbert's *Love III*, as is, surely, the inspiration for some punning lines in Hopkins' *The May
Magnificat* on Mary's literally magnifying the Lord). Hopkins' own epithet for the peculiar characteristic of Herbert's
poetry is "fragrant sweetness."[2] And it is certainly this characteristic which is stressed in the early poems.

One of the problems with the early poems is the diction; it
is in a curious middle-high register, a dreamy mixture of the
sensuous and the moral. It suffers, in fact, from what Hopkins would later come to call medieval keepings. Experience
is filtered through a rosy, aureate tapestry, whose warp is
Christina Rossetti and Tennyson, and whose woof is Her-

[1] Letter of July 5, 1909; quoted in part in G. F. Lahey, S.J., *Gerard
Manley Hopkins* (London, 1930), p. 19.

[2] See Hopkins' letter to Dixon, February 27, 1879, *Letters II*, pp.
23–24, in which he holds Herbert above Henry Vaughan as the better
poet.

bert, blended under their common strand of goodness and sweetness, the kind of thing we see again and again in visual terms in Dante Gabriel Rossetti's *The Girlhood of the Virgin Mary* (1849) or *The Wedding of St. George and Princess Sabra* (1857), or in William Holman Hunt's *The Scapegoat* (1854).

The majority of Hopkins' early poetry exists in two identical small copybooks (4.9 by 2.9 inches) with dark green covers, designated by Fr. Bischoff as C I and C II. These served as Hopkins' diaries from late September 1863 to late January 1866, a period which covers his first twenty-eight months as an Oxford undergraduate. Most of the poems are fragmentary, often with alternative readings, scattered among a miscellany of word lists, books to be read, lecture notes, wine parties, bills, budgets, nature descriptions, drawings of stone tracery, addresses. In the Fourth Edition, Gardner has for the first time included "every scrap of English verse which can be ascribed with certainty, or reasonable certainty, to Hopkins." [3] This means over one hundred pages of English poetry from the early period, of which nearly seventy are transcribed from these two small diaries. The other early poems exist in various places: letters sent to friends, prize poems, copies in the hands of his friends or parents or a few that were printed, and a number of separate sheets found in sundry scattered places. All of the finished English poems and most of the fragments will be treated here, but the fragments do present a problem. Many are no more than a few lines; others show little sense of a curve of development. The plan here, then, is to discuss most of these fragments and to comment on the others, so that the pattern of Hopkins' early development and achievement can be established. The order of treatment will be chronological, except that certain groupings, such as the sonnets, will be treated together to show their development more clearly.

[3] *Poems,* p. xvii.

The Escorial, dated Easter 1860, is a school-prize poem in Spenserian stanzas which Hopkins wrote when he was only fifteen. It bears a pale resemblance to Keats's *The Eve of St. Agnes* in its stanza form, use of narrative, luxurious descriptions, and oblique but nevertheless strong moral undertone. It demonstrates the young poet's precociousness and preciousness, but it is too sententious to manifest any personal involvement with the material. It remains what it is, a fine school exercise.

Hopkins' *Il Mystico* is a long (142 lines) fragment of a poem which he copied out in a letter to his school friend E. H. Coleridge in early September 1862. Hopkins was still on holiday and had been "writing a good many poetical snatches lately," but *Il Mystico,* he felt, was "the best thing" he had recently done.[4] It is, as he himself says, in imitation of Milton's *Il Penseroso.* There are strong echoes here not only of Milton but of two of Hopkins' early favorites, Tennyson and Keats. It is a good imitation, but Milton is made to don Pre-Raphaelite robes; the rhythm is Milton's but the music Tennyson's.

As in *Il Penseroso,* the opposite of what the poet praises is first exorcised. That Puritan strain in Hopkins, that uneasy suspicion of the sensuous which was to nag him throughout his life, blares forth in the opening lines. Sensual gross desires are clotted, filthy, slimy, feverish, spawned in "some sickly hovel." They are earth-bound and alien to that fledgling spirit which would ascend unencumbered. He calls on the mystical spirit to raise him, a spirit which in description and tone recalls one of Rossetti's angels. *Il Mystico* is, like *Il Penseroso,* a haunter not of night but of the dark before Matins, when hope quickens and "tide of ill is out." It is then, when silence is most deep, that the veil which "covers mysteries" is thinnest. But like *L'Allegro,* he is a haunter of the day, from before sunrise till after sunset. If *Il Penseroso*

---

[4] *Letters III,* p. 8.

sought Musaeus or Orpheus or Chaucer, *Il Mystico* asks for the "close-folded peace" of Galahad and the radiant vision of Ezekiel. Fifteen years later Hopkins' heart would "stir for a bird," for the "brute beauty" of the windhover gliding against the "big wind." Here he wishes too that he might fly freely like the lark, drifting in the air, spread out against the sun, and there, alone, to "fill / The airy empire at his will," to sing until he has spent himself at sunset. With the word "sunset," the naturalist instinct in Hopkins is in danger of throwing over the balance of the entire poem. The last fifty lines of the fragment describe a dramatic sunset with shower, "sapphire-pale" skies and "amber" west. The light and mist create a magnificent rainbow which seems to be an incarnation of angels' wings, for the spiritual and the mundane seem harmoniously intertwined here in a "sweet uncertainty / 'Twixt real hue and phantasy." Goethe's Faust laments:

> Alas that I have no wings to raise me into the air!
> Then I should see in an everlasting sunset
> The quiet world before my feet unfold   [I, 1074–1079].

And Hopkins' naturalist-mystic wishes to be melted into the vision of a world in harmony with the heavens, meeting "in mid-air" in the "dizzy bow." [5] But Hopkins' mystic is no more a mystic than Wordsworth was when he composed his sonnet on Westminster Bridge. He is a Romantic with a strong (and vague) religious sensibility and an extremely sensitive eye for a view. And for an eighteen-year-old, that may have been close enough to mysticism. It seems to have been enough for a number of Pre-Raphaelites.

In the same long letter to E. H. Coleridge, Hopkins included two other original fragments and a translation of some lines from *Prometheus Bound* that he copied out of his

---

[5] See *The Caged Skylark*, which closes with the image of the rainbow over the meadow-down as a symbol of the resurrected body now in full harmony with the soul.

schoolbook. The first of the two original pieces is *A Windy Day in Summer,* a nature description in ten lines of octosyllabic couplets. Elms, willows, chestnut trees, aspens, pools, and clouds are all vexed or swept or smitten by the mastering azure skies. Hopkins has his eyes on adjectives here, on color (blue, argent, sapphire, white, silver, azure), and on action as epithet (vex'd elm-heads, laboring willows, mastering heaven). It may be unfair, but it is enlightening, to see how much he had developed when he presented rather than described another windy day in summer in the opening lines of *That Nature is a Heraclitean Fire* twenty-five years later: "Cloud-puffball, torn tufts, tossed pillows."

A Fragment of Anything You Like is a nine-line poem written in tercets. Hopkins compares the pale, delicate sorrow of a woman to the late-rising and forlorn moon wandering aimlessly in broad daylight across the heavens. It is an image which calls Shelley to mind. But it is the same pale moon which travels across the morning landscape in Ford Madox Brown's *Carrying Corn* (1854). And if we transpose the time to late afternoon, it is the same moon which Hopkins evokes in *Winter with the Gulf Stream* a year later.

A Vision of the Mermaids is dated Christmas 1862, some three months later. It is written in heroic couplets and, again, the influence of Keats is noticeable, the Keats of *Endymion,* especially in the lush imagery. Here is the young naturalist's description of the phenomenon of color compensation; as the eye stares at the sunset, it substitutes greens for the strong reds. But in the process of staring hard the eye plays tricks on the mind, signaling "Keen glimpses of the inner firmament." This looking hard at nature opens into a surrealistic spectacle of sporting, singing mermaids. The artistic execution is quite good. Hopkins handles the epic simile adequately; he employs an extensive vocabulary, and he is successful at evoking a (very) mild sensation of pathos. Matthew Arnold's evocation of the sea's inhuman strangeness in *The Forsaken Merman* (1849) is echoed here, especially in the following:

> it is a pain
> To know the dusk depths of the ponderous sea,
> The miles profound of solid green, and be
> With loath'd cold fishes, far from man.

Hopkins is playing in this poem with what he was to present in all earnestness some fourteen years later. Then, instead of precious mermaids in a calm bay, there was to be Christ's giant striding over the Kentish Knock one December night to take home his brides.

Winter with the Gulf Stream (February 1863) is a nature piece describing a mild winter scene. Hopkins' use of *terza rima* is respectable if uncharacteristic. The final couplet neatly reflects the completion of the finished day, so that the poem finds a natural, if prosaic, resolution in form and idea:

> Into the flat blue mist the sun
> Drops out and all our day is done.

Spring and Death, undated but about 1864, foreshadows the later *Spring and Fall* in its theme and use of the octosyllabic couplet. The last lines are especially similar in tone to the later poem in their bittersweet evocation of the passing of all things. Hopkins creates here a dream-vision in which the poet meets Death in "a hollow lush and damp," where there is, as in Baudelaire's *Les Fleurs du Mal,* "too much fragrance everywhere." The speaker is aware, even while he enjoys the flowers in all their promise, of the knowledge that they too must pass away. And this knowledge makes the inevitable even more regrettable.

She schools the flighty pupils of her eyes (no. 82 in the Fourth Edition), entered in Hopkins' copybook for June 1864, is in form a Spenserian stanza lacking a final line. It is a picture of a young woman struggling to maintain self-control over a heart which would run "riot" at the thought of her lover. There is a sustained effort to extend the ideas both of schooling (as in the pun on schooling the pupils of the eyes in line 1) and of leashing the passions as one would leash an untrained dog. It is a thoroughly Victorian treatment, but its erotic impulse is uncharacteristic of the young Hopkins in its intensity and restraint. It almost teases us with its oblique sensuousness.

The Lover's Stars, which Hopkins called "a trifle in something like Coventry Patmore's style," [6] exists only in a series of fragments in his copybook for mid-July 1864. The poem turns on a simple contrast. If Fate or the stars favor him, even though there seem to be insurmountable obstacles, the lover will win his mistress. On the other hand, if the stars show their "swart aspect," then no matter how close he is to his beloved or how apparently favorable are the circumstances, he cannot win her. Hopkins uses a number of spatial images: images of great distance ("Antipodes apart," "8,000 furlongs in advance") , and of small (the "garden chair," the closeness of dancing) . There is a touch of the metaphysical here, especially of Andrew Marvell's *To His Coy Mistress,* combined with a touch of *Lycidas,* especially in the "ill-launchèd hope / In unimperill'd haven . . . wreck'd." The special appeal of this poem, though, along with fragments 82, 87, and 94, is that it shows a young man's interest in the opposite sex; but it is a tautly controlled erotic impulse. Number 87 describes the experience of love as a winged Cupid ascending into the "blue element," but the experience is described only and not presented.

During the eastering of untainted morns (84) is a six-line fragment in heroic couplets on a favorite theme of Hopkins': sunrise with rainbow as seen from a moist garden. There is something sacred in such a natural vision, in "the cloister-light of greenhouse vines." For the young Hopkins as for Wordsworth, the "vernal impulse" is of itself a religious

[6] *Letters III,* p. 213.

response. *The Peacock's Eye* (86) is an artistic-scientific analysis of the protean color pattern of the peacock's eye. The precise descriptions characteristic of Ruskin and the Pre-Raphaelites are behind these pieces, as behind so many of Hopkins' journal entries articulating what the eye has recorded. Such precise delineation of natural things is an impulse which, chastened, remained with Hopkins till the end of his life, when the haggard eye could still start before the pretty chervil growing along a small stream in Ireland in early spring.

A Soliloquy of One of the Spies left in the Wilderness (July 1864) perhaps owes something to Browning's *Soliloquy of the Spanish Cloister.* One of those who followed Moses out of Egypt and on the long sojourn into the desert debates within himself whether or not simply to give up the struggle. The steps by which this spy surrenders to despair are etched logically and dramatically. First, Moses' authority is questioned and rejected. God's heaven-sent manna and water no longer satisfy. Finally the speaker's thirst and tiredness condition him to recall the relative security of Egypt's bondage through a cool, liquid prism; the Nile's water blazes, he sucks "the full-sapp'd vine-shoot," and the slavery of making bricks is remembered only as cool feet plashing "clay juicy soil." The exodus struggles on but he cries he can no more. It is hard not to see Hopkins' own uneasy sense of moving away from Egypt—the Anglican Church (see no. 20)—and into an uninviting but nonetheless compelling exodus into the unknown. The fragment *Pilate*, in rhyme royal stanzas, and contemporary with the *Soliloquy*, is also a soliloquy which deals with the theme of alienation and isolation, but here Pilate seeks to be forgiven by the crucified Christ by crucifying himself with sharp stones.[7]

[7] That Browning's poetry was on Hopkins' mind at this time, see *Poems*, p. 133, for a delightful couplet, "By one of the old school who was bid to follow Mr. Browning's flights": "To rise you bid me with the lark: / With me 'tis rising in the dark."

Barnfloor and Winepress, written in July 1864 and printed in *The Union Review* in 1865, is a religious poem in octosyllabic couplets which in tone and theme owes something to George Herbert's *The Bunch of Grapes.* The poem is generated by a series of metaphysical conceits revolving around the bread and wine of Christ. The title, taken from II Kings 6:27 in the King James Version, links Christ's great sacrifice with wheat-threshing and grape-treading. Christ is "Scourged upon the threshing-floor," the vine is "fenced with thorn," the wine is "rackèd from the press." Christ is there in the Communion service each morning, "on a thousand altars laid" and "in our altar-vessels stored." In the last lines Hopkins turns the thought, for when we partake of the "banquet food" Christ's blood becomes "our blood," and we, like branches, are grafted on the vine of the cross, "on His wood." Hopkins handles the couplets with mastery here; what could have degenerated into doggerel is kept vigorous and crackling from opening to close.

New Readings is, in fact, a reworking of *Barnfloor and Winepress,* which it follows in the copybook. It too shows the influence of Herbert. Metaphysical in nature, the poem playfully reverses both Christ's words that grapes do not grow from thistles and Christ's parable of the seed that fell upon rocky ground. For from the crucified Christ's bloody head, surrounded by thorns, "drops of wine" and grains are indeed shed. And in feeding the five thousand on the barren hillside, Christ does manifest his fruits. There are some good lines here, but Hopkins is straining too hard, and the poem falls flat in the last two lines, especially with the intrusion of the Keatsian lushness of "easeful wings."

He hath abolished the old drouth follows immediately after *New Readings.* It is a song of joy, of affirmation in the resurrection, and it was probably inspired by a passage from Revelations describing the chosen hundred and forty-four thousand in heavenly bliss, singing a "new song" of praise

(Rev. 14:1–4).[8] The speaker sees himself and another as among the "shocks" of "corn" (wheat) "stored" in the final "harvest" and "garnering." The image of the garnered wheat was a favorite with Hopkins; he was to use it again, for example, in stanza 31 of *The Wreck of the Deutschland* ("does tempest carry the grain for thee"), in *The Starlight Night,* and in *Carrion Comfort.*

Heaven-Haven, also written in July 1864, is a minor masterpiece, a finely finished lyric. It is a haunting evocation of the peace of the cloistered life, away from the storms of life and "out of the swing of the sea." As such, the soft anapests serve as a counterpoise to the sprung rhythms in the terrifying re-creation of

$$\text{the sea flínt-fláke, bláck-bácked}$$

of the *Deutschland.* The title, as Gardner points out,[9] is taken from Herbert's *The Size:* "These seas are tears, and Heaven the haven." But the poem also owes much to Tennyson's description of Avilion in *Morte d'Arthur:*

> Where falls not hail, or rain, or any snow
> Nor ever wind blows loudly; but it lies
> Deep meadowed, happy, fair with orchard lawns
> And bowery hollows crown'd with summer sea
> [ll. 311–314].

There is a counterpiece to this poem's desire for stasis, which follows immediately in the diary, and which is printed among the fragments (88). Using the same formal pattern,

---

[8] The passage in Revelations specifically addresses those who have remained innocent virgins for Christ's sake. Had Hopkins determined already on a life of chastity, as Newman early had? The theme of chastity for Christ is a constant in a number of Hopkins' poems and in his letters; see *St. Thecla, The Bugler's First Communion,* and *The Leaden Echo and the Golden Echo.*

[9] *Poems,* p. 248. Cf. p. 300, where Gardner notes that the title could also have come from Thomas More's address to Fortune.

the speaker here calls for a life of heroic adventure, for extending one's limits, imaged here in terms of landscape: the eagle's mountain home and the frozen wastes "Not so far from the pole."

During August Hopkins traveled by train and omnibus to Wales, Maentwrog, Merionethshire with two Oxford companions on a reading holiday. Hopkins had his little diary with him, and fragments 89–97 were written during this period. Number 89 is a satire on gloomy, lugubrious, and anti-Christian Victorian funerals. Using the Spenserian stanza, the poet chastises the funereal rites as more suited to ravens for offering thanks that their curses have prospered. Black death impales the body, and the rosy cross, with its sign of hope, is banned. Number 90 is a short description of a heavy, dismal storm, probably at Bala, since this name is written beneath the piece. "I have had adventures," he wrote Baillie early in August, jokingly identifying himself with St. Paul. "I was lost in storms of rain on the mountains between Bala and Ffestiniog. . . . I took refuge in a shepherd's hut and slept amongst the Corinthians." [10]

The next fragment (91), which follows immediately, is in heroic couplets and discusses one of those favorite chestnuts of undergraduates: do we create the rainbow by our perception of it or is the rainbow "out there"? Both are true, the young poet insists. We do not invent the rainbow; it is the "sun on falling waters writes the text," yet the bow needs a point of perception to be interpreted, which makes, therefore, as many rainbows as perceivers, but *none* without sun and water. Fragment 92 (and 93) seems to echo I Samuel 14:24 and following, as the notes to Hopkins' journal point out. In Samuel, Saul curses whatever man shall eat before the day's battle is won. His son Jonathan unwittingly eats of

[10] Letter to Baillie of July 20–August 14, 1864, *Letters III*, p. 212. This letter should be read to see how many different poetic projects the young Hopkins could have underway at any one time. Nor was he concerned about finishing many of the things he had begun.

"the lawless honey" and is saved from death only by the people. But Hopkins' passage is too fragmentary to make more sense of than this.

Fragment 94, *Miss Story's character,* is an imitation of Pope's satire in heroic couplets, particularly *Of the Characters of Women,* which Hopkins quotes in his letter to Baillie at this time: "We have four Miss Storys staying in the house, girls from Reading. This is a great advantage—but not to reading." [11] Hopkins was having one of those flirtatious duels with one of the young ladies. He sketches "Miss Story's character" to present her to her confidante "Miss May." For the most part Hopkins' criticism is harsh but without that stinging wit of Pope or of Molière's Celimène. There are some good bits here. There is a double-edged thrust aimed at Miss May as well as Miss Story:

> No: [this epistle] shewn to her it cannot but offend;
> But candour never hurt the dearest *friend.*

Another bon mot is this line: "And, thinking that she thinks, has never thought." But most of the lines become slack because Victorian Hopkins keeps moralizing and holding back where the sting of wit is demanded by the genre itself. In the last two lines the twenty-year-old Hopkins comes close to showing some interest in the young lady.

Hopkins also tried his hand at several epigrams. Three, particularly, are of interest in that they are concerned with poetry. *Modern Poets* likens poets to swans who sing, but, instead of dying as they should, kill their hearers. Another is supposedly spoken by a poet "of the old school who was bid to follow Mr. Browning's flights." [12] The best, however, is *On a Poetess:*

> Miss M.'s a nightingale. 'Tis well
> Your simile I keep.
> It is the way with Philomel
> To sing while others sleep.

[11] *Ibid.,* p. 213.   [12] See note 7 above.

The "Hopley" of *By Mrs. Hopley* is a combination, no doubt, of the names Hopkins and Manley. As with *Miss Story's character*, the fragment is in heroic couplets and satirizes the Victorian father who lives with his theory and neglects his children except to bestow pains upon them, in the less charitable sense of that phrase.

Hopkins told Baillie in September that, besides working on his *Floris in Italy*, he had written little since July "except three verses, a fragment, being a description of Io (transformed into a heifer). It sounds odd." [13] *Io* (99) is in three staves of six lines each, rhyming ababcc. It is a rich and luxuriant description, but completely static. It is a cow that we see, a pretty cow, but a cow only. That mastery of presenting an actual transformation, as in the protean shaping of the speaker and God in *Carrion Comfort*, was still a long way off.

In the same month Hopkins wrote a number of other fragments. One (100) is in blank verse describing a rainbow seen over "Havering church-tower" and "the Quickly elms." There is a piece (101) for two voices in which the second voice crumbles the first's "morticed metaphors." If the two (lovers?) hold together as the cup holds the acorn, the glove the hand, the duct the water, in time the cup drops the fruit, "the hand draws off the glove," and "the duct runs dry or breaks." Six months earlier Hopkins had recorded in his copybook that his friend Addis had told him that he often colored his arguments with his feelings. Here Hopkins seems to direct an ironic scrutiny against the validity of his own metaphors. The resulting ambivalence is thoroughly Victorian.

I am like a slip of comet may be a speech intended for Giulia in *Floris in Italy*. The speaker, presumably a woman, likens herself to a comet attracted to the sun (her lover), which grows in its presence, and then fades into death. Num-

---

[13] *Letters III*, p. 221.

ber 104 is a description of a powerful army which may also have been meant for *Floris in Italy*. Number 105 is a fragment of a hymn to early autumn—"a song to the decaying year." It captures a moment of precarious balance before the trees turn color, when the skies are grey and clear and the harvest is ready to be gathered in.

For a Picture of St. Dorothea has survived in several forms. Gardner prints three versions in the Fourth Edition: an early version written about November 1864, a version in sprung rhythm which can be dated about spring 1868,[14] and a third (and expanded) version in dramatic form which was written probably mid-way between the other two. The poem centers on St. Dorothea's apparition before the skeptical Theophilus bearing a basket of "Sweet flowers" grown in heaven. In its treatment of a religious subject in sensuous terms it is very much in the vein of the Pre-Raphaelite painters and could serve as a poetic commentary on one of Dante Gabriel Rossetti's graphically sensual-innocent women. Take the first four of the regular octosyllabic lines:

> I bear a basket lined with grass;
> I am so light, I am so fair,
> That men must wonder as I pass
> And at the basket that I bear.

And compare them with their sprung counterparts:

> I bear a basket lined with grass.
> Í am só líght and faír
> Men are amazed to watch me pass
> Wíth the básket I béar.

[14] In a postscript to a letter to Bridges of August 7, 1868, Hopkins writes: "I hope you will master the peculiar beat I have introduced into St. Dorothea. The development is mine but the beat is in Shakspere— e.g., Whý should thís desert be?—and Thoú for whóm Jóve would swear —where the rest of the lines are eight-syllabled or seven-syllabled" (*Letters I*, p. 24). The point here is that Shakespeare is using four stresses in a six-syllable line, thereby packing stresses next to one another without reversing feet.

Hopkins' sprung effects draw at least moderate attention to the words themselves by their nervous energy. The thematic treatment of the poem is too light to carry the weight of more than a moderate number of such stresses, and Hopkins is for the most part careful not to use too many six-syllable, four-stress lines. Still, there is something intolerably artificial about some of the lines, such as "Sérvèd bý méssengér?" In the long run, the poem counts more for what it points to in terms of metric experimentation than for the intrinsic merits of the lyric itself.

The Queen's Crowning (December 1864), placed among the fragments (109) although complete in sense, is an imitation of a Scots border ballad. Each of the thirty-nine stanzas employs the same long *e* rhyme in the second and fourth lines. Hopkins' ballad owes something, as Humphry House explains, "to the ending of Sweet William's Ghost." [15] Lord William, the king's son, weds, beds, and then leaves his bride Alice to go to sea, promising to return "in two years or in three." But he is killed by his brothers, ostensibly out of rage for having married beneath his station, in reality for the crown. They return to Alice, the dead king's wife, at the allotted time, but she will have nothing to do with them. Finally the wraith of her dead husband comes to her with a rose, a crown, and "kisses three." The kisses send her into death and she is crowned queen—in paradise. It is a saccharine product, certainly respectable, but too long. And there is a touch of Victorian melodrama. The aloof, objective, bald narrative is suffused here with a tinge of Pre-Raphaelite preciosity. It is a creditable imitation of the ballad, but it remains that: an imitation.

Stephen and Barberie is a fifteen-line fragment of a projected narrative poem which Hopkins entered into his copy-

---

[15] *The Note-Books and Papers of Gerard Manley Hopkins* (Oxford, 1937), p. 358.

book in January 1865. A young lady sits beneath a sycamore tree at Martinmastide, while the leaves shower into her lap. She weeps and sings, fittingly, a "country song of *Willow*," which also tells of a poor soul *"sighing by a sycamore-tree."*

Richard is a longer fragment of another narrative poem. The pastoral setting is Hopkins' own contemporary Oxford countryside. Hopkins worked on this poem intermittently, shaping it first into stanzas in May–June 1864, but then rewriting it in heroic couplets in October–November 1864, and continuing with the couplets in the following July. The setting, with its modern shepherds who act more like Oxford undergraduates on a reading tour in the Long Vacation, recalls those other Oxonian shepherds' songs, Matthew Arnold's *The Scholar Gypsy* (1853), and A. H. Clough's *The Bothie of Tober-na-Vuolich* (1848). Richard is unmistakably Hopkins, lying in the summer grass of the beautiful Cumnor hills, examining minutely the local flora of the meadows and river banks. And for Richard, as for Hopkins, there is "a spiritual grace / Which Wordsworth would have dwelt on, about the place." Like one of Hopkins' reading companions, the shepherd Sylvester reads Keats's letters while sheep bleat drowsily in the summer fields.

Among the odd fragments Hopkins wrote in early 1865 is one of some eight lines describing a woodland stream (112) and another (113), a Spenserian stanza, describing the music of a lark. *The Summer Malison* (114) is a two-stanza catalog of summer curses—a malison or malediction. The fields shall be dry, mother will have no milk for child, the ships shall lie useless upon the still seas, the soldier will learn to "hate his faded red, / Grown wicked in the wicked wars." It is a curse upon all that Hopkins held dear, lover of nature and country that he was. It seems to be a document of the "blackguard" strain which Hopkins, like most men, had lurking somewhere. But *O Death, Death, He is come* (115), written in early March, sings of Christ's harrowing of hell to bring the saved into heaven. It is a hymn which in spirit anticipates Hopkins' entry of the twelfth of that month: "A day of the great mercy of God."

Easter Communion is Hopkins' earliest extant sonnet and was entered in his diary in early March of 1865. In the next seven months he wrote all of his early sonnets (fourteen pieces, most of them fairly complete, a number existing now only in fragments). We know from a letter he wrote in January of that year that he was reading and enjoying Charles Tennyson Turner's sonnets, and this volume may have been the inspiration for his own attempts in the form.[16] As with all of the early sonnets, including the apparent formal design of the fragments, it is written in the Italian or Petrarchan mode, following Milton in a majority of instances in disregarding the strict turn or *volta* in the argument between the octet and the sestet. Even the sonnet fragment *Shakspere* (126) uses the Italian form. The son-

---

[16] Two months before this first draft, Hopkins had commented in passing to Baillie: "Have you read Turner's sonnets? They are the things to read now; but again I had forgot that you have a standing interdict against new poetry, the unhappy books being put on the *Index Expurg.* at once after birth" (January 5, 1865, *Letters III*, p. 225). Charles Tennyson Turner (1808–1879), an older brother of the Poet Laureate, had published in 1864 a slim volume of his sonnets, composed in both the English and Italian modes. Many of them possess real poetic merit. Were Turner's sonnets the immediate cause of Hopkins' experimenting with the form? We cannot be sure, but the following lines from Turner's sonnet, *Summer Gloaming,*

> The bat is circling softly by my door,
> And silent as the snow-flake leaves his lair,
> In the dark twilight flitting here and there
> Wheeling the self-same circuit o'er and o'er

may have been echoed in these lines from Hopkins (19):

> Let me be to Thee as the circling bird
> Or bat with tender and air-crisping wings
> That shapes in half-light his departing rings,
> From both of whom a changeless note is heard.

nets are best treated together, and this can be accomplished without doing much violence to the chronology.

Easter Communion is made up of a series of six parallel contrasts between severe forms of Lenten self-chastisement (including, probably, self-flagellation),[17] and the resultant spiritual rewards, rewards which evoke the sensual phrasing of D. G. Rossetti's *The Blessed Damozel* rather than echoes of the Anglican prayer service. The adjective count here is quite high: twenty-three, including five hyphenated compounds, such as "ever-fretting," "myrrhy-threaded," and "scarce-sheathed," recalling the early Keats. Language here is vitiated and languorous. We think rather of Walter Pater enjoying the aroma of expensive myrrh as he watches at a distance the Anglican Communion service. The poem is a good example of one extreme of Hopkins' esthetic sensibility.

Hopkins' next sonnet, *Confirmed beauty will not bear a stress* (April 24), swings to the other extreme. It is a good imitation of Shakespeare in its diction and presentation of an intellectual argument. It is clearly in the Italian mode, despite the condition of line 4, which is so badly smudged as to make the rhyme-word illegible and so mar an otherwise complete sonnet. Probably for this reason Gardner did not print it until his Fourth Edition, where he places it among the unfinished poems as number 117.[18] The sonnet shows a noticeable tightening and complexity of argument: major

[17] In the Lenten season of the year before (March 1864), Hopkins had written to Baillie: "My mother does not let me fast at all, and says I in particular must never do it again, and in fact I believe I must not" (*Letters III*, p. 207). Self-flagellation, then, was probably not one of Hopkins' Lenten practices. But cf. *ibid.*, p. 395, a letter of June 13, 1890, from C. N. Luxmoore to Arthur Hopkins, which recalls Hopkins' powers of stoical abstinence at Highgate, and all for a small wager.

[18] Gardner and MacKenzie accept Fr. Bischoff's reading of the last word of line 4 as "expressionless." Since they do, the sonnet might be transposed to the early complete poems, as Hopkins did complete the sonnet.

statement, development by examples, and resolution. The major statement—"Confirmed beauty will not bear a stress" —is a favorite of Hopkins', and was to be reiterated, for example, in *The Leaden Echo and the Golden Echo*. It is the lament that beautiful things inevitably vanish even as we attempt to keep them. Three examples of vanishing beauty are given: color, sky, and (surprisingly) the sonnet itself. With the *volta* in line 11, the speaker reverses the traditional Elizabethan stance that the poet's muse can adequately capture in words his beloved's beauty. Beauty inherent in the object is a better thing than its pale imitation in the artist's work, and "The sweetest sonnet five or six times read / Is tasteless nothing." Only by turning from art to her "not-staled unchartered memory" can the speaker hope to capture his beloved's beauty, for that is so complex that it will always reveal fresh facets to explore.

There is a noticeable academic flavor to this sonnet, especially in the way in which it displays its biblical and classical allusions, which is no more than to be expected in the poetry of a mid-nineteenth-century Oxford undergraduate. The early Arnold and Clough come immediately to mind. But Hopkins' conceit to his anonymous beloved's "unchartered memory" was to take fire in the profound devotional compliment at the close of *God's Grandeur* (1877):

> There lives the dearest freshness deep down things
>   . . . . .
> Because the Holy Ghost over the bent
>   World broods with warm breast and with ah! bright wings.

Without pressing too hard on Hopkins' few, rather thin-blooded erotic sonnets, it seems that even in them the hint of God as the beloved is never too far from his mind.

The next sonnet, *Where art thou friend, whom I shall never see*, written a few days later (April 25–27), has been explained by Humphry House as referring to Digby Mackworth Dolben, a highly devout, highly unstable young man who seems to have won the deep friendship of both Hopkins and Bridges. However, Gardner's explanation that "the poem was addressed to some fascinating stranger," a recurrent theme in Hopkins' poetry (for example, *The Lantern out of Doors* and *The Candle Indoors*), seems better to explain the internal evidence of the poem.[19] The poem is difficult and unsatisfactory because its syntax is tortuous and its pronoun references uncertain. The whole sonnet is made up of only two sentences, the second of which drags its slow length along for twelve lines. And the delicate mechanism of the sonnet is nearly swamped here, not so much by an intrinsic complexity in the argument as by the confusion of the thought itself.

Still, the sonnet represents a clear example of one direction toward which Hopkins was working, as *Easter Communion*'s languorous, honeyed, and highly emotional diction and urgent rhythms represents a second. Here, despite serious flaws, there is a striving toward a tightly controlled, intellectualized argument. There is only one adjective, the "dear" of "God's dear pleadings" in line 10. Its uniqueness draws attention to itself, thereby focusing on the essential attribute of the central figure of the poem. And the series of five dashes in the second sentence, which serve as loose syntactic connectives, gives the effect of impassioned and earnest pleading rather than the studied impression of a set speech.

The Beginning of the End is the start of what appears to have been an abortive sonnet sequence which, in theme, recalls George Meredith's sequence of fifty sixteen-line sonnets entitled *Modern Love* (1862).[20] Hopkins' entire se-

---

[19] See *Poems*, p. 250.

[20] Gardner (II, 87) says that there is direct evidence in one of Hopkins' unpublished confessional entries scattered throughout his early notebook (C II) that Hopkins had read the sonnets. It is interesting to note how an older Hopkins approached Meredith. Two one-time students of Hopkins' at University College, Dublin, recalled years later the following characteristic anecdote from early 1884. There

quence, composed May 6–8, numbers three Italian sonnets
and the fragment of a fourth, probably jettisoned as too
imitative. In point of form, syntax, and especially archaic
diction, however, the sonnets recall the Elizabethan sonnet
sequences. It is in their imitative diction that Hopkins' sonnets most noticeably fall short. The archaic astrological ter-
minology of the second sonnet is so artificial as to short-cir-
cuit any sincerity of tone. No amount of sympathy can
salvage such lines as

> no recorded devilish thing was done

> With such a seconding, nor Saturn took
> Such opposition to the Lady-star
> In the most murderous passage of his book.

And the simile in the final lines of the third sonnet overrides
the subject for which it is supposed to serve as comparison:

> What have I come across
> That here will serve me for comparison?

> The sceptic disappointment and the loss
> A boy feels when the poet he pores upon
> Grows less and less sweet to him, and knows no cause.[21]

---

was an attempt by the students to establish "a society for the study of
Meredith. . . . Father Gerard Hopkins, just appointed by the Senate to
his Fellowship in Greek, also attended the proceedings. One evening
the promised writer of a paper was not ready and they began to read a
portion of *The Egoist*. Hopkins, though an admirer of the author, was
so irritated at the ideas expressed in the passage read that he could not
endure to listen and by way of showing his displeasure took an abrupt
departure. The Society hardly survived this hard blow" (*A Page of
Irish History: The Story of University College, Dublin, 1883–1909*,
compiled by Fathers of the Society of Jesus [Dublin, 1930], p. 117). As
Hopkins grew older he saw, as he put it, that while art is of itself
neutral, "right must seek a side / And choose for chieftain one."

[21] Hopkins wrote to Baillie on September 10, 1864: "Do you know, a
horrible thing has happened to me. I have begun to *doubt* Tennyson."
And later in the same letter, "I think one had got into the way of
thinking . . . that Tennyson was always new, *touching*, beyond other

There are no further sonnets until the Long Vacation of 1865, following Hopkins' second year at Oxford. And then there is a burst of sonnet activity recorded in his copybook between June 24 and 26. Hopkins entered *Myself unholy, from myself unholy, To Oxford* (consisting of two sonnets and what Hopkins could remember of a third—first printed by Gardner in the Fourth Edition as fragment 119), which had already been sent to his classmate Vincent Coles, and *See how Spring opens with disabling cold. Easter Communion* was also revised to its final form.

Myself unholy, from myself unholy resembles in theme the arcane *Where art thou friend* of two months before, although there is now a stricter syntactical control. The sonnet is generated on a series of parallel contrasts; the speaker turns from his "unholy" self to his more virtuous friends, which action he compares to one's turning to the brighter and fresher things of nature. But none of his friends is perfect, and the absence of a worthy model to emulate confuses and depresses him. Line 12 "turns" the argument simply: while all of his friends are *better* than himself, only Christ will serve as *best*.

But if Hopkins' mastery of the argument shows improvement, the strain of lush Rossettian diction is a flaw, and several words are obvious compromises made to meet the strict requirements of end-rhyming. The most glaring example of this is Hopkins' choice of the unhappy first end-rhyme with "unholy," a choice which finally marred the entire sonnet. For in line 4, possibly thinking of the Victorian industrial cities, he compared "white clouds to furnace-eaten regions coaly," and then changed this to an equally weak "Or unsalt streams to teasing waters shoaly." But "unsalt streams" is too cumbersome a negative, and "teasing" is an

---

poets, not pressed with human ailments, never using Parnassian [uninspired craftsmanship]. So at least I used to think" (*Letters III*, pp. 215–218).

ambiguous modifier at best. Hopkins compromised by finally adjusting this to the firmer "Fresh brooks to salt sand-teasing waters shoaly." The Keatsian-Miltonic inversion of "waters shoaly" still troubles the line, but Hopkins does not appear to have seen any solution to the difficulty. In the middle of line 8, he seems to have chosen "sultry" more for the alliteration with "seize" than for any precision of meaning. And the imperfect eye-rhyme of "melancholy" with "solely" Hopkins would never have allowed in his later poetry.

The problem with the sonnets *To Oxford,* besides their rough or incomplete state, is that they are abstruse and even hermetic. They are written as if they were meant to be personal entries in an undergraduate's journal, for perusal by none or by only a few close friends at Oxford. The first sonnet turns on the mild paradox that what especially endears Oxford to the speaker can be as fully shared by all of Oxford's other admirers, without loss to any. For "all like me may boast, impeached not, / Their special-general title to thy love."

In the second sonnet, the speaker describes, in painfully minute fashion, a special vantage point of Oxford, where "none besides me this bye-ways beauty try." But even if they do try it, he argues, he is made even happier, for then "unknown" others have only confirmed the peculiar pleasure which he has experienced and of which he has written. The *volta* is both strained and tedious, and makes much ado about nothing.

The third sonnet (fragment 119) is unclear, even cryptic, although it seems that the name "Belleisle," an island off the coast of Brittany, is here used as a pun for Balliol. This inference is supported by another loose scrap of poetry (116) which seems to be the beginning of an intended Petrarchan sonnet, entered in Hopkins' notebook for some time near April 24, while he was still at Oxford:

> Bellisle! that is a fabling name, but we
> Have here a true one, echoing the sound;

> And one to each of us is holy ground;
> But let me sing that which is known to me.

The meaning of the incomplete third sonnet of *To Oxford* is tied up with the initiate, Hopkins' coterie, and with some happy news which seems to have reached Hopkins from Balliol about some of his friends. Tennyson is paid homage in line 9, which is borrowed from *A Dream of Fair Women*. Did Hopkins' poem have to do with some religious news concerning his friends? However tempting to speculate, it is difficult to be sure just what Hopkins is alluding to, for unfortunately none of his letters or poems have been discovered among the papers of Vincent Coles, to whom the sonnet was sent.

See how Spring opens with disabling cold is a somber lament for wasted years which might have been spiritually profitable. Gardner has noticed some similarities with Milton's Italian sonnet *On His Being Arrived to the Age of Twenty-three,* which Milton composed in his last year at Cambridge, shortly before he took his master's degree. Hopkins' sonnet opens with an extended simile; the image of Spring's late arrival is compared to the speaker's spiritual condition:

> See how Spring opens with disabling cold,
> And hunting winds and the long-lying snow.
> Is it a wonder if the buds are slow?
> Or where is strength to make the leaf unfold?

The lines are a more leisurely unfolding of Milton's terser metaphor:

> My hasting dayes flie on with full career,
> But my late spring no bud or blossom shew'th.

One difference between the two sonnets lies in their respective resolutions; Milton's speaker is convinced that however slowly his talents appear to be ripening, he trusts that he will be equal to whatever task his great Taskmaster sets.

This note of assurance is missing from Hopkins' poem. Here the speaker turns within himself to survey the lack of "yield" in his "poor and stinting weald." His depression is all the more severe because of his knowledge that the "good sower [Christ] once did sow" good seed within him, seed which he has failed to cultivate. He is specifically and painfully aware that his ties with his past have retarded his moving toward the Roman Catholic Church, a subject which his diary and letters at this time show to have been foremost among his concerns. The speaker has loaded "with obstruction that threshold / Which should ere now have led my feet to the field." The parallel between one's spiritual state and the farming of a crop is, of course, one of the recurring similes in the Gospels, and Hopkins seems also to have had in mind the parable of the talents. The final rhetorical burst of "Therefore how bitter, and learnt how late, the truth!" is, despite the emphatic parallel placement of the double "how," a somewhat melodramatic resolution after the markedly controlled self-excoriation of the preceding lines. Over-all, however, this sonnet shows clear signs of improvement over Hopkins' earlier experiments.

Between this and the next sonnet, two and one-half months elapsed, during which time Hopkins, among other things, was touring the Devonshire countryside. In his notebook for September 13, he composed an octet of a Petrarchan sonnet called, simply, *Shakspere* (126). It is surprisingly good; the syntax is tight, the conception pleasingly complex. Shakespeare's final place among the great masters, argues Hopkins, despite our inability to judge that place absolutely while there are future artists to be judged, must nonetheless be considered near the summit. For just as there are saints who do not have to await the final "Doomsday" to be judged, but "start" / Upwards at once," Shakespeare's canon has already been canonized. The diction, syntax, and modulated rhythms approximate normal speech patterns, an effect created by several stress adjustments. Of the eight lines, only three have end stops. The reversed first foot of lines 3, 5, 7, and 8, together with the masculine rhyme-ending and heavy enjambment, create a virtual spondaic packing. And all working together create the movement of natural speech. In a surprisingly short time Hopkins had learned what the syllabic-stress system could do in freeing poetic rhythms from the pitfalls of a sing-song musical facility.

Let me be to Thee as the circling bird (19) was composed on October 22, almost six weeks after the *Shakspere* fragment, when Hopkins was back at Oxford for his third term. Like *See how Spring opens,* this sonnet is an attempt to articulate his spiritual condition. The entries immediately surrounding his poem throw considerable light on the poem itself. Just before, Hopkins had written, "Note that if ever I should leave the English Church the fact of Provost Fortescue is to be got over." Provost Fortescue was a High Anglican churchman with strong Roman Catholic leanings who for a time managed to reconcile himself to his church with the Branch Church theory, which saw the English Church as a viable branch of the older religious body. In 1871 he became a Roman Catholic. What is most important about this note is that the sonnet itself celebrates Hopkins' virtual acceptance of worshipping God as a Roman Catholic, knowing "infallibly which I preferred." And this was a full year before his conversion.

Immediately following the sonnet is *The Half-way House* (October 1865), in which the speaker calls on Love, that is, Christ, to come down and be caught. The position that Christ was only symbolically present in the Eucharist, held by many prominent members of the Anglican Church ("My national old Egyptian reed"), gives way, for Hopkins, to the Roman Catholic doctrine of the Real Presence: "He is with you in the breaking of the bread." If there is any one doctrinal point which seems to have fired the intellect and imagination of Hopkins, it is precisely the doctrine of the Real Presence. Nearly seventeen months before, Hopkins

had written to E. H. Coleridge: "The great aid to belief and
object of belief is the doctrine of the Real Presence in the
Blessed Sacrament of the Altar. Religion without that is
sombre, dangerous, illogical, with that it is—not to speak of
its grand consistency and certainty—*loveable*. Hold that and
you will gain all Catholic truth." [22] This passage can serve as
Hopkins' own best gloss on the closing lines of his sonnet:

> The authentic cadence was discovered late
> Which ends those only strains that I approve,
> And other science all gone out of date
> And minor sweetness scarce made mention of:
> I have found the dominant of my range and state—
> Love, O my God, to call Thee Love and Love.

There is a double meaning to "ends" in line 10, for the
speaker has found his own proper *end* or goal, which thereby
ends all further searching.

In the octet the speaker prays for unerring constancy and
likens his call to that of "the circling bird" or the bat with its
"departing rings." The "changeless note" is then altered and
carried as a musical metaphor, "perhaps," as Gardner comments, "too cleverly sustained." [23] The entire sonnet builds
up to the speaker's "music in a common word," his "authentic cadence" and "dominant" in the crescendo of the final
line, whose alpha and omega is simply and powerfully
"Love." The emphatic repetitions and the delayed apostrophe to God have the authentic note of fine devotional
verse. The sonnet has the characteristic ring of, and is indeed
every bit as good as, most of the religious sonnets of Christina Rossetti.

Let me be to Thee is the last sonnet we know Hopkins to
have written for eleven years and four months, until he
created the splendid *God's Grandeur* on February 23, 1877.
The period of the early sonnets (March–October 1865),
when Hopkins was in his late twentieth and early twenty-

first years, has its own small but defined curve of religious
and artistic development and maturation. But while Hopkins' early sonnets show "a considerable mastery of the traditional sonnet form," [24] most of his best early work is in other
poetic forms.

The Alchemist in the City is among Hopkins' better
poems. It is entered in his copybook-diary for May 15, 1865,
in the midst of the sonnet period. It is written in the long
ballad form, each stanza being four lines of iambic tetrameter and rhyming abab. Gardner is correct in seeing the
autobiographical bias of this poem.[25] The alchemist who
must labor so long and so fruitlessly is a projection of the
Hopkins who was to become the classical scholar, the duty-
bound Jesuit, the dray horse with the yoke around his neck.
If there is gold, it will not be found in his lifetime. What
Hopkins is aware of is the long afternoon of the process
itself, the steeling oneself to perseverance, to patience. Because most men do not set their goals so high, they have the
succour and satisfaction of seeing their plans brought to
completion. The alchemist will not go their way, for it is not
that he envies other men so much, but that they show that
goals *can* be reached. What he most desires is "the wilderness / Or weeded landslips of the shore." As he strolls Faust-
like along his "breezy belvedere" high over the city, his heart
stirs for the "city pigeons" and the "tower swallows." He hun-
gers for the distance, to meet with the sunset, to replace the
tedious step-by-step dialectic of his books with the intuitive
grasp of God's untamed wilderness. What he has been looking for in books, the golden treasure, might be found there if
he could count on "prediluvian age," but he is painfully
aware that there is a short cut to that golden treasure of "the
yellow waxen light" if it could only be grasped intuitively, by
melting into it. Hopkins seems to be hungering here for the
prelapsarian world of angelic knowledge, for God's traces of

[24] Ritz, pp. 479–481.   [25] Gardner, II, 87–88.

that Edenic world are still to be found in nature's untouched wilderness. But the leap is not made, and the alchemist is left with his longing only. Of course if the leap were made, we would have no poem, since the poet would have transcended the very limitations of poetic syntax and logic within which he must create.

At the close of his long essay "On the Origin of Beauty: A Platonic Dialogue," written probably in May 1865, Hopkins' fictive Professor of Aesthetics summons Richard Garnett's *Nix* as typical of "what a poet expressed as a poet, in the transparent, almost spontaneous, artifice which alone can make a genuinely simple subject palatable." [26] The Professor proceeds to demonstrate that the beauty of the poem to a large extent is a result of parallelism and antithesis. About a month later Hopkins tried to capture the sense of pure poetry in his *Continuation of R. Garnett's "Nix"* by employing the same formal pattern and principle of antithesis. Garnett's poem shows ability, but it is pale next to Keats's *La Belle Dame sans Merci* and Arnold's *The Merman,* poems which *The Nix* immediately calls to mind. There are a large number of parallel phrases in Hopkins, as in line 2—"She loves his face, she knows the spot"—and lines 11–12—"And relish not her loveless kiss / And wonder at her shallow smile," or the syntactical antithesis of the entire last stanza, where the first three lines are set against the final line. Hopkins even presents a dilemma as a kind of culminating antithesis, for the hapless young lady who is the speaker is not recognized by Fabian, her lover. Nor can she leave without in turn leaving Fabian to the Nix's deadly charms. But in spite of his critical theory, Hopkins must have realized that successful poetry cannot be constructed by formula alone, however satisfactory it seems and even if a "professor of aesthetics" proposes it. Hopkins himself came to realize that inspiration was essential and that this came from without.

[26] *Journals,* p. 112.

There are a few fragments for August: a short description of streams and mosslike clouds (121) ; a rather forced description (122) of the special beauty of the skylark's "traverse flight" and heavenly music breaking against the sweet silence of the wilderness (an image which was to be used again in *The Caged Skylark;* and a piece of tortuous logic (123) which compares the relative nature of happiness:

> Mothers are doubtless happier for their babes
> And risen sons: yet are the childless free
> From tears shed over children's graves.

My prayers must meet a brazen heaven was entered in Hopkins' book on September 7, 1865. The stanzaic pattern is the common octave, with iambic tetrameter lines. There is in this poem a sense of the conviction of sin and of the speaker's unworthiness to receive God's love. His heart is not only clay, but iron. Try as he will, he will not allow a change of heart. There is a spiritual dryness here which the poet acknowledges but which he cannot change.[27] A sense of terror, and certainly a self-loathing, pervades the poem. We notice a clarity and sharpness of thought: the few images of brass, iron, and clay are severely controlled; the syntax is handled firmly except perhaps in the last two lines. There is no experimentation in rhythm, no lusciousness of diction, no sophistication of argument. But the poem is instructive in telling us something about Hopkins' poetics. When he experiences a religious depression, as here in his sense of sin and damnation or in his heroic effort in his last years to seal his

---

[27] What malaise Hopkins is referring to in this poem is not certain. It may be simply a sense of his own unworthiness, a feeling he experienced deeply and periodically. Or it may be his refusal to accept Catholicism outwardly, for it is clear that he had already, probably since the preceding March, seen its validity for him, although it took a year more to make the assent outwardly. Notice that by late October, as numbers 19 and 20 suggest, Hopkins had moved closer to Catholicism, especially because of the doctrine of the Real Presence, which was of central importance to him.

will totally to God, Hopkins without exception employs a severe style in which each word is weighed, like chiseled stone fitted into place. At such times there is little place for play in his language.

As with his later *St. Winefred's Well,* Hopkins' undergraduate *Floris in Italy* and *Castara Victrix* are also fragments of verse plays. The first is composed of two short soliloquies and a monologue, which add up to about 125 lines, including variant readings. The second is a series of three disjointed scenes that amount to 58 lines, although *Daphne* (124) may have been meant to be a song for a character of that name in this play. *Floris in Italy* is mentioned in Hopkins' long letter to Baillie of July 1864, where Hopkins speaks of it as having a narrative form, rather than its extant dramatic one.[28] And this earlier form was probably on some of the twenty-one pages torn from Hopkins' copybook for the period of June and July 1864.[29] The fragments of this play are scattered in the copybooks over a thirteen-month period, from August 1864 to September 1865. *Castara Victrix* coincides with the latter date and seems to have been conceived only in the previous month.

The two fragments of verse plays have a number of similarities. Both are imitations, in plot, diction, and blank-verse form, of Elizabethan and Jacobean drama. Both have young lovers in whom the dramatic tension is generated by a misunderstanding of the loved one's motives or by the fear of being so misunderstood.

In the first fragment of *Floris in Italy,* Giulia assumes the disguise of a young man (perhaps of Floris himself), with moustache and all—"This downy counterfeit upon my lip" —in order to pass through the sentries around the camp.

---

[28] "I have added several stanzas to *Floris in Italy* but it gets on very slowly" (*Letters III,* p. 213). In September he told Baillie, "It occurred to me that the story of *Floris in Italy* is dramatic, and all of a sudden I began to turn it into a play. It is a great experiment" (*ibid.,* p. 221).

[29] See *Journals,* p. xviii.

Before she leaves she passes a lantern over the sleeping Floris' hand, removes his ring, and ties it by a "ribbon" around her neck. In true Elizabethan fashion, Giulia displays her powers of conceit by her sustained punning on Floris' name. He is "this flower, this Floris," over whom Giulia's tears fall, as rainclouds "spill o'er fields of lilies." He is a "jacinth," the "late-found All-heal" (heal-all) with its many "virtues" (medicinal powers as well as character).

The second fragment is a speech, perhaps by the same Floris, who upon waking, angrily finds his "sweet Deserter . . . marching to false colours." The speaker recalls that the skies of Britain once raged and stormed in protest against the infidelity of Arthur's wife, Guinevere. England itself has turned "black and blasted" for having so mistreated the "mint of current courtesies." We hear Hopkins scolding here, too.

In the third fragment Floris argues against returning Giulia's love. Despite her beauty, he reasons, unless he loves freely, he cannot love. What is clever about the monologue is the metaphysical conceit of the drawing compass, which Donne uses so well in *A Valediction Forbidding Mourning*. In Hopkins' poem beauty becomes "the meet of lines," with one term of the arc in Giulia's beauty and another in "the looker's eye." If there is to be any circle which would "compass . . . the all-starr'd sky," the symbol of perfection and harmony, the fixed center must be in Floris' heart. It is a clever if somewhat strained and cold conceit, which, as Henry says, "ties spider's web across his [Floris'] sight."

The fragments of *Castara Victrix* (or *Castara Felix,* an earlier title which Hopkins proposed) make up even less of a story. In the first fragment (fifteen lines), we learn that Castara, led by her Esquire to attempt a shortcut through a mountain, has been separated from the main body of horses and men. In the second fragment (fourteen lines), Castara acts coldly and haughtily toward a wooing Daphnis. In the third fragment, Daphnis soliloquizes about the power that Castara holds over him. Castara's face, her very self, is fairer than other ladies', whose beauty is but as fever spots to her "rain or breeze or spring."

It seems clear that the drama was too ambitious a form for Hopkins to complete successfully. But the form did serve as a way of objectifying and chastening his poetic excesses. And if his short snatches of dialogue continually fall flat, they do seem to have helped to purge Hopkins' syntax of unnecessary connectives, of the stuff of prose. There is a growing muscularity in the language and a stepping away from the languorous style. Hopkins turned to Shakespeare to purge himself of Keats's music. But, then, Keats did the same.

A Complaint (128) is, as Gardner says, Hopkins' way of apologizing to his eldest sister Millicent for forgetting her birthday, probably her sweet sixteenth in 1865.[30] The complaint was written obviously after October 17, Millicent's birthday, and before Christmas, as the penultimate line suggests. Hopkins composed the "birthday letter" in Alexandrine couplets spoken in Millicent's own voice, to show that he understood her grievance and so forestall any further criticism. The tone is light, the rhythm jouncy, and the poem shows Hopkins' love of conceits, as in his comparison of a letter to "lily-white" leaves "charactered over with blacks."

On Christmas Day of 1865, Hopkins wrote out a short prayer-poem (129) to Christ, asking to be freed from "the self that I have been." It is a petition which he was to continue to make all his life, and more passionately as his "self-taste" brimmed within him. The intention of number 130, dated January 5, 1866, is unclear. But there is a strong contrast between the static "all-accepting fixèd eye" of the speaker and the swallow which hurls itself upon the gale, escaping "weight or pain" in motion.[31] And so the speaker too

---

[30] *Poems*, p. 307.

[31] The image of the bird moving effortlessly through the gale or the wind is a favorite of Hopkins'. There is "the dare-gale skylark" of 39, the falcon's rebuffing the big wind in 36, and the storm fowl hurling itself into the wind as it ascends in 45.

wishes to pass into the impermanent and away from the too "solid world." But in the scrap of poetry 132, Hopkins hears "the cold wind blowing" in the darkness and is glad to have a home.

The Nightingale (January 18–19, 1866) is quasi-ballad narrative in the worst tradition of mid-Victorian melodrama. The speaker is Frances, a young woman whose sailor-husband has quietly left to go to sea. The burden of her forty-nine-line speech is that because of the nightingale's song, upon which Hopkins lavishes two full stanzas of description, Frances did not hear her husband depart. And now, while she lies in bed alone with her "sad visions," he, poor Luke, is being washed "from on deck," victim of a storm at sea. What Hopkins is struck by, it seems, is the disparity between Frances' nostalgic regrets and the simultaneous death of her husband, of which she is unaware. The idea is paralleled in Section VI of Tennyson's *In Memoriam,* which of course Hopkins knew:

> O mother, praying God will save
> Thy sailor,—while thy head is bow'd,
> His heavy-shotted hammock-shroud
> Drops in his vast and wandering grave.

Suffering is a lonely thing. Hopkins was to treat this problem again in *The Wreck of the Deutschland,* for he was deeply impressed by the fact that people were being washed overboard off the east coast of England while he slept peacefully in Wales.

The Habit of Perfection, contemporary with *The Nightingale,* and written in the long ballad form, is among the handful of Hopkins' best Oxford undergraduate poems. Each of the stanzas is a self-contained unit shaped in the form of a command. The first six stanzas are addressed to one of the sense organs: ears, lips, eyes, tongue, nostrils, and hands. In each case the speaker chooses self-denial for the senses in order to prepare himself ro receive the spiritual life. In the last stanza the poet chooses to wed himself to self-denial in the form of poverty. Recalling Christ's words about

trusting in God—"And as for clothing, why are you anxious?
Consider how the lilies of the field grow; they neither toil
nor spin, yet I say to you that not even Solomon in all his
glory was arrayed like one of these" [32]—the speaker asks for
the wedding garment (the habit of perfection) from his
bride, poverty.

It should be noticed that in each stanza ascetic denial
leads to a spiritual insight manifested in lush, sensuous imagery. For example, the speaker addresses his hands and feet:

> O feel-of-primrose hands, O feet
> That want the yield of plushy sward,[33]
> But you shall walk the golden street
> And you unhouse and house the Lord.

What is interesting here is Hopkins' presentation of the
habit of self-denial not in its negative but rather in its
positive aspects, as leading to a cleansing and chastening of
the senses. Self-denial leads to such paradoxes as "elected
silence" singing, the eloquence of "lovely-dumb" lips, and
the darkness which is prelude to "the uncreated light." The
poem is tight, the progression smooth, the ending right.

Nondum, dated "Lent 1866," is, like *My prayers must
meet a brazen heaven* of six months before, a poem of darkness, a cry in the wilderness to a God who will not show
himself. Apparently Hopkins was undergoing another of
those periods of intense self-revulsion which accompanied an
overwhelming sense of sinfulness. The consequences of sin,
Milton writes, are "distance and distaste, / Anger and just

---

[32] Matthew 6:28–29. I have used the Confraternity of Christian Doctrine translation throughout; it is a more modern version of the
Douai-Rheims translation available to Hopkins. Hopkins himself, of
course, could read the Latin (and Greek).

[33] The contrast between walking bare-foot through the summer grass,
of kicking off one's shoes in unrestrained freedom, and the call to do
one's duty imaged in the figure of being shod recurs frequently throughout Hopkins' poetry. It is to be found, for example, in *God's Grandeur,
The Caged Skylark, Felix Randal,* and *Epithalamion.*

rebuke" (*Paradise Lost*, IX, 9–10). And the distance is very great in Hopkins' poem; our words seem "lost in desert ways," or they die in the "vast silence." The abysses are infinite; we search the "blackest night" and are met only with "being's dread and vacant maze." Stanza 2 sketches a particularly harrowing image of a hiding God. All about us we see proofs of a majestic design, as in the myriad stars above us like a "lighted empty hall," which invites us but which is discovered to be appallingly empty.

But the distance is not only spatial; there is the awareness in this post-Darwinian world of the "unbroken silence" of untold ages, which recalls the domain of Chaos and of Night. So God remains silent, while we mortals zealously uphold our contradictory creeds, shaping the "King" in our own images, uncertain of the truth, which has become as a "moaning voice among the reeds." And what is worse, we move swiftly, unavoidably "along life's tomb-decked way" toward the final silence, the final darkness of death.

The speaker can do nothing but surrender, to admit that he is, as Newman had said in *Lead, Kindly Light,* a child in the darkness, or as Tennyson had written in *In Memoriam* (LIV), "An infant crying in the night." [34] He asks for patience—that virtue Hopkins was to pray for so often as a Jesuit—to sustain him until God not only shows Himself to exist but also that He is near. Against the backdrop of a terrifying universe which had suddenly exploded both outward and backward beyond the imagination's ability to grasp, Hopkins calls on God not as a father but as a mother to still her child's fears with "One word." That, he feels, can sustain him until he can "behold Thee as Thou art." [35]

---

[34] Hopkins copied out the full text of *Lead, Kindly Light* into his copybook in mid-October 1865 (see *Journals*, p. 71). Newman's own religious struggles were very much on Hopkins' mind in 1866, the year of his conversion to Catholicism.

[35] See *The Blessed Virgin compared to the Air we Breathe* (1883) for a similar tension between God's infinite awesomeness and the Blessed

Hopkins was to return to this theme a decade later in dramatically similar terms in *The Wreck of the Deutschland*. There too, facing the encroaching chaos figured, as Milton had seen it, as a black storm-tossed ocean, Hopkins prayed to find meaning and was answered with "One word"—the Logos, Word, Christ, *Ipse*.

Easter, written probably at Easter 1866, is a hymn of joy, unrestrained, exclamatory, opulent. The first stanza recalls Lazarus' sister Mary anointing Christ's head with the expensive spikenard; she does not reckon the cost (cf. John 12:10). Easter is not a time of stinting; it is a time of giving freely, of celebration, as the skies themselves warm up and earth is decked with flowers opening heavenward. Lenten austerity gives way to the time of feast, of the Communion banquet at God's table. Let every morning, the speaker puns, be an eastering, a rising, "an Easter Day" in us.

While most of Hopkins' early poetry exists in the rough drafts of his two small diaries, some of the very early poetry exists in copies written out by others, and some remains in autograph. Bridges had already begun copying out Hopkins' poetry in 1866 and so we have some of the poems for the period after the copybooks end. But Hopkins meant what he wrote in his diary for May 11, 1868: "Slaughter of the Innocents." For it was on this day that he gathered together all the finished copies of his poems and burned them because he did not believe that writing poetry would be compatible with his priestly vocation.[36]

Mother's human tenderness. Hopkins needed the latter as he needed the Incarnation, to be able to grasp the "too huge godhead" in personal terms.

[36] He did, however, keep corrected copies of some things he had sent to Bridges, since Bridges already had them in an earlier form. But he destroyed all those finished poems which no one had yet copied. So, for example, he must have shocked his friend when he wrote him that he had burned his *Summa,* probably an extensive poem. See *Letters I,* p. 24.

So, for example, his 175-line fragment (longer with fragment 118, which belongs in sense with it) of *A Voice from the World* (81), which has been meticulously pieced together and edited, was in fact finished, probably, in late 1866. But there is no finished version extant. It is an answer to Christina Rossetti's *The Convent Threshold* of 1862, a monologue by a young woman who has seen "the far-off city grand" of heaven, and bids her lover, with whom she has "sinned a pleasant sin," to repent and rise heavenward with her. Her love has been transformed from eros to caritas. The poem, which received a sympathetic reception among her mid-Victorian audience, falls flat on our ears. It lends itself to the same kind of unintentional humor that William Holman Hunt's *The Awakened Conscience* does, in which the young lady, having fallen already with the young beau seated there, suddenly springs up, her eyes filled with what is to be taken for ecstasy. Whatever the expression on her face, the young man looks unmistakably disappointed. What is annoying about Miss Rossetti's poem is the assumed superior morality of the female speaker, her histrionics, her Beatrice complex. Hopkins began his reply as a serious answer from the point of view of the young man who wants to be understood, who feels rejected, who has moved from center to periphery of the woman's vision. While he finally does repent, he still wants to remember his sweet past; yet how can he when God has so freely offered His forgiveness? And more. By January 1867 Hopkins could no longer subscribe to the egocentric and unrealistic morality of his reply. "I have ceased to care for *Beyond the Cloister* [the final title of his poem] being put into a magazine," Hopkins wrote to his friend, the Reverend E. W. Urquhart:

Too many licenses are taken for a beginner, but the objection is on the score of morality rather than of art, and as the licenses in themselves I still think justifiable I need not alter what I cannot publish. . . . I did send this piece first to *Macmillan's* wh. is always having things of Miss Rossetti. Part of it was written two years and a half ago [June 1864] and though that does not sound much one changes very fast at my age and I shd. write better now, I hope.[37]

Hopkins twice mentioned his *Summa* to Bridges. The first mention is in a letter of December 22, 1866, two months after his conversion. "I will copy out the *Summa* for you shortly, but I intend to add a good deal to it some day and your copy will be a very imperfect version in other ways." [38] What Hopkins sent was the sixteen lines printed as fragment 133; how much he added to it over the next seventeen months will never be known, although it was probably a sizable amount. The conception, according to the title, was certainly impressive. But he burned the poem in the general slaughter of his innocents because, he felt, "they wd. interfere with my state and vocation." [39] The fragment we have argues that there must be a heaven because something must "supply / All insufficiencies." With our hindsight we can see that some of the lines refer uncannily to Hopkins' own priestly ministrations, especially the image of those who might have passed the time in the delight of the good life but who are confined to the "sordidness of care and crime" of the cities, cities like Manchester, Leigh, Glasgow, London, and Dublin.

The fragment of *St. Thecla* was discovered, with a Latin version facing it (180), in Dublin in 1952 by the Reverend Burke Savage. It is undated, but was probably written in 1866 while Hopkins was still at Oxford. St. Thecla is, in *Margaret Clitheroe,* "the plumed passion flower, / Next Mary mother of maid and nun." Hopkins was also ordained a priest on the virgin-martyr's feast day, September 23. Thecla's story is told in the apocryphal *Acta Pauli et Theclae,* composed by a priest about A.D. 180. The fragment is written in taut, energetic heroic couplets. Hopkins begins by con-

---

[37] Letter of January 16, 1867, *Letters III*, p. 36.
[38] *Letters I*, p. 15.   [39] *Ibid.*, p. 24.

demning time for being a smothering river which has obliterated Thecla's name, she whose name was once surpassed only
by Mary's. Pegasus and Bellerophon, who flew heavenward
from Tarsus, are evoked only to be dismissed, for St. Paul,
hurled by God from his horse while on the road to Damascus, is Tarsus' "true Bellerophon." Thecla is sketched; she is
a Greek beauty and bride-to-be. But Paul's preaching on
"the lovely lot of continence" and his dark saying that "the
world was saved by virgins" win her over. Again Hopkins
celebrates the positive values of chastity, as Thecla joins the
line of Hopkins' good but lively virgin-heroines: Dorothea
and Winefred.

Sometime between mid-February and early April 1868,
Hopkins contributed a poem, *The Elopement,* to *The Early
Bird or The Tuesday Tomtit,* a short-lived weekly journal
written at and for Newman's oratory, where Hopkins was a
junior master. The original of this poem is gone, and only
the fragment published as number 135 by Gardner exists, as
printed in an essay in *The Oratory School Magazine* in 1895.
Written in a rhythmic variation of the stave of six (ababcc),
it is a form popular with Matthew Arnold, used in *Stanzas
from the Grande Chartruese* and his *Marguerite* poems. The
speaker is a young woman who sneaks from her bed and out
into the night to meet Stephen, her lover. But the woman
seems more preoccupied with the "burly wind" and the
beauties of the young spring night:

> The stars are packed so thick to-night
> They seem to press and droop and stare,
> And gather in like hurdles bright
>   The liberties of air.

The piece is amusing if we think of Hopkins, twenty years
later, losing himself again in the natural splendor evoked by
his muse and forgetting his subject matter. For in the *Epithalamion* which he began to write for his brother but which
turned into a vivid re-creation of a summer's swim he called

himself up short by admitting he "should be wronging longer leaving" his sacred matter. So too the subject of the elopment here is recalled only in the last two lines of a thirty-six-line fragment, and poor Stephen still waits in the limbo of unfinished actions for his beloved.

Except for his Highgate translation of lines 88–127 of Aeschylus' *Prometheus Bound* (1862) and an anonymous Greek epigram (161) in March 1865, Hopkins' handful of English translations of passages from the classics or of Catholic hymns all date from the seven months during which he tutored in classics at Newman's Oratory School (September 1867–April 1868), having graduated from Oxford with a double first in "Greats" in the previous spring. There are two passages from Horace's odes which are certainly competent and based on the best Victorian models in the art of translation. Both pieces (165 and 166) urge the simple pleasures rather than the effete "Persian-perfect art." For why, Horace-Hopkins asks, "should I change a Sabine dale / For wealth as wide as weariness?" It was at this time that Hopkins was giving serious consideration to entering the priesthood, and these Horatian passages are in line with his thinking.

The translations of the popular Latin hymns are adequate, the rhythms are regular and true to the originals. Three (167, 168, and 170) are the hymns Hopkins would have sung or said often at Mass or Benediction. The other (169) is a translation of a prayer by Fr. Condren of the French Oratory of St. Philip Neri which Hopkins seems to have admired, perhaps because it asks Christ to help the petitioner to become more like him, especially, in words which have become signposts of Hopkins, in "the fullness of thy force and stress."

From the few fragments we have which Hopkins wrote in 1867–1868, it is clear that he was writing better. In fact, we can see a development during the eight-year period in at least three areas: a movement away from early Keatsian lushness toward a severer diction; a greater control of syntax and of the methodology of presenting an argument or idea poetically; and an early experimentation with sprung rhythm. But the development is not great, nor are there great strides forward. There is competency, but no inspiration. Much of his early poetry suffers, in fact, from that Parnassian tinge which Hopkins complained of in Tennyson in September 1864. We glance at the early poetry, we may be struck by images or a phrase, but we are not tempted to remain among those bright shards. Despite Yvor Winters' harsh judgment on them, it is to the poems written after the seven years of silence that we turn again and again.[40]

From Hopkins' seven-year period of silence there are only "two or three little presentation pieces which occasion called for." [41] Two of these pieces are Marian poems, written, in all probability, to be hung on the statue of the Blessed Virgin at St. Mary's Hall, Stonyhurst, where Hopkins studied philosophy between 1870 and 1873. *Ad Mariam* is a good imitation of Swinburne's diction and rhythms, although quite different in content. And *Rosa Mystica* also has the predominant anapestic lilt of Swinburne. That Hopkins should imitate Swinburne's flowing rhythms is not surprising; whatever their weaknesses, they mark a new direction, an energetic break with the languorous and nostalgic lyricism of Keats and Tennyson on the one hand and the grating roughness of Browning's dramatic verse-speech patterns on the other.

"Swinburne's genius is astonishing, but it will, I think,

[40] Winters sums up Hopkins' achievement this way: "It would appear that the most nearly successful poems are the following: *The Habit of Perfection, The Valley of the Elwy, Inversnaid, St. Alphonsus Rodriguez,* and *To him who ever thought with love of me.* . . . If one were to name the twelve or fourteen best British poets of the nineteenth century, Hopkins would certainly deserve a place among them, and I think his place will be permanent; but the place is not the place of the greatest nor even of one of the greatest" (*On Modern Poets* [New York, 1959], pp. 190–191).

[41] Hopkins' letter to Dixon of October 5, 1878, *Letters II,* p. 14.

only do one thing," Hopkins told Bridges in 1879.[42] The rhythms are too forceful to allow the treatment of all kinds of subject matter. But for the celebration of Mary's month, May, their lilting freedom was appropriate. Again, the use of the anapest demands great care by Hopkins that the accents not fall on the weak syllables, for this impairs the balance between sound and sense. It is one reason why Swinburne so easily degenerates into empty doggerel, why it is so hard to keep our minds on his meaning. Another thing we notice in Hopkins' poem is the absence of archaisms—"*untos* and *thereafters* and -*eths*" [43]—so characteristic of Swinburne. In *Ad Mariam* Hopkins uses a variation of *ottava rima* in anapestic tetrameter, the same stanzaic form that Swinburne employed, for example, in the chorus "When the hounds of spring are on winter's traces" from *Atalanta in Calydon* (1865), which Hopkins had read. The openings are quite similar, and Hopkins seems to be deliberately substituting Mary, "Maid yet mother as May hath been," for Swinburne's Diana, "mother of months."

The first stanza personifies May Day as a "sweet child" lying "in the breast of the young year-mother," so fair that men ask if there is any one fairer "to brighten our day." The "sons of Winter" have ruled oppressively, but their day is past; there is "joy for to-day and hope for to-morrow." Mary, like May, is "proud mother and much proud maiden," and dwells, like Diana, in a grove: Eden ("Aidenn"). Stanza 4 elaborates a bright analogy: just as May succeeds the storm months, so did Mary succeed the line of warrior-kings with a son whose name is peace. The final stanza is a hymn of praise to her who is "as dew unto grass and tree," and who is asked to be our "May-hope."

Rosa Mystica is also written in anapestic tetrameters, but in three couplets to a stanza, the last two lines forming a

---

[42] *Letters I*, p. 79.
[43] Letter to Baillie of September 15, 1867, *Letters III*, p. 229.

refrain. It is not as successful as *Ad Mariam,* and it is almost a self-parody as the other is not. The grafting of a metaphysical conceit in the tradition of Herbert upon Swinburne's meter was not a wise choice, for it lends a lack of seriousness to a serious subject. Mary is the mystical rose, "made of earth's mould" but now "shut in the skies," who bloomed two thousand years ago in Galilee. Christ is Mary's immaculate white blossom which flushed crimson "down the crosswood." Christ's wounds are like five rose leaves which have multiplied in their effects throughout the world. This Christ-bloom now gives off a sweet odor of grace in heaven, the grace which is love. Besides its merit as a prayer, *Rosa Mystica* points to stanza 22 of *The Deutschland* in its image of the rose bloom with "cinquefoil token" and "ruddying . . . rose-flake."

In that long period of silence, then, it is clear that Hopkins continued to deepen his theological sensibility and to cultivate religious paradoxes in the English metaphysical tradition. He was also looking for a new rhythm which Swinburne helped to supply. A number of lines in *The Deutschland* do recall Swinburne. But Hopkins needed a viable form to articulate the Word, and Swinburne's prosody was, he soon found, inadequate for carrying the heavy burden that he would demand of it. Here is how Hopkins characterized Swinburne's strengths and defects in a letter to Dixon in 1888:

For music of words and the mastery and employment of a consistent and distinctive poetic diction, a style properly so called, it [Swinburne's poetry] is extraordinary. . . . I shd. think it could only be in Persian or some other eastern language that a poetical dialect so ornate and continuously beautiful could be found. But words only are only words.[44]

And Hopkins wanted words which would point beyond themselves to the Word.

[44] *Letters II,* pp. 156–157.

The paucity of comment on Hopkins' early work in stark contrast to the voluminous criticism on the later speaks for the relative merits of the two periods. Had he continued in the direction indicated in this examination of his early work, Hopkins might have become a silver-age George Herbert, or he might have been relegated to a few pages in a respectable anthology of Victorian poetry following John Keble and John Henry Newman and Richard Watson Dixon in a section on devotional verse. But he did change. In fact, *The Deutschland* signals more than a change. It points to a transformation of the poet into one of the most dynamic and distinctive voices not only of his time but of all times. And for all that has been said here, most of that transformation occurred within the silent cocoon of the Stonyhurst, Roehampton, and St. Beuno's years.

2 ⤷ The Wreck of the Deutschland: 1875–1876

The Wreck of the Deutschland virtually explodes when placed within the landscape of Victorian poetry and poetics. It is an anomaly, a sport, an idiosyncratic performance in an era of highly individual performances. No wonder, then, that the poem should so often be shuffled by critics and teachers out of the time period in which it was written and into the twentieth century, an age which sees it as a harbinger of poetry in our own time, and should give it, by the very fact of its technical experimentation, a more sympathetic hearing. Like every long poem of achievement, it is singular. But it is also uncharacteristic of its age in a way that *In Memoriam* or *The Ring and the Book* or *The Scholar Gipsy* are not. It is uncharacteristic in its intensity, its prosodic techniques, its language, its range of emotional and religious responses, its intellectuality, its depth of structure, and its sense of organic unity achieved by the welding torch of Hopkins' imagination.

By uncharacteristic I mean that *The Deutschland* is not in keeping with our assumptions—aesthetic, intellectual, moral, and even tonal—about the mainstream of the Victorian period. There is missing, for example, that stance of ironic ambivalence, of the mind watching suspiciously and nervously its own movements. Nor is there an uneasiness or conflict of belief in a body of doctrine, or even in God. Nor, even, is there the attempt to work out the artist's own emotional purgation by the use of the dramatic persona or mask so that part of the self is exposed for scrutiny and part either safely shelved away or commenting on the part exposed. But a forthrightly religious poem is always uncharacteristic of a secular age. It leaves no doubt where it stands, and so it is intellectually accepted or rejected, even though it may be and often is salvaged by being enjoyed aesthetically. Still, Hopkins' *Deutschland* demands at least a momentary (fictive) assent to what it says or else the emotional intensity is bound to strike the reader as not only strange but wearying and even repulsive. Thus both Bridges and Patmore, two poets, one an agnostic and the other a Catholic, could be repelled by the ode.

But if the poem is uncharacteristic in its Christian affirmation and, more particularly, in its Catholic sacramental vision, it is in a number of ways a child of its age. In its twofold vision of the forces of nature it calls to mind immediately Tennyson, Newman, Carlyle, Ruskin, and Arnold. And it is Victorian in its fascination and repulsion with the self, which is both god- and wombat-like. Hopkins is kin to Diogenes Teufelsdröckh.[1]

Shipwrecks seem always to have fascinated Hopkins. Several of his early poetic fragments deal with or mention them. Sitting at table with his family at Hampstead, he must often have listened to his father, a marine insurance adjustor, discussing wrecks and salvaging operations. And literature, of course, is filled with accounts of shipwrecks. But even closer, perhaps, is the influence of Joseph M. W. Turner's seastorm paintings and their dynamic verbal representations in John Ruskin's art criticism. There is an obvious parallel, for example, between the description of those aboard the

---

[1] For a helpful (and rare) discussion of Hopkins in his time see especially Chapter 1 of Wendell Stacy Johnson's *Gerard Manley Hopkins: The Poet as Victorian* (Ithaca, N.Y., 1968). Professor Johnson sees Hopkins as sharing with the other Victorians "an oblique, often nervous, constantly self-questioning manner" and an "ambivalence" toward "the whole Romantic landscape" (p. 44).

"Deutschland" in the narrative center of the ode and Turner's "Slaves Throwing Overboard the Dead and Dying—Typhoon Coming On." [2] But there seems to be an even closer analogy between Turner's later impressionistic paintings of a strong, blinding, and suffusing source of light transfiguring a storm at sea and Hopkins' vision of Christ as the beacon light transfiguring that chaotic snow-driven night on the Kentish Knock.

Hopkins' muse ended its seven-year silence in December 1875, when Fr. Jones, his superior at St. Beuno's, suggested that Hopkins might write a poem on the shipwreck of the North German steamship "Deutschland" which had foundered on a sand shoal in the mouth of the Thames early in that month. Of the two-hundred-odd passengers (the exact number is not known) aboard who were going to America, a quarter became victims of the storm and the sea, among them five German nuns who had been exiled from Germany by Bismarck's anti-Catholic Falck Laws. But Hopkins did not create a masterpiece simply because he had an opportunity to write. The account of the wreck, he wrote his mother that Christmas Eve, "made a deep impression on me, more than any other wreck or accident I ever read of." [3]

Hopkins' mother sent him the newspaper accounts of the shipwreck, probably those in *The Times* and the *Illustrated London News*, and many of the incidents of the narrative are drawn directly from these,[4] such as the description of the brave sailor who was crushed to death when he fell to the deck attempting to help the women below, and the words of the gaunt six-foot nun who called out, "Christ come quickly," before she perished. And Hopkins insisted that "what refers to myself in the poem is all strictly and literally true and did all occur; nothing is added for poetical padding." [5]

[2] *Ibid.*, p. 59.   [3] *Letters III*, p. 135.
[4] For the newspaper accounts see *ibid.*, pp. 439–443, and the fuller Appendix in Norman Weyand's *Immortal Diamond* (New York, 1949).
[5] Letter to Bridges of August 21, 1877, *Letters I*, p. 47.

Bridges read *The Deutschland* only once and refused to read it again. Hopkins remonstrated with him at the same time that he sympathized with Bridges' difficulties. Hopkins suggested a method for reading the poem in a letter to Bridges:

Granted that it needs study and is obscure. . . . You might, without the effort that to make it all out would seem to have required, have nevertheless read it so that lines and stanzas should be left in the memory and superficial impressions deepened, and have liked some without exhausting all. . . . [You can get] more weathered to the style and its features—not really odd. . . . When a new thing, such as my ventures in the Deutschland are, is presented us our first criticisms are not our truest, best, most home-felt, or most lasting but what come easiest on the instant.[6]

Hopkins' poem is difficult primarily because of its intellectual and emotional depth. And there is no escaping the task of wrestling long and hard with a task that was long and hard for its creator. Hopkins has said, in Coleridgean fashion:

The further in anything, as a work of art, the organisation is carried out, the deeper the form penetrates, the prepossession [the connotations and emotional complexities aroused in the artist by contemplating a word or idea as thing] flushes the matter [i.e., the thing contemplated], the more effort will be required [by us] in apprehension, the more power of comparison, the more capacity for receiving that synthesis of (either successive or spatially distinct) impressions which gives us the unity with the prepossession conveyed by it.[7]

In short, Hopkins would warn us, if you want to know *The Deutschland* you will have to do more than read it; you will have to live with it.

[6] Letter of May 13, 1878, *Letters I*, p. 50.
[7] *Journals*, p. 126. It is in grasping the prepossession that we also grasp the distinctiveness of the artist, the very self of the creator. See, for example, *Henry Purcell*.

Hopkins called *The Deutschland* an ode and also suggested its affinities with Pindar,[8] but it does not have the
strophe-antistrophe-epode stanzaic movement of the Pindaric ode. It is like the later odes of Keats in employing a
fixed stanzaic pattern throughout, a pattern which Hopkins
apparently developed himself. The stanzas are eight lines
long and use the rhyme scheme ababcbca, a pattern which
returns on itself. The lines are in sprung rhythm; the stress
pattern in Part the First is 2-3-4-3-5-5-4-6. There is an extra
stress in the first line of each stanza in Part the Second. The
stresses, properly read, emphasize the meaning. In a note to
the poem Hopkins asks his readers to "let the stress be made
to fetch out both the strength of the syllables and the meaning and feeling of the words." [9]

The Deutschland is divided into two unequal parts: the
first part has ten stanzas, the second twenty-five, so that the
poem has a neat ratio of 2 to 5. Part the First is autobiographical. It recalls an actual time when the speaker himself
was pushed under the great stress of God to acknowledge His
mastery.[10] Part the Second moves outward from the self to
the objective world of the moment of the shipwreck, when
the nun was also confronted with God's awesome power and
likewise acknowledged His mastery. The conclusion turns to
England itself with the prayer that she too may acknowledge
God. We have a general movement, then, from the self to
another to a larger community, but the larger framework is
God Himself, the first word ("Thou") and the last word
("Lord") of the poem, the alpha and the omega.

Part the First

Stanza 1. Pindar often directly addresses the athletic champion in his victory odes. And here at the very opening of Part
the First Hopkins addresses the champion of his ode: God

[8] *Letters I,* p. 49.   [9] See *Poems,* pp. 255–256.
[10] See letter of August 21, 1877 to Bridges, *Letters I,* p. 47.

Himself. God is addressed as the master, as the creator and sustainer of the world and of the speaker as well. He creates the world's strand, nature's ground of being, and controls as well the limits of nature's shifting, terrifying, ungraspable forces. Job-like, the poet chides the giant shaper, God, who has knotted him together as man by inscaping him—that is, shaping, creating, and sustaining him. The speaker is like a length of rope which has been twisted and then unraveled. The speaker remembers how he had seemed to fall apart as his "momentary stay against confusion" (to quote Frost) gave way under a new onslaught, a new religious crisis.[11] As the "Deutschland" itself will be, the speaker is again forced onto another strand and buckled by a new sway of waves. He is terrified by the new confrontation. But he reads the signs aright; he finds God's presence (although overwhelming) here in the events of the sea disaster. And what many would call merely chaos and chance the speaker sees to be God's plan of salvation for men.

Stanza 2. The speaker remembers that he had acknowledged God's design and mastery working within him, not as he looked at the beauty of bluebells or landscapes, but when confronted by "lightning and lashed rod"—two terrors which call to mind the frightened child. He confessed, proclaimed, God's terror. "O Christ" is a prayer which in its emotional stress sounds like a strong expletive as well. God knows where, before what altar, and when the speaker gave his assent. Like the later yes of the nuns, it was given in the night when the terror of God was about him. His sense of utter helplessness is like falling from a great height (as those felt who were pitched downward from the masts of the "Deutschland"). God is seen here as a giant, as he was to be

[11] See Hopkins' journal entry for August 16, 1873, for another image of the self unraveling: "In fact being unwell I was quite downcast: nature in all her parcels and faculties gaped and fell apart, *fatiscebat,* like a clod cleaving and holding only by strings of root. But this must often be" (*Journals,* p. 236).

pictured again in *Carrion Comfort*. The speaker is a wreck whose "midriff" (heart) is strained but is also "laced" (bound together) with the fire of God's stress. So even as he feels torn apart by God, he is sustained by Him.

Stanza 3. Before him the speaker had seen a justly angry God; behind him was the plunge into despair and hell. His agitation and bewilderment are echoed in the repetitiveness of "where, where was a, where was a place." He fled not to the face of God—His stern justice in which no man is found worthy—but to the heart of God, relying on His mercy. That heart of the Host is the Communion bread, Christ incarnated in the bread rather than God confronted directly. The heart has reasons that the mind does not understand, and it can choose its resting place all in a moment. It is like a dove, the symbol of faithfulness, and like a carrier pigeon with its inherent homing instinct.[12] Like St. Paul, he too will boast, for Paul had also suffered shipwreck and had been miraculously saved, as Hopkins had suffered spiritual shipwreck and found God.[13] All in a moment Hopkins had flashed from the flame of hell and of divine anger to the Sacred Heart of Jesus. He had grown, spiraled upward from the prescient grace of an awareness of the *need* for God to the grace of fully accepting Him, of *wanting* Him. For we only tower by God's grace; otherwise we are nothing.[14]

Stanza 4. There is a shift to the present moment and a commentary. For what am I in and of myself, the speaker asks. I am soft sand sifting in an hourglass. I am bound fast at the wall (see stanza 1, fastened flesh, bound bones), at least in appearance. But within I cannot sustain myself because I am constantly drifting and "mined with a motion"

---

[12] See also *The Handsome Heart,* where the heart is again likened to a "carrier" in its "homing nature," and *In Memoriam,* section xii.

[13] See Paul's second letter to the Corinthians, 11:19–33, 12:1–9, which is the Epistle for Sexagesima Sunday.

[14] See the tower imagery of *The Shepherd's Brow* written in the last months of Hopkins' life.

(also, his *mind* is in a constant turmoil and flux). I drift with time (like the rudderless "Deutschland" of the second part), and this motion goes of itself in one direction continuously, gathering to the fall (the Fall). My own drift or bent of mind is always away from God.

Still, "I steady" (used here in its verb sense primarily) like water in a well, for I am roped always (see stanza 1) with a fresh supply, freely given, of Christ's gift: grace. This is a spiritual vein (see stanza 1), like streams of water from a "voel" (hill) which sustain me. It is a supernatural stream of grace from that hill of Calvary which keeps the well of my being constantly full, steadies me, and stops my drifting. Christ is the living water, the gospel proffered to me. He is the pressure, the "principle" (the first, as well as the payment given in buying me back). The image here is one of great height, for man, Hopkins implies, is roped, sustained, at every moment by God's hand. So while life ebbs out, Christ's life sustains him and steadies him; it is the "yes" given to Him which poises the speaker. Hopkins has found a perfect image of God's paradoxical dynamic stasis in the apparently steady water that is at every moment constantly circulating and being freshened from unseen sources.

Stanza 5. This stanza is a further clarification of the nature of the pressure exerted by God. He is there in the world about us. The poet acknowledges this presence; he bears witness to it in kissing his hand to the stars. God is there in the gentle starlight as well as in the thunder and lightning of storms, thus manifesting both his gentleness and his power through the things of nature. I kiss my hand, the poet repeats, to the beautiful sunset. For since God is the world's strand (stanza 1), he is "under the world's splendour and wonder." Still, we do not always see this; it is an insight into reality freely given by God. Spiritual beauty is "stressed" in upon us by God's pressure in our apprehension of physical beauty. And it must be continuously stressed in us to make its indelible mark. So that is why I kiss my hands to nature, for I am acknowledging having met Christ there. And I bless Him when I understand what God has freely offered me. The poet literally understands, for he "stands under" the appearance of the world's beauty and meets its Creator.

Stanza 6. But the stress of Christ on the speaker's heart does not spring (in its senses of water and of eastering) out of Christ's bliss. Nor does the stroke of the stress on his heart swing first from out of heaven. That stroke (with its dual meanings of a harsh blow as well as of soft petting) and stress of God are delivered by both soft stars and harsh storms (see stanza 5); it hushes guilt and flushes and melts our hearts. God's stress rides time like "riding" (going with the current, but also ruling) a river. The Christocentric nature of history is clear to only a few; the faithless misinterpret it altogether, and even the faithful waver in accepting the full implications of the Incarnation.

Stanza 7. That divine stress dates historically from Christ's Incarnation, from his "going" or riding in Galilee. The earthly life of Christ led from the womb to the grave, for the very carrying of Christ within Mary is a microcosm reflecting the daily existence of Christ, a gray "womb-life." "Manger" and "maiden's knee" led irrevocably to the frightful sweat of the Passion. The Passion is likened to the cloudburst of a storm which discharges its living waters amidst lightning and thunder. And the Incarnation is like a gathering storm which was felt in the Old Testament prophecies, discharged in the Passion and Redemption of man, and is still in high flood in the world itself.[15] But men do not understand this unless they are driven to it by some powerful religious crisis of the heart, unless the hart (heart) is hounded (by the hunter Orion of stanza 21). It is only under great mental and physical stress that we are raised from our diurnal affairs

---

[15] One of the corollaries of God's intersection with time is the shadowing forth of that event in the things of the world. For if **God** made and sustains the world, there must be some trace of Him in His creation (*ex opere operantis*).

to answer not only with our reasoning or esthetic faculties but with the whole man. There may also be a homophonic pun in the last line of stanza 7 on "none," for it is the nun also who was hounded by Christ and was "hard at bay" in the Kentish Knock.

Stanza 8. This stanza is linked by syntax (and thought) to stanza 7. The first line is a spillover, a release, and a completion of the sentence unit which takes up all of the previous stanza. The pressure and release of the syntax imitates the pressure and release of the uttered Word itself. We imitate that terrible stress of the uttered Word in our own struggle to utter the right word (Word). We bind ourselves with our choice, and by our acceptance or rejection Christ becomes either expletive or answer, joke or salvation. It is as when we bite into a ripe "sloe" (a plum-like fruit). We respond to that first pressure, to the sourness or sweetness of the fruit, with our whole beings. And this we do in an instant, "Brim, in a flash, full!"

So this is where men go—some early, some only at the very last: to the feet of the cross, to Christ, the hero of Calvary. We go even if we hadn't meant to or hadn't wanted to or even if we had no prior warning that this was where we were all the while tending. There we are. For men admire the heroism of Jesus whether or not they accept the significance of his sacrifice.

Stanza 9. The last two stanzas of Part the First utter praise to the Trinity. Like the ode itself, stanza 9 begins ("Be adored among men, / God") and stanza 10 ends ("be adored King") by focusing on the act of adoration. Hopkins picks up the hart imagery again. Man's maliciousness and rebelliousness must be wrung, "dogged in den." Like Donne in *Batter my heart, three person'd God,* Hopkins asks God to wring man from his evil propensities, from his motionable mind, with wrecking and storm, whether that wrecking take place on the Kentish Knock or in the knocking breast.

More than tongue can tell, God is sweet; He is both

lightning and love, both a winter and warm. For we perceive God's action on us in different and even paradoxical ways. God is a "Father," a "fondler" who has wrung men's hearts back to Him. In His dark and stormy descending, God most shows his mercies.

Stanza 10. Like a smith, God wrings the adamant self-bent man on the "anvil-ding" with the fire of stress. (There is also the hint here of the storm in the thunder of the anvil and the lightning of the fire.) But in this very stormlike stress, God steals in as a gentle spring, melting our hearts. The two stresses are really two aspects of the same divine stress and stroke, and both end in mastery (cf. stanza 1). God can make his mercy in all of us, whether it be abruptly, as with St. Paul on the road to Damascus who was blinded by a light and heard the thundering voice out of the heavens, or slowly and gently, as with St. Augustine, whose conversion was a matter of many years and backslidings. Make mercy in us, the speaker asks, so that we may be Your willing servants caught with kindness. But even more, make us adore You, which is our principal reason for being.

Part the Second

Stanza 11. Hopkins begins Part the Second abruptly amidst banging drum and blaring bugle. This is Death's cacophonous song, and everyone must listen to it. To some, Death comes as a cutting edge, whether it be the sword or the edge between flange and rail, or the biting flame, or animal fang, or flood. And on that note of presentiment Death's short song ends. Storms bugle Death's name, as they did when the "Deutschland" was wrecked. We dream that we are rooted, fixed in this world, in this earth, and that this is our home. But the only sense in which we are rooted here is in the dust from which we sprang and to which we shall return. All around us we see Death, but we wave with the meadow of flowers, the mass of humanity, and forget that in this part of the meadow also the scythe (Death) will "cringe" us, lop us off, and stain itself with our sour juices. It is our grim lot, our "share," to be sheared. The manner is uncertain, but not the end. Hopkins has thus established a tone with which we can all empathize, for no one escapes.

Stanza 12. Hopkins begins the narrative of the wreck of the North German steamer "Deutschland," which sailed on Saturday, December 4, 1875, from Bremen, bound for America (New York and Canada). There were over two hundred souls aboard her but the exact number will probably never be known. Many of these people were not under God's "feathers," the protection of the Holy Spirit and the Father. Nor did they realize that a fourth of them would be drowned on the shoal of the Kentish Knock. Still, the speaker asks (as he is to assert more positively in stanza 33), even though most were not ready, did not the inscrutable "bay of Thy blessing" vault even them in? Hopkins plays on the architectural meaning of vault and bay in the sense that God houses and bends over these souls. And there is a play on "round" and "rounds," for while the two hundred may be a large number to be cared for, they are but a fraction when compared to God's millions of rounds of mercy, His infinity. Surely all of this mercy could reeve in, fasten in, even these? And so Hopkins juxtaposes God's doom of stanza 11 against God's mercy of stanza 12. Death's terror is not compromised but it is seen under the corrective adjustment of God's infinite power.

Stanza 13. Here Hopkins moves into the heart of the narrative. The "Deutschland" hurls the haven of Bremen behind and goes too boldly into disaster, relying too much on itself. So too is the German state going in the wrong direction, away from the haven and into the storm in rejecting religion in favor of secularism and antichurch feeling. The snowstorm keeps up; the "infinite air is unkind," alien to mankind. There is a foretaste of hell in the infinite storm. Like a rope, the snow is "Wiry and white-fiery," like ice-cold flames. And the snow, like Fate itself, "spins" to the depths. Hopkins stresses the complete isolation that the ship experienced once it had left its harbor of refuge. Those deeps mean death; they are "widow-making," "unchilding," and "unfathering." Here is the terror of loneliness which the speaker experienced in Part the First.

Stanza 14. In the dark and apart from God, the ship strikes not a "reef or a rock" but a smother of sand, which recalls the image of sand as time running out in stanza 4. The ship is stopped dead on the Kentish Knock, and try as she may to break away from the shoal, she is helpless and at the mercy of other forces much as the speaker's own "midriff" had been "astrain with leaning" in stanza 2. The compass is now useless, for maintaining direction is out of the hands of the crew. Nor is the canvas, the "whorl" (propeller), or the ship's wheel of any help. For she can not be wafted (floated) nor can she be set going by the wind.

Stanza 15. By reiterating the word "hope," Hopkins suggests the hopelessness of the situation aboard the "Deutschland." The ship had stranded about 5 A.M. on December 6. And all day, until 5 P.M. when nightfall began to set in, the passengers looked for some sign of hope. But there was no rescue. Hopkins alludes ironically to rockets on shore and signals from a lightship which acknowledged the distress signals of the "Deutschland." But no help was sent out in the storm. Lives were literally "washing away" overboard. Finally, with nightfall and the rising tide, the people climbed to the sails, transformed now into shrouds, and shook there in the freezing wet air.

Stanza 16. Hopkins recalls (from the newspaper accounts) how one man stirred from the rigging above to save some screaming women on the decks below. He was strong, handy, brave. But all this man could do by himself (see stanza 4) was—nothing. In stanza 12 Hopkins speaks of God's mercy reeving in these poor souls aboard the wrecked ship, that is, fastening them in with the rope (vein) of His graces. But it is different with this sailor. The waves killed him "at a blow" and sported with him as in some macabre cat-and-mouse game. He was brave, but against the terrifying perspective of the manic storm he made but a poor *deus ex machina* transformed suddenly into a headless manikin swinging from a string, a grotesque pendulum for the others to "tell" the terrible "hours" by. There is added terror in the gay, boisterous indifference of the "cobbled foam-fleece" playing with its gruesome burden. It is a terrifying glimpse of what happens to those who rely on their own strength, even for good.

Stanza 17. It was God's cold against which these victims fought helplessly. The very decks and the water seemed to join actively in the conspiracy of crushing and drowning them. It broke the hearts of some to hear the broken-hearted other passengers, reduced to "rabble" by the storm. Amidst the general chaos and confusion of the romping sea and roaring night were mingled the "woman's wailing" and the child's frightened cries. But beyond all this cacophony and terror, this babble, this tumult, there is the telling, the effective utterance, of the virginal and prophetic tongue towering above the rest. There is a pun here on "told" and on "virginal," for it is music, both percussive (tolled) and melodic, which arises above the discord and confusing noises. And Hopkins may be playing on the story of the Tower of Babel, for the frightened shouts are unable to reach anything like succour, as opposed to the prophetic tower of the nun who does find markedness, meaning, inscape, in the general catastrophe. (Hopkins too is a virginal tongue telling the significance of the shipwreck.)

Stanza 18. The crescendo of the poem, like the crescendo of the storm, breaks now, midway through the poem. A deep, religious calm surfaces here as the poet is surprised by what his own breast has told him (it is what the nun's breast had told her). For he knows what it is the nun told, what she uttered (which the newspaper accounts, of course, passed over). In chiding himself for the tears which threaten to overcome him, he also calms us down. As in *Brothers* and *The Handsome Heart,* he is surprised at what the heart can know. Unteachably seeking "after" evil, never seeming to learn even when it should know better, it can still utter truth. Oh come now, tears? he chides himself. But the heart melts into a "madrigal start," into music, into the poetry of the ode. The speaker is glad for the insight and for his sensitive response. But he is embarrassed by his tears. You are always the child, the river of eternal youth, he chides his heart. But this feeling is not revel; this is *glee*—this is good —"an exquisite smart," a happy cry, that instinctive knowledge of the heart's good. Stanza 18 serves literally as an emotional release before the ode pitches upward again to its emotional climax.

Stanza 19. Hopkins, having evoked at the end of stanza 17 the central figure of Part the Second, the lionlike nun, now focuses on her, freezing her in the moment of her utterance. He hovers about this moment, backtracking and approaching but stopping at that moment until stanza 24, where the "word" is finally uttered. It is the technique employed in classical literature, as in the Homeric epics where, for example, the narrative is stopped to describe an artifact or weapon at some length. Hopkins' reason for freezing the moment is to focus on the "word" which gives meaning to the entire shipwreck and, by extension, to an apparently dark, stormy, hostile universe in which we are all shipwrecked, isolated, and helpless.

Hopkins dwells on the significance of the appellation "sister" in its meaning of a nun as well as of a relative (since both he and she have the same Father). He focuses on the crazed onslaught of the sea. Although blinded by the "rash smart sloggering brine," she does see one thing, she does have one "fetch" (breath, tack or course, contrivance, stratagem) in her. Like the lioness she is, she rears herself to call on "divine ears," and this call rides over the storm's own noise.

This call is to Christ and it rides time like riding the river (see stanza 6), for the ship is in the mouth of the Thames. But it is a call which summons and startles the men in the tops and, by extension, us, the readers.

Stanza 20. Hopkins summarizes the history of the German nun. She was the Superior of five Franciscan nuns. He interjects a six-line parenthesis to dwell on Germany (Deutschland) and its quite opposite offspring. As he was to associate the "Eurydice" with a foundering England, so here he connects the ship with its namesake: the morally foundering Germany of Bismarck. "Deutschland" is "double a desperate name," first, because of the desperate condition of the ship, and second, because of Germany itself which initiated the Reformation and which signaled the breakup and foundering of traditional Western Christianity. It is a paradox that the city of Eisleben, in Saxony, should have had two such diverse children as the thirteenth-century nun and mystic St. Gertrude and the Augustinian friar Martin Luther, who both gained nourishment from Mother Church.

But so it has always been, he realizes, since the very beginning of mankind, for Cain and Abel too "sucked the same" breasts, yet one made a sacrifice which was found pleasing to God and one was cast out into the wilderness. St. Gertrude is of central importance to the ode, especially in light of her devotion to the Sacred Heart of Jesus. And Hopkins himself versified, probably in 1877, a passage (no. 140) from her *Life and Revelations* which sheds a great deal of light on the poem's Christocentric resolution:

> To him who ever thought with love of me
> Or ever did for my sake some good deed
> I will appear, looking such charity
> And kind compassion, at his life's last need
> That he will out of hand and heartily
> Repent he sinned and all his sins be freed.

Stanza 21. By a perverted irony, however, these nuns were hated for their love and cast out into the wilderness from the land of their birth. Two rivers were responsible for their death: the Rhine expelled them, and the Thames killed them. The elements themselves were sinister hounds gnashing at a cornered quarry. But beyond the storm clouds are the serene stars. And prominent among the stars in the winter sky is the constellation Orion the hunter, who is Christ-Orion, the hunter of souls after his quarry of hearts. The speaker acknowledges Christ's hand in this storm. You, oh master of martyrs (and yourself the supreme example for martyrs), had ferreted the ship from its sanctuary and were weighing the true mettle of these souls simultaneously with your poising and steadying them. The terrible snowstorm, seen through eyes that can read these signs, becomes a sweet shower of lilies sent from heaven.

Stanza 22. Metaphysical Hopkins plays with the figure five. It is as though it had been divinely ordained that five nuns should be sacrificed. For it is a sacred number which particularly helps to explain Christ's own suffering. Five is a *sake*—Hopkins' own coinage for a recognizable, distinctive, and external manifestation—of Christ. Five is a cipher, that is, a message in code as well as a symbol of the absence of all quantity and magnitude, for Christ's sacrifice was an emptying of himself. Mark, the speaker puns, the marks were made by men, and made in the flesh of God-as-man. These five marks *mean,* are "word of," Christ's great sacrifice. Christ's sacrifice, however, was willed, was accepted gladly, as the necessary price which fallen men would demand and which Christ would give to buy men back for the Father (in the market-place diction, the buying-back was "dearest prizèd and priced").

These five scarlet wounds were, paradoxically: a royal stigma (the slave's brand marked in kingly scarlet); a signal —here meant as an act agreed upon as the occasion of the Trinity's concerted action for man's redemption, a token inciting to action, an object used to convey information beyond the range of the human voice, and a sign; and, finally, a cinquefoil (five-leaved) token and royal coat of arms for "lettering" (branding) Christ, the unblemished lamb who was sacrificed. Christ's wounds redden the rose-flakes (the cinquefoil is a five-leaved rose) which is a traditional Christian symbol for those who are witnesses in death to Christ. So the nuns' sacrifice recalls Christ's.

Stanza 23. Hopkins turns to the founder of the Franciscan Order, to one who had the stigmata: St. Francis of Assisi. May you be showered with joy, the speaker prays, for you were yourself drawn to Christ, to the source of life ("I am the Way, the Truth, and the Life") who, as man, died. After seeing in a vision a seraph bearing the crucified Christ, St. Francis received the stigmata, the impress of Christ's five wounds in his hands and feet and side—in short, Christ's own lovescape, the very wounds etched forever into his own body as a manifestation of his love, and the seal and guarantee of his love for men. And here aboard the wrecked "Deutschland" were five Franciscan nuns, "thy daughters," who held each other's hands, sealed themselves into one another to become "a five-leavèd favour," a flower for Francis to wear. They are sealed in death to form a new cinquefoil, a new stigmata. The terror of the scene dissolves as they bathe in Christ's "fall-gold mercies." That is, the storm is transfigured into a shower of bright autumn leaves as well as into a shower of Christ's bountiful graces won in his own fall to redeem the first Fall. Now, too, the drowning nuns breathe in the presence of Christ, the passionate bridegroom, by breathing into themselves his life-giving graces.

Stanza 24. While the nuns were experiencing their final agony in the winter storm, Hopkins was comfortably asleep in the dormitory of the theologate at St. Beuno's in northern Wales, situated on "a pastoral forehead." And that nun was calling out into the black night beyond the waves breaking over the ship, beyond the storm, to Christ to come quickly. As St. Francis had before her, she was calling the crucified Christ to her. And so she "christens," that is, names and sanctifies this ordeal in the name of Christ, so that the worst becomes the "Best" when she sees God's presence giving meaning to the apparent chaos.

Stanza 25. Hopkins has again circled around to the moment of the nun's utterance. And again there is no forward movement of the narrative in the subsequent stanzas until the close of stanza 28. The four intervening stanzas are concerned with the significance of the nun's utterance. What did she mean?

To inspire him in this prophetic undertaking, Hopkins invokes the Holy Spirit to breathe into him, as He had breathed into the nun that night (stanza 23), and to reveal to him her meaning. (1) Did she want to become selflessly more like her model lover, the crucified Christ, to sacrifice herself in order to identify more fully with him? No, he decides, for even those disciples who had Christ there in the body with them were terrified when threatened with shipwreck when the squall broke over Lake Gennesareth. They hurried to wake Christ to tell him they were perishing. All their thoughts were on survival then. Direct confrontation with such danger short-circuits thoughts of selflessness and makes us think only of survival. (2) Did she wish to suffer more keenly in her final agony in order to win a greater crown and comfort for herself in heaven?

Stanza 26. We know how we rejoice when the local gray fog or mist which hugs the ground like some furry animal moves off and the larger mottled May skies reveal themselves. Or even beyond that, how the vaster heavens of night manifest themselves with their "belled fire" (with its connotations of harmony) and "moth-soft Milky Way." But, paraphrasing St. Paul, however one imagines heaven, its beauty and grandeur and splendor surpass anything eye has seen or ear heard.

Stanza 27. No, Hopkins concludes, men don't seek greater suffering when they are actually confronted with imminent destruction. For it is being day after day after day yoked like a work horse to the galling, chafing, workaday world that makes the heart so heavy that we ask for escape.[16] It is then that we dream of heaven's ease. But in the direct confrontation with horror our natural response is only toward self-preservation, Hopkins shrewdly notes. It is in prepared meditations, when the heart is made tenderly receptive, that Christ's suffering appeals to us. No, he concludes, in the midst of the wind's terrifying uproar and the sea's dragon-filled (unknown and therefore all the more frightening) dangers, the burden (heavy load, cargo, and recurring theme) of her mind was quite different. "Measure" and "Burden" reinforce the idea that in the nun's mind the Word is a tune or melody played over against the chaos of the howling, discordant wind and seas. "Measure" carries the further meaning of a standard or criterion by which the nun could gauge her experience.

Stanza 28. What, then, is the meaning, the thought, the harmony which the nun found in the eye of all that surrounding chaos? Here the heavy ellipses reflect the poet's labor in struggling to bring forth *his* burden, to give birth to his tremendous insight. It is the center, the climax of the ode. What did she see?

It is the Word which gives meaning to all else. It is the Master, Christ *Ipse*,[17] King, Head. It is Christ who had cast the nun into her extremity, this farthest reach, and it is Christ who comes to cure, to save her. Echoing the opening lines of the ode, the speaker gives his fiat to the Lord to "lord

[16] For similar imagery, see the discussion of *Felix Randal*, in Chapter 5. Hopkins also employs this imagery in speaking of his duties as a priest: "One of our Fathers, who was for the best part of two years my *yokemate* on that laborious [Liverpool] mission, died there yesterday night after a short sickness, *in harness* and in his prime" (letter of New Year's Day 1882, *Letters III*, p. 162; italics mine).

[17] At the conclusion to the Canon of the Mass, the great Eucharistic prayer, all honor and glory are offered to God, the central Self, "per ipsum, et cum ipso, et in ipso" (through him and with him and in him).

it with living and dead." Let him who is her pride and whom she has summoned forth "ride" (travel toward and rule over them) in his triumph. For it is Christ, the Incarnated, who rides time like riding a river. With the vision of Christ in complete mastery of the situation, the doom itself (in its sense of judgment), which has been held in suspension since the end of stanza 17, now crashes over like a wave, dispatching them. But the doom now drops to the place of an afterthought, defanged of its horror.

But in what sense was Christ glimpsed? In terms of the emotional crescendo which has been building up to this point, it is clear that Hopkins is suggesting that what the nun saw in her last extremity was Christ himself literally walking the waves toward her. Regardless of how hard this reading is for most readers of whatever religious sensibility to accept, this is what the stanza certainly points to. Elizabeth Schneider is essentially correct in her reading of the ode,[18] for at this point all of the imaginative theological play on the Word comes down to this: the Word *is* Christ, with a human personality and nature, who actually walked across the breakers of the Kentish Knock on that particular stormy December night in 1875, as he did at Galilee nineteen hundred years before. Literary mythos is dissipated entirely at this point.

Certainly the lines can be read in part as a realization that it is the Word which gives meaning to the "unshapeable" (lacking scope or form) terrors. And certainly this is the realization which Hopkins wishes to stress upon his readers:

---

[18] See *"The Wreck of the Deutschland:* A New Reading," *PMLA,* LXXXI (1966), 110–122, reprinted with changes as ch. 2 of Schneider's *The Dragon in the Gate: Studies in the Poetry of G. M. Hopkins* (Berkeley and Los Angeles, 1968). Her reasons are forceful and cogent, especially her explanation of "fetch" in stanza 19, in which she quotes from Hopkins himself (*Sermons,* p. 200), who makes a distinction between "real fetching, presentment, or 'adduction,'" a real presence, and "mere vision."

the optimistic view that at the center of existence is not *nada* but a divine ordering. But what the nun saw was something more: her hero-bridegroom coming to take her home. And this interpretation most likely accounts for Hopkins' anxiousness that it would be better if the ode's full implications were not immediately comprehended by a Victorian reading public.[19]

Stanza 29. This stanza and the next dwell on the nun and her final utterance, praising and admiring her for having had her heart poised in the right direction, for having the "single" (healthy, undeviating) eye. She read and interpreted the chaos of that "unshapeable shock night" and saw its real meaning. She knew the "who" (Christ) and the "why" (Christ the lover was coming for his bride). She uttered the Word which all heaven and earth mutely proclaim because they were created and are sustained as a by-product in time of God's own selving when He worded Himself. Like Simon Peter (*petros*-rock), she answered "Thou are the Christ" when put to the test. Like the Tarpeïan rock, the place of execution in ancient Rome, the doomed nun was unshakable in the face of the storm. By Christ's grace she was so steady that she became a "blown beacon" (blown in the wind, but also growing in light), giving light and offering refuge to the others in that dark night.

Stanza 30. There is significance, the poet says, in the fact that the nun's vision and death occurred on the eve of the Feast of the Immaculate Conception (December 8), "Feast of the one woman without stain." For Mary first of all conceived Christ. It was fitting that Christ's dwelling place be without blemish, and so Mary was herself without the stain visited on all men since the Fall. The nun's virgin-birth was a parallel shadow of Mary's birth; it was a "heart-throe" and "birth of a brain," where Mary's was a physical bearing forth. But here too the Word was conceived in the mind and

[19] "I was not over-desirous that the meaning of all should be quite clear, at least unmistakeable" (*Letters I*, p. 50).

nurtured and "uttered . . . outright." The nun is Zeus and Christ the offspring from her head in this reversal of the ancient myth. In this utterance of the Word from the heart the Incarnation is constantly renewed in time.

Stanza 31. For her long patience and her final agony she has won Christ, but what of those others who perished without the comfort of Christ, without confessing their transgressions, and without confessing Christ? Stanzas 31–33 deal with this problem of Christ's *other* sheep. "Heart," the speaker cries, "go and bleed at a bitterer vein" (of thought) for them. But abruptly the poet reverses himself. No, they were not uncomforted, for Providence is so "lovely-felicitous" that God's feathery delicacy (see stanza 12) so touched the nun's breast that she could act as a bell, as a signal of Christ's proffered comfort, to "startle the poor sheep back" into the fold of the Good Shepherd. Is not, then, the "shipwreck" in fact a harvest of souls for Christ? And did not the tempest let the chaff fly and carry off the grain for him? [20]

Stanza 32. The speaker can only admire the ways in which God works. For the same God who could inundate the earth in the Yore-flood and who allows the year to fall and time to pass and autumn to come—there is a play here on the root similarities of time and tide—that same God controls the tides and recovers the year with spring. He sets the limits beyond which the sea shall not pass; He is the wharf and the wall of the flood. And He is also the ocean which quenches and stanches the motionable mind (see stanza 4). It is in Him that our minds find their rest. For He is the ground and granite too, the foundation of being itself, finally beyond our grasp to ever fully understand. He is the sovereign *behind* death, who heeds our prayers though he hide from us. He "bodes but abides," that is, He has told us what He as King demands, but He still stays by his rebels, watching and waiting, bearing patiently with us.

Stanza 33. Having stressed God's power, Hopkins now

[20] See the similar imagery of *Carrion Comfort.*

focuses on His mercy, which outrides "The all of water," the depths of the sea as well as time. Christ's mercy is an ark (the symbol of the covenant and of the Church's safe journey through time) for the listener who hears God's word and obeys. Christ's love for men glides even into death and the profound dark for "the lingerer," he who has gone largely on his own way but who fluctuates, never fully turning his back on God.

But even beyond and lower than that, Christ has a channel ("vein") for those sinners who cannot now help themselves but who with their last breath called penitently on Christ. He reaches to the very gates of hell to snatch them up. That prison is likened here to the cold, dark, and lonely ocean depths (an image Hopkins uses again in *The Loss of the Eurydice*).

As Hopkins frequently does with his syntax, he has made a sentence purposely ambiguous and capable of two viable readings. Lines 6–8 may be read in two ways. (1) The uttermost, those sunk deepest and closest to hell, "mark" (remark, watch) Christ the Redeemer and are "fetched" (reached, fished for) by the "passion-plungèd giant" who strides across the deep waters toward them, which giant striding is experienced by these desperate souls as a condition of storm. (2) Or—perhaps better because syntactically less strained—Christ's harrowing of hell after his passion and death and before his rising from the dead is the uttermost "mark," the furthest limit, that Christ won in buying souls back again. It is the furthest limit which he "fetched" for men in the stormy passion of his stride into hell. Since it is for men to give the final "yes" or "no," beyond this point Christ himself cannot go.

Stanza 34. Hopkins praises the Incarnated Word with a string of epithets rounded off in the magnificent crescendo of the closing lines of the ode. Christ the Light is asked to burn, having been once again reincarnated, refleshed, in the nun's utterance of the Idea into sound. He is the double-natured name of the God-man, and the antithesis of the "double a desperate name" of the "Deutschland." God has flung Himself once again from heaven and taken on a physical nature. The Second Person of the Trinity, of the awesome "thunder-throne," is a miracle of flame born of Mary. Christ came to these victims of the wreck not as lightning ("dooms-day dazzle") as he will at his Second Coming, nor darkly, as he came that first time to Bethlehem. He came to these souls kindly, in his man*kind*. But he is also King, and so he came "royally reclaiming his own." He did not come as a terrifying electrical storm but rather as a "released shower," a soft summer storm, bringing relief to the shire.

Stanza 35. So, as Milton did in *Lycidas* with Edward King, Hopkins makes the German nun a *genius loci* of the Kentish Knock and addresses her. Drowned at the doorway of the Thames, "among our shoals," our smothering sands, our English perils both physical and spiritual (for England, like Germany, lives in heresy), remember us where *you* are now, "in the roads," the protected, enclosed waters where ships may ride safely at anchor. For you are now in "the heaven-haven of the reward." [21] And that reward is Christ.

In the last five lines Hopkins turns directly to Christ and to those who are still struggling amidst the stormy shoals of life. He wants his King, exiled first by heresy and robbery and later by the indifference of secularism, to return "upon English souls." Christ is the rising sun, source of renewal and resurrection. The dark night of the ordeal is over (Hopkins specifically remarks in the subtitle that the nuns were "drowned between midnight and morning"), and God's light and warmth have returned. Let Christ easter, dawn, be a dayspring to our own dimness. Let his royal scarlet wounds, the sign of his love for us all, shine like a "crimson-cresseted east." Let him brighten "rare-dear Britain" as he brightened the nun, that "blown beacon of light."

[21] See *Heaven-Haven*, "where no storms come."

The last two lines have, in fact, something of the echo of the onward roll and surge of the ocean, and of a sustained drum roll. The epithets are a forceful recapitulation of the ways in which Christ has been treated throughout the ode. Christ is our "Pride, rose, prince, hero of us, high-priest." He must become the fire of charity in our English ("hearth's") hearts, and it must be he to whom all our noblest thoughts are addressed. The ode ends where it began, focusing on God, but with fuller joy and praise at having understood an event which had threatened to unmake the speaker. And, as in T. S. Eliot's *Little Gidding*, the fire resulting from the German bombing raid over London becomes the purgative force of Divine Love, so here the "fire of stress" in the speaker's heart in stanza 2 becomes finally the fire of Christ's charity spreading in the hearts of all.

The ode is certainly splendid, brilliant, emotionally charged; all of its strands are carefully interwoven, braided together, reeved in. It is an impressive poem, and despite its flaws of rhyme ("grubs in amber" Hopkins called them) and patches of flatness, the ode is a masterpiece. English literature, as Hopkins noted, "is not rich in odes." [22] And *The Deutschland*'s music and sheer intellectual manipulation of images and wordplay are uncharacteristic of the traditional English ode (Ben Jonson, Andrew Marvell, Abraham Cowley, John Dryden, and Wordsworth come immediately to mind) . So the accolade for England's finest ode is often given to Wordsworth for *Intimations of Immortality*. Certainly the music and movement, the serenity and tone of elevated celebration in that poem are more even-keeled and balanced than in *The Deutschland*. And Hopkins knew that Wordsworth had touched on something here which was original and seminal to English literature itself. [23]

But Hopkins' ode is, for all its grubs in amber, certainly equal to Wordsworth's. *The Wreck of the Deutschland* is

[22] *Letters II*, p. 147.   [23] *Ibid.*, p. 148.

unique: it is the one English ode to have captured the Pindaric spirit. Hopkins, like Pindar, is a metaphysical in his shaping power, for the most diverse and seemingly disparate subjects and ideas are interwoven, or better, welded into an artistic whole. Richmond Lattimore has said of Pindar's *Sixth Olympiad* that it "is exceptionally complicated; but the difficulties are met with triumphant, challenging, and almost perverse brilliance." This description fits Hopkins' ode just as well.[24]

[24] *The Odes of Pindar,* translated by Richmond Lattimore (Chicago, 1964), p. 152.

3 Musing in Wild Wales: 1876–1877

After the great effort of *The Deutschland,* and for the rest of 1876, Hopkins wrote only two fragments, *Moonrise* on June 19 and *The Woodlark* on July 5, and two occasional pieces, *The Silver Jubilee* in July and *Penmaen Pool* in August. *Moonrise* is pure description; it evokes a scene of a midsummer's crescent moon rising quite late over Mt. Maenefa as seen from St. Beuno's situated on the mountain itself. The moon still clings like a cusp or fluke to the mountainside, and it is this lovely sight, "unsought, presented so easily," which greets the poet as he awakens in the early morning. *Moonrise* is an important piece in charting Hopkins' prosodic development during this crucial year. It is written in anapestic heptameter unrhymed lines with an occasional reversed foot added for a spondaic or sprung effect, as in the second line:

The moón, dwíndled and thinned to the fringe . . . .

Hopkins has marked a strong caesura after the fourth foot, and he meant to change the lines to octometers, as his revision of the first line indicates. What we notice here is that he seems to be grafting Swinburne's anapests onto a long line more suitable for prose, as though he were regularizing Whitman's poetic prose. We know that he had read excerpts of Whitman's *Leaves of Grass* in 1874, perhaps earlier. In one sense, this fragment is a swing backwards from his just-completed *Deutschland* ode in sprung rhythm. But it also looks forward to his experiments in his verse drama, *St. Winefred's Well*, begun early in 1879, where he employs a carefully modulated sprung-rhythm line varying from six to eight stresses, and to the eight-stress lines of *Spelt from Sibyl's Leaves* (1885).

Two weeks later, on July 5, Hopkins experimented with a radically different form in the unfinished *The Woodlark*. This piece was left in disorder. It was arranged and three lines added by the Reverend Geoffrey Bliss, S.J., and printed in *The Month* in June 1936.[1] Hopkins uses a four-stress sprung line rhyming, for the most part, in couplets; it is patterned after the form he had used in his early *Spring and Death*, but the execution is radically different. It is Hopkins' first use of the sprung line employed simply for the play and *joie de vivre* of the thing itself: the woodlark's song. The poet hears the bird's tiny "trickle of sóng-strain" but cannot spot the bird itself. The larger part of the lyric is the woodlark's (and the poet's) joy in existence. There is a catalogue of the local flora: the corn, the "crush-silk poppies," "Sunspurge and oxeye," and "fumitory." The bird sings until "the longing is less and the good gone." The lyric ends like *Binsey Poplars* and *Inversnaid*, two other pieces about nature's wildness, with a haunting, sensitively modulated echo:

> With a sweet joy of a sweet joy
> Sweet, of a sweet, of a sweet joy
> Of a sweet—a sweet—sweet—joy.

Within probably two weeks, Hopkins wrote the short piece in honor of Dr. James Brown's twenty-five years as First Bishop of Shrewsbury. He was pleased with *The Silver Jubilee*, and he wrote to his father proudly about its being printed along with a sermon by the Reverend John Morris, S.J., and even of its being "sung as a glee by the [seminary] choir."[2] He also wrote two other addresses to the Bishop, one

[1] See the note in *Poems*, p. 310.
[2] Letter of August 6, 1876, *Letters III*, p. 140.

in Welsh and one in Latin, which are printed with translations as 172 (*Cywydd*) and 173 (*Ad Episcopum Salopien-
sem*) in the Fourth Edition.

Hopkins uses a forceful and sprightly four-stress sprung
line. The four-line stanzas have a rhyming couplet, followed
by a third line, in which the word receiving the second stress
rhymes with the word stressed at the end of the line. The last
line in each stanza acts as a refrain. Though the bells of
Wales do not ring out the Bishop's twenty-five years of service, other things do, like the fountain of twenty-five years of
grace. Shrewsbury may keep other feasts, but this is her
true silver jubilee, the twenty-fifth year of the re-establish-
ment of the Catholic hierarchy (actually it was the twenty-
sixth) . The Bishop's grey head is a visible sign of his having
spent his life well, it is "Silver but for Jubilee." And if the
Welsh bells have not chimed their welcome, let the chiming
of this rhyme, this poem, "Utter Silver Jubilee." Hopkins is
punning here on his use of internal rhyming, which is called
in Welsh poetry *cynghanedd,* or chiming. It is a tight little
lyric which, as Hopkins said himself, hits "the mark it aims
at without any wrying." [3]

Penmaen Pool was composed in August 1876 while Hopkins was enjoying a holiday at this North Wales mountain
retreat. Written in the long ballad form, it employs a standard iambic tetrameter line. Since each of the ten stanzas ends
with the same words, "Penmaen Pool," and an abab rhyme
scheme is used, Hopkins had to find a large number of
rhyme words. He succeeds by using only two impure rhymes,
"wool" and "full." He seems even to have used "renewal,"
but dropped this, and in a letter to his mother in late
September he admits that "it must be looked at partly as a
freak, partly as a necessity." [4] The stanzas are developed as a
sightseeing guide might be: attraction gives way to attraction, always turning on the pool itself. There in the pool

[3] *Letters I*, pp. 77–78.   [4] *Letters III*, p. 141.

sculls swing, Dyphywys and the Giant's Stool and "sheep-flock clouds" are reflected during the day, "Charles's Wain" by night. Even in rainy weather there is beauty in the rain-drops lacing the pool's surface, and in winter the "Furred snows" cover it "tuft above tuft." Hopkins' closing stanza is a variation of the opening, reinforcing the invitation to come to this section of wild Wales. If he had not become a priest, Hopkins would certainly have made a fine travel agent.

Hopkins wrote nothing further until 1877, when he was in his final year of studies at St. Beuno's in North Wales pre-paratory to the priesthood. In the months leading up to his ordination as a priest of the Society of Jesus, an event he had been preparing for since the autumn of 1868, poetic and religious inspiration, that "fine delight that fathers thought," welled up again within him. This year was to become, in effect, his *annus mirabilis,* when he created ten religious sonnets, all of considerable brilliance and at least one, *The Windhover,* a recognized tour de force.

The chronology of the 1877 sonnets cannot, unfortunately, be determined with absolute assuredness. Unlike Hopkins' undergraduate poems, which can for the most part be dated with some accuracy by checking his Oxford diary and his letters on literary matters, the 1877 sonnets were dated by the poet himself with widely varying degrees of precision. Half are handily dated to the day, two by the month; one is dated "Summer," and two carry only the year. Furthermore, it is important to remember that, as with Yeats, no matter how often or how much later he revised his sonnets, Hopkins never changed the original date of the poem.[5] So, for exam-

---

[5] "G. M. H. dated his poems from their inception, and however much he revised a poem he would date his recast as his first draft," Bridges noted in his Preface to the First Edition (*Poems,* p. 234). The only exceptions to this of which I am aware are Hopkins' dating of his revision of 31 and 32 from February to March 1877. Even then, he later replaced the February date for 31.

ple, while he considerably revised *The Sea and the Skylark,*
with which he was displeased, about 1883, he still retained
the May 1877 date.

Nevertheless, there is enough evidence to plot, with some
degree of confidence, the probable order of the sonnets. For
this task we have two primary sources: the manuscript poems
themselves, and the letters, particularly those to Bridges.

The earliest draft of *God's Grandeur* is precisely dated
February 23; *The Starlight Night* is dated the next day,
February 24. *In the Valley of the Elwy* can now also be
dated, because of a fortunate discovery, to the day: May 23,
1877.[6] *The Windhover* carries the date May 30, 1877; *Hurrahing in Harvest* is dated September 1, 1877. Both *Spring*
and *The Sea and the Skylark* are dated May 1877. The
curtal sonnet, *Pied Beauty,* is simply dated Summer 1877.

Finally, both *The Lantern out of Doors* and *The Caged
Skylark* are dated only "1877," but since, like all the other
sonnets, they were composed at St. Beuno's, both were defi-
nitely written before mid-October, when Hopkins was assigned to Mount St. Mary's College, Chesterfield. Furthermore, *The Caged Skylark* had to be written before July 24,
when Hopkins left St. Beuno's for a three-week holiday,
because in a letter to Bridges of August 8 from Hampstead,
he sends him a correction of the last three lines of the sonnet
already in Bridges' possession.[7] One final piece of evidence is
Bridges' note to *In the Valley of the Elwy,* which is there
marked as "contemporary with No. 39."[8] If I construe this
remark correctly, then *The Caged Skylark* may be dated
around late May of 1877.

---

[6] Norman H. MacKenzie (in "Hopkins MSS: Old Losses and New
Finds," *Times Literary Supplement,* March 18, 1965, p. 220, and in
"Gerard and Grace Hopkins: Some New Links," *The Month,* n.s. xxvii
(1965), pp. 347–50) explains how a copy of number 34 with the May
23 date was recently discovered among the literary remains of Lady
Pooley, Hopkins' niece. The sonnet was originally sent to Grace,
Hopkins' "musical sister."

[7] *Letters I,* p. 42.   [8] *Poems,* p. 265.

This appears to be as far as we can reasonably conjecture given the extant manuscript evidence of the poems themselves; it is possible, as Professor MacKenzie and others have suggested, that further manuscript poems may turn up, but this is the dating as we now have it. One final conjecture from internal evidence is that *Spring* may have been written for May 1, "Mayday" (line 13) ; in tone and spirit it is like Hopkins' Marian poems.

Hopkins' letters can now provide us with an interesting if fragmentary background to this dating of the sonnets. In reconstructing the background we can follow, as in a mist, the setting for this period of generous and intense poetic activity. Some of the sonnets are well documented in the letters, especially the first two, which thus fittingly inaugurate Hopkins' mature composition in the form. But after an auspicious beginning there are lamentable gaps when we have no letters. This is especially true of May, when Hopkins probably wrote six of the ten sonnets. Still, there are valuable comments scattered throughout Hopkins' correspondence for this period, and when these are collated with other evidence, a clear pattern does emerge.

If we rearrange the sonnets according to the partial dating thus far established, and if we analyze Hopkins' crucial remarks appended to the manuscript sonnets themselves as pointing the direction in which he was developing the rhythms of his sonnets, I think that we will have sufficient evidence to reconstruct the sequence of these ten sonnets. I cannot, for reasons which should become apparent, accept Professor MacKenzie's proposed rearrangement of the 1877 sonnets as they appear in the Fourth Edition. My objections are more than merely theoretical.

In his "Foreword" to the Fourth Edition, Professor Mac-Kenzie sees the 1877 sonnets as forming "a sequence related with unusual immediacy to the flow of the changing seasons." But he would place *The Lantern out of Doors* (40), because of its "sense of bereavement," sometime in the early

autumn, after Hopkins had learned, to his great disappoint-
ment, that he would not be taking an additional year of
theology at St. Beuno's, as he had expected, but would be
assigned to Chesterfield. While the mood of the sestet of this
sonnet is somewhat restrained in tone, it is less so than that
of *The Sea and the Skylark,* written in May. Besides, if we
can judge by such a fleeting thing as a mood, *Hurrahing in
Harvest* is an extremely enthusiastic piece, and this was
composed at the beginning of September, where Professor
MacKenzie would fit 40. Furthermore, only six days after his
ordination (September 23), Hopkins was confined to his
bed, where he remained until shortly before his transfer, and
probably he did not feel like composing sonnets. Moreover,
there is internal rhythmic evidence, as I hope to demonstrate, which points to an earlier date for the poem, probably
May.

On April 3, two days after Easter, Hopkins confessed—for
the first time since his Oxford days—that he, like Bridges,
had been writing sonnets, but he carefully avoided any mention of the more radical experiments of *The Wreck of the
Deutschland.* Like Hopkins, Bridges had also been experimenting with Milton's prosody, and it was this coincidence
which may have caused Hopkins finally to speak about his
own poetry:

It happened that the other day, before you had written to me on
the matter, I composed two sonnets [31 and 32] with rhythmical
experiments of the sort [based on Milton's prosody], which I
think I will presently enclose. How our wits jump! Not but what
I have long been on metrical experiments [*The Wreck of the
Deutschland* in sprung rhythm] more advanced than these. You
will see that my rhythms go further than yours do in the way of
irregularity. The chiming of consonants [*cynghanedd*] I got in
part from the Welsh, which is very rich in sound and imagery.[9]

In a letter to his mother on April 20, he calls attention to a
slim volume of lyrics by Bridges and remarks that they are

[9] *Letters I,* p. 38.

"beautiful" and designedly written in Miltonic rhythms *but not violent like mine.*" [10]

From April 20 to June 13—a period of almost eight weeks —there are no extant letters either from or to Hopkins. This is unfortunate, especially since it was in May that he composed *Spring, The Sea and the Skylark, In the Valley of the Elwy, The Windhover,* and very probably both *The Lantern out of Doors* and *The Caged Skylark.* He had written six sonnets in one month in a spurt of creative energy. Moreover, in his short letter of June 13 to Bridges, he does not even hint at what he had composed in May.

One subject much on Hopkins' mind at the time was Welsh phonetics and etymology, a concern which we would suspect from the rich assonance and chiming of the 1877 sonnets themselves. Hopkins' sharpened interest in Welsh is manifested in his May poems, in *Pied Beauty,* and in *Hurrahing in Harvest.* In a letter to Bridges dated November 26, 1882, Hopkins admits that the "sonnet [35] you ask about is the greatest offender in its way that you could have found. It was written in my Welsh days, in my salad days, when I was fascinated with *cynghanedd* or consonant-chime, and, as in Welsh *englyns,* 'the sense,' as one of themselves said, 'gets the worst of it'; in this case it exists but is far from glaring." [11]

Hopkins' next note to Bridges is dated August 8 and sent from his parents' home at Oak Hill, Hampstead. He mentions that he is now forwarding his *Deutschland* manuscript, which has just turned up, and then, to "complete the set" he encloses "the sonnet you have already got, a little corrected. [12] It seems clear, then, that Hopkins waited until he saw Bridges before he gave him the rest of the sonnets to make up "the set." And it is probable that Bridges now had eight of Hopkins' sonnets.

In his last letter to Bridges from St. Beuno's, written

[10] *Letters III,* p. 146 (italics mine).
[11] *Letters I,* p. 163.   [12] *Letters I,* p. 42.

August 21, Hopkins deals primarily with the sprung rhythm of *The Wreck of the Deutschland,* a poem which Bridges had read once through and then had attempted to parody. The only mention by Hopkins of his sonnets is a comment that he has combined counterpoint and sprung rhythm in some of them and that this combination "is the most delicate and difficult business of all." [13]

Hopkins spent the time between Friday, September 14, and Friday, September 21,[14] in retreat preparing for his ordination on Sunday, September 23. And then, six days after being ordained, he became so ill that he was forced to take to his bed completely until October 9. The nature of the illness is not clear; it may have been any number of things, but the high-strung Hopkins may have had a severe attack of nervous prostration at the realization, now that classes were actually beginning (probably on October 1), that he was leaving Wales. It seems likely that Hopkins was in no mood to write poetry at this time.

There are two sonnets whose dating remains to be considered: *Pied Beauty* and *Hurrahing in Harvest,* the second written on Saturday, September 1, which was still vacation time at St. Beuno's. Writing to Bridges in 1878, he recalls "The Hurrahing Sonnet was the outcome of half an hour of extreme enthusiasm as I walked home alone one day from fishing in the Elwy." [15] As for *Pied Beauty,* it is merely dated by Hopkins "Summer, 1877" at St. Beuno's. But when Hopkins saw Bridges at the end of July 1877, he does not seem to have had this poem with him. Nor is mention made of this

[13] *Letters I,* p. 45. "Your parody," Hopkins wryly commented, "reassures me about your understanding the metre. Only remark, as you say that there is no conceivable licence I shd. be able to justify, that with all my licences, or rather laws, I am stricter than you and I might say than anybody I know" (*ibid.,* p. 44).

[14] There is no evidence for these dates in his letters, but ordination was regularly preceded by an eight-day retreat ending on the Friday before. On Saturday the minor orders would be administered to those beginning their theology studies at St. Beuno's, and on Sunday ordination into the priesthood was conferred.   [15] *Letters I,* p. 56.

"experiment" in his long letter of August 21, in which he expounded at such length on *The Deutschland*. Further- more, since *Hurrahing in Harvest* begins "Summer ends now," it is probable that *Pied Beauty* was written shortly before *Hurrahing in Harvest,* perhaps in late August. That the two were written at about the same time seems probable from Hopkins' letter to Bridges of July 16, 1878:

> You will learn that I have just called at Bedford Sq. I brought with me a basket of clean linen [his sonnets] but did not deliver it. It comes now between these sheets. [Here is] The Hurrahing Sonnet. . . . I am going to send you a slightly amended copy of the Falcon sonnet [*The Windhover*]. The Curtal Sonnet explains itself, for an experiment in metre (that is, in point of form it is an experiment). I have several things unfinished and one fin- ished, if I could find it.[16]

This is the background which we can, with our present knowledge, reconstruct for the 1877 sonnets. The excitement and enthusiasm of the poems reflect the excitement which the Welsh countryside and language generated in Hopkins. The tensions of the poems are in part generated by Hopkins' meditation on and anticipation of his forthcoming ordina- tion.[17] Besides, he had discovered that Bridges was also work-

---

[16] *Ibid.* Perhaps this last is a reference to *The May Magnificat* written two months before, in May 1878.

[17] Since Hopkins would have spent a good portion of his time meditating on the responsibilities and special nature of the priesthood, it would appear that his daily immersion in the Roman Catholic missal and breviary would be reflected in his sonnets. Robert Boyle, S.J., makes several fruitful connections along this line of investigation. But there is no attempt to give a systematic presentation of the connection between the given date of a poem and the Mass or Office for that day. Little has been published dealing with this relationship, but Ronald Bates ("Hopkins' Ember Poems: A Liturgical Source," *Renascence,* XVII [1964], 32–37) has uncovered what seem to be direct sources for several of the images in both *The Windhover* and *God's Grandeur.* Although not specifically connected with the Mass of the day, several images have a probable origin with the Ember Days which occur four times a year at the beginnings of each of the four seasons. They are

ing with new rhythms based on his study of Milton. Finally, he had found in Bridges a responsive (if often antipathetic) audience.

If we plot this information, then, and follow the notes on the rhythms of the sonnets which Hopkins himself has supplied, a clear pattern of increasing rhythmic complexity from "standard rhythm counterpointed" to "sprung and outriding rhythm" emerges. And if we accept a curve of increasing rhythmic complexity as Hopkins' concern, the vaguely dated sonnets fall neatly into the positions I have given them. The sequence, together with the notes on the rhythms of the poems supplied by Hopkins, follows, with comments on this schema. The numbers refer to Gardner and MacKenzie's Fourth Edition.

31. *God's Grandeur*. February 23, 1877. "Standard rhythm counterpointed."
32. *The Starlight Night*. February 24, 1877. "Standard rhythm opened and counterpointed." (Bridges explains that " 'opened' means that both octave and sestet are opened with a 'sprung' line." [18])
33. *Spring*. May 1877. "Standard rhythm, opening with sprung leadings." (Probably May 1.)
40. *The Lantern out of Doors*. St. Beuno's, 1877. "Standard rhythm, with one sprung leading and one line counterpointed."
35. *The Sea and the Skylark*. Rhyl, May 1877. "Standard rhythm, in parts sprung and in others counterpointed."

"intended to consecrate to God the various seasons in Nature, and to prepare those who are about to be ordained." Some of these connections will be considered when we come to the readings of these two poems. Another more general connection between the liturgy and the poems was made by Bro. Adelbert Scheve, E.S.C., in a brief analysis of the sun image in stanza 33 of *The Deutschland* (*The Explicator*, XVII [1959], Item 60). He noted that the sun image recurred also in numbers 31, 37, and 38, and suggested that they referred to Psalm 18. This psalm appears at various times among the Introits of the Mass throughout the year.   [18] *Poems*, p. 264.

34. *In the Valley of the Elwy.* May 23, 1877. "Standard rhythm, sprung and counterpointed."

39. *The Caged Skylark.* St. Beuno's, 1877. "Falling paeonic rhythm, sprung and outriding."

36. *The Windhover.* May 30, 1877. "Falling paeonic rhythm, sprung and outriding."

37. *Pied Beauty.* Curtal Sonnet. Summer 1877. "Sprung paeonic rhythm."

38. *Hurrahing in Harvest.* September 1, 1877. "Sprung and outriding rhythm."

It seems reasonable to expect that Hopkins, in working with a poetic form as formally conditioned by centuries of tradition as the Petrarchan sonnet, would lead into his radical sprung rhythms carefully and by degrees. In *The Wreck of the Deutschland* of the preceding year, Hopkins had largely created his own poetic form based on his study of the Pindaric ode, and had there employed his sprung rhythm freely, although many of *The Deutschland*'s lines are simply traditional anapests. But with the sonnet Hopkins, conservative that he was in some matters, would feel the weight of tradition on him and so move more carefully to graft his new rhythms onto the sensitive Italian form.

Hopkins begins, then, with "standard rhythm counterpointed" in *God's Grandeur,* and then experiments in *The Starlight Night* with "standard rhythm opened and counterpointed." Hopkins explains to his mother on March 1 that the two sonnets "are not so very queer but have a few metrical effects, mostly after Milton, as in his—

> Light from above, from the fountain of light—

or

> God hath performed for His people of old—

or

> But to vanquish by wisdom hellish wiles.

These rhythms are not commonly understood but do what
nothing else can in their contexts." [19] A month later, in his
long letter to Bridges on, among other things, his new
rhythms, he repeats the first and last examples and gives two
more,[20] remarking that "these are the lines, I suppose, which
. . . folks think will not scan. . . . The choruses of Samson
Agonistes are still more remarkable." And then he adds, "I
think I have mastered them and may some day write on the
subject. . . . I composed two sonnets with rhythmical experiments of the sort." [21]

Despite the fact that both of these sonnets (31 and 32)
were altered, the rhythms have remained unchanged. And it
is fairly easy to see what Hopkins found of interest in Milton's counterpointed rhythms, if we compare two of the
given examples of Milton which find parallels in Hopkins.
Compare Milton's

God hath performed for his children of old

with Hopkins'

The world is charged with the grandeur of God.

And this from Milton:

By the waters of life, where'er they sat

with Hopkins'

[19] *Letters III,* p. 144; scansion mine. The first and third examples are
from *Paradise Regained,* the second is from *Samson Agonistes.* Although this last is incorrectly quoted by Hopkins, what is important is
the rhythm in which he was interested.

[20] The two new examples are:

"By the waters of life, where'er they sat" and

"Home to his mother's house private returned"

(from *Paradise Lost,* XI, 79, and *Paradise Regained,* IV, 639; scansion
mine) .   [21] Letter of April 3–8, 1877, *Letters I,* p. 38.

/ x / x x / x / x /
Generations have trod, have trod, have trod

or with his earlier, somewhat harsher version

/ x / x   x / x / x /
Generations have hard trod, have hard trod.

In *The Starlight Night* Hopkins takes a further step beyond counterpointing [22] and employs sprung rhythm in two lines. Compare, for example,

/ x x / /   x / x x /
Look at the stars! look, look up at the skies!

with Milton's line ("which . . . folks think will not scan") :

/   x   x /   /   x   / x   x /
Light from | above, | from the | fountain | of light.

But Hopkins did not want his line to be read as a bold mixture of trochees and iambs:

/ x   x /   /   x   / x   x /
Look at | the stars! | look, look | up at | the skies!

The rhythm, rather, is sprung, and its energy is only released if read as a sprung line, the way Hopkins insisted:

/ x x   /   /   x   / x x   /
Look at the | stars! | look, look | up at the | skies!

The first scansion stumbles and starts; the second rhetorically emphasizes the meaning, placing the stress where the meaning demands it. The opening line of the sestet has an even more pronounced sprung line:

/ x   /   x   x   /   / x   x /
Buy then | bid then!—What?— | Prayer, | patience, alms, | vows.

The Starlight Night has sixteen exclamations in its fourteen lines, which is profuse even for one as enthusiastic about the beauty of nature as Hopkins was. But one reason Hopkins may have been so free with his hyperboles was to demon-

[22] Counterpointing occurs, for example, in line 3:

/   /   /   /   /   /
"The bright boroughs, the circle-citadels there!"

In "standard" counterpointing the second foot is the least inverted foot after the fifth.

strate to the Victorian sensibility the need for sprung rhythm where a more conventional rhythm would not have been able to carry the electrical charge of the enthusiastic as well as earnest speaking voice.

In point of rhythm, *Spring* is similar to *The Starlight Night;* it too employs sprung leadings grounded on a poem mainly in standard rhythm.[23] *The Lantern out of Doors* has only "one sprung leading" (line 9) and "one line counterpointed" (line 4).[24] *The Sea and the Skylark* and *In the Valley of the Elwy* have almost identical rhythmic descriptions; they are both structured on standard rhythm, but both use sprung rhythm and counterpoint more freely.[25]

The Caged Skylark and *The Windhover* have similar directions for their rhythms; here the standard iambic rhythm has been discarded altogether for a "falling paeonic rhythm, sprung and outriding." The first paeonic, a stress followed by three unstressed syllables, is a standard Greek foot, and Hopkins seems to have been holding onto this traditional term for reasons of maintaining a seemingly formal structure. *Pied Beauty* has the amphibious rhythmic direction, "sprung paeonic rhythm." And finally, in his tenth sonnet, *Hurrahing in Harvest,* Hopkins breaks through to a full-blown sprung sonnet which carries the directions, "sprung and outriding rhythm."

[23] Lines 1 and 9 may be scanned:

/ x / x / x / x   /
"Nothing is so beautiful as spring" and

/ x / x / x / x /
"What is all this juice and all this joy?"

These are not rising rhythms (iambs) with an acephalous first foot but sprung in their falling rhythms.

[24] Line 9 is exactly like the sprung leadings of *Spring* and is scanned:

/ x / x / x / x /
"Death or distance soon consumes them: wind . . . ."

[25] "[In] some of my sonnets I have mingled the two systems [counterpointed and sprung rhythm]: This is the most delicate and difficult business of all" (*Letters I,* p. 45). The sonnets Hopkins referred to are *The Starlight Night, The Lantern out of Doors, The Sea and the Skylark,* and *In the Valley of the Elwy.*

In the note to his last poem, Hopkins explains the subtle difference between the smoother paeonic rhythm and the more heavily stressed outriding rhythm: "Take notice that the outriding feet are not to be confused with dactyls and paeons, though sometimes the line might be scanned either way. The strong syllable in an outriding foot has always a great stress and after the outrider follows a short pause. The paeon is easier and more flowing." [26] The great beauty of the mimetic rhythms of *The Windhover* has frequently been applauded; however, the paeonic rhythm as a grounding is best suited for special effects, such as the glide or hurl of the kestrel.

But the sprung rhythm with its more emphatic stress is better suited to embody the charged emotion of the speaker. Take, for example, the second quatrain of *Hurrahing in Harvest:*

I | walk, I | lift up, I | lift up | heart, | eyes,
Down | all that | glory in the | heavens to | glean our | Saviour;
And, | eyes, | heart, what | looks, what | lips yet | gave you a
Rapturous love's | greeting of | realer, of | rounder re | plies?

Hopkins was, then, consciously working toward a new metric which would free his rhetoric. He was attempting to employ in his sonnets a rhythm which would smoothly yet precisely capture the stress of his personal poetic voice. Sprung rhythm, he explained to Bridges in late August.

is the nearest to the rhythm of prose, that is the native and natural rhythm of speech, the least forced, the most rhetorical and emphatic of all possible rhythms, combining, as it seems to me, opposite and, one wd. have thought, incompatible excellences, markedness of rhythm—that is rhythm's self—and naturalness of

---

[26] *Poems,* p. 269. While outriding feet "belong to counterpointed verse, which supposes a well-known and unmistakeable or unforget[t]able standard rhythm" (*Letters I,* p. 45), Hopkins has in *Hurrahing in Harvest* assimilated outriding feet to a basic sprung-rhythm grounding.

expression. . . . My verse is less to be read than heard, as I have told you before; it is oratorical, that is the rhythm is so. I think if you will study what I have here said you will be much more pleased with it and may I say? converted to it.[27]

Time has sadly demonstrated that he had more than just Bridges to convert. In any event, by September 1877 Hopkins had successfully mounted a sprung rhythm on the normally iambic pattern of the Italian sonnet. He had, in effect, created a viable and fresh rhetoric for a traditional form haunted by the powerful voices of nearly three and one-half centuries of sonnet writing.[28]

Readings which consider only the discrete images of a poem no doubt have their value as criticism, but Hopkins' mature sonnets ask to be read as organic entities operating at once on the levels of natural perception and supernatural vision. All the images of any one of Hopkins' mature sonnets elucidate, although often in an olique fashion, the theological insight at its white-hot core. It is a simple fact that Hopkins' poems must be read and reread until the meaning —the religious insight of the poem—manifests or reveals itself. We are not at the crucial center of Hopkins if we only add our own extrinsic meanings and glosses, or demonstrate a string of literary or biblical allusions, or even untwist the complexity of a particular metaphor. If the sonnet does not "explode" in upon us, we have "fabled and missed" the central meaning. The 1877 sonnets, therefore, by their own

[27] Letter of August 21, 1877 (*Letters I*, p. 46). While Hopkins is here specifically defending his *Deutschland* ode, his comments apply equally to what he was attempting in his sonnets.

[28] Hopkins perfectly demonstrates the truth of T. S. Eliot's comment that in "a perfect sonnet, what you admire is not so much the author's skill in adapting himself to the pattern as the skill and power with which he makes the pattern comply with what he has to say" (from "The Music of Poetry," a W. P. Ker Memorial Lecture delivered at the University of Glasgow, February 24, 1942.)

sacramental and poetic logic, should and will be read primarily to glean from them what Hopkins believed *he* had gleaned from nature: ontological and concrete traces of the Incarnation in the countryside of Wales.

For Hopkins, the central fact of the world is the mystery of the Incarnation, Christ the Word (the Logos or Idea) become flesh by assuming matter. The Incarnation is operative in time and space, in Hopkins' time as in Christ's, in Wales as in Galilee. Therefore God's workings can be discerned in the phenomenological world; there is spiritual meaning, news of God everywhere for those who are properly receptive. Sometimes this central mystery is "instressed," "wafted" freely in on us by God, and then we become aware of His presence. At other times *we* must do all the work, we must attempt to "glean" Christ from out of our surroundings.

There is no guarantee that we will find Him, and it will do no good to fool ourselves—it is finally Christ who must *reveal* himself, and we who should "bless" when we "understand." But one point cannot be emphasized too strongly: this "gleaning" Christ is not a mythopoetizing of nature, nor is it a vague impulse toward a Wordsworthian Romantic transcendentalism, although this did have its appeal for the young Hopkins. For Hopkins, Christ—"*Ipse*"—is himself manifested in and under the beauty of nature. And it is this emphasis that we must consider in reading many of his sonnets.

T. S. Eliot has called Hopkins a "nature poet," and this he is, for his artist's eye, influenced by his reading of John Ruskin, carefully and continually scrutinizes the designs of nature. Besides his poetry, his notebooks, journals, correspondence, and even letters to the editor of *Nature* all show an honest and clear perceptivity of natural phenomena. But nature observation is not an end in itself for Hopkins. He is searching for real traces of God, of the presence of the Incarnation, and sometimes he has his vision in a flash of insight. His sonnets imitate this same twofold natural perception and supernatural vision.

The sonnets may be read for their celebration of nature: the stars on a clear late-winter's night, the springing dawn, the gliding kestrel, the "piecemeal" windswept clouds. But something more—another meaning—sometimes impinges, even forces itself, upon the periphery of our vision in reading these sonnets. We know we are reading in *The Windhover* about a kestrel, but we become increasingly aware that the kestrel is not only analogically *like* Christ; in its existence, insofar as it shares this with Christ's existence, it is linked with Christ. Or again, in *Hurrahing in Harvest,* we are reading about fields and clouds, but Christ's "world-wielding" shoulder is suddenly glimpsed among the hills of the valley of the Clywd. And when the spiritual meaning is finally glimpsed, there is a far greater immediacy to the spiritual reality than any symbol is likely to discharge.

This immediacy strikes us like a *gestalt* exploding into meaning, bringing with it a psychological impact greater than we receive from our knowing the traditional associations of a religious symbol. Knowing, for example, that the Holy Ghost is traditionally represented as a dove does not satisfy the meaning of the final image of *God's Grandeur* in more than a superficial way. It is only when we see that the Paraclete *is* the dawning sun—its breast the warming sun, its wings the spreading rays—that the immediacy and force of the image strike the reader.

This approach is not to presume any final understanding of Hopkins' sonnets; they are rich enough and "charged" enough that there will always be something to say about them, and informative glosses will continue to appear. Furthermore, the thesis about the central importance of the Incarnation has been discussed with varying degrees of complexity and illumination in several places.[29] Of the impor-

---

[29] For an excellent, refreshing, and enlightening discussion of the importance of the Incarnation to Hopkins' poetics, see David Downes's

tance of the Incarnation for Hopkins there have been apolo-
gists enough. But of how this insight informs the very
structure and meaning of his sonnets, little has been said.
What I am particularly stressing is that Hopkins' poems
imitate the natural-supernatural structure which he believed
all phenomena revealed, without compromising the reality
of either.

It should be made clear that not all of Hopkins' sonnets
are equally successful in revealing to us Christ's presence in
nature, and some of the later ones are concerned with other
religious questions and stress other poetic practices. But the
1877 sonnets will very clearly yield this twofold reading, and
it is the special excellence of these poems that the words
intentionally reveal the Word with, when at last it flashes,
the immediacy of lightning.

God's Grandeur has continued to intrigue critics and explicators. The "ooze of oil / Crushed" image regularly finds
its glosses and explanations in the scholarly periodicals. And
the very fact of its recurrence testifies to both the attractive-
ness and the elusiveness of the image. Rightly, most commentators attempt to link it up with a moral message about one
or another attribute of God, but the connection often seems
to be an afterthought. Or, as with Gertrude White's imaginative reading, the emphasis is placed on the secondary or
symbolic level without fully providing the reader with the
ground of the literal meaning.[30]

From my own reading of Hopkins, it has become clear to
me that all images of a particular sonnet (both their "thing-
ness" and their dynamism) serve to illuminate each other, so
that when Hopkins told Bridges that the image of the shook
foil in *God's Grandeur* was of paramount importance, we

Victorian Portraits: Hopkins and Pater (New York, 1965), pp. 84–101.
Although I read him only after this chapter was written, my readings of
the poems here assume Downes's view wholeheartedly.

[30] Gertrude White, "Hopkins' 'God's Grandeur': A Poetic Statement
of Christian Doctrine," *Victorian Poetry*, IV (1966), 284–287.

must assume that this was no hyperbole and that he meant exactly what he said.[31]

Syntactically, the first quatrain of the sonnet speaks of God's grandeur as being manifested in two ways, or, more precisely, as two parts of the same operation. God's grandeur, that is, His glory and benevolence, are concretely manifested in and through the phenomena of nature. But Hopkins does not mean this in any vague, Wordsworthian sense; it is demonstratively true for those psychologically prepared to receive this news of God.

God's grandeur is, appropriately enough, manifested in terms of light and density. His glory can reveal itself of its own accord and with lightning rapidity, as in the shook foil image. Or his glory may also gather in us by trickling increment, as oil is crushed from olives by an applied pressure, collecting its dense meaning slowly under our applied psychic pressure (our stress) until finally the spiritual significance within the phenomenal is discharged. For God wills to appear to Paul in one fashion and to Augustine in another. This image of the process by which God's grandeur is manifested is presented in terms of small, common objects, and is held in check in the structure of the poem while the speaker contrasts this grandeur with man's own grubby, grimy, earthbent inclinations. But the final tercet relies for its full impact on recalling the first quatrain:

> Oh, morning, at the brown brink eastward, springs—
> Because the Holy Ghost over the bent
> World broods with warm breast and with ah! bright wings.

If we can picture the dawning sun before it breaks over the horizon, we may recall how the rich light seems precisely to "gather to a greatness" in density and brightness (one of the meanings of greatness is brightness) , until the orb of the

[31] "With more truth might it be said that my sonnet might have been written expressly for the [shook foil] image's sake" (letter to Bridges of January 4, 1883, *Letters I,* p. 168) .

sun itself seems to spring forth, and then the sun flames out in strong rays like wings from its center. Hopkins is equating ontologically, not pantheistically or even analogically, the rising sun with the glorious manifestation of the Triune God in the Person of the Holy Ghost, the Paraclete who descended in the shape of a dove over Christ at his baptism in the Jordan, and who appeared in the form of tongues of flame on Pentecost Sunday.[32]

Hopkins tells us in the very first line that the "world is charged with the grandeur of God." In the same way that potential electricity is stored in clouds or trees, the world is "charged" with God's glory and needs only a proper receptor to discharge and epiphanize this grandeur.[33] On December 8, 1881, the Feast of the Immaculate Conception, Hopkins wrote in his private spiritual notes, "All things therefore are charged with love, are charged with God and if we know how to touch them give off sparks and take fire, yield drops and flow, ring and tell of him." [34]

Secondly, the "world is charged with" telling of God's grandeur. It is for this reason that it was created, as the Jesuit Hopkins felt instressed so deeply: to give greater glory to God.[35] And because the world can only give back, reflect,

---

[32] Brooks Wright has given a similar but analogical reading of the final line of *God's Grandeur* in *The Explicator,* X (1951), Item 5: "Indeed, the dove, sun, and tongues of flame are so intimately merged that one can almost say that the warm breast is the disk of the sun itself, and the bright wings its rays." Rather, insofar as the sun shares in God's Being, it reflects that Being. In matters ontological, Hopkins inclines toward Scotus rather than St. Thomas.

[33] Hugh Pendexter III comments that the "electrical potential of a charged earth-cloud and of a Leyden jar is . . . compared to the spiritual potential of a world overcast by the materialism of trade . . . apparently gloomy but constantly on the brink of a glorious flaming out of spiritual energy" (*The Explicator,* XXIII [1964], Item 2) .

[34] *Sermons,* p. 195.

[35] This reading is certainly suggested by the double stress Hopkins gave to "chárged wíth."

God's own glory, the word "charged" here has not two separate meanings but rather one meaning seen from two points.
The world *must* manifest the beauty of God, a beauty so
radiant, so charged, that it needs only to be perceived aright
to discharge its light upon us.

"God is holiness," Hopkins explained in a sermon for
October 5, 1879, "loves only holiness, cares only for it, created the world for it (which, without man, if churned or
pressed would yield God none)." [36] But men do not "reck his
rod." *All* generations, not only Hopkins' contemporaries in
industrial, Victorian England, "have trod," have stamped or
crushed the earth, but *wrongly,* so that it discharges neither
meaning to man nor the glory to God for which it was
created. The positioning of "then" in line 4 does splendid
double service. Besides its meaning of therefore (Why do
men therefore . . .), Hopkins inscapes the sense of all the
passing generations in the yoking together of "then" with
"now" (Why do men then now . . .).

Tread ("trod") and "trade" have more in common than
cynghanedd; they are related etymologically, for "trade" derives from "tread," and originally meant a "path traversed."
Man has "seared" all with his plodding trade. By working
God's creation without taking cognizance of the Creator,
man withers and burns everything, unlike nature, which
"flames out" God's glory. Man has "bleared, smeared" all, so
that everything wears his "smudge," and hides God's brightness. These three quoted words all have the meaning of
dimming, blurring, or lessening light, and all work counter
to the images of natural light which reveal the Light. Man is
"shod" like a workhorse; he is dull and insensitive to the
richness and wetness of fresh soil as he treads his well-worn,
down-looking path.

Nevertheless, "nature is never spent" (depleted, tired, and
financially exhausted) because there "lives the dearest

---

[36] *Sermons,* p. 29.

[sweetest, most expensive] freshness deep down things." And now the deeper significance of the poem yields itself. For the "dearest" gift by which nature itself, as well as man, is kept from becoming bankrupt is to be found in Christ's Redemption, literally, his buying-back-again of man and nature with his life. And although the world remains bent (out of its correct alignment, following its own inclination or "bent"), some are also "bent" in anguished supplication, so that the world is also the Holy Spirit's bent nest (thick with rushes, reeds, or heather), over which Love broods, concerned about its young, hovering over them protectively.[37] And it is also the "deep down" of things, the intrinsic grounding of things in God's love, figured here in the Holy Spirit as dove with its deep down or soft feathers, which insures continual renewal, a continual spring.

The liturgical overtones of this poem are plentiful. There is Psalm 18 for Saturday of the second week in Lent. "The heavens show forth the glory of God: and the firmament declares the work of his hands." And there is the scriptural link in Leviticus 24:1–3, read for the Mass during the Lenten Ember Days, of the crushed oil for the lamps shining before the sanctuary of Jahweh, which shall be administered always by His people, His generations:

And the Lord spoke to Moses, saying: Command the children of Israel, that they bring unto thee the finest and clearest of olives to furnish the lamps continually, without the veil of the testimony in the tabernacle of the covenant. And Aaron shall set them

---

[37] For a deeper theological reading of the poem, see Gertrude White's comments, *op. cit.* She holds that the crushed oil refers both to Christ's agony on the Mount of Olives and to his crucifixion, when he was "literally crushed at Gethsemane and on the cross for the sins of men." Furthermore, the darkness refers to the darkness which eclipsed the world at Christ's death, and the glory of the rising sun refers to his resurrection as well as to the Holy Ghost and the Father-Creator. The Incarnation *will* flame out, even through the density of some of these images.

from evening until morning before the Lord, by a perpetual service and rite in your generations.[38]

But all the generations have not listened and have followed their own bent.

The Christian themes of God's manifest glory and man's black indifference, of Christ's incredible condescension in becoming man and of the paradoxical greater glory he achieved in his great sacrifice, of Christ's continual concern for men, whom he bought back at the cost of his own life, all of these supply the underthought as well as the plainly stated thought of *God's Grandeur*. And it is these themes which recur, in one degree or another, in all of the 1877 sonnets.

The Starlight Night opens with the speaker looking up into the clear winter heavens to see the stars flaming with all the intensity of Van Gogh's "Starry Night." Hopkins stresses the dynamic vibrancy of this diamond-bright world, with its "bright boroughs" and "circle-citadels" inhabited by "firefolk sitting in the air." But then Hopkins does something which, to my knowledge, has not yet been pointed out. He radically changes the point of vision and while we are still looking *up*, up has become "Down" in line four. The reason this has escaped comment, perhaps, is that we may also be said to be looking *down* a field at a point on the distant horizon. But here Hopkins is deliberately reversing our vantage point, literally turning us on our heads (or perhaps lifting us "above" the sky) to see the unity of all creation and to glean Christ operative in all nature.[39] The dark heavens studded with stars become "dim woods" studded with diamond mines, as well as grey lawns studded with myriad droplets of quivering, translucent dew ("quickgold"). The stars vibrant in the heavens are white undersides of "white-

[38] Ronald Bates, *op. cit.*, also quotes this scriptural reference.

[39] In *Hurrahing in Harvest*, which in its unmitigated enthusiasm is cousin to *The Starlight Night*, the same device of radically altering our common vision by turning things on their heads is again used, to even better advantage.

beams" and "airy abeles" stirred up and shaking brilliantly and unsteadily in the wind. Again, they are frightened doves scattering in the distance into so many flakes of light.

This beauty and this vision, the speaker tells us, "is all a purchase, all is a prize." But what currency will buy it? what is offered for it? the speaker asks, in auction-room terms. Not money but "Prayer, patience, alms, vows." Insofar as we can possess fleeting beauty, we can best do this by sacrificing ourselves freely and by buying for ourselves eternal beauty —Christ. For all of this beauty was bought back by Christ's purchase, by his Redemption.

Then the speaker, like a good auctioneer, asks us to look again at the starlight night, up for bids, which is like the light, white May blossoms of an "orchard," or like the spotted, golden, young willow leaves of March. These stars are the barn, the edifice; within is housed the garnered grain. The stars in the heavens ("This piece-bright paling") form a fence (paling) shutting home Christ and Mary and "all his hallows." But a paling also has ecclesiastical overtones; a "pale" is a territory within which one is spiritually protected. "These" in line 12 also refers to the "Prayer, patience, alms, vows" as well as to the stars. This ambiguity of the reference pronoun is, in fact, intentional because the stars and the spiritual currency are identified. Like money, both the stars and the spiritual goods are desirable, but both are means of buying God. Now "May-mess" (May Mass, Mary's month; as well as May feast) and March-bloom (Lent, with its fastings, but also giving us pieces of gold, rewarding us—"mealed-with-yellow") become the exterior currency—the bright pieces ("piece-bright") —by which we, too, buy our way home.

The stars then, creation's beauty itself, provide a means, a bright currency, not for hoarding up but for freely spending to buy eternal beauty—heaven, of which the heavens themselves are but a reflection. The stars cannot be bought, nor do we want them; they are husks, Hopkins says. What we do want, rather, is the beauty they reflect, the grain within, Christ.

The larger unified pattern of images discoverable in the starlight night flashes upon the attentive observer all in a moment. But what may escape notice is the presence of an interlocking pattern of assimilative consonants chiming down the alphabetical scale. The assimilative pairing is not unbroken, and its fragmentary nature is probably indicative of the fragmentary nature of God's evidences in the world about us. Still, once we notice it, the pattern is there in "bright boroughs," "circle citadels," and "down in dim woods the diamond delves," this last echoed in "elves-eyes." Everything in nature, for all its quaint distinctiveness, forms part of a larger pattern. It is a good example of Hopkins' delightful yet serious word-playing.

Spring, while having excellences of its own, does not appear to have the complex underthought of the previous two sonnets. The octet is a beautiful, vital recreation of the joys of spring. And Hopkins, as usual, has a perceptive eye for nature. In line 2 he describes the species of lily called Solomon's Seal which still grows profusely and wildly in the Valley of the Elwy.[40] The sky-blue eggs of the thrush "look little low heavens," and the thrush singing through the "timber" of the woods is echoed by the "echoing timbre." The blossoming pear tree touches the blue which comes down to meet it; the blue "is all in a rush" and the lambs too are "racing." Hopkins is clearly identifying all of nature again; everything is dynamic. To do this he has carefully chosen his verbs and his adjectives derived from verbs: "shoot," "echoing," "rinse and wring," "strikes," "rush" of blue, and "racing lambs."

This spring is a strain, a fragment of what nature was

[40] John Driscoll, S.J., notes that in a visit to St. Beuno's he saw the Solomon's Seals whose heavy flowers hang down at intervals of several inches, bending the stem into an arc so that they "look so much like the spokes of a wheel" (*The Explicator*, XXIV [1965], Item 26).

before the Fall (for even Christ's Redemption did not restore nature to the beauty of God's first kingdom) in "Eden garden." The speaker, intoxicated by this "juice" and "joy," prays that this innocence be not blasted:

—Have, get, before it cloy,
Before it cloud, Christ, lord, and sour with sinning,
Innocent mind and Mayday in girl and boy,
Most, O maid's child, thy choice and worthy the winning.

The syntactical beauty of this sentence is that it operates in two ways simultaneously. Paraphrase may best bring these dual and, in fact, interweaving meanings out: (1) "Oh, Christ, lord, have, get the innocent mind and Mayday in the young, before it cloys, clouds, and sours with sinning, for they, O Mary's son, are your first choice and most worthy of winning (since they have not yet been blasted by sin)." But the lines also mean (2): "Oh, condition of innocence found in the young, have, get Christ, your lord, before this quality in you cloys, clouds, and sours because of sinning, for he, O you creatures of innocence, is (or should be) your first choice and most worthy of winning." This syntactical ambiguity precisely reflects the interaction between Christ and man; this intertwining occurs again in the final lines of *Carrion Comfort*, composed eight years later:

Cheer whom though? the hero whose heaven-handling flung me, fóot tród
Me? or me that fought him? O which one? is it each one? That night, that year
Of now done darkness I wretch lay wrestling with (my God!) my God.

Hopkins' theme of our buying Christ, because Christ first bought us, as seen both here and, not so obviously, in the previous two sonnets, is a thought he never tired of reiterating.[41] It appears again in a sermon he preached two years

[41] On this theme of who loved who first, see Hopkins' sermon on Mary Magdalen (*Sermons*, p. 83). Here, in baroque fashion, he at-

later, on August 31, 1879: "[The] man or woman, the boy or girl, that in their bloom and heyday [their "Mayday"] in their strength and health give themselves to God and with the fresh body and joyously beating blood give him glory, how near he will be to them in age and sickness and wall their weakness round in the hour of death!" [42]

The Lantern out of Doors deals with two of Hopkins' favorite themes: with the fascination he had for the striking physical, mental, or spiritual beauty of a person,[43] and with Christ's especial interest in those he bought with his life's blood. The speaker's eye is attracted by a lighted lantern moving away from him in the dark; he begins to wonder "who goes there," where is that person "from" and "bound . . . where / With, all down darkness wide, his wading [walking] light?"

Then in the second quatrain the speaker turns within, recalling that a rare few with bright beauty in "mould or mind" rain like "Rich beams" against our "much-thick and marsh air" until something happens and they are "consumed" (bought and swallowed up) by either death (time)

---

tempts to unravel the fine thread between the proper cause and effect of Christ's love and man's response: "[Mary Magdalen] not only loved because she was forgiven, she was also forgiven because she loved: both things are true. When she came as a sinner, she had heard no forgiveness spoken, she came to get it, and to get it she shewed all that love: in this way then she was forgiven because she loved. On the other hand she knew of Christ's love, she knew he *offered* mercy to the sinner, . . . this love of his was first, mercy, forgiveness, *offered* forgiveness, on Christ's part came first and because he forgave her, that is[,] offered to forgive her[,] she loved: So then she loved because she was forgiven."

[42] *Sermons*, p. 19. See also *Morning, Midday, and Evening Sacrifice*, written at the same time as this sermon.

[43] See, for example, Hopkins' comment in an early letter to Bridges on the striking countenance of an Oxford student: "His face was fascinating me last term: I generally have one fascination or another on. Sometimes I dislike the faces wh. fascinate me but sometimes much the reverse, as is the present case" (Letter of September 24, 1866, *Letters I*, p. 8) .

or distance (space). The solicitous speaker is painfully aware of his limitations; no matter how he should strain after such persons, he cannot "be in at the end," cannot follow them after they cross the threshold of death. Moreover, he is bound even to forget them as other objects or other people come into his consciousness. The old maxim remains true, that "out of sight is out of mind."

The powerful and exact image which Hopkins uses for man's journey through this world should be examined more closely. The image remains in the foreground throughout the octet, except that in the second half, the second quatrain, the image assumes a wider scope. The single winding light against the encircling "marsh air" gloom which the speaker sees moving in the valley is a fine, existential image for the unsteady flickering quality of life as we see it even in those closest to us. No matter how we may try to pierce through the darkness, a particular life will at best present only a fragmented picture with large gaps between bright flickerings, and with life's final phase enshrouded in isolation and darkness, the last act known only to God and the soul.

It is only in the final tercet that we have the Christian resolution of the sonnet. For there is someone who does care and who, furthermore, is without the speaker's mortal limitations: Christ. For "Christ minds" (he cares; but also he minds or keeps his property constantly before him). It is in Christ's "interest" to follow man; like a prudent owner he is interested in man because man is the interest constantly accruing from Christ's life investment. Because man is his property, it is in Christ's interest to avow what is good in man and to amend what needs repair. He is a lover—a jealous lover—who eyes his "rare" possessions, who is haunted by care for them, whose foot follows after his kind (his people —and does it *kindly*). For he is their ransom; having paid for them with his life, he is their rescue "and first, fast, last friend." Christ, then, the Alpha and Omega, was in at the beginning and will be "in at the end."

The Sea and the Skylark was originally entitled *Walking by the Sea,* but the original version, with its heavy imitation of Welsh *cynghanedd* or consonant chime, internal rhyme, and assonance, was altered about 1883. These chimes are perhaps most obvious in the original second quatrain of *Walking by the Sea* which reads:

> Left hand, off land, I hear the lark ascend
> With rash-fresh more, repair of skein and score,
> Race wild reel round, crisp coil deal down to floor,
> And spill music till there's none left to spend.[44]

There is an ingenious example of *cynghanedd* in "wild reel round" and "coil deal down t———." Rhyming occurs in "hand" and "land," "more" and "score," "spill" and "till," "hear" and "repair" and "there's." Consonance is present, for example, in such combinations as "left" with "off," "rash" with "fresh," "more" with "repair," "skein" with "score." [45]

Although Hopkins noticeably toned down the chiming in his later revision, he kept the finely wrought unraveling image to present vividly the skylark's song. There are two aural images of natural freshness and regeneration developed in the octet—the sea ramping on the shore and the skylark's song. The speaker walks westward along the shore. (The place of composition is given as Rhyl, a small Welsh mining town which faces the Irish Sea.) On his right, from

---

[44] As quoted in *Letters I,* p. 163.

[45] Writing to Bridges on November 26–27, 1882, Hopkins explains the meaning of these lines in great detail, adding: "There is, you see, plenty meant; but the saying of it smells, I fear, of the lamp, of salad oil, and what is nastier, in one line somewhat of Robert Browning. [It is impossible to be sure, but perhaps the line he is referring to is "Race wild reel round, crisp coil deal down to floor," which has something of the clogged consonantal tongue-twisting of Browning's "Irks care the crop-full bird? Frets doubt the maw-crammed beast?" in his *Rabbi Ben Ezra* of 1864.] I felt even at the time that in the endless labour of recasting those lines I had lost the freshness I wanted and which indeed the subject demands. 'As a dare-gale skylark' is better in that respect" (*Letters I,* p. 164) .

the sea, the waves lift up and crash against the shore, like a ramping steed. On his left, from the land, he hears the lark singing its heart out as it spirals upward. The moon is seen to "wend" its way in unending and ever-fresh cycles across the heavens as the skylark's song is "re-winded" again and again to "pour / And pelt music."

In the sestet, the speaker turns to "this shallow and frail town" which "these two shame." They, "Being pure," ring out their contrast with the town. The times themselves are made "sordid" and "turbid" (heavy with smoke and mist, but also confused and muddled in thought), fitting epithets to describe the overemphasis of even this small, bleak Welsh mining village on profits at the expense of health, beauty, and especially human dignity. Man has soiled more than his skin. How different the rhythm of the town's life from the rhythm of nature.

The argument, however, is more complex than this. We, the speaker laments, we are the pride of life, we are the crown of creation, cared for by our Creator, and it is *we* who have "lost that cheer and charm of earth's past prime," that is, in our post-Edenic world, where spiritual values have been passed over. It is not the mine-working which is sordid; it is rather that in this burrowing into the ground we find an expression of the modern condition of man. For man has also, in the post-Darwinian era, attempted to see himself, his own "make," as only a naturally evolved higher species of animal without an immortal, personal soul. If, therefore, his very existence is a matter of chance and man is not "life's pride," in his despair he also finds no value in his "making," his works. Therefore he replaces the dignity of work with the dreadful working conditions of the poor, entrapped by a utilitarian economic philosophy based on personal selfishness rather than on communal welfare. Men live out their lives appropriately in the dust of the brick tenements and factories which blight England, and they return to the dust from which they came and from which they could not escape in life.

In this utilitarian philosophy, man's end is to return to dust, as he drains away steadily ("fast") to the primordial "slime" from which his life, according to the Darwinians, began. But there is also a suggestion of ore, man's making, also disintegrating into ore dust and ore slime, for man and his works (including his offspring) are identified by the same word ("make and making") since at bottom man, without any marked distinctiveness, slides back into matter, slime. Man has identified himself with his industry and trade and is chillingly satisfied, when his vein is worked, to be quietly reduced to a similar annihilation. "I see the *Academy* no more," Hopkins wrote to his mother three years before, "but among the last things I read in it was Tyndall's address. I thought it interesting and eloquent, though it made me 'most mad.' It is not only that he looks back to an obscure origin, he looks forward with the same content to an obscure future—to be lost 'in the infinite azure of the past' (fine phrase by the way) ." [46]

What is saddest for Hopkins, however, is that this philosophy has destroyed man's "cheer and charm," those regenerative qualities possessed by even the lower creation—the ramping sea and the singing lark. Man has willed to follow the deterministic philosophies of the times and to accept every degradation to his own human dignity, even as nature itself gives the lie to this pessimistic philosophical view.

In the Valley of the Elwy is also concerned with the failure of man to recognize and live under the sway of God. Hop-

[46] Letter of September 20, 1874, *Letters III*, pp. 127–128. See Hopkins' comments in *Journals*, pp. 76, 84, 104, 118–121, on chromatism, gradual or sliding change, as opposed to diatonism, abrupt, marked change imposed on matter (inscaped) from above by the Creator. J. Hillis Miller has made some astute comments on the central importance of the two kinds of changes for Hopkins in "Gerard Manley Hopkins" in *The Disappearance of God: Five Nineteenth-Century Writers* (Cambridge, Mass., 1963) , pp. 276–317. Reprinted as "The Univocal Chiming" in the Twentieth Century Views volume on Hopkins edited by Geoffrey H. Hartman (1966) , pp. 89–116.

kins' Englishness comes through in this sonnet as he compares the very air (in the sense of both atmosphere and
manner) of an English home, and its correspondingly good
people, to the beautiful air of Wales and the failure of its
"inmate" to correspond. Writing from Oxford two years
after he had written the sonnet, Hopkins explained its structure to Bridges in this way:

The kind people of the sonnet were the Watsons of Shooter's
Hill, nothing to do with the Elwy. . . . The frame of the sonnet
is a rule of three sum *wrong,* thus: As the sweet smell to those
kind people so the Welsh landscape is NOT to the Welsh; and
then the author and principle of all four terms is asked to bring
the sum right.[47]

The air is the central image of the poem, as it is also in
The Blessed Virgin compared to the Air we Breathe, written
six years later. The speaker again begins by giving us a
specific composition of place; once he was treated well,
through no merit of his own. There is a cordial (warm, from
the heart—*cors*) air, a smell that seems "Fetched fresh, as I
suppose, off some sweet wood." It is not only "fetched" in
being gathered, but the sweet air of nature also provides the
very atmosphere of the home with its own "fetch" (a dialect
word for "spirit") , with its own penates. This air forms a
hood, a protective and gentle covering for its inmates, as a
nesting bird will for its unhatched young or the mild spring
nights will for her "new morsels." The atmosphere of kindness pervading the house is literally incarnate and made
manifest in the particular atmosphere of the place.

So, too, in his beloved "wild Wales" there is in the heady

[47] Letter of April 8, 1879, *Letters I,* pp. 76–77. Shooter's Hill is in
Blackheath, six miles southeast of London. What kindness these people
showed to Hopkins we do not know, but it is possible that he saw them
when he was home sometime in 1875, for on June 10 of that year he
wrote his mother: "Remember me very kindly to Mr. Manley, and to
Watson and Tom Turner when next seen—and all Cristen soules"
(*Letters III,* p. 134) .

scents of spring a protective and gentle covering. But while nature does her part, "Only the inmate does not correspond," neither corresponding in the sense of responding to the beauty of Wales and thence to the beauty of its author nor corresponding in the mathematical sense of agreement. The equation will not work out:

$$\frac{\text{sweet smell}}{\text{kind inmates}} \;::\; \frac{\text{sweet Welsh landscape}}{\text{? Welsh inmates}}$$

God is then addressed as both "lover of souls" (mercy, charity) and as judge, "swaying considerate scales" (heavenly justice). There may be an allusion here to the constellation Libra ($con + sidera$ = made up of stars; and Libra, scales), in which case the majesty and grandeur of God is presented against the backdrop of the universe as a counterbalance to God's mercy. And the Creator is asked to complete the sum by bestowing on the Welsh kindness and cordiality, in short, an abundance of Christian charity. For though he is "mighty a master," God is also "a father and fond." That is, as a father he loves his people, it would seem, to the point of fondness, of foolishness. And it is only in this way that God can make that intractable equation finally come right. The final line is all the more aesthetically pleasing because it is also a theologically exact phrasing of God's complete identity and unity with what appear to be disparate attributes: "Being mighty a master, being a father and fond." God *is* both justice and mercy, master and father; the parallel phrasing beginning with God's essential quality, his name for himself—"Being"—superimposes the two attributes upon each other as complementary, ending on that finest chord and final note of love.

The Caged Skylark is a perennial favorite among teachers and students because of the relative ease with which it lends itself to explanation. Hopkins makes a comparison, as with the last sonnet, using four terms: (1) "Man's mounting spirit" in (2) his "bone-house, mean house" is compared to

(3) "a dare-gale skylark scanted" (4) in a "dull cage." The captured songbird lives now not even recalling its original nesting place deep in the woods; man lives for the most part in drudgery, living out from day to day his life, looking only to his work for the day, like a day laborer.

The second quatrain expands the analogy to include the range of moods through which both man's spirit and the bird struggle. Both are sometimes up and sometimes down; both sing sweetly; but both may fling themselves against their own prisons, man against his imprisoning flesh and the bird against his cage, out of either fear or rage.

Even the free skylark cannot always be singing aloft; he too returns for rest to his "own nest, wild nest, no prison." And so does man's spirit need a place for rest, for even "when found at best," in the resurrection of body and soul, he will be "flesh-bound." But then his body will be no bone house or "mean [lowly, half-way] house" but "uncumbered." His body will be to him as the wild nest to the free skylark— "no prison." To present immediately and forcefully the condition of the resurrected body, the spirit's best home, Hopkins employed one of his finest and most vivid analogies: "meadow-down is not distressed / For a rainbow footing it nor he for his bónes rísen." Just as fresh, wet "meadow-down" (perhaps the grain) is not weighed down, made slack, troubled, or unbound by a rainbow which rests upon it, neither is man's spirit—"he"—distressed or weighed down or troubled by his "bónes rísen." Then, like the rainbow itself (a symbol of hope) , the body will be weightless, beautiful, luminous, no longer bound by time or space, a fitting home for the spirit. The analogy is felicitous, and so too is the epithet "flesh-bound," for while man's soul by its very nature requires the body to be complete, that body, that flesh, "bounds," jumps, leaps freely, is dynamic, and neither "droop[s]" nor lives now "day-labouring-out life's age."

Referring to *The Wreck of the Deutschland*, Robert Bridges warned his readers to circumvent this dragon at the entrance to Hopkins' poetry and to go another way. There was no real dragon in that poem, but there is another dragon, "a billion times told" bulkier, which has been conjured up by two generations of critics and which sits before the gateway to *The Windhover,* the poem Hopkins thought "the best thing I ever wrote." [48] This undoubtedly complex sonnet has had so many glosses in the past forty years that it is difficult to separate the grain from the chaff. Discriminating students of Hopkins are often amazed and irritated at the flimsy webs of introspection spun out from very little of the poem's real substance; there are usually some brilliant hits scattered throughout too many pages of clear misses. There will be no attempt here to collate the explications of this poem, which would be a large task in itself. But there are, thankfully, several interesting and competent readings of *The Windhover* which do the poem justice. [49]

As with the majority of his other sonnets, Hopkins here maintains the original eight-six structure and resolution of the Italian sonnet. Briefly, the structure is as follows: in the octet, the speaker observes the majestic flight pattern of the kestrel; [50] in the first tercet of the sestet, the kestrel changes

[48] Letter to Bridges of June 22, 1879, *Letters I,* p. 85.

[49] One especially good reading is that of F. X. Shea, S.J., "Another Look at 'The Windhover,' " in *Victorian Poetry,* II (1964) , 219–239. Fr. Shea points out that "an agreed principle of *hermeneutics* is that further meanings be firmly grounded on the literal." Hopkins' poetic, he believes (as I do) , was based on "philosophic realism and exact rendering of the object," and that while "classical theoreticians of poetry saw objectivity as merely a necessary condition of writing, Hopkins saw it as the almost unattainable end to be striven for, mightily and passionately."

[50] The marvelous rhythmic imitation of the windhover in flight has been commented upon frequently by critics of the sonnet. It should be emphasized just how closely Hopkins' eye was on a real windhover in flight, a sight he could have seen from the Rock Chapel located a half-mile from the central complex of St. Beuno's, on the slopes of "dark Manaefa." It was here that the Jesuit seminarians traditionally assisted at morning Mass throughout May. Of the chapel Hopkins

from glide to downward swoop. Its wings buckle in a V-shape, and the speaker remarks on its beauty. Then, in the final tercet the speaker comments that beauty in such buckling is not surprising, for even a plough buckling up the earth will flame out more brightly, as will seemingly dead embers when they collapse, buckle through the grate, and burst into vivid fire. This is what a literal reading of the poem reveals. And, as I have tried to show in the other sonnets, a literal reading must come first. As Shea explains, "The realism of Hopkins drove him to place meaning in *things* first, to seek to utter *things* in such terms that they remain fully themselves while revealing the very pattern of being in all its orders." [51]

The religious significance in this sonnet is so continually bursting through the natural scene that many commentators have spent most of their time on the secondary meaning without grounding it in the perceptual world. The essential religious meaning here expressed seems to me to be the earthly beauty of the God-man Christ. By self-mastery he was able to keep himself in perfect balance with all of the external forces to which he was subjected. And in those three years of his public ministry, he seemed always to be victorious against those who came out to oppose him. For Hopkins, soon ready to begin his own public ministry, the example of Christ is enough to make his heart both withdraw "in

---

noted in his journals, "The Rock is a great resort of hawks and owls." (See Eugene R. August, "The Growth of 'The Windhover,'" *PMLA*, LXXXII (1967), 465.) Thomas P. Harrison has accurately described the flight of this small twelve-to-fourteen inch falcon ("The Birds of Gerard Manley Hopkins," *Studies in Philology*, LIV [1957], 458). If we follow Harrison's explanation of the kestrel's flight, it follows the exact pattern of lines 1–10 of *The Windhover*. It is also interesting to note that the kestrel is blue-gray above ("blue-bleak" as are embers and the steel plow) and russet red beneath, so that in swooping in the brilliant morning sun it could appear to be a buckling ember.

[51] *Op. cit.*, p. 239.

hiding" and yet desire to emulate "the achieve of, the mastery of the thing!"

And yet for all of Christ's "Brute beauty and valour and act, oh, air, pride, plume," the speaker is drawn to that final sacrifice of Christ on the cross. It is in his giving of his life for his people, in the V-shaped collapse of his out-pinned arms, when his body buckled under its own weight, it is *then* that a fire (the unleashed graces of Redemption for billions of souls) "a billion / Times told lovelier, more dangerous" broke from this gallant knight, God's minion, His dauphin, this chevalier.

There is nothing really strange here, the speaker now comments, for those who keep face forward and hands to the plough, although their lives, like Hopkins', seem to have no more adventure or seeming consequence than that of a day laborer or a plow horse. For they also make themselves receptors of the Light. Even "blue-bleak embers," with the fire all within (it is a fitting image of the ideal of St. Ignatius Loyola), when they buckle, as did the "blue-bleak" corpse of the dead Christ, will fall (die), and gall themselves (Christ's great sacrifice was a self-willed breaking). But they will also "gash gold-vermillion," flaming into red and gold, as Christ's blood flames out into gold, for it was this great sacrifice, which he wears so proudly, that was the price for buying men back again.

Against the "dapple-dawn-drawn" natural light—the necessarily variegated light of God's creation, and not the intense, terribly blinding light of God in Himself—Christ's "Brute beauty," his human beauty, is breathtaking. This was especially so to Hopkins, who was sensitive to physical beauty and wrote one of his best sermons on Christ's mortal beauty.[52] But just as the dynamic fire of the bird is best

[52] See the entire sermon prepared for November 23, 1879, for his congregation at Bedford Leigh in *Sermons*, pp. 34–38. Especially pertinent to *The Windhover* are the following passages: "I leave it to you, brethren, then to picture him, in whom the fulness of the godhead

caught as it plunges downward so that the fire seems to generate from the bird itself and not from the sun, so in falling, Christ's especial beauty as he offered himself up to his Father generates a more brilliant flame by his human willingness to make the sacrifice. And just as the sun's light is always on the kestrel, so God's grace continually sustains Christ-as-man. *The Windhover* is a tremendously complex poem. Hopkins could go no further in the direction of re-creating in words the spiritual significance of a natural phenomenon. It is perhaps for this reason that Hopkins next experimented, in a radical manner, with the very structure of the sonnet, again, it is probable, for reasons of a new rhythm.

Pied Beauty is a curtailed or "Curtal-Sonnet," of ten and one-half lines, with the critical ratio between the octet and sestet carefully maintained. Hopkins defended his Curtal-Sonnets (*Peace* and *Ashboughs* are the others) in his "Author's Preface," written probably in 1883, as "constructed in proportions resembling those of the sonnet proper, namely 6 + 4 instead of 8 + 6, with however a half-line tailpiece (so

---

dwelt bodily, in his bearing how majestic, how strong and yet how lovely and lissome in his limbs, in his look how earnest, grave but kind. In his Passion all this strength was spent, this lissomness crippled [buckled], this beauty wrecked, this majesty beaten down. But now it is more than all restored, and for myself I make no secret I look forward with eager desire to seeing the matchless beauty of *Christ's body in the heavenly light.* . . . Poor was his station, laborious his life, bitter his ending: through poverty, through labour, through crucifixion his *majesty of nature more shines"* (pp. 36–37, italics mine). The tremendous condescension of the Incarnation is also figured in the image of the small kestrel. Ronald Bates ("The Windhover," *Victorian Poetry*, II [1964], 63–64) notes that in falconry "there was a strict hierarchy of rank and degree. . . . [At] the very bottom—lower even than priest, holy water clerk, yeoman and poor man—[was] the knave or servant. The falcon designated for this class was the kestrel." See also Sir Toby Belch's speech in *Twelfth Night* (I, iii, 37–38): "He's a coward and a coystrill that will not drink to my niece till his brains turn o' th' toe like a parish top."

that the equation is rather $12/2 + 9/2 = 21/2 = 10\frac{1}{2}$).'' [53]
Another way of saying this would be simply to make "come right" the equation $\dfrac{8}{6} :: \dfrac{6}{x} = (8x = 36) = (x = 4\frac{1}{2}.)$

Pied Beauty is beautiful in its, for Hopkins, relative simplicity. It is a prayer, a meditation, a *Laus tibi Deus* for the variety and individuality of all of creation, which is founded on the eternal bedrock of permanence, on Being itself. And yet, although there is such variety, there is also a subtle interweaving of identity, as individual patterns are likened to other individual patterns.

In the first line the speaker sets the theme: "Glory be to God for dappled things." And then, in the rest of the first part of the sonnet, he presents specifically variegated objects: dappled skies like dappled cows; the rows of rose-colored spots on trout; the beautiful coal-fire glow of the inner husks of freshly fallen chestnuts, which are identified with coals themselves; the wings of finches; the dappled landscape; and "all trades, their gear and tackle and trim."

In the second part the speaker continues to praise God for nature's variety, but now he does so in terms of abstract classification and by pairing opposites:

> All things counter, original, spare, strange;
> Whatever is fickle, freckled (who knows how?)
> With swift, slow; sweet, sour; adazzle, dim.

For all of these are the dappled creation, the variegated lights, of the uncreated and eternal, pure, white dome of God's radiance:

> He fathers-forth whose beauty is past change:
> Praise him.

The rhythm, the slow, measured tempo of those final two words which take up, in musical time, a full three beats, has a quality of serenity, of rest, of finality which is brought out

[53] *Poems,* p. 49.

perfectly by the poetic form itself. Even if that form cannot be completely defined as a sonnet,[54] still it is as perfect a prayer in miniature as the ancient canticle of Daniel, which Hopkins would have recited so often in his Office:

> Benedicite omnia opera Domini Domino:
> Laudate et superexaltate eum in saecula.
> Benedicite aquae omnes quae super caelos sunt Domino:
> Benedicite omnes virtutes Domini Domino.

Hurrahing in Harvest, probably the last of the sonnets of 1877, although much admired, has received relatively little attention from the explicators. It is an enthusiastic performance; its rhythm, correctly read, captures the ecstatic yet controlled voice of the speaker. But the meaning is more complex, more radical, more surprising than has so far been demonstrated. The sonnet contains a fleeting glimpse of Christ's presence in nature which is more exciting, I believe, than the accepted reading of Christ's "world-wielding shoulder" being glimpsed in the "azurous hung hills."

Attracted by the harvested fields and the fragmented cirro-cumulus clouds, the speaker looks hard at nature to "glean our Saviour." In his choice of words Hopkins is clearly seeking to identify the fields of cut grain and their "barbarous" (wild, bearded, barbed) stooks (the bundled sheaves of the freshly cut grain), with the "wind-walks" and the "silk-sack," "Meal-drift" clouds. Furthermore, there is

[54] Apart from my defense of the form of *Pied Beauty* as allowing for the resonance, finality, and resolution of the last line, I am in agreement with the remarks of Paul Fussell, Jr. (*Poetic Meter and Poetic Form* [New York, 1966], p. 132), that neither this poem nor *Peace* "justifies itself as a structure—neither performs the fundamental Petrarchan action which is implicit in the formal disproportion of their two parts, an action of complication and resolution. . . . Indeed the two parts of "Pied Beauty," despite their difference in weight and shape, are pretty much of a piece in substance. . . . [The] only thing that takes place in the white space between the two parts is an ascent to a slightly higher plateau of abstraction."

the verbal and adverbial confluence of "the stooks rise / Around; up above, what wind-walks," which forces the image of grain upward and the cloud image downward.

In lines 6 and 7 the merging of field with heavens is reinforced:

> I walk, I lift up, I lift up heart, eyes,[55]
> Down all that glory in the heavens to glean our Saviour.

The heavens become the fields in which "to glean," to collect fragments of information piece by piece, and the sense of direction becomes hazy and heady as the speaker lifts up his eyes to look down all that glory. As in *The Starlight Night,* Hopkins is not only suggesting the distant perspective which seems to vanish downward on the horizon, but by his syntax he is forcing a reversal of directions. By giving us a radically altered viewpoint, we see how the artist and the saint (as well as the madman) look upon the world. The search is successful for the speaker:

> And, éyes, heárt, what looks, what lips yet gave you a
> Rapturous love's greeting of realer, of rounder replies?

But what *is* the vision, the gleaning of Christ which the speaker has gathered from this looking hard at the fields and clouds? If we see the vision of Christ's round, world-wielding shoulder reflected in the round hills, there seems nothing particularly exciting or even imaginative about such a conceit apart from the presentation. Furthermore, if the hills stretch up from the earth, how do they wield or support the world? But if we follow the up-down reversal, then it is the sky which at the confluence of two hills would form a curve, an inverted hill or hump; seen upside down these curves

---

[55] The rhythm of this sprung line Hopkins may have first heard suggested in Swinburne's halting "Lift úp thy líps, turn róund, look báck for lóve," from the opening line of the first of his *Hermaphroditus* sonnets. See also John 5:35: "Why, lift up your eyes, I tell you, and look at the fields, they are white with the promise of harvest already."

become "azurous hung hills" (sky hung between hills), formations formed by the "world-wielding shoulder / Majestic"
of God manifested in nature. Again, the tremendous power
and yet apparent airiness of the gravitational forces support-
ing the world would be "as a stallion stalwart, very-violet-
sweet." This *gestalt* once seen explodes upon the reader in
the same manner as the original vision exploded upon the
speaker of the poem.

Such gleanings of Christ were always here, "wanting," that
is, lacking or needing only the proper receiver—a person
"wanting," desiring, to find God in nature. When these two,
the (for Hopkins) real presence of God in nature and the
receptive human, "once meet," when they converge and are
harmoniously identified,

The heart rears wings bold and bolder
And hurls for him, O half hurls earth for him off under his feet.

Like the ending of *Spring*, lines 12–14 are brilliant in
their double significance. They mean that when the beauty
of the Incarnation and the beholder meet and greet, the
heart half-hurls the world off from under the beholder's feet
in an ecstatic vision. But the lines also mean that the heart,
in glimpsing Christ, is so drawn to him that the heart half-
hurls earth for the sake of Christ to place it under Christ's
feet for his greater honor and glory. The world is half-hurled
and not fully hurled because Christ is present *in* the world.
Again there is the suggestion in the "heart rears wings" of
the plodding horse being transformed into the airy steed
Pegasus, rising above its surroundings, a transforming image
Hopkins perhaps implied in the "plow down" image of *The
Windhover* and used to great effect, as we shall see, in *Felix
Randal*. Here too there is the suggestion in "hurls earth for
him off under his feet" of being literally turned on one's
head to see the world not as we normally see it but from a
radically new and exciting viewpoint. With *Hurrahing in
Harvest*, vision and voice meet in a mature, sensitive union.

Hopkins was to continue with this poetic style in his next series of sonnets.

These are the extremely powerful, necessarily complex, and dynamically beautiful ten sonnets which Hopkins composed between the late winter and late summer of 1877. They are intricately bound up with several factors: Hopkins' deep love for the Welsh countryside, his approaching ordination to the priesthood after nine years of preparation, the crystallization of rhythms which had been haunting his ear for years, and the need of a priest-poet to sing of God's creation. And when these delicate threads were unwoven abruptly with Hopkins' transfer to smoky Chesterfield, his "muse turned utterly sullen" for many months. It was to take another disaster at sea and a full half-year before she could be coaxed into singing again, and longer before she would sing a medley.

4 ⌖ Chesterfield, Stonyhurst, Oxford: 1878–1879

Between September 1877, when he wrote *Hurrahing in Harvest,* and late February 1879, a period of nearly a year and a half, Hopkins wrote only two poems. *The Loss of the Eurydice* was written in late March and early April of 1879, at Chesterfield, and *The May Magnificat* was composed in the following month at Stonyhurst. The disaster of the "Eurydice," like that of the "Deutschland," affected him sensibly, and he felt compelled to write something about it. *The May Magnificat* is more of a religious exercise, a poem honoring the Blessed Mother and meant as a popular piece for the Jesuit school at Stonyhurst. It was not until he was at Oxford, both dear and strange to him now (an attraction and repulsion shared also by that other Oxonian convert, Newman) and where so many of his earlier poems had been written, that his creative vein yielded anything like a steady flow of song.

Hopkins' second shipwreck poem is a narrative, less than half the length of the *Deutschland* ode. Perhaps because of Bridges' criticisms of the first wreck poem, Hopkins concerned himself more directly with making a popular poem and so concentrated more on the events of the shipwreck itself.[1] *The Loss of the Eurydice* (March–April 1878) is a far less complicated poem, although the art is surer and in some ways as bold as it was in the earlier poem. The concerns of

---

[1] See *Letters I,* p. 49.

119

the *Eurydice* are those of the *Deutschland:* the fate of those who went to their deaths apparently without confessing Christ; the fate, by extension, of the large segment of England which also seemed to be going to its spiritual ruin; the mercy and generosity of the hero Christ; and the efficacy of prayers said for the dead.

Hopkins insisted to his brother Everard and to Bridges that the poem had to be declaimed properly if it was not to seem intolerably artificial. "To do the Eurydice any kind of justice," he warned Bridges when he sent him the poem in late May 1878 (after *The Month* had refused this poem as well),

you must not slovenly read it with the eyes but with your ears, as if the paper were declaiming it at you. For instance the line "she had come from a cruise training seamen" read without stress and declaim is mere Lloyd's Shipping Intelligence; properly read it is quite a different thing. Stress is the life of it.[2]

So intense is the pitch of the poem that it must be read a number of times with the ear if it is to be understood. Hopkins himself admitted to Bridges that, on rereading the *Eurydice* only with his eyes after it had been returned to him, he was struck by "a kind of raw nakedness and unmitigated violence I was unprepared for." [3] But reading with the ears is essential to an understanding of Hopkins' poem, especially if we are to feel the excitement and immediacy and drama of the shipwreck—and this through the heightened awareness of a religious sensibility.

The nature of Hopkins' boldness is at least threefold: in the mimetic nature of much of the verse, in the run-over rhythms, and in the run-over rhymes. For the measure which Hopkins is working with here (as in a number of his mature poems) is not the line alone but the strict line played against

[2] *Ibid.,* pp. 51–52.   [3] *Ibid.,* p. 79.

the unit of the stanza. Rhyme and rhythm play thus together, for example, in one of the boldest stanzas, the sixth:

> And you were a liar, O blue March day.
> Bright sun lanced fire in the heavenly bay;
> But what black Boreas wrecked her? he
> Came equipped, deadly-electric.

Here "electric" is made to rhyme with "wrecked her? he / C
——," where there is a primary stress on "wrecked" and a
secondary stress on "he / C——." The first letter of the
fourth line belongs, in the reading, to the end of the third
line, and the light syllables following "wrecked" are satel-
lites of the first stress of the fourth line (since the "feet" here
are rising). So that in fact "Came" is drawn out, by being
dwelt upon, to almost a dissyllable. Still, in the reading,
"electric" is forced to be read "electeric" to equal its partner.
"The run-over rhymes were experimental, perhaps a mis-
take," he admitted to his brother Everard seven years after
he wrote the poem:

I do not know that I should repeat them. But rhyme, you understand, is like an indelible process: you cannot paint over it. Surely
they *can* be recited but the effect must have been prepared, as
many things must. I can only remember one, the rhyme to
electric: it must be read "startingly and rash." It *is* "an effect." [4]

The imitative rhythms are present in a number of places,
but perhaps most noticeably in the eleventh stanza, where
the lurching of the "Eurydice" is caught in the lurching or
encountering rhythm of the line itself: [5]

> Then a lurch forward, frigate and men.

[4] From an unpublished letter of November 5, 1885, quoted in *Poems,*
p. 243 n.

[5] See Hopkins' remarks on this line in *Letters I,* pp. 52–53.

And again, there is the sense of encircling, twisting, and suffocating in the repetitive rhyming phrases of the fourth line of that stanza; where the ship was "around them, bound them, or wound them with her" with, of course, a fourth echoic rhyme in "drowned them."

The "Eurydice" was a training ship with some three hundred sailors aboard, most of them young men, and was returning from a six-month training cruise in the Bermudas. The ship was only about an hour from its home port and was opposite the Isle of Wight on the afternoon of March 24, 1878, when, suddenly and without warning, a squall swept from the north across the land and out to sea. Before the captain could have his sails taken in the ship was caught in a blinding hail- and snowstorm. When the squall passed a short time later, the ship had disappeared, taking with her her captain, Marcus Hare, and all but two of the crew— Sydney Fletcher and Cuddiford (the "other" of line 70).

The 120 lines of the narrative break into eight sections. The opening apostrophe to Christ presents the framework within which the shipwreck is viewed: it is a religious meditation on a human tragedy that has the potential for being seen as a comedy in the Christian sense of that term. That is, while the disaster is viewed in all of its stark, realistic terror, Christ, like Orpheus, descends to bring these souls literally out of the depths.

The opening line sounds the theme: Christ's concern with the "Eurydice," which swiftly and without warning foundered, even as many slept, carrying with it three hundred sailors and trainees into eleven fathoms of water. Like tall and stalwart English oaks, they were felled by a freak storm and twisted beneath the sands of the ocean floor—and this within very sight of land. On the pastoral Boniface Down of the southern tip of Wight, the sound of bells from flocks of sheep tolled the knell of the burial. Here was no ship filled with "Bounden bales or a hoard of bullion" but with something far richer, "lads and men."

In the next eight stanzas (ll. 13–44) the poet narrates the actual events of the disaster. The "Eurydice" had come from a cruise where she had been training seamen, men and brave "boldboys" who would soon be men. But the storm blasted both the "bole" (the experienced, hardened oak-like sailors) and the "bloom" (the young, handsome trainees). The weather on that Sunday afternoon was "worst" not only because it took the young with the old, but because it came not from the Atlantic or from the Bay of Biscay, where it might have been spotted, but from off England itself when the ship was within sight of home.

And that beautiful blue March day was a "liar," for while the bright sun shone in the bay, the black winds of Boreas blew down over the ship. It was a snowstorm ("wolfsnow") and hailstorm which mingled and conspired to destroy the "Eurydice." As the storm proceeds south, the poet calls off the places on the Isle of Wight over which the savage cloud passed: Carisbrook, Appledurcombe, Ventnor, and finally the high cliffside of Boniface Down.

But the royal ship was too proud; dressed in her full sail, she was too puffed up, so that when the treacherous black gale was sighted, it was already too late to take in the sail. The capsized ship might have righted herself after the first onslaught of the storm, but the portholes had been left open and Death (the sea) teemed in, eating up "messes of mortals." The ship and her men lurched forward swiftly, and the captain gave the order, "All hands for themselves." The "Eurydice," which had housed and kept the men in their journey, now became their tomb as she bound those within her or wound others, both those in the shrouds and those who had jumped overboard and were then sucked down in her pull.

The next ten stanzas (ll. 45–84) focus on three of the crew. First, Captain Marcus Hare, who went down with his ship as he felt duty-bound to do. Second, Sydney Fletcher, one of the two survivors of the calamity. Third, an unnamed "sea-corpse cold." Lines 45–56 describe Hare, who, drowned in cares and wrapped in despair, followed his "Eurydice" to her sandy grave in the English Channel, like a pale, modern-day counterpart to Orpheus, thinking it his duty so to go down with her. Only *this* Orpheus, unlike Christ-Orpheus, does not return. Well, the poet reflects, even a man much less responsible than Captain Hare, a man who is "time's something server" and a "duty-swerver," may, when confronted with the stark choice of "No or Yes," drive like Hare for the right.

Lines 57–72 focus on young Sydney Fletcher. Hopkins captures the terror and strangeness of the sailor's ordeal. Nineteen-year-old Fletcher of Bristol had jumped overboard as the ship plunged "sheer down." Sucked downward in the ship's "after-draught," he had wrung, wrestled, twisted for air as the sea, that "deathgush brown," gripped him downward. Finally, the lifebelt he had held to, and God's will, lifted him to the surface—a return from hell. Trying to keep afloat in that wintry ocean, he sees no land about him, only the sea and the snowstorm which cut his vision. Finally, "after an hour of wintry waves," a schooner sights and saves him and the other survivor near him. But so great has been the ordeal and the joy of being picked up that he cannot remember what happened next.

The next three stanzas (ll. 73–84) describe one of the three hundred drowned sailors. This corpse was once a fine sailor, the poet laments, whose whole being had been "strung by duty . . . strained to beauty," shaped by the elements among which he lived: "brine and shine and whirling wind." Here lies potential for "leagues of seamanship" which will never be actualized, never wakened.

The poet draws a lessson, a sermon (ll. 85–96), from this dead young seaman. England, like the "Eurydice," is spiritually foundering and taking with it Hopkins' people, his generation. He, the Catholic priest, might let bygones be bygones, forget the curse visited on the English for desecrating the old Catholic shrines, the chapels, churches, cathedrals, monasteries. These shrines are, in these secular times, frequently unvisited. And worse, many of them have been seized by the heirs of the Reformation and are cared for by "Robbery's hand." [6] But the worst is that the English, these living, breathing temples of the Holy Spirit, with their natural beauty so in evidence ("wildworth blown so sweet"), this handsome crew (people) of England, are in "Unchrist," living away from Christ, away from grace, and heading toward their doom.

Yes, the poet laments in the next two stanzas (ll. 97–104), this foundering of an entire nation, of which the "Eurydice" is but a type, is to be deeply deplored. Why, he wonders, did Christ bear this division of a people who at one time were all so at home, familiar, at one, with Christ's "truth and grace." Once this island was *all* so Marian that a pilgrim traveling by the stars and looking up at the marvelous Milky Way thought of it rather as the Walsingham Way, pointing the way to Mary's famous shrine. (And it was another Englishman, the "one" of line 103, the Franciscan philosopher Duns Scotus, who so splendidly defended the Immaculate Conception.) But let that be, for the future has promises of even greater things than these from our glorious medieval tradition.

In the last four stanzas (ll. 105–120) the poet turns from the dead sailors to those women who mourn for them. By implication, all humanity is included here. You have done well, the poet says, in weeping for your lost sons, husbands, and sweethearts. And while your grief can not help them, still, weeping is what "sad truelove should" do. But if you would help your lost ones, he advises, kneel low before Christ, "lord of thunder," [7] and pray: Christ, who art holiest, loveliest, bravest, save *my* hero, O Hero that saves. The

---

[6] These are the lines that Hopkins was referring to when he wondered how Canon Dixon, an Anglican churchman, could desire to print the *Eurydice* and "stand godfather to some of the stanzas in that poem." (*Letters II*, p. 31). See also *Letters I*, p. 28.

[7] See *The Wreck of the Deutschland*, st. 34.

prayer that thou hearest me making *now* have heard *then* at the moment of foundering; have heard and have granted grace *then* when grace was needed. (For God, the past, present, and future are one, so that we can pray after the fact that God shall have heard us before the fact.)

The poet knows that for those who are already damned there is no redemption. But until God has passed final judgment, against which prayer is useless, for those who are sunk in seemingly fresh death, prayer is efficacious and can "fetch pity eternal" (that is, Christ himself). The underthought here is the Orpheus-Eurydice myth. Christ is Orpheus and sinks into the bleary, watery depths in a new harrowing of Hades to bring the crew of the "Eurydice" from death into eternal life.

It is no wonder that *The Month* rejected his poem, addressed as it was to the families and loved ones of the shipwrecked men. For the remedy is no halfway consolation, but a plea for his countrymen to pray seriously to a living Christ who could actually visit the icy brackish waters three miles off the English coast and save the souls of the dead. Hopkins' proposed measures, in both senses of that word, were too bold for the editor of *The Month* to print.

Hopkins wrote *The May Magnificat* soon after he was sent to Stonyhurst to teach classics. While studying philosophy here in the early 1870's he had written *Ad Mariam* and *Rosa Mystica*, and now, in May 1878, he tried his hand at another Marian poem. He used a stanzaic form and meter similar to those he had used in *The Loss of the Eurydice* the month before, except that the fourth line of that poem had four stresses, while here there were only three. *The Eurydice* uses sprung rhythm, with four stresses to the line in the first couplet and three in the second. The poem is unexceptional but for the rhythm, which Hopkins thought good because free,[8]

[8] *Letters I*, p. 65.

and for its delightful eighth stanza, with its outrageously innocent punning:

> Their magnifying of each its kind
> With delight calls to mind
>   How she did in her stored
>   Magnify the Lord.

But the rest of the poem lacks inspiration; it is Hopkins' own brand of Parnassian.[9] We can see him struggling to get the poem under way, as he asks why he muses at Mary's month. The pun on "muse" (create, wonder) may be consciously ambivalent, for Hopkins' occasional verse here lacks that poetic spark which his Stonyhurst May lines of 1883, *The Blessed Virgin compared to the Air we Breathe,* so abundantly display. Here he seems to be writing in two veins, in the Herbertian tradition, as the stanza above shows, and in a mood of exuberance over nature's plenitude, as in

> azuring-over greybell makes
> Wood banks and brakes wash wet like lakes
>   And magic cuckoocall
>   Caps, clears, and clinches all.

But he does not fully align the two strains, which remain uneasily juxtaposed. The closing lines are a slackening, a grating on the ear. This ecstasy of May, the poet says, tells Mary

> To remember and exultation
> In God who was her salvation.

Hopkins' rhymes are often ingenious and very often "work." But these rhymes are a compromise, a stopgap conclusion, and they come dangerously close to being Hudibrastic. Except for a few lines, the poem is journeyman's work.

---

[9] Hopkins himself found "something displeasing" about the poem; see *ibid.*, p. 77.

In early December of 1878 Hopkins was transferred to Oxford. This time he was sent as a preacher to St. Aloysius' Church, St. Giles' Road, administered by the Jesuits, where he was stationed for ten months. During his first three months there he wrote no poetry, but with late February and the promise of spring his muse revived, and he wrote an impressive number of lyrics—impressive, that is, if we remember how busy he was kept because of his parish duties— including six new sonnets. He already had "two sonnets soaking," as he told Bridges in late February,[10] when, walking along the Thames River from Oxford to Binsey and Godstow on March 13, he saw that a great number of aspens had been cut down along the riverbank.[11]

On that same day he wrote his wistful lyric *Binsey Poplars*, inscribing "felled 1879" immediately after the title to emphasize the irreplaceable loss of these particular trees. The title itself suggests that these poplars gave Binsey its local beauty, and that in destroying them, something of Binsey, too, was irrevocably lost. The poem is composed of two unequal stanzas. In the first stanza the poet presents the scene at Binsey; in the second he comments on what we do when we hack at "growing green." Paraphrase is easy here, but paraphrase too hacks and hews, for this is a musical piece, haunting the ear with its soft rhymes and diction.

In the first stanza, the poet presents the liveliness, playfulness, and power of the aspens whose branches ("airy cages") seemed to quell, quiet, and pacify, and whose leaves seemed to quench the leaping sun itself. But they are all, all felled. Of the whole line of them none have been spared, which used to spread their "sandalled / Shadow" on the meadow or river or along the banks where weeds wind and wind wanders.

The poet turns to the reader in the second stanza, with something of desperation, anger, and sorrow in his tone.

---

[10] *Ibid.,* p. 73.   [11] See *Letters II,* p. 26.

Country scapes are delicate, tender, slender. They can be disfigured as easily as our eyes can be with a single jab of the needle. We cannot hack and rack the wild of the landscape; even when we wish only to mend her, we destroy the delicate, aesthetic balance, the exquisite self of the scene, and later generations cannot even guess what the beauty of the land-scape must have been. Only a few axe strokes create havoc where once there was living beauty. In the last lines the repetition of "rural scene" serves as an echo in the reader's memory of a distinctively beautiful local country scene for-ever lost.

The first of the six Oxford sonnets of 1879, *Duns Scotus's Oxford* is written in the sprung and outriding rhythm which Hopkins had employed in his last sonnet of 1877, *Hurrahing in Harvest*. But *Henry Purcell,* written in sprung Alexandrine lines, is a marked departure from all of Hopkins' earlier sonnets, which, for all of their experiments, maintain a "standard" five-stress line. Yet, having made the break, he continued to employ this line, writing *Peace* in "standard Alexandrines." And *Felix Randal,* composed at Liverpool a year after the Purcell sonnet, is also written in wonderfully free sprung and outriding Alexandrines. Hopkins wrote three of his Oxford sonnets, however, in a strict counter-pointed iambic pentameter, or what he called "common rhythm counterpointed": *The Candle Indoors, The Hand-some Heart,* and *Andromeda.*

Although *Duns Scotus's Oxford* and *Henry Purcell* were conceived in February, they are dated March and April respectively. Duns Scotus, of course, was Hopkins' favorite philosopher, as is abundantly clear from his journals, his spiritual notes, and from Hopkins' poetry itself. "After all I can, at all events a little read Duns Scotus," Hopkins had written Bridges from Wales in February 1875, "and I care for him more even than Aristotle and more *pace tua* than a dozen Hegels." [12] Hopkins had made his discovery of the Subtle Doctor in the August vacation of 1872, when he came upon Scotus' two-volume commentary on Peter Lombard in the Badeley Library at Stonyhurst's House of Philosophy. In his journal for August 3 of that year he wrote:

At this time I had first begun to get hold of the copy of Scotus on the Sentences [*Scriptum Oxoniense super Sententiis*] in the Baddely [*sic*] library and was flush with a new stroke of enthusiasm. It may come to nothing or it may be a mercy from God. But just then when I took in any inscape of the sky or sea I thought of Scotus. [13]

Hopkins had alluded to Scotus in *The Loss of the Eurydice* as the "one" (l. 103), and gave his own gloss on the line in a postcard to Bridges on April 8, from Oxford:

The One of the Eurydice is Duns Scotus. . . . The thought is: the island [England] was so Marian that the very Milky Way we made a roadmark to that person's shrine and from one of our seats of learning (to wit the above) went forth the first great champion of her Immaculate Conception, now in our days made an article of faith. [14]

In fact, 1879 marked the twenty-fifth anniversary of the dogma, and Hopkins was always aware of religious anniversaries. His sonnet makes a contrast between the old Catholic Oxford of Scotus' day, with its "grey beauty" seeming to spring directly out of the meadows, and the modern brick architecture of the newer colleges springing up without proper planning or concern for preserving the "neighbour-nature" of trees and fields.

In a letter to Dixon of February 27, 1879, Hopkins, speaking as one fond alumnus of Oxford to another, had lamented that "that landscape the charm of Oxford, green shouldering grey . . . is already abridged and soured and perhaps will

<hr>

[12] *Letters I*, p. 31.   [13] *Journals*, p. 221.

[14] *Letters I*, pp. 77–78. "The above" refers to Oxford, from which the postcard was sent.

soon be put out altogether." [15] This destruction of nature's wildness signified for Hopkins, as a similar lack of concern on the part of men for natural and architectural beauty did for Ruskin, the very change in outlook between Hopkins' Oxford contemporaries and the Oxford of nearly five hundred years before.[16] The polluted upper reaches of the Thames—Oxonians call it the Isis—now form "a brickish skirt," a river polluted with industrial refuse by a society that condones, for a price, the destruction of its own natural resources.

One facet of the genius of Oxford which is specially dear to Hopkins is its closeness to the freshness of nature; blur that by hacking the "rural keeping," the surrounding landscape which forms an integral part of Oxford, and Oxford itself must suffer. Hopkins' inscaping of Oxford, his capturing of its inner spiritual design or significance, leads him to focus on this precise harmonious counterpoint between city and country. In the first quatrain of the sonnet the speaker remarks on this organic interrelationship:

Towery city and branchy between towers;
Cuckoo-echoing, bell-swarmèd, lark-charmèd, rook-racked, river-
    rounded;
The dapple-eared lily below thee.

It was in the University itself that the distinctive powers of country and town once met, but both kept their individual nature in balance, touching but separate, "coped and poisèd." But all has since been soured and confounded, all is now "graceless growth."

In the first tercet of the sestet, the speaker reflects that

---

[15] *Letters II*, p. 20.

[16] "I should not have thought that Cobbett [the historian] was merely a utilitarian. His seemingly heartfelt remarks about love of country for instance (I mean patriotism) and its dependence on beauty of buildings and historic monuments are those of a man who has other ideals than utility" (letter to Dixon of February 1, 1882, *ibid.*, p. 103) .

there still does linger a shadow of that earlier Oxford in which a spirit like Duns Scotus' could be nurtured, could thrive and grow. It is because of these ever-fresh elements that the speaker's spirit can identify with the spirit of Scotus, for they breathe the same air and haunt the same "weeds and waters" and the same grey stone "walls." And the distinct self of Scotus, felt in these, "most sways my spirits to peace."

Then, in the final tercet, the speaker focuses on Scotus himself, who went from Oxford in 1301 to Paris to fire all of France with his "not / Rivalled insight" into the nature of the Immaculate Conception, of Mary's necessary freedom from any trace of sin in order to house worthily the Incarnated Word of God. And this insight into the central mystery of the life of God and the nature of the Incarnation found its equal, its "rival," neither in the vast theophilosophical learning of classical Greece nor in the Neoplatonic doctrines of Renaissance Italy. The poem, then, is a salute not only to Scotus but to Oxford itself, which could nurture a spirit like the Subtle Doctor's.[17]

But having said this, we have still to get to the core or underthought of the sonnet, to its "echo or shadow of the overthought . . . an undercurrent of thought governing the choice of images used."[18] There is, first of all, a shadow of Mary to be found in the very description of Oxford which Hopkins gives us. In the Litany of Loretto, which dates back to 1587 and which Hopkins would have prayed frequently,

[17] On December 5, 1879, Hopkins obliquely referred to the role of Scotus in a sermon on the Immaculate Conception delivered at Bedford Leigh: "It is a comfort to think that the greatest of the divines and doctors of the Church who have spoken and written in favour of this truth came from England: between 500 and 600 years ago he was sent for to go to Paris to dispute in its favour. . . . [This] wise and happy man by his answers broke the objections brought against him as Samson broke the thongs and withies with which his enemies tried to bind him" (Sermons, p. 45).

[18] Letter to Baillie of January 14, 1883, which discusses the underthought to be found in classical literature, Letters III, p. 253.

we find "Tower of David," "Tower of Ivory," "Seat of Wisdom," and "Mother undefiled," as well as "Regina sine labe originali concepta, ora pro nobis" (Queen conceived without original sin, pray for us). And the sonnet echoes these praises in its opening and closing lines, for Oxford, also a seat of wisdom, is "towery city and branchy between towers," which inspired Scotus to defend "Mary without spot." And in the fourteenth century, Hopkins' Oxford was also a mother undefiled, unpolluted. In Mary, as well, are to be found "coped and poisèd powers," for Mary is creature, but also mother of, tabernacle of, God.

Medieval Oxford, too, had "coped and poisèd powers"; not only was the town set off yet complemented by the gown, but Oxford's teachers, the early and great generations of scholastics, were equipped to make fine but true distinctions and discoveries about the nature of the human and the divine, while maintaining the real distinctions governing each. This is sadly not the case today, the second quatrain suggests, when theological distinctions have collapsed and are "skirt[ed]," avoided because of difficulty or fear of controversy. They have become cloudy, and philosophy has degenerated into a concern for utilitarian matters, for industry. And cheap "brick" in place of the beauty of natural grey stone externally reflects this decay in the level of thought of Victorian England. Oxford has become a "graceless growth," without its earlier natural grace or that "neighbour-nature," God's grace, to keep pace with its physical growth. Oxford's "folk, flocks, and flowers," which contributed to its distinctive beauty, have been "confounded," that is, blended together and perhaps also theologically spoiled and confused by blurring the real distinctions between them.

If any one image is the center around which the other images coalesce, it is Hopkins' strategical employment of the word "realty." Most commentators understand it to mean, simply, reality. And this it does mean. But it quite properly refers to fixed, permanent, or immovable things, as in "real estate," as well as to that which is not artificial, fraudulent, or illusory. For Scotus, as Hopkins was well aware, was the "rarest-veinèd unraveller" of "realty," of the inscapes in all of nature, and he lived on "these weeds and waters, these walls." And by looking hard into the untarnished nature of Oxford around him, he glimpsed his "not / Rivalled insight" into the untarnished nature of Mary. Oxford's "realty" has suggested a spiritual "realty."

There is one other underthought flowing through the sonnet, the image of a stream at the root of several key words. For "rarest-veinèd" (l. 12) can describe a submerged narrow water channel as well as a line of thought, and "rival" itself originally referred to a stream (as in "rivulet"). And in the *Deutschland,* Hopkins speaks of Christ's Incarnation as present in the world, in time, riding time "like riding a river" (st. 6, l. 8). For the Incarnation and the Immaculate Conception are inextricably bound up, as a stream to a river:

The first intention then of God outside himself or, as they say, *ad extra,* outwards, the first outstress of God's power, was Christ; and we must believe that the next was the Blessed Virgin. . . . The sacrifice would be the Eucharist, and that the victim might be truly victim like, like motionless, helpless, or lifeless, it must be in matter. Then the Blessed Virgin was intended or predestined to minister that matter. . . . She followed Christ the nearest.[19]

Hopkins, then, while drawn to Oxford, is also alienated from it. Scotus had been able to fire all France for "Mary without spot" half a millennium before, but in 1879 Hopkins had to complain to Bridges that, "small as Oxford compared to London is, it is far harder to set the Isis on fire than the Thames."[20]

[19] *Sermons,* p. 197.

[20] Letter of January 19, 1879, *Letters I,* p. 61. It must be remembered that, strange as Oxford now was to Hopkins, it had a special meaning for him. In October 1878, before being sent to Oxford, he had written to Dixon saying, "Of Oxford . . . I was very fond. I became a Catholic there. But I have not visited it, except once for three quarters of an

On April 22, Hopkins finally sent Bridges *Duns Scotus's Oxford* and *Binsey Poplars,* along with that second sonnet which had been "soaking," *Henry Purcell.* "What do you think of the effect of the Alexandrines?" Hopkins asked. "That meter unless much broken, as I do by outrides, is very tedious." [21] We can only surmise what Bridges thought of Hopkins' latest innovation in the sonnet. Hopkins seems to have employed the longer line to give formal structural support to the density of the thought and to approximate more closely the longer length of his Italian models. But Bridges was puzzled by the thought, and in the next four years Hopkins had to answer at length Bridges' queries about a sonnet which Hopkins thought "one of my very best pieces." [22] In fact, in his very next letter after sending Bridges the sonnet, Hopkins explained the meaning of the sestet, showing the relation of the sea bird to Purcell's genius. He followed with an extended crib on the word "sake" and two short glosses on "wuthering" and "moonmarks." [23]

---

hour, since I took my degree" (*Letters II,* p. 12). And writing to Baillie in May 1880 from Liverpool, he took pains to pay his debts to his University. His remarks help to pinpoint his tone toward the present-day Oxford of his sonnet: "Not to love my University would be to undo the very buttons of my being. . . . And in that stay [December 1878–October 1879] I saw very little of the University. But I could not but feel how alien it was, how chilling, and deeply to be distrusted. . . . Religion, you know, enters very deep; in reality it is the deepest impression I have in speaking to people, that they are or that they are not of my religion" (*Letters III,* pp. 244–245).

[21] *Letters I,* p. 80.   [22] *Ibid.,* p. 171.

[23] "*Sake* is a word I find it convenient to use. It is the *sake* of 'for the sake of,' *forsake, namesake, keepsake.* I mean by it the being a thing has outside itself, as a voice by its echo, a face by its reflection, a body by its shadow, a man by his name, fame, or memory, *and also* that in the thing by virtue of which especially it has this being abroad, and that is something distinctive, marked, specifically or individually speaking, as for a voice and echo clearness; for a reflected image light, brightness; for a shadow-casting body bulk; for a man genius, great achievements, amiability, and so on. In this case it is, as the sonnet says, distinctive quality in genius" (letter of May 26, 1879, *ibid.,* p. 83).

Still, Bridges failed to catch Hopkins' inscaping of Purcell's particular genius as objectively seizing on "the very make and species of man." "By the by your remark on Purcell's music does not conflict with what my sonnet says," Hopkins replied in June, "rather it supports it. My sonnet means 'Purcell's music is none of your d——d subjective rot' (so to speak). Read it again." [24]

In January 1883 the sonnet had again to be defended, this time at even greater length. It is worth examining how Hopkins precisely marks off the development of the thought within the 4-4-6 formal structure of the Italian sonnet. His crib outline suffers, unfortunately, by being too rigidly precise. How Bridges must have started when he read:

The sonnet on Purcell means this: 1–4. I hope Purcell is not damned for being a Protestant, because I love his genius. 5–8. And that not so much for gifts he shares, even though it shd. be in higher measure, with other musicians as for his own individuality. 9–14. So that while he is aiming only at impressing me his hearer with the meaning in hand I am looking out meanwhile for his specific, his individual markings and mottlings, "the sakes of him." It is as when a bird thinking only of soaring spreads its wings: a beholder may happen then to have his attention drawn by the act to the plumage displayed.

Then he explains more fully and thereby softens somewhat his gloss on the first quatrain of the sonnet: "May Purcell . . . have died a good death . . . so that the heavy condemnation under which he . . . nominally lay for being out of the true Church may in consequence of his good intentions have been reversed." He also confesses that it is "somewhat dismaying to find I am so unintelligible." [25]

There was, however, for Hopkins a more particular question, not about the theological, but about the grammatical validity of his opening line, "Have fair fallen, O fair, fair

[24] Letters I, p. 84.   [25] Ibid., p. 170.

have fallen. . . ." Hopkins' concern for the precise correctness of the line hints at that scrupulous concern for grammatical precision we have seen so frequently in his sonnets:

One thing disquiets me: I *meant* "fair fall" to mean *fair (fortune be) fall;* it has since struck me that perhaps "fair" is an adjective proper and in the predicate and can only be used in cases like "fair fall the day," that is, *may the day fall, turn out, fair.* My line will yield a sense that way indeed, but I never meant it so. Do you know any passage decisive on this?

Hopkins did not want the line read as merely a fond, sentimental hope; he is praying to God in his sonnet that Purcell's soul shall truly "have parted from the body and passed away, centuries since though I frame the wish, in peace with God!" [26]

A month later Hopkins again, and for the last time, defends the sonnet to Bridges, who had once more written that Hopkins still made himself misunderstood:

This is a terrible business about my sonnet "Have fair fallen." . . . *Have* . . . is the singular imperative (or optative if you like) of the past, a thing possible and actual both in logic and grammar, but naturally a rare one. As in the second person we say "Have done" or in making appointments "Have had your dinner beforehand," so one can say in the third person not only "Fair fall" of what is present or future but also "Have fair fallen" of what is past. The same thought (which plays a great part in my own mind and action) is more clearly expressed in the last stanza but one of the *Eurydice.*[27]

The sonnet itself is an exciting as well as a precise piece of work; in its preoccupation with the exact nature of Purcell's

---

[26] *Ibid.,* pp. 170–171.

[27] Letter of February 3, 1883, *ibid.,* p. 174. The lines from *The Loss of the Eurydice* have not only the same thought, but use the same past optative construction (ll. 113–116). The same concern for rescuing even those long dead by prayers offered to an eternal God is found in stanza 33 of the *Deutschland.*

idiosyncratic genius it stands beside *Duns Scotus's Oxford*. But whereas the Oxford sonnet implies or obliquely points to the underthought of medieval Oxford's appropriateness as a setting for Scotus' insight into the nature of the Immaculate Conception, the Purcell sonnet is based structurally on a more explicit analogy between Purcell's distinctive characteristics and the markings of the sea gull. Even so, there is here also a submerged metaphor, and one key to the metaphor may be found explicitly in Hopkins' spiritual notes for the feast of the Immaculate Conception, 1881. In making the Ignatian "Contemplation for Obtaining Love," Hopkins wrote:

"Faciens me templum, cum creatus sim ad similitudinem et imaginem"—The word Temple at first sight hides the thought, which is, I think, that God rests in man as in a place, a *locus*, bed, vessel, expressly made to receive him as a jewel in a case hallowed to fit it, as the hand in the glove or the milk in the breast. . . . And God *in forma servi* rests *in servo*, that is / Christ as a solid in his member as a hollow or shell, both things being the image of God; which can only be perfectly when the member is in all things conformed to Christ. This too best brings out the nature of the man himself, as the lettering on a sail or device upon a flag are best seen when it fills.[28]

The opening quatrain, with its deeply sincere wish that Purcell's soul be at peace with God, then, is not a pious introduction; it is essential to the artistic logic of the sonnet. For Purcell's sacred music and the distinctive voice in which he pronounced his art touch Hopkins as the authentic voice of man's ascendency toward God. If the echo or sake of Purcell's spirit can so earnestly move Hopkins now to thoughts of God, surely it would be tragic if that spirit itself

[28] *Sermons,* p. 195. (Slash marks in quotations from Hopkins' prose are here reproduced as he used them.) Christopher Devlin, S.J., notes in his comment on this passage the similarity of the last tercet of *Henry Purcell* to the line from the *Deutschland,* "I whirled out wings that spell"; *ibid.,* p. 305.

were not to be with God. Unless Hopkins can reasonably hope that this correspondence between the sacred voice and the spirit of Purcell exists, the sonnet suffers prolapsis in more than its form. And while this religious consideration may be aesthetically irrelevant by the dicta of modern criticism, Hopkins' sonnets are colloquies or prayer-forms. Furthermore, Purcell possessed one of those rare geniuses whose voice "seems something necessary and eternal," [29] who has, as Hopkins wrote in the prose argument at the head of the Purcell sonnet, "uttered in notes the very make and species of man as created both in him and in all men generally." It is

> Not mood in him nor meaning, proud fire or sacred fear,
> Or love or pity or all that sweet notes not his might nursle.

Rather it is in the particular accent, in the unexpected and spontaneous repetitions of Purcell's canons, and in the unforced sincerity and joy that the "forgèd feature" of his music reveals itself.

"Rehearsal" has three meanings that work simultaneously within the poem. The word has its strictly musical meaning of a preparation for a musical performance. Something of Purcell's self is recaptured in his music whenever it is played. And in its meaning of presenting an account of oneself, it refers to the repetition of the particular "sakes" of Purcell's spirit which are intrinsically bound up with his music; it refers also to that other rehearsal of Purcell's spirit before God, that other presenting an account of oneself.

Hopkins' extremely perceptive eye had noticed the peculiar "crescent shaped markings on the quill-feathers" of storm fowls, "either in the colouring of the feather or made by the overlapping of one on another." [30] The "stormfowl" Hopkins

[29] Hopkins remarked in a letter to Dixon six months before he wrote this sonnet: "[Milton's] verse as one reads it seems something necessary and eternal (so to me does Purcell's music)" (*Letters II*, p. 13).

[30] *Letters I*, p. 83.

is referring to is probably the common black-headed sea gull which is to be found along the seashores of Britain, as well as along the Thames River. Hopkins, of course, had closely observed the flight pattern of the kestrel in Wales. And he has given us a fine word picture of sea gulls on the Mersey River at Liverpool in a letter to Bridges of late January 1881.[31]

But why did he choose the soaring sea gull as an analogy for Purcell's soaring spirit? Perhaps Hopkins wanted to draw attention to the contrast between the clumsily wobbling earth-bound bird and its effortless, graceful beauty in flight, and to suggest the contrast between "Man Jack" (man in and of himself) and the ability of his spirit to soar in divine song. It is only when the breath of the wind lifts and supports the bird that its gracefulness is made manifest. At the same time its *haecceitas*, its particular self, also clearly flashes forth. And it is only when man works in harmony with the Holy Spirit that his grace-ful-ness is made manifest. And yet, his spirit is not absorbed by the Spirit of God; rather it is in identifying with God that the particular self is made most manifest. Hopkins explains this polarity of individuality and identification in this way:

The universal mind being identified not only with me but also with all other minds cannot be the means of communicating what is individual in me to them nor in them to me. . . . The universal cannot taste this taste of self as I taste it, for it is not to . . . him, that the guilt or shame, the fatal consequence, the fate, comes home. . . . *And for all that this universal being may be at work in mine it leaves me finite.*[32]

Besides the majesty of the bird and the majesty of Purcell's music, there is, finally, the joyous humanity of the man. For Purcell does what neither animal nor angel can do, what the bird only fancifully does; he scatters "a colossal smile / Off him" in singing "his air of angels."

[31] *Ibid.,* p. 116.   [32] *Sermons,* pp. 125–126 (italics mine).

It is probably because he was so busy with parish work that his next two sonnets, written between mid-April and mid-June, are not exceptional poems. "I enclose you two sonnets, capable of further finish," he tells Bridges on June 22, referring to *The Candle Indoors,* the companion piece to *The Lantern out of Doors* of 1877, and the autobiographical *The Handsome Heart.* "I am afraid they are not very good all through. One is a companion to the Lantern, not at first meant to be though, but it fell in. The other is historical, autobiographical, as you would say, or biographical. Remark what strikes you." [33]

In his next letter, almost two months later, the harried parish priest apologizes that he "must try and tersely scribble you something." He defends the analogy in *The Candle Indoors* of the candle to the human spirit. Bridges never could understand Hopkins' deeply instressed religious feeling, and he was to complain in his 1918 Preface that Hopkins' poetry suffered from this mannerism of trying "to force emotion into theological or sectarian channels." [34] "Though the analogy in the Candle sonnet may seem forced," Hopkins writes, "yet it is an 'autobiographical' fact that I was influenced and acted on the way there said." [35] He also sends

[33] *Letters I,* p. 84. In a letter to Bridges of August 14, 1879, Hopkins said of the *Handsome Heart:* "The story was that last Lent, when Fr. Parkinson was laid up in the country, two boys of our congregation gave me much help in the sacristy in Holy Week. I offered them money for their services, which the elder refused, but being pressed consented to take it laid out in a book. The younger followed suit; then when some days after I asked him what I shd. buy answered as in the sonnet" (*ibid.,* p. 86). As a postscript to this narrative, Hopkins wrote Bridges in October of the same year that "the little Hero of the Handsome Heart has gone to school at Boulogne to be bred for a priest and he is bent on being a Jesuit" (*ibid.,* p. 92).

[34] Bridges' "Preface to the Notes" of the first edition of Hopkins' poems (January 1918), reprinted in *The Poems of Gerard Manley Hopkins,* ed. W. H. Gardner (3rd ed.; New York, 1965), p. 204.

[35] *Letters I,* p. 85.

along a recast of *The Handsome Heart*, and defends the run-on rhymes with their "overreaving," rising and falling rhythm. Still, he is "somewhat surprised at your liking this sonnet so much. I thought it not very good."

By comparison with *Duns Scotus's Oxford* and *Henry Purcell*, it is "not very good." There is a noticeable decline in finish in these next two sonnets. They are contemporary with *The Brothers, The Buglar's First Communion,* and *Morning, Midday, and Evening Sacrifice,* all composed within four months of each other. *Andromeda*, dated August 12, was written just before *Morning, Midday, and Evening Sacrifice*. But it shows a radically new direction for Hopkins' sonnets in the treatment of its content and will be best discussed apart from these two sonnets.

Hopkins' short narrative pieces are not among his most successful poems, and *The Handsome Heart: at a Gracious Answer* is no exception. The first quatrain opens with two lines of dialogue that capture the rhythms of an energetic colloquial speech between priest and altar boy:

> "But tell me, child, your choice; what shall I buy
> You?"—"Father, what you buy me I like best."

The boy is "plied and pressed," but he continues to return to his first generous answer, as the needle of a compass, "plied and pressed" from its true reading, will continue to swing back to its "first purport of reply."

In the second quatrain, the priest turns within to muse on the nature of the uncorrupted heart, likening it to the homing instinct of a carrier pigeon, an image of unswerving tendency toward a fixed point clearly related to the first image:

> What the heart is! which, like carriers let fly—
> Doff darkness, homing nature knows the rest—
> To its own fine function, wild and self-instressed,
> Falls light as ten years long taught how to and why.

Just as the carrier pigeon will fly to its home once the physical darkness has been removed, so the heart would naturally and instinctively follow the right path, its own self, were it not for the crippling scar of original sin and man's perverse propensity for evil. "Rest" has two simultaneous meanings: for the spirit, once darkness is lifted, knows what *remains* to be done, and it also knows that its true resolution or rest is to be found in the good.

The speaker marvels at the triple graces found in the boy's handsome face, in his handsome, maturing mind, and, most importantly, in his handsome heart:

> Mannerly-hearted! more than handsome face—
> Beauty's bearing or muse of mounting vein,
> All, in this case, bathed in high hallowing grace.

In a letter to Bridges written in October 1879, there is a passage which serves as a prose paraphrase of these lines:

I think then no one can admire beauty of the body more than I do, and it is of course a comfort to find beauty in a friend or a friend in beauty. But this kind of beauty is dangerous. Then comes the beauty of the mind, such as genius, and this is greater than the beauty of the body and not to call dangerous. And more beautiful than the beauty of the mind is beauty of character, the "handsome heart." [36]

An aposiopesis follows line 11 as the priest considers that the best thing he could buy the boy would be the reward of heaven itself: "Of heaven what boon to buy you, boy, or gain / Not granted!" But the line also means that it is for such a reward as this boy that Christ was willing to spend his life, and in fact Christ will grant any gain he has made to have him. It is one of those fine, meaningfully ambiguous lines in which Christ and man reciprocate and interact upon one another, as in the "O which one? is it each one?" of *Carrion Comfort.*

[36] *Ibid.,* p. 95.

But a second hiatus follows closely on the first, for that instinctive goodness may be darkened, the magnetic pitch toward true north may at any time be distorted by Satan, the master of crooked paths: "O on that path you pace / Run all your race, O brace sterner that strain!" The internal rhyming of "pace," "race," and "brace" with "grace" in line 11 reinforces the note of urgency and alarm. Again, the emphasis is on staying on the straight and undeviating line, of running, as St. Paul says, to win the race.[37] The opening lines of dialogue assume a deeper significance, for the priest's offer to buy the child something also echoes the central fact for Hopkins of the redemption of Christ, a theme which runs just below the surface throughout much of Hopkins' poetry.

The Candle Indoors is the obverse of *The Lantern out of Doors.* The speaker is out walking randomly during a mild evening and stops to muse at a light shining out from a window, cutting back the all-devouring, "blear-all black." The candle light is "yellowy moisture," and the "to-fro tender trambeams truckle at the eye"—that is, the fine, delicate beams of light, like loose strands of silk, bend and are subservient to the slightest motion of the speaker's eyelashes. But these fine lines of light are most noticeable when the eyes are moist, and the point of perception in this poem is Hopkins' own tear-filled eye. The harsh yet lyrical percussion of the line calls insistent attention to itself: tender tears *will* well up and bend ("truckle") the lines of light ("trambeams").[38]

In the second quatrain the lonely priest turns within to ask himself if the people indoors are magnifying God in-

---

[37] St. Paul's racing metaphor seems to have been in Hopkins' mind in his letter of exhortation and deep concern to Bridges in January 1879, when he laments that "not to have the faith is worse than to have sinned deeply, for it is like not being even in the running" (*ibid.,* p. 64).

[38] See Sr. Rosemarie Julie Gavin, "Hopkins' 'The Candle Indoors,'" *The Explicator,* XX (1962), Item 50.

doors within themselves. Are these common folk, these human representatives, doing that for which they were created, he asks. For in just performing their duties, they do honor God. "It is not only prayer that gives God glory but work," Hopkins wrote in his private spiritual notes on the "Foundation" of the *Spiritual Exercises:*

Smiting on an anvil, sawing a beam, whitewashing a wall, driving horses, sweeping, scouring, everything gives God some glory if being in his grace you do it as your duty. . . . To lift up the hands in prayer gives God glory, but a man with a dungfork in his hand, a woman with a sloppail, give him glory too. He is so great that all things give him glory if you mean they should.[39]

Hopkins in this sonnet is playing on the root meaning of "ply," which means to work at a task, but also to interweave the threads of yarn suggested by "tram" in line four. "Tram" derives from the Low German *traam,* meaning a wooden beam, and from the Latin *trama,* meaning woof or silk thread. "Trambeam" ("beam" from *baum,* meaning tree) suggests the holy tree or rood upon which Christ was hung, as well as the silky, delicate, crossing lights formed on the retina of the tearful eye. These people, then, give God glory by manifesting a clear if small external light, a sign of the cross, in plying at their lowly task. But the speaker is impatient and wants God's glory increased, aggrandized.

In the sestet, the speaker realizes what he has been doing. As John Pick aptly puts it, "Hopkins turns upon himself and closes with a terrifying question that echoes all the priest's own yearning for perfection and his anguished fear that he has himself failed in himself to live up to what he expects of others."[40] It is not the manifestation of Jack or Jessy's spiritual light that he should now be concerned with; he recognizes the humbling fact that this concern may be merely a

---

[39] *Sermons,* pp. 240–241.

[40] *Gerard Manley Hopkins: Priest and Poet* (2d ed.; London, 1966), p. 97.

tactic to divert attention from his own "fading fire." And as if he were calling to a reluctant dog, tail between legs, he orders his spirit to come home for a tongue-lashing:

> Come you indoors, come home; your fading fire
> Mend first and vital candle in close heart's vault:
> You there are master, do your own desire;
>
> What hinders? Are you beam-blind, yet to a fault
> In a neighbour deft-handed? are you that liar
> And, cast by conscience out, spendsavour salt?

This is terrible self-chastisement, and the lines echo loudly with Christ's warning to his disciples against spiritual complacency and the judging of others.[41]

Hopkins plays again on the word "beam," asking himself if he is blind to the "beam" in his own eye, and also blind to the slender cross-like beams shining outdoors from Jack and Jessy. His overzealousness, his eagerness and impatience for any manifestation of the cross, the beam, has as its deepest motivation the unwillingness to look at the unpleasant reality within. The poem, then, is an unflinchingly honest particular examination of Hopkins' own "close heart's vault." This preoccupation with inner purity of motive and self-scrutiny had been with Hopkins from his student days, and it was to become central to his later sonnets, which for their searing examination into the void within were to gain the name "terrible."

The Bugler's First Communion, dated tentatively by Hopkins "July 27 (?), 1879," was "not quite finished" in mid-August and not sent until October.[42] It is a narrative poem in twelve four-line stanzas in sprung rhythm, with five stresses in lines 1, 2, and 4, and three in line 3—a meter, Hopkins commented, "something like the Eurydice." There is the same overreaving of rhyme and rhythm as in the earlier poem, the same boldness and startling freshness. In the first

[41] See, for instance, Matthew 7:1–5, and 5:13–16.
[42] *Letters I,* pp. 86–87, 92.

stanza, for example, "Irish" is made to rhyme with "sire (he / Sh—. . .)"; in the second stanza, "Communion" rhymes with "a boon he on." But these are the boldest. Most of the other rhymes are tame by comparison.[43]

The poem is largely narrative, with a personal commentary for coda. The priest-poet relates the story of a particular "bugler boy from [Cowley] barrack" who "this very very day came down to us" (to the Jesuit Church of St. Aloysius in Oxford) to receive his first Communion from the priest's hands. The poet praises the handsomeness of the boy, who shares the "best gifts" of his English father and Irish mother. On the priest's recent visit to the barracks, the boy had asked to receive the sacraments, and today he knelt "in regimental red" to receive the "Boon" of Christ in the Eucharist. "Fetched" from the "cupboard" (the tabernacle), the Eucharist, the frail Communion wafer ("housel") which is now the body and blood of Christ himself—"Low-latched in leaf-light housel his too huge godhead"—is the "treat" administered to the young soldier.

The priest offers his own prayer with Christ's gift, that the heavens may send through the sacraments their sweetest divine gifts to the lad, which are: to give him a "dauntless" heart and so make him "Christ's darling," and to make him neither deceitful, bragging, nor insulting—"Tongue true, vaunt- and tauntless." The leaf-light housel is asked to continue breathing the bloom of chastity into this young knight. This sacrament, this "angel-warder," messenger and guardian against evil, is asked in military terms to "squander," scatter, "the hell-rook ranks" which "sally to molest him." Christ is the "kind comrade" (gentle, but also partaking of human nature—mankind) who is asked to march abreast of this soldier (in close order and also within his breast), and to keep his days in the same good order as the stars themselves.

---

[43] Hopkins' bold rhymes almost always include a hard *h* which is unaspirated in the reading.

He considers the other young men—"limber liquid youth" —at the barracks, who yield to his teaching as a tender peach bears the imprint of the finger's pressure. "Headstrong" (impetuous, but also intelligent), they rush after their own well-being, for they still have the flexibility of going after, of willing, what they intuitively know is best for their wisest selves. For days after, the priest walks on soft "tufts of consolation," which is *his* own reward for having served God in serving Christ's "royal ration"—a military metaphor for the body of Christ the King—to "just such slips of soldiery." Slip has its meaning of a slender youth, but it also means a small shoot or twig cut for grafting, in this passage, to the "leaf-light" Body of Christ.

The botanical image is continued in stanza 8. There is nothing like seeing the young, so "fresh," "limber liquid," and "fretted" (that nervous unfolding of new leaves in spring) in a "bloomfall" (that time in spring when the first blooms of the trees, blown by the wind, drop to the ground like a snowfall). It is this sweet season which portends that even sweeter end; that end in time when men shall have their youthful beauty forever in Christ, and also man's spiritual end, his reason for being, when natural beauty is "fretted," interlaced, with spiritual beauty, for then Christ reigns in the human temple to which he is the natural heir.

May that sealing sacred ointment of the Sacrament act, the poet hopes, as a charm to make the lad charming. May it arm him against and seal him *off* from evil and seal *in* charity. Let me never again, he asks, see this young chaste Galahad who is today given to God, either in or out of uniform, rather than be disappointed in those sweet hopes for him, whose least realization or quickenings (as of a tender shoot) can stir and quicken my spirit. Hopkins feels that this child's direction is channeled by God, and that he is not headed toward a moral disaster, that he will not wreck himself on the shoals of evil.

Nevertheless, he knows by sad experience that, even though the young soldier is on the right road bound for home (heaven), he can still "rankle and roam / In back-wheels," that is, wander, err, stray off the road and so "ran-kle" God. Hopkins may also be playing here on the connec-tion between "rankle," which comes from *dracunculus,* the diminutive of *draco,* serpent, and the wandering, devious motion of the Devil, "thrower of things off the track."[44]

Well, Hopkins remarks, the future of this young man must be "left to the Lord of the Eucharist." He rests his case, but not altogether. For he will record this: that he has prayed so strongly to heaven that his pleas would, continuing the mili-tary analogy, throttle even a fortress-heaven with the "ride and jar" of a cavalry charge, if his prayer were to go disre-garded. It may seem brazen or "Forward-like" to speak in this manner about heaven, he admits, but in any event, it is likely, and *like* heaven, both that such prayers as these were given a favorable hearing and that heaven's favors (those special privileges given to Knights) were bestowed on this young Galahad, this chaste knight in Christ's service.

This young soldier was much in Hopkins' mind, and he does seem to have lost sight of him as he suspected he would and as so often happens in relations between a parish priest and his spiritual charges. Both left Oxford at the same time, the young soldier having been ordered to Mooltan in the Punjab, Hopkins to Bedford Leigh. But so caught up was Hopkins with the idea of radical innocence, of unsullied purity, that he could confess to Bridges that "I am half inclined to hope the Hero of it may be killed in Afghani-stan" before that innocence was lost.[45]

Sometime early in August, Hopkins finished "a little song" in three stanzas and sent it on to Bridges. *Morning, Midday, and Evening Sacrifice* forms a three-part progres-sion urging the reader to give the best gifts of youth, middle, and old age back to God. (The theme is similar—giving back beauty to God—but the treatment is different in *The*

---

[44] See *Sermons,* pp. 198–199 and Milton's *Paradise Lost,* IX, 510–518, 631–633.   [45] *Letters I,* p. 92.

Leaden Echo and the Golden Echo.) Here Hopkins uses an extremely tight measure (ababccc), a three- and four-stress sprung rhythm line, and a correspondingly concentrated diction.

In the first stanza, the poet dwells on the beauty and harmony particular to a child's countenance: the redness of the cheeks melding into the whiteness of the skin, the exquisitely chiseled upper lip, the light golden hair, the grey eye. While all this young beauty is still fresh, the poet urges, even while it is still fuming and drifting away like smoke, it should be offered as the first fruits to God.

In the second stanza, the poet dwells on the young man in full possession of his physical health and mental faculties. When our bodies "beat and breathe" in their towering pride and strength, let us remember that they are meant to be tools used in doing Christ's work, and that they are not primarily meant for our own pleasure.

The third stanza focuses on the wisdom and intellectual powers of the older man, whose mastery is not physical but "in the mind." In a metaphysical conceit, the poet likens the old man's grey hairs to "silk-ash" within which there is a hot core of thought. Again, thought is ripest under the rind, the balding head. Do not delay, the poet urges, for death is already lifting the latch to take away your intellectual gifts. Therefore, he advises, dispatch with your offering, and do it with dispatch.

Hopkins composed *Andromeda* on August 12 and enclosed it with his lyric in a letter to Bridges of August 14–21. "Lastly," Hopkins wrote, "I enclose a sonnet on which I invite minute criticism. I endeavoured in it at a more Miltonic plainness and severity than I have anywhere else. I cannot say it has turned out severe, still less plain, but it seems almost free from quaintness and in aiming at one excellence I may have hit another." [46]

---

[46] *Ibid.*, p. 87. When, in April 1881, at Dixon's pleading, Hopkins sent three sonnets to Hall Caine for possible inclusion in Caine's

If the Incarnation rides time like a river, this central act of history must in some dark way be foreshadowed in pre-Christian times. Certainly many of Hopkins' arcane and sometimes brilliant insights into classical and Egyptian antiquity are at least partially related to his search for shadowy correspondences between Christ's "great sacrifice" and ancient ritualistic sacrifice. In 1886, for example, Baillie was swamped by a deluge of letters from Hopkins asking for specific information on possible influences of Egyptian religious practices on the early Greeks. And in March 1889, just a little more than two months before he died, Hopkins wrote his brother Lionel that he was busy tracing the significance of a sacrificial pagan rite performed annually by priests on May 14 in ancient Rome.[47]

Hopkins sees in the mythological story of Perseus and Andromeda a foreshadowing of Christ's protection of his Church.[48] Andromeda, the myth goes, is a beautiful young

---

anthology of sonnets, he included his *Andromeda* in case Caine was troubled by Hopkins' rhythmic novelties in his other poems. Early in May Hopkins told Bridges that he would not be printed, but added, "However [Caine] had Andromeda and one cannot say there is any novelty in rhythm there" (*ibid.,* p. 128).

[47] *Letters III,* p. 193.

[48] Hopkins comments on Greek mythology in his letter to Dixon of October 23, 1886: "Mythology is something else besides fairytale; it is religion, the historical part of religion. . . . I cannot enter on this consideration without being brought face to face with the great fact of heathenism. . . . [What] are we to say of it? For myself literally words would fail me to express the loathing and horror with which I think of it and of man setting up the work of his own hands, of that hand within the mind[,] the imagination, for God Almighty who made heaven and earth. But the Greek gods are rakes, and unnatural rakes. . . . But I grant that the Greek mythology is very susceptible of fine treatment, allegorical treatment for instance, and so treated gives rise to the most beautiful results. No wonder: the moral evil is got rid of and the pure art, morally neutral and artistically so rich, remains and can be even turned to moral uses" (*Letters II,* pp. 146–147).

maiden tied to a rock on the seashore to be sacrificed as an innocent victim to a terrifying sea monster. The gallant Perseus, flying above on wings given him by Mercury and carrying the severed head of Medusa, sees Andromeda below and is attracted by her beauty. After gaining the consent of Andromeda's parents to wed her if he saves her, the bridegroom-to-be slays the beast after a terrible battle and marries Andromeda. The analogy of the bridegroom Christ looking over his beloved Church in distress below, who will, when "no one dreams," descend to rescue her and slay the beast of sin is of course clearly intended, as Gardner's incisive notes on the poem make clear. The clarity of *Andromeda* is in part due to the poem's allegory, which is more pointed in this (and in *Peace*) than is usual for Hopkins. "Time's Andromeda" is the militant and persecuted Church of Christ working out its salvation in time, in the present, "Now." She is founded "on this rock rude," on Simon Peter the fisherman, by Christ's own punning command, "Thou art Peter [*petros* = rock], and upon this rock I will build my church; and the gates of hell shall not prevail against it" (Matthew 16:18). She who has "not her either beauty's equal or / Her injury's, looks off by both horns of shore," both behind her to her scarred past and before her to her uncertain future. "Her flower, her piece of being," is "doomed dragon food"; that is, she seems destined to be sacrificed to the dragon (Satan), but we should not forget that the dragon has also been "doomed" already. And although he is the prince of the world "Now," he will eventually be defeated here as well.

Although the Church has been frequently attacked and cursed throughout her long past, there are newer "wilder" forces arising out of the west, which are "more / Rife," "more lawless, and more lewd." Among these, Gardner points out, would be "rationalism, Darwinism, [and] the new paganism of Swinburne and Whitman." [49] For all of these, as

---

[49] *Poems,* p. 277.

well as utilitarianism, liberalism, Irish nationalism, Gladstone, and the general weakening of moral fiber among his own countrymen, were constant sources of worry in Hopkins' letters.

But there is another meaning of "wilder beast from West" almost certainly suggested here, and to understand this we must turn first to a long passage in Hopkins' spiritual notes. In writing his exegesis on Chapter 12 of the Apocalypse during his tertianship in November 1881, Hopkins makes some profound theological and mythopoetical comments which help to more fully explain several ideas in *Andromeda:*

As the woman is compared to the earth in the solar system so the dragon is to the constellation Draco, the tail of which sweeps through 120° or a third of the sphere and which winds round the pole (. . . a star in the head of Draco was then the polestar), this world's seeming axis and the earth's real one, so as to symbolize how Satan tried to possess himself of the sovereignty of things, taking . . . the culmination of the firmament towards the pole, as a throne and post of vantage and so wreathing nature and as it were constricting it to his purposes . . . , though he was foiled, cast from heaven, and left master only of the material world, by a figure [symbol] the earth. . . . The snake or serpent [is] a symbol of the Devil. So also the Dragon. . . . And therefore I suppose the dragon as a type of the Devil to express the universality of his power, both the gifts he has by nature and the attributes and sway he grasps, and the horror which the whole inspires.[50]

Hopkins is here interested in the correspondence between the ancient mythopoetizing of the constellations and the imagery of Sacred Scripture, both in the Old Testament and the Apocalypse, and it seems clear that the constellations of Perseus and Andromeda, as well as of Draco and Cetus, are all involved on one level of *Andromeda.* The constellation Perseus kneels with "barebill" drawn just beneath Androm-

[50] *Sermons,* pp. 198–199.

eda. To the northwest lies Draco, coiled around the North
Pole. Far away and to the east in the southern hemisphere
lies the constellation Cetus, the sea monster (or, more specifically, whale) whom Perseus destroyed. It is not the sea
monster Cetus who is the real threat to Andromeda, but the
dragon Satan sitting "towards the pole."

The action of the time in the sestet is both sensitive and
complex, for if Perseus-Christ *now* "treads a time," he will
"then," when he sees fit, descend to save Andromeda and slay
the beast. But while we are given assurances of the outcome
of the struggle, and the action of rescue appears to be happening within the poem, the "then" of line 13 makes it clear
that this remains a future event. In the meantime, although
seemingly forsaken, Andromeda must maintain her patience,
which is being fragmented and nibbled at by the evil around
her. But at the same time her patience "Mounts." For while
her patience is racked by excruciating tenseness, it is also
learning by necessity to ascend toward its only help, Perseus-
Christ. And when her savior does come, he will "alight
disarming," coming to disarm in one way his people by
winning them over with his "disarming" mercy and kindness, while he appears simultaneously to his enemies as a
matchless warrior "disarming" evil of its "fangs" and his
people of their "thongs" or prisoner's chains.

Christ-Perseus evokes also St. George protecting his distressed Britannia. The legend of St. George, England's patron saint since 800, would, of course, have deep significance
for the priest eager for the reconversion of England.[51] We

---

[51] In fact, there is evidence that the legend of St. George slaying the
dragon was borrowed from the Perseus-Andromeda myth and attrib-
uted by English crusaders fighting in Asia Minor to their own national
patron. In *The Dragon in the Gate* (Berkeley, 1968) Elizabeth Schneider reads *Andromeda* as referring pointedly to the growing threat of
Irish nationalism, that "wilder beast from West . . . , more / Rife in
her wrongs, more lawless, and more lewd." It is a shrewd and totally
acceptable gloss.

have only to turn to the Epistle for the feast day of St. George and the adjacent passages from St. Paul's Second Letter to Timothy to see the echoes in the poem:

Fix thy mind on Jesus Christ . . . who has risen from the dead; that is the gospel I preach, and in its service I suffer hardship like a criminal, yes, even with chains [*ad vincula*—thongs]; but there is no imprisoning the word of God. . . . [In] firm resolve, in faith, in patience, in love, in endurance; all my persecutions and suffering, such as those which befell me at Antioch, Iconium, Lystra; what persecutions I underwent! And yet the Lord brought me through them all safely. And indeed, all those who are re-solved to live a holy life in Christ Jesus will meet with perse-cution; while the rogues and the mountebanks go on from bad to worse, at once imposters and dupes. It is for thee to hold fast by the doctrine handed on to thee, the charge committed to thee [II Timothy 2:8–10, 3:10–14].

Finally, *Andromeda* can be read as Christ's abiding con-cern for each Christian in distress who is fighting the terrify-ing battle against evil, and who, in his seeming abandon-ment by Christ, is perfecting the gift of patience. In the end, Christ descends, bringing with him for his Andromeda a lasting peace and freedom from the wars without and within.

It is this last thought, this deeply felt need for spiritual peace and its prior condition of learning patience, which leads directly to the last sonnet of this second Oxford period, the curtal sonnet *Peace*. It does not seem likely that Hopkins sent this sensitive and personal poem to Bridges till some years later, for the autograph copy is found in Hopkins' own collection of manuscript poems. Bridges had copied out those of Hopkins' manuscript poems in his possession and had given the copies to Hopkins in late 1883, in the manu-script book Bridges calls B. But this poem is in Hopkins' hand, dated "Oxford, 1879" and an early draft of the poem is dated more precisely October 2, 1879, the day before Hopkins was sent to the Bedford Leigh mission as preacher.

Furthermore, there is only one explicit reference to the sonnet, and that is in Hopkins' letter to Bridges written from Dublin in August 1884, almost five years after he had composed *Peace*.[52]

The meaning of *Peace* is relatively straightforward throughout, certainly, at least, on the surface of it. Peace itself, in the form of a "wild wooddove," is the prize desired. The speaker, picturing himself as a tree, pleads with the dove to settle in his boughs. And although Peace does sometimes rest there, it is easily alarmed and then flies away. There is, then, a real distinction between Peace, with a capital *P*, and the other peace in lower case. For the peace which can be easily shaken is "piecemeal peace" and "poor peace." It is the peace which relies on external events and which is gone when those conditions change, as they are forever doing in the flux of time.

His letters frequently suggest how often Hopkins' peace was broken by "Alarms of wars, the daunting wars, the death of it." "I am very sad at heart about the battle of Majuba," he wrote his mother in March 1881. "It is a deep disgrace, a stain upon our arms; which indeed have not shone of late. The effect will, I am afraid, be felt all over the empire. Would that we had some great statesman, a patriot and not a truckler to Russia or the Freemasons."[53] Hopkins may have been concerned also about the Berlin Conference of June–July 1878, when Disraeli demanded and got a "peace with honour." As chaplain, he had been close to at least one young British soldier at the Cowley Barracks, who had been ordered to fight in the Second Afghan War two days before Hopkins wrote *Peace*.[54] And in November, about six weeks later, he sadly noted to Baillie that "the Government is

---

[52] See *Letters I*, p. 196.

[53] *Letters III*, p. 158. The "truckler" is Gladstone.

[54] Note appended to *The Bugler's First Communion* by Hopkins and quoted in *Letters I*, p. 92 n.

arresting Irish agitators, that will do far more harm in prison than on the stump." [55]

Hopkins always considered himself a great patriot. He composed martial music to a poem he wrote for British soldiers, *What shall I do for the land that bred me.* And several of his piano melodies sound like variations on "The British Grenadiers." But Hopkins knew that it was another kind of peace he was looking for, the *pax Christi.* "Peace I leave with you, my peace I give unto you: not as the world giveth, do I give unto you. Let not your heart be troubled, nor let it be afraid " (John 14:27). This is that perfect Peace which Hopkins so desired and which is so difficult to attain.

Such Peace is the reward for patience, for aligning the self-bent of the soul to the will of God. For the speaker must first learn the very difficult lesson that he cannot receive any spiritual consolation except as the gift and grace of God. As the *Spiritual Exercises* explain, God sometimes makes us desolate "to teach us not to build our nest in another's house." [56] Patience, itself the gift of the "reaving Lord," will later be transformed into Peace. But patience is not simply a passive state of mind; it is a willingness to make oneself a more perfect receptor of the Dove, the Holy Spirit, who is God's Peace.

Critics have commented on the inversions in the opening lines of the poem:

When will you ever, Peace, wild wooddove, shy wings shut,
Your round me roaming end, and under be my boughs?
When, when, Peace, will you, Peace? I'll not play hypocrite

To own my heart: . . . .

Part of the reason for the transposition is to make the lines, as Hopkins said, *tamquam exquisitius,* all the more exqui-

---

[55] Letter of November 19, 1879, *Letters III,* p. 243.
[56] *Sermons,* p. 205.

site. As Jean-Georges Ritz explains, "Over against the anxious questions that stress the inversions of the second line, over against the numerous and varied pauses of the opening line, he gives us the calm, rising rhythm of the last two lines." [57] But perhaps there may be another reason for the most awkward, seemingly, of the inversions: "under be my boughs." If we remember that the wood dove, or wood pigeon, builds its nest within the heart or trunk of the tree,[58] and that Hopkins is not talking of an external peace but rather of a transforming Peace, then the dove also acts as a protection to the tree, and its wings become the boughs of the tree. Further, there may be a pun on "leave" in lines 7 and 8; as the dove Patience "plumes to Peace," its wooden temple likewise "leaves" into a proper receptor of Peace, for the two *must* grow together.

This underplay of metamorphosis depends on a delicate punning similar to that which we find in the transformation of the souls of suicides into the barren wood in Dante's *Inferno*: "Quando si parte l'anima feroce / dal corpo ond 'ella stessa s'e disvelta" (when the ferocious spirit leaves the body from which it has uprooted itself—XIII, 94–95). Still, if this underlying punning complexity is suggested in *Peace*, it is not as developed as is the underthought of *Duns Scotus's Oxford* or *Henry Purcell*.

Besides these finished sonnets and lyrics, there are four fragments of varying length which Hopkins wrote at Oxford. On May 20, Walter Pater, Hopkins' friend and tutor from his Oxford days, sent the Jesuit priest a note accepting his invitation to dinner. It is on the back and sides of this note that Hopkins scribbled the poetic fragments that are number

[57] Ritz, p. 491. All translations from Ritz are mine.
[58] In his journal for October 17, 1873, while teaching rhetoric at Roehampton, Hopkins noted that "wood-pigeons come in flock into our field and on our trees: they flock at this time of year" (*Journals*, p. 239).

148.[59] Bridges called this *On a Piece of Music,* but that the piece deals with music as other than a metaphor is open to question. If we look at the stanzas, it seems rather that Hopkins is talking about a piece of architecture (perhaps Balliol College). The informing mind which shaped these thick stone walls manifests in rough fashion something of itself in the matter it worked with. The walls form, in fact, a sake of the mind, some evidence of the mind exterior to itself. But the walls (chosen because they present a fine example of the intractability of the materials the artist works with) are only the mind's "ruder-rounded rind." The artist's execution is necessarily something less than his conception, as the wax cell is less than the bee behind it. Yet, no matter how sweet or good the shaping spirit of a man, Hopkins insists, it is a God-given gift. Man may will to create or not, but if he does, what he creates is determined by his very nature and by the nature of his materials. He may sing, but he must use the air which overvaults his voice.

The sixth stanza is quite good, for it can be read in two ways. Man the maker is himself made (genetically, environmentally) and must himself make or create within his limitations. But man has free will and so can choose, not how well he will create, but what he will *make* of his creations. It is up to him to decide for what purpose he makes beauty. Abstractly, beauty is wild and good. It is amoral of itself, and therefore any and all subject matters can be treated.

But man has a moral sense as well as an esthetic sensibility, and "right must seek a side / And choose for chieftain one." Hopkins seems to have been working toward an analogy here. We are limited in our free creativity by our own natural limitations as well as by the nature of the materials we use. So, too, are we limited in what we create by the fact that we are governed by a sense of the right as well as of the good.

[59] In H (Bridges' scrapbook of Hopkins' poems), p. 101, in the Bodleian Library. The year is not given, but 1879 is most likely.

It is interesting that Hopkins should have written on the theme of morality in art on the back of a note from Pater, and it is probable that they discussed this topic a number of times. For while Pater did in fact have a refined moral taste, he was not popularly so understood. And certainly Pater's views, no matter how we squint, were not Hopkins'. Hopkins was all his life concerned with the scandal which art could give rise to. "With regard to the morality it is true no doubt ʽαπλῶς [absolutely] that any subject may be chosen for its art value alone and so will not, or rather need not, be any scandal in the writer or the reader. The question however is the practical effect, and is of course one of degree, where no line can be drawn." [60] Hopkins was willing to have his own poetry consigned to oblivion rather than cause scandal. In this regard, he was closer to Ruskin than to his tutor.

Fragments 143 and 144 were probably written about the time of *Binsey Poplars,* for there is a draft of that poem on the reverse of these two fragments. In the first, Hopkins seems to have begun to sketch a contrast between Denis' sharp wit and quick answers, and Arthur's slower wit but charming earnestness, whose deliberate shafts hit their target.[61] The second (144) is a word painting of a young man. There are some good lines here, and the fragment will bear comparison with *Harry Ploughman* of eight years later, as in this dynamic description of the young man's hair:

> His locks like all a ravel-rope's-end,
>   With hempen strands in spray—
> Fallow, foam-fallow, hanks—fall'n off their ranks,
>   Swung down at a disarray.

Cheery Beggar (142) may be later than these two, for it describes a scene which Hopkins probably experienced in

[60] Letter to Baillie of September 15, 1867, *Letters III,* p. 228.

[61] This interpretation is based on manuscript evidence in Norman White's letter in the *Times Literary Supplement,* August 22, 1968, p. 905. White gives two lines; he does not think their rhythm and tone similar to 143. But they help to give point to that fragment.

the early summer of 1879, perhaps while on his way to the Cowley Barracks beyond Magdalen Bridge. The subject of the cheery beggar recalls Wordsworth's *The Old Cumberland Beggar,* which also portrays a contented beggar in a harmonious natural setting. What strikes Hopkins about the man is that "struggling should not sear him," and that a few pence should be able to "cheer him." The attitudes here were to be reinforced in *Tom's Garland* (1887). There is something so light and carefree and spontaneous about *Cheery Beggar* that it is a pity Hopkins did not complete it.

Hopkins was sent on October 3 to fill in temporarily at St. Joseph's in Bedford Leigh, an industrial town near Manchester. In the period of nearly three months that he spent here he wrote only one little lyric, and perhaps the narrative fragment *Margaret Clitheroe* (145).

The little lyric *At the Wedding March* is dated October 21, 1879. It is in sprung rhythm, in three four-line stanzas, with four stresses to the line. It is a personal poem, as Hopkins noted years later, and plainspoken.[62] The priest-poet hopes that the new couple may have "lissome scions" and that they may grow more deeply into each other—more deeply than they might even suspect—through their mutual love for one another. Then, as the wedding march plays, the priest, moved to the point of tears by the ceremony, recalls that he, too, is locked in marriage to Christ, and that the fruit of that "wonder wedlock" is eternal life with him.

In the same month Hopkins wrote both Bridges and Dixon from Bedford Leigh that he was contemplating a drama on the martyrdom of Margaret Clitheroe along with one on St. Winefred.[63] We have fragments of the latter, but nothing of the former. What we do have is a sixty-one-line fragment of a narrative poem, without title, final arrangement, or date. Bridges supplies the most natural title, *Mar-*

---

[62] Letter to Dixon of June 30, 1886, *Letters II,* p. 132.
[63] *Letters I,* p. 92, and *Letters II,* p. 32.

garet Clitheroe, and Gardner and MacKenzie have done a skillful job of rearranging the fragments in their most logical order. One has only to compare the fragments as they appear in the Third Edition with their new arrangement to see what has been thus gained. We now have a nearly complete story. My own guess (and, judging by the place they gave it among the mature fragments, Gardner's and MacKenzie's) is that the poem was probably composed in the latter part of 1879, for all of Hopkins' references to Margaret Clitheroe are from October and December of that year. In a sermon preached at Bedford Leigh on December 14, 1879, Hopkins used her as an example of Christian cheerfulness in the face of heavy trials:

Margaret Clitheroe as she went through York streets, to be pressed to death on Ouse Bridge [Lady Day, 1586], all along the road as best she could with her pinioned hands dealing out alms to the poor, looked, it is said, so marvellously cheerful and happy that her murderers, like those Pharisees who of Christ her master said that he cast out devils by Beelzebub, had nothing for it but to pretend she was possessed by "a merry devil." [64]

Hopkins uses a seven-line stanza which is similar to the one he had employed in *Morning, Midday, and Evening Sacrifice* (August 1879). The pattern is a four-stress line rhyming abbaccc, with the last line of every stanza ending with the martyr's name. Stanza 1 focuses on God's foreknowledge and determination that Margaret be pressed to death. Hopkins reinforces this idea with several images of weight: the weeks are "weighty" and "Heaved drum on drum." Hopkins characteristically compares Margaret's preparations for her death with the way water seems to prepare itself before being sucked down. He puns on the name of Clinch, the judge who sentenced Margaret to death, for he was "clinching-blind" to her virtue and therefore had no eyes for her "mould of features." Those self-appointed judges whom Hopkins likens

[64] *Sermons,* p. 48.

to the Pharisees in his sermon are here "Fawning fawning crocodiles" crying for her to repent. But Margaret listens instead to the crying of God—"The Utterer, Utterèd, Uttering"—to bear witness to Him. The martyrs, and especially Mary and Thecla,[65] in fact all heaven, turn their "starlight eyes below." Margaret's arms are outstretched, and Hopkins naturally identifies her death with Christ's crucifixion. God's son died long ago, now it is God's daughter. Hopkins is bitterly severe against Margaret's "murderers," and yet he remarks, in words which recall the crucified Christ's, that "they did not know" what they did. Again, in the last line, Hopkins' "It is over" recalls Christ's "It is consummated." Two images here are quite harrowing. The first is Margaret's last bit of sewing: a shroud for herself. The other is the image of the heavy weights smothering the "quick" child in Margaret's womb. This last image occurs in an unfinished stanza. "Her history is terrible and heartrending," he told Dixon.[66] Perhaps it was too much so for him to finish the poem.

Hopkins may not have been at ease in his return to Oxford, but despite his heavy work load he found time to compose more poetry in the eight months between late February and early October 1879 than he wrote in any other comparative period of his maturity except for 1885. But the lyrics, and especially the sonnets of the middle period, for all their excellences, cannot as a group match either the lyric intensity of the 1877 sonnets or the hard brilliancy of the sonnets of 1885. After *Henry Purcell*, Hopkins' diction in the remaining lyrics of 1879 becomes plainer, more severe, less quaint, and there is no further prosodic experimentation. For he is consciously striving for a Miltonic severity, which seems in part the result of Bridges' dissatisfaction with the Purcell sonnet and in part the result of his own fears of

---

[65] See Hopkins' early (1866?) fragment, *St. Thecla*.
[66] *Letters II*, p. 32.

5 ☙ The Lean Years:
1880–1884

There are a number of reasons for Hopkins' silence or near silence between 1880 and 1884. After Oxford and Bedford Leigh (his happiest post, but one of his shortest), he served his longest single assignment as parish priest at St. Francis Xavier's in Liverpool, where he stayed from the end of December 1879 until early August 1881, a period of nineteen and one-half months. During this time he wrote only three poems: the sonnet *Felix Randal* in late April 1880, the narrative *Brothers* in August, and *Spring and Fall* on September 7. He rewrote *Brothers,* the longest of the pieces, at Hampstead during his holidays. After he had left Liverpool and while filling in at a parish church at Glasgow, he spent a few days in the Scottish highlands, near Loch Lomond. Here he conceived and wrote *Inversnaid,* a poem in praise of that wilderness of which he now saw so little, on September 28, 1881.

From late September until the following August Hopkins wrote no more poetry. The ten months from early October 1881 until July 31, 1882, he devoted entirely to his tertianship, voluntarily giving up all poetic composition.[1] He may have written the sonnet *As kingfishers catch fire* in the following August, or he may not have.[2] But in September, when

[1] Letter to Dixon of November 11, 1881, *Letters II,* p. 89.

[2] John Pick tentatively dates the sonnet as August 1882, and quotes from the passage below on page 178 in support of this dating. The close correspondence between the final tercet of the sonnet and this close

he was again at Stonyhurst, Hopkins probably wrote the sonnet *Ribblesdale,* and the following October he composed *The Leaden Echo and the Golden Echo.* Five months later he had three comic triolets published in *The Stonyhurst Magazine* (March 1883). And finally there is the powerful *The Blessed Virgin compared to the Air we Breathe,* his best Marian piece, written in May 1883. From that month until sometime in October 1884, nearly a year and a half later, he seems to have written no poetry. In the latter month he began rough drafts of Caradoc's soliloquy for *St. Winefred's Well* and *Spelt from Sibyl's Leaves.* But that begins another period in another place: the agony of the desolate sonnets written in Dublin. The period, then, is particularly lean, and for two reasons: first, Hopkins found Liverpool and Dublin unsuited to his muse; and second, there is the period of elected silence. But much of what we do have is quite good, especially the rich echoic music of *The Echoes* piece, and the superb mastery of tone, diction, imagery, and underthought in *Felix Randal,* which may very well be the single best lyric Hopkins ever wrote.

Felix Randal, written April 28, 1880, at Liverpool, is the artistic culmination of *Duns Scotus's Oxford* and *Henry Purcell,* for all three "quaint" poems are specifically concerned with delineating the distinctive inscape of a person. The deeply human qualities of the blacksmith in his wild and random hardiness and the underlying spiritual drama of sheep and shepherd are precisely and tenderly caught by Hopkins. "I will send what else I have whenever I can find an opportunity of copying it," he wrote to Dixon on May 14, 1880. "The parish work of Liverpool is very wearying to mind and body and leaves me nothing but odds and ends of time. There is merit in it but little Muse, and indeed 26 lines

---

paraphrase is the strongest piece of evidence for thus dating the sonnet. But see MacKenzie's introduction to *Poems,* p. xlii, which suggests an earlier dating. It may very well have been written in late 1879 or 1880.

is the whole I have written in more than half a year, since I left Oxford." [3] A month later he sent the twenty-six lines with a short letter to Bridges. Playing on his favorite parallel between poetic and human gestation, he ended his letter with the comment, "I will enclose a sonnet and a little lyric, the only things I have written in nine months." [4]

The lyric was *At the Wedding March. Felix Randal,* while written during his labors among the poor in the slums of Liverpool, "of all places the most museless," seems to have been based on his experience at Bedford Leigh, whose people he especially loved. But *Felix Randal* is no slight piece. It is, rather, an astonishingly complex emotional performance which succeeds simultaneously as elegy and as Christian celebration of the final victory over death.

It is surprising that *Felix Randal,* although widely admired and read, has been so little analyzed, compared with other of Hopkins' poems, such as *The Windhover.* And the glosses which have been given *Felix Randal,* despite their value, have not properly marked the poem's complexity of vision. An analogical and anagogical interpretation, as with *Duns Scotus's Oxford* and *Henry Purcell,* is needed to show the organic center of the poem and to articulate the poem's underthought.

Felix Randal has most often been read as the poignant elegy of a priest for a dying and now dead blacksmith under his spiritual care. Recalling the confrontation of the grim and unalterable fact of death which he shared with the blacksmith, the priest remembers that he had given the dying farrier, along with the sacraments, consolation and hope, that he had been touched himself in the terrible encounter. This two-way exchange of a love matured in adversity is reflected in the parallel phrasing and in the dual repetition of three key words: "endear," "tears," and "touch."

---

[3] *Letters II,* p. 33.   [4] Letter of June 18, 1880, *Letters I,* p. 103.

This seeing the sick endears them to us, us too it endears.
My tongue had taught thee comfort, touch had quenched thy
    tears,
Thy tears that touched my heart, child, Felix, poor Felix Randal.

In the final tercet, the priest turns back in memory to the blacksmith's healthy prime, which assumes an aura of radical innocence in the image of the blacksmith shoeing the powerful workhorse with "bright and battering sandal." Read in this way—and this is only the skeletal outline—the sonnet assumes a curve similar to, if shorter than, the resolution of *Thyrsis,* or to one of the curves of *In Memoriam:* a confrontation with the fact of loss in death and then a moving back in time to a happier memory and a brighter landscape. Both Arnold and Tennyson realize that the final darkness is inscrutable and so are poetically justified in turning back to memory. And Hopkins too, as a man, must turn backwards into memory to breathe a life into Felix Randal again. But such a reading leaves unanswered Hopkins' radically felt Christianity and the significance for him of the Incarnation. And while this reading may at first satisfy us, its success depends upon separating Hopkins as priest from Hopkins as a "modern" man. If it satisfies the conditions of an elegy, it does violence to Hopkins' theology.

The rhythm and the tone of the poem are our first clues to a different interpretation. These point away from a solely elegiac mood; there is a consistent refrain of comfort throughout, which surges through in the final lines into the "roll, the rise" of sheer strength and a primal joy. Furthermore, if the priestly comfort is found precisely in the priest's role as ministrant of the sacraments, and if there is no evidence within the sonnet that these prepare the soul to meet God—if they are essentially empty forms—then the comfort is simply a sham and so, therefore, is the ministrant. And so, too, is the poem itself, for the success of the poem rests on our acceptance of the priest-speaker's sincerity and intelligence.

Felix Randal is actually a journal of the loss of a loved one, which carries a note of quiet elation and of controlled exuberance. It is a journal of the priest-speaker's care for the farrier, who was tendered the sacrament of holy viaticum by the priest. Both shepherd and sheep have been "touched," in fact, changed, by the terrible encounter. The priest has been touched by Felix's childlike incomprehension and terror before death. And Felix, in a more profound spiritual metamorphosis, had been changed when "a heavenlier heart began" through the efficacy of the holy viaticum—"our sweet reprieve and ransom." The final change has taken place in Hopkins the poet-priest, who has been touched by the terrible joy of not only knowing but realizing the consequences of this change in Felix Randal.

In fact, the whole poem suggests metamorphosis, both natural and supernatural. For the underlying structure of the sonnet rests on the following analogy: the image of the farrier who shielded the "great grey drayhorse" is a figure on the natural level for the priest who has shielded the "hardy-handsome" farrier. The first is a prefiguring, a "forethought," of the second. Holy viaticum (spiritual provision for a journey) is precisely a sacramental "shield" to help protect the soul in its final journey into and beyond death.[5] And the priest has prepared the hardy tough farrier for that road out of the "random grim forge" of a fatal and fevered sickness, much as the workingman Felix "Didst fettle for" the workhorse, preparing and protecting it for a more humble road.

If this is the correct underthought of the poem, as I believe it is, then each of the details—every word, in fact—should contribute to this core of poetic underthought. Even the wish in Lancashire dialect, "Ah well, God rest him all road ever he offended," appropriate as it is as a benediction for a

---

[5] "[Viaticum] means money, provision, for a journey, that is / the journey to the other world" (*Sermons*, p. 248).

Lancashire blacksmith, now flashes into its theological significance: the road is the age-old metaphor for the spiritual
struggle through life, of direction rather than randomness.[6]

Now, too, the title assumes its real significance. For *Felix
Randal* is probably not the farrier's name.[7] Hopkins had too
fine a sense of Victorian gentlemanly decorum to use it, and
in all of his poems he almost never gives us a contemporary's
name. "Randal" is of Anglo-Saxon origin and means a
"shield," as well as a strip of leather placed on the heels of a
shoe. Both meanings reinforce one another here.[8] *Felix,* of
course, is Latin for "happy" or 'blessed," so that the far-

[6] In a sermon (December 14, 1879) to a congregation made up
largely of Lancashire working people, Hopkins uses this Lancashire
coinage: "There is a crowd of you, brethren, and amidst that crowd
some must be in this road—I mean are out of your duty, out of God's
grace, and in mortal sin"; see *Sermons*, p. 47 and its accompanying
note.

[7] It should be emphasized that the poem is almost certainly autobiographical. But whatever the blacksmith's name was, it does not seem to
have been Felix Randal. The tone of the first line of the poem strongly
suggests that Hopkins had learned the news of the blacksmith's death at
second hand, as if he had ministered to him for a while, then had not
heard from or of him, and only afterwards heard of his death. This
suggests that the blacksmith was not from Liverpool, where Hopkins
had been stationed for less than four months when the poem was
written, but was rather from Bedford Leigh. Devlin too is certain that
Hopkins experienced the emotions of *Felix Randal* at Leigh (*Sermons*,
p. 5). Fr. Charles J. Horan, P.P., of St. Joseph's checked the registries at
Leigh and found that there was no Randal listed. The poet, in his
onomastic stance, probably got the genesis for the farrier's name in
"genial Randal Lightbound," mentioned in his letter to his mother two
days after he wrote *Felix Randal* (*Letters III,* p. 157).

[8] See the *Oxford English Dictionary* under "Rand." The "Worcester
Exhibition Catalogue" for 1882 describes a "Rand turning machine . . .
[which] delivers the rands . . . in a horse-shoe form ready for use." A
rand is a strip of leather (or iron) placed under the quarters of a boot
or shoe. "Randall," significantly, was also an obsolete variation of
"random," meaning a gallop, a rapid headlong course, and a disorderly
life. Felix's boisterous, random life is given direction by the viaticum,
metamorphosing randal to "bright and battering sandal."

rier's name both harks back to his "more boisterous years," when he plied his trade with rough good nature, and simultaneously points ahead to the purer and permanent joy of the "heavenlier" blacksmith, now sacramentally shielded and protected for the final journey into eternity. The metamorphosis of the "great grey drayhorse" into a light, supple, Pegasean steed with "bright and battering sandal" is an exact parallel of Felix Randal's spiritual transformation. The movement of the entire sonnet toward transformation is telescoped in the two halves of the final resounding line. And the rhyme words "Randal" and "sandal" also suggest this transformation, as the humble leather strip becomes the light and elegant footwear with which the blacksmith will batter his way through whatever threatens to bar him on his last road.

It is worth emphasizing what Hopkins has done with time in the structure of this sonnet. In the final tercet, he moves away from the contemplation of Felix's death. The note is struck in line eleven with the word "child." The sonnet then moves elegiacally back in time to recapture the "more boisterous years" of Felix's prime. But this lively and happy scene, so filled with the sense of strong animal vitality, is a recapturing in a double sense, for it simultaneously looks forward to Felix's promised state in terms which preserve the distinct inscape of Felix's childlike vigor.

As has been stressed before, for Hopkins the very core of the Incarnation is to see everywhere in the reality of concrete and seemingly trivial objects and actions the instressed presence and activity of Christ. One of Hopkins' most striking comments on the central importance of the Incarnation in the daily and humble affairs of men comes in an early letter, written while he was still at Oxford, to E. H. Coleridge (January 22, 1866):

I think that the trivialness of life is, and personally to each one, ought to be seen to be, done away with by the Incarnation. . . . It is one adorable point of the incredible condescension of the

Incarnation (the greatness of which no saint can have ever hoped to realize) that our Lord submitted . . . to the mean and trivial accidents of humanity. . . . It seems therefore that if the Incarnation cd. *versari inter* [dwell among] trivial men and trivial things it is not surprising that our reception or non-reception of its benefits shd. be also amidst trivialities.[9]

Felix Randal translates this theological insight into lyric poetry of the highest order. Hopkins' vision is to have seen in the daily shoeing of horses by a common blacksmith, without "forethought of" its spiritual significance, the abiding presence of Christ. And Christ's presence is not more discernible to men only because men do not care to stress or instress the spiritual potential of all things to shout glory to God.

This spiritual vision of man's Godlike worth, without mitigating any of his apparent trivialness, gives to Hopkins' poems of the common man their spiritual intensity and profoundly personal charity. He has certainly caught the exact tone of resignation and restrained sorrow in his colloquial diction and remarkably free-sprung and outriding Alexandrines:

Felix Randal the farrier, O is he dead then? my duty all ended,
Who have watched his mould of man, big-boned and hardy-
    handsome
Pining, pining, till time when reason rambled in it and some
Fatal four disorders, fleshed there, all contended?

Here is a poetic voice with no parallel among the Victorian poets. And this voice had to be first fired and tempered in the slums of the Victorian industrial cities. By constant exposure to misery this young priest from a respectable and comfortable middle-class background, who was temperamentally unsuited by his delicate sensibility to such

⁹ *Letters III,* pp. 19–20.

raw work, found a new and more mature voice. For Hopkins had an astonishing capacity for love, a deep strain of humility beneath his assertiveness, and a truly courageous desire to be transformed literally into an *alter Christus* whatever the personal cost to himself. And the one thing most needful for Hopkins was to cultivate an ever greater patience as a prelude to peace. ("Impatient he cursed at first.") The inscrutable finger of God seems to have been at work in the harried and gallied Hopkins as well as in the victorious blacksmith.

Brothers (or *The Brothers*) was rewritten or revised by Hopkins at least five times. He first wrote the narrative in "something" like "Wordsworth's manner," which, he admitted, was "inimitable and unapproachable." He meant to enclose the poem in a letter to Bridges, but thought better of it, for he was aware that the entire piece turned on the pathos of the experience, and that pathos had "a point as precise as jest." [10] This first version was written by mid-August 1879, while Hopkins was still at Oxford.

The second version was written a year later (August 1880) when Hopkins was at home on holiday. He seems to have shown a draft of the new version to Bridges at this time, for he mentions the new draft familiarly in a letter in early September, when he was back at Liverpool: "[*Brothers*] was first written in Stanzas in Wordsworth's manner, but when I compared it with his inimitable simplicity and gravity I was disgusted and meant to destroy it, till the thought struck me of changing the metre, which made it do." [11] He enclosed a revision of the new version with this letter. And it was corrected yet again in late January 1881, at the urging of both Dixon and Bridges. [12] The published version in *Poems* incorporates all of Hopkins' latest revisions and removes Bridges' "improvements."

[10] All of these quotations are from *Letters I,* p. 86.
[11] *Ibid.,* p. 106.
[12] See *ibid.,* pp. 114–116, 118, and *Letters II,* p. 49.

Written in the difficult three-foot couplet form and employing sprung rhythm throughout, this narrative uses many double rhymes successfully, but without the overreaving which had been used in the earlier narrative poems, *The Loss of the Eurydice* and *The Bugler's First Communion*. The poem is based on an experience Hopkins had while stationed at Mount St. Mary's College, Chesterfield, in 1878. "I find within my professional experience now a good deal of matter to write on," he wrote Bridges in August 1879.[13] And twice he mentioned that the incident did really occur at Mount St. Mary's, once in this letter and again a year later.[14]

The poem treats a tender and unconscious display of love by an older boy for his younger brother, and it deals with this precariously sensitive subject neither sentimentally nor mawkishly. The narrator begins by exclaiming how Henry, the elder brother, is laced, tied, to his younger brother, John, by love. He recalls what he had seen "two years gone" during the school festivities held at Shrovetide, the three days before Ash Wednesday. John is chosen to play a comic part in one of the school plays, and Henry feels both joy that his brother has been chosen and fear that his brother will not act his part well. On the night of the performance the priests, boys, and guests of the school crowd the hall, and Henry calls the narrator over to watch John's performance with him.

We are not told what play is being performed, nor does it matter, for the narrative focuses on the speaker's glancing often at the human drama unfolding beside him as the boys' play is performed, "making mý play / Turn most on tender byplay." Henry is unaware and "lost in Jack"; his exquisite and obvious unrest reflects his inward brotherly concern as he frets and awaits Jack's entrance in the third act. Against this tenseness and concern Hopkins counterpoints young Jack's impishness and "roguish . . . vein," in playing his "bráss-bóld" part. The movement changes here to the pizzi-

---

[13] *Letters I,* p. 86.   [14] *Ibid.,* p. 106.

cato of a more noticeable sprung rhythm, and the diction too
changes, to the colloquialness of

> Theré! the háll rúng!
> Dog, he did give tongue!

The suspense mounts as Henry, seeing his brother, looks
down, awaiting the audience's verdict, afraid to see his
brother hurt. But young Jack's nonchalant self-confidence
assures his success, and "Harry" breaks into hot tears of joy
and relief, and embarrassment, too, at unexpectedly catching
himself crying.

The speaker turns to human nature itself in the closing
lines. Nature, "framed in fault" because of the original Fall
so that its natural proclivity is toward evil and perversity—
"Nature, bad, base, and blind"—can still be kind. Here is
that salt, which Christ speaks of, that flavors human nature.
The last four lines modify the couplet form, using an echoing repetitive pattern which evokes the tenderness of the
remembered scene—a device Hopkins had used in *Binsey
Poplars* and was to use in *Inversnaid*.

A few weeks later Hopkins was again at his duties in
Liverpool. On September 7, while walking back to the city
from a country house of a Catholic family at Lydiate where
he was regularly sent to say Mass, he composed his poignant
and tender *Spring and Fall*. "I enclose a little piece composed since I began this letter," he wrote Bridges, "not
founded on any real incident. I am not well satisfied with
it." [15] Nevertheless, the fifteen-line lyric in four-stress sprung
lines is one of Hopkins' most anthologized pieces.

Everything about the poem has an exquisite rightness
about it. The diction is quite straightforward, as we would
expect, since it is addressed "to a young child" with the
diminutive name Margarét (Margarette). The title strikes
the chord of tension in Margaret between her spring of life
and her imperfect understanding of the curse common to all

[15] *Ibid.*, p. 109. He "improved" it the next day.

things as she weeps over the falling leaves—and herself. The beauty of the autumn leaves, flaming into gold before giving way to the spareness and starkness of encroaching winter, the death of the year, recalls the final image of *The Windhover,* where dying embers momentarily flash out into golden-red. But here the emphasis is on the loss, not on the glory. The speaker, catching the child "grieving" over the fallen leaves, is surprised by this display of tenderness. But age, he knows, brings an increasing toughness to such sights, and though she grieves now, someday she will not even "sigh" when whole forests lie lifeless and their dead leaves lie scattered piecemeal ("leafmeal") about.

Still, the child is not consoled and insists on some kind of explanation: "yet you *will* weep and know why." The speaker does not tell her that all things must die as a result of man's fall from grace. This is no place for a theological explanation of the consequences of that Fall, one of them being the fall of the year. Hopkins was to show in *Ribblesdale,* as Milton had in *Paradise Lost,* that nature herself had been brought down, bent, in man's general fall. Intuitively, without naming nature's and man's blight, the child has felt the need to weep for herself.

"Goldengrove" recalls, of course, the prelapsarian Edenic state.[16] And the barren trees reflect nature's suffering. Hopkins ties the trees' dissolution with man's through the "blight," the disease, which has visited and crippled both. With the close of the poem, Margarét, knowing intuitively now the fact of evil and of death, has grown into Márgaret. But it is a knowledge of good and of evil dearly bought.

Between September 1880 and September 1881 Hopkins seems to have written nothing. Then there is one lyric, *Inversnaid,* and then nothing again for another year. *Inversnaid* seems to have been carried in embryonic form in Hopkins' mind for two and one-half years before it was finally given its

---

[16] "Goldengrove" is the name of an actual estate near Lydiate.

final sixteen-line form on September 28, 1881. He told
Bridges in February 1879 that he was laboring to give final
shape to

something, if I could only seize it, on the decline of wild nature,
beginning somehow like this—

> O where is it, the wilderness,
> The wildness of the wilderness?
> Where is it, the wilderness?

and ending—

> And wander in the wilderness;
> In the weedy wilderness,
> Wander in the wilderness.[17]

These lines are contemporary with *Binsey Poplars;* and
the close of that lyric also laments, if not a wilderness,
certainly a wildness gone. It was only after his Oxford and
Liverpool years, while he was filling in at St. Joseph's in
Glasgow, that Hopkins escaped the city and found the wilderness he needed so much. He spent a well-earned rest at
Loch Lomond and Inversnaid and here he wrote his lyric.

Inversnaid is a poem in four stanzas, each consisting of
four four-stress sprung lines in double couplets. Hopkins,
using Scottish words for Scottish things, celebrates the world
of "wildness" and "wilderness," of "wet" and "weeds." The
focal image is Inversnaid, a swiftly moving "burn" (brook)
which empties into Loch Lomond. It is the "fleece of . . .
foam" which catches the poet's eye, for this "fawn-froth"
plays over pitch-black pools and drowns black Despair in its
passing. As it flows it sprays the heather and fern and "bead-
bonny ash" near its "braes" (banks and slopes), transforming everything with a freshness and iridescent joy.

If there was one natural scene which could rekindle Hopkins' flagging spirits, it was a brown brook or river, whether,
as here, the "horseback brown" burn, or the "gluegold-
brown / Marbled river" of the *Epithalamion,* or the "burl-

---

[17] Letter of February 22, 1879, *Letters I,* pp. 73–74.

ing Barrow brown" as seen at Monasterevan, Ireland. For a few hours in early autumn Hopkins recaptured here in the Scottish highlands something of what had stirred him in "Wild Wales." It was enough to deliver him of a stark, joyful lyric with its lines lightly bubbling, like the brook itself, over deep, dark recesses.

As kingfishers catch fire is the first mature sonnet which Hopkins did not send to Bridges. The single draft, with corrections and variants, was found among Hopkins' literary remains sent to Bridges in 1889. There is a prose paraphrase of the final tercet of the sonnet,

> Christ plays in ten thousand places,
> Lovely in limbs, and lovely in eyes not his
> To the Father through the features of men's faces,

in his spiritual notes for late December 1881, "from thoughts arising in the Long Retreat":

Grace is any action, activity, on God's part by which, in creating or after creating, he carries the creature to or towards the end of its being, which is its selfsacrifice to God and its salvation. It is, I say, any such activity on God's part; so that so far as this action or activity is God's it is divine stress, holy spirit, and as all is done through Christ, Christ's spirit; so far as it is action, correspondence, on the creature's it is *actio salutaris;* so far as it is looked at *in esse quieto* it is Christ in his member on the one side, his member in Christ on the other. It is as if a man said: That is Christ playing at me and me playing at Christ, only that it is no play but truth; That is Christ *being me* and me being Christ.[18]

Hopkins had focused on creation and the self during his Liverpool retreat in late August 1880. In his notes he remarks that selving, the concomitant action of existence and of individualizing a predetermined nature, is a perfection which, by the finite nature of things, points to God's operation in bestowing and sustaining this selving from without:

Now to be determined and distinctive is a perfection, either self-bestowed or bestowed from without. In anything finite it cannot

---

[18] *Sermons,* pp. 152, 154.

be self-bestowed; nothing finite can determine its own being, I mean its being as a whole; nothing finite can determine what itself shall, in a world of being, be. For to determine is a perfection, greater than and certainly never less than, the perfection of being determined. It is a function of a nature, even if it should be the whole function, the naturing [*natura naturans*], the selving of that nature. It always in nature's order is after the nature it is of [*natura naturata*].[19]

Hopkins came back to these thoughts again after his tertianship. He added an important postscript to his August 1880 notes on August 12, 1882: "Remark that the assumption [to identify as closely as possible the Self of God with the individual person's self] . . . is to assume in oneself a hypostatic union."[20]

In fulfilling one's distinctive nature, any object gives glory back to God. In the action of their very selving, in proclaiming their nature, all things great and small speak of God's gift of creating them in their distinctiveness, just as the sun (God) turns static receptivity (*natura naturata*) into dynamic activity (*natura naturans*), as in the images of the first line: "As kingfishers catch fire, dragonflies draw flame." Even inanimate objects tell of themselves; and Hopkins has caught precisely, in the echoing long vowels and soft *n*'s, *m*'s, and *s*'s, the echoing ring of a stone falling into a well: "As tumbled over rim in roundy wells / Stones ring." He catches both the sharp metallic notes of plucked strings in the sharp dentals of "like each tucked string tells," as well as the oscillating pounding of swinging bells in the heavy rhythm and internal rhymes and assonance of "hung," "swung," "tongue," and "fling" in his next lines:

> each hung bell's
> Bow swung finds tongue to fling out broad its name.

In the second quatrain Hopkins translates into poetic statement the Scotistic philosophical dicta of the particular and dynamic natures of all creation:

[19] *Ibid.*, pp. 124–125.   [20] *Ibid.*, p. 129.

> Each mortal thing does one thing and the same:
>   Deals out that being indoors each one dwells;
> Selves—goes itself; *myself* it speaks and spells,
>   Crying *What I do is me: for that I came.*

The biblical echo of Christ's reply to Pontius Pilate is unmistakable. "What I was born for, what I came into the world for, is to bear witness of the truth. Whoever belongs to the truth, listens to my voice" (John 18:37).

But while all creation can do "one thing and the same," man himself, in acting in his *human* capacity, has in all of his actions a supernatural dimension, for man in acting as man "keeps grace," since man's own proper end is, as the Ignatian *Spiritual Exercises* state, "to praise, reverence and serve God Our Lord, and by so doing to save his soul."[21] A man's state or condition is revealed in his actions; as long as he wills to do what is properly his to do, he is in the state of grace. Furthermore, this grace is frequently manifested in a man's exterior gracefulness. The sprung lines capture the dynamism of each man's being:

> I say more: the just man justices;
>   Keeps grace: that keeps all his goings graces;
> Acts in God's eye what in God's eye he is—
>   Christ.

For in fulfilling his own individuality, he is a living temple of God, he is another Christ, who is most himself "when the member is in all things conformed to Christ. This too best brings out the nature of the man himself, as the lettering on a sail or device upon a flag are best seen when it fills." For the self, that about the individual "which is more distinctive than the taste of ale or alum, more distinctive than the smell of walnutleaf or camphor" is not annihilated by Christ's presence, but rather brought to its most perfect stress of

[21] *Ibid.,* p. 122.

pitch, to the actualizing of its fullest human potentiality.[22] For since the self is the individuating existence of a nature, God's presence, which is existence itself, can hold that self at its highest quivering stress without absorbing it.

Ribblesdale, written sometime between September and the end of December 1882 (probably in September), has many affinities to *As kingfishers catch fire.* But whereas the earlier poem is a brilliant and exact synthesis of a philosophical and theological insight without any underthought—there are no multiple levels there—*Ribblesdale* is like *Duns Scotus's Oxford* in its multilevel structure.

In a letter to Bridges on September 26, 1882, Hopkins described the surrounding topography of Stonyhurst, where he was preparing to teach Latin and Greek. "There are acres of flat roof which, when the air is not thick, as unhappily it mostly is, commands a noble view of this Lancashire landscape, Pendle Hill, Ribblesdale, the fells, and all round." [23]

In late March of the following year he sent the sonnet to Bridges, and on June 25 he also sent it to Dixon: "I enclose one sonnet, meant as a companion to one beginning 'I remember a house' [*In the Valley of the Elwy*], which perhaps you have. You will see that the first words begin a lyric of yours—or perhaps those are 'Earth, *sad* Earth.' " [24]

Both Bridges' and Dixon's copies are prefaced by the following Pauline commentary: " '*Vanitati enim creatura subjecta est, non volens sed propter cum qui subjecit eam in spe*' *cum praecc. et sqq.* Rom. viii 20." It will help in understanding this sonnet to quote this passage from St. Paul with what precedes and follows:

If creation is full of expectancy, that is because it is waiting for the sons of God to be known. Created nature has been condemned to frustration; not for some deliberate fault of its own, but for the sake of him who so condemned it, with a hope to look forward to; namely, that nature in its turn will be set free from

[22] *Ibid.,* pp. 123, 195.   [23] *Letters I,* p. 151.   [24] *Letters II,* p. 108.

the tyranny of corruption, to share in the glorious freedom of God's sons. The whole of nature, as we know, groans in a common travail all the while [Rom. 8:19–23].

As in *As kingfishers catch fire*, Earth can only give glory to God in being itself, in simply revealing its beauty and goodness. But men have made of earth a dimmed beauty, a crippled goodness. The scene is autumn, the leaves lie in throngs around the bases of their trees, and the grass is bent; both leaves and grass are in the posture of humble supplication, crying out their fallen beings as well as they can. Who is he who has "dealt" nature this blow? Biblical commentators are divided on this poetical passage of St. Paul. It can refer to Adam, and therefore generic man, who in falling dragged down earth itself with him. Or it can refer to God Himself, Who has made the straight ways crooked and Who cursed the very ground on which Adam stood. At the root of the curse of earth, in either event, is man's "selfbent," his sin and fall. The creature earth, even if wearing "man's smudge" (from *God's Grandeur*), still continues good in God's eyes.

It is only man, nature's most distinctive self, her "clearest-selvèd spark" (from *That Nature is a Heraclitean Fire*), who can voice the praise due to the Creator of all this beauty. But man, turned to his "selfbent," continues to rob or misuse this world's wealth without any concern for his fellow man or for using the goods of this world as means to buying the next.

A key verb in *Ribblesdale* is "bids" in lines 7 and 13, for if God "bids" the beautiful river to run twisted, it is man who first broke the covenant. And in the sestet it is clearly man who "bids" Earth wear "brows of such care." For Hopkins the verb has a specifically theological meaning:

God first entered into relations (or what I used to call bidding) with man in Adam and a commonweal arose—with its sovereign and one subject; its membership . . . ; its distribution of the common goods . . . ; its justice, *original justice;* and so on. This commonweal may be looked on as not only a polity of sovereign and subject but also in the light of property, where God is the landlord, man the tenant, and this indeed not only as touches property strictly so called but also life and other *bona* or blessings. Then sacrifices, tithes, and so on will be rents, real or conventional; acknowledgments of dependence.[25]

The tenant, however, does not pay his rents. As in *God's Grandeur*, he is self-bent, he is selfish. And innocent earth is made to suffer. In the earlier *In the Valley of the Elwy*, the companion of *Ribblesdale*, Hopkins had presented a beautiful picture of nature where only man did not seem to fit:

> Lovely the woods, waters, meadows, combes, vales,
> All the air things wear that build this world of Wales;
> Only the inmate does not correspond.

In *Ribblesdale*, however, the earth itself suffers and lies bleeding with brows of care. Gardner thinks that it was the just man knitting "his brows with pain and sorrow at the sight of sin and ugliness [that made] the Earth [appear] to 'wear brows of such care, care and dear concern.' "[26] But Boyle is right in his insistence that it is the earth itself which Hopkins sees as frowning, as a concerned mother frowns over her prodigal son, and he points to Hopkins' letter printed in the January 3, 1884, issue of the journal *Nature*. Describing a weird series of sunsets, caused by volcanic ash, Hopkins writes, "while these changes were going on in the sky, the landscape of Ribblesdale glowed with a frowning brown."[27]

While I agree with Boyle that we must look to the landscape upon which Hopkins himself is looking for an understanding of the poem, there is an alternative reading for the final lines of *Ribblesdale*. If, in the second quatrain, Hopkins stresses the crookedness of nature, in the sestet it is man's bleeding of the earth, his unselving of it that concerns

---

[25] *Sermons*, pp. 165–166.   [26] Gardner, II, p. 352.

[27] See Boyle, p. 169. Hopkins' letters to *Nature* are printed in *Letters* as Appendix II, pp. 161–166.

the speaker most. In a short but perceptive note, George Goodin remarks that "Hopkins' association of physical crookedness and moral wrong can be seen in the Comments on the *Spiritual Exercises,* where crookedness is spoken of as the influence of Satan." He then quotes a passage which also finds echoes in *Andromeda:*

God gave things a forward and perpetual motion; the Devil, that is / thrower of things off the track, upsetter, mischiefmaker, clashing one with another brought in the law of decay and consumption in inanimate nature, death in the vegetable and animal world, moral death and original sin in the world of man.[28]

In the sestet, man, "the heir / To his own selfbent so bound," the son of Adam, who perversely desires to set himself up as the highest good rather than acknowledge his dependence on his Creator, is tied to his own little turn, treading in his own tracks. This self-bent is so strong in him that, selfish prodigal that he is, he robs "our rich round world bare," and he gives thought neither to the afterworld ("world after") nor to the provision or conserving of nature's goods for his own heirs (the "world after" he is gone). He therefore "bids" only in his own perverted interests, he buys up what was properly meant for him to use as the tenant of God's earthly beauty. And he leaves the rich round earth with brows that have been caused by "such care" (man's care) and "dear concern" (an enterprise expensive and costly to the very earth itself). Man is primarily interested only in translating the earth's treasures into financial capital. He has by his negligence scarred the land with brows, cliff edges, for he has made gaping wounds in the hills to mine and quarry the land, and thus left his own "manmark" on the face of the earth.

Possibly there is an allusion to these "brows" made by

[28] "Man and Nature in Hopkins' 'Ribblesdale,' " *Notes and Queries,* VI (1959), p. 454; this passage is quoted from *Sermons,* pp. 198–199.

such ill "care" in the letter of late September 1882 written to Bridges from Stonyhurst:

There is always a stirring scene, contractors, builders, masons, bricklayers, carpenters, stonecutters and carvers, all on the spot; a traction engine twice a day fetches stone from a quarry on the fells; engines of all sorts send their gross and foulsmelling smoke all over us; cranes keep swinging; and so on.

And a little further on in the same letter he describes the fells and Ribblesdale as "bleakish but solemn and beautiful." [29] A passage from Hopkins' spiritual notes is also relevant here:

[God] meant the world to give him praise, reverence, and service; *to give him glory*. It is like a garden, a field he sows: what should it bear him? . . . it should yield him glory. . . . The creation does praise God, does reflect honour on him, is of service to him. . . . But man can know God, *can mean to give him glory*. This then was why he was made, to give God glory and to mean to give it; to praise God freely, willingly to reverence him, gladly to serve him.[30]

Hopkins had made a similar cry of man's refusal to "reck" God's "rod" almost six years before; then, however, the poet had the consolation that "There lives the dearest freshness deep down things." But here his vision is darker, reflecting his new awareness of the blight that man has imparted to the earth itself. Hopkins' youthful outlook shows signs of corroding before his brooding on the horrors and miseries of unregenerate but still dear man.

The Leaden Echo and the Golden Echo was to be, as the subtitle tells us, the "Maidens' song from St. Winefred's Well," a proposed verse play on the life of the Welsh virgin-martyr, which Hopkins never completed. Except for this cho. ral song and three fragmentary scenes nothing else was done. But this song has its own completeness and is rightly placed among Hopkins' finished pieces. It deserves special attention

---

[29] *Letters I*, p. 151.   [30] *Sermons*, pp. 238–239.

because it represents that side of the poet which enjoyed the sheer pleasure of words tumbling vibrantly over one another and breaking into ecstatic melody. Here is that same exuberance that Hopkins was to catch in his beautiful *Epithalamion* fragment of 1888 and, more somberly, in *Spelt from Sibyl's Leaves.* "I never did anything more musical," he once confessed to Dixon.[31] The music, though, is fairly strange to the modern ear, for its antecedents are the choral strophes of the Dorian mode, especially as these are present in Pindar's epinician odes and in plainsong. And there is something here too of the Welsh strategies of repetition and echoic vowel chiming that haunt the ear in, say, Dylan Thomas' *Under Milkwood.*

Although the finished piece is dated October 17, 1882, Hopkins seems to have begun writing it more than two years before, when he was on holiday at his parents' home in Hampstead in August 1880. Writing to Bridges in September of that year, he speaks of *The Echoes* familiarly, so Bridges must have seen a rough draft of it when he met Hopkins in August. "You shall . . . see the *Leaden Echo* when finished," he promises. But "museless" Liverpool was not the place to compose so lyrical a piece, and then the tertianship, when Hopkins gave up all poetry, intervened. But two months after his long retreat Hopkins did finish the piece in substantially the form we have it, and he admitted to being pleased with it.[32]

Bridges liked *The Leaden Echo and the Golden Echo,* as he told Dixon, but he bantered Hopkins on being false to his

[31] *Letters II,* p. 149.

[32] Only with the opening line was Hopkins dissatisfied. In the copy sent to Bridges this line is thinner than the revision:

How to keep—O is there any any, is there nowhere known any

any brooch or clasp, catch, key to keep
Back. . . .

(printed in *Letters I,* p. 161, note 1) .

own poetic voice and on sounding too much like Walt Whitman. A testy letter was shot back to Bridges, a "de-Whitmaniser" which Hopkins confessed was "a bit of a mouther." [33] Hopkins realized he had protested too much. Still, his comments provide a valuable key to the surprisingly light form of his song.

There is a direct antecedent for *The Leaden Echo and the Golden Echo* in his own *Binsey Poplars* of March 1879, as Hopkins is careful to point out. Both poems are composed of two stanzas in the ratio of 1 to 2. "The Leaden Echo" consists of sixteen lines, followed by the reply of "The Golden Echo" in thirty-two lines, as the first, eight-line stanza of *Binsey Poplars* had been followed by a second stanza of sixteen lines. Both poems are in pure sprung rhythm of varying line lengths. *Binsey Poplars* employs lines of from two to six stresses. And *The Echoes* song uses lines, if my ear is correct, of from two to twelve stresses. As in Greek choral poetry, there is a strophe followed by an antistrophe. In *Binsey Poplars* the movement is from observation in stanza 1 to commentary and homily in stanza 2. In *The Echoes,* "The Leaden Echo" is answered and reversed by "The Golden Echo." Both poems employ end-rhyme in a complicated scheme. But while there is no overlapping of rhymes in the earlier piece, there is significant echoing in the second poem. This tightness of form generates an anticipation of the word-chiming, an anticipation which is considerably weakened in Whitman because the metrics and rhyming are purposely frustrated in the interest of an unrestrained freedom and a "savage beauty." [34]

---

[33] *Letters I,* p. 158.

[34] Hopkins' comments on Whitman's prosodic techniques are quite good and critically sound. Like D. H. Lawrence and Samuel Beckett after him, Whitman was constantly approximating a traditional metrical form and then assiduously avoiding it. Hopkins knew that Whitman's techniques were founded on a viable principle, but that principle was directly opposed to his own. For Whitman, nature was organic, its

There seems to be an inverse ratio between the amount of meaning and the amount of musicality which the public ear can grasp in poetry. If the meaning is complex and deep, the artist attempts to demonstrate his melodic virtuosity at the risk of seeming garbled. It is only when the line of meaning is relatively simple and repetitive that the poet can go on to display his verbal fireworks. Such is the case with *The Leaden Echo and the Golden Echo,* which Hopkins said was "dramatic and meant to be popular." [35] In one sense, the poem may be thought of as a lyrical scholium to a text in St. Matthew: "Are not sparrows sold two for a penny? And yet it is impossible for one of them to fall to the ground without your heavenly Father's will. And as for you, he takes every hair of your head into his reckoning" (10:29–30). Hopkins is treating here a theme similar to that in both *Morning, Midday, and Evening Sacrifice* and *To what serves Mortal Beauty?* There is a moral danger in attempting to freeze our

---

creations determined by inner necessities which revealed themselves in the process of working themselves out. Nature's design was there even if it could not be grasped by the human perceiver in other than a fragmentary way. But for Hopkins, design in nature was constantly revealing itself. If left to itself, it could ring news not only of itself, but of its Designer. So, too, in their respective poetics: for Whitman, poetic design was ever changing, ever tenuous, evolving always from an ever-changing creator of poetry. For Hopkins, words were signatures of God, and rhyme words could be shown to reveal something of their internal necessity, of their meaningful correspondences with other things, as pointers to a larger unity of which they partook. Hopkins' rhymes are always significant and often point to the deeper significance of a poem. Whitman, therefore, can acknowledge the "Spirit that form'd this Scene"—the Platte Cañon, Colorado—as the same spirit that shaped his own poetry, his own "formless wild arrays." But Hopkins' rhymes reveal the metamorphosis of one form, for example, the "Randal," into another precisely defined form to which it is linguistically rooted, the "sandal." See, in this connection, David Sonstroem's "Making Earnest of Game: G. M. Hopkins and Nonsense Poetry," *Modern Language Quarterly,* XXVIII (1967), 192–206.

[35] *Letters I,* p. 106.

physical beauty, for by its very nature it is fleeting and cannot be contained. To become unduly attached to it is a dead end, which leads inevitably to despair. It is only in the paradox of freely giving this beauty back to the source of all beauty—to God—in an act of sacrifice and worship, that we can hope to regain our transitory freshness. We regain it, the song tells us, in the resurrection of the body, when we will be an "all youth" having regained forever our "own best being." Though we forget this promise of eternal beauty, God does not. "Now when we love God," Hopkins wrote in notes for a sermon he delivered on December 14, 1879,

he first loved us . . . as a ruler his subjects before we loved him as subjects their ruler; so when we love Christ with a fonder love than that / he with a fonder love than that ["Fonder a care kept than we could have kept it, kept / Far with fonder a care . . ."] first loved us. . . . Are they [men and women] handsome, healthy, strong, ableminded, witty, successful, brave, truthful, pure, just? He admires them more than they can, more than they *justly* can, themselves, for he made all these things. . . . But we admire ourselves and pride ourselves: we should leave that to him, he is proud enough of us.[36]

If we remember that the song was written to be sung by a chorus of maidens, the images fit beautifully; the maidens are concerned with "frowning" away wrinkles and with "waving off" the encroaching grey of their locks. Certain of the rhyme words call attention to these concerns: "fair"—"despair"—"hair"—"despair" in "The Leaden Echo," and then "Spare!"—"there"—"hair"—"care" in "The Golden Echo." In fact, it is not too much to say that the lyric is, at least in part, generated on a gigantic but quite serious pun: the search for a lock to keep our locks.

Another poetic effect is the internal chiming and sliding of one word into a cognate which also sounds similar. In the opening there is the play on "none . . . nowhere known"

---

[36] *Sermons,* pp. 48–49.

and the verbal sliding of "bow or brooch or braid or brace, láce, latch or catch or key to keep," and we are back to the beginning with "keep." And there is this sliding: "sweet looks, loose locks, long locks, lovelocks," and then, "gaygear, going gallant, girlgrace." Hopkins ends the first part by locking on the word "despair"; it is as if the word were being rebounded off the imprisoning walls of a leaden coffin:

> Be beginning to despair, to despair
> Despair, despair, despair, despair.

This then bursts into the golden echo's returning echo, which shatters the word itself in denying it: "Spare!"

Where the first movement ends in a deadly turning inward, the ending of the second opens out toward infinity:

> —Where kept? do but tell us where kept, where.—
> Yonder.—What high as that! We follow, now we follow.—
> Yonder, yes yonder, yonder,
> Yonder.

At this point the chorus would seem to follow, that is, follow both the golden echo's meaning and her direction, probably off stage. But there is no such direction, because there is no scene to follow. For Hopkins' poetic genius was of that nineteenth-century egocentric kind, and whatever his muse's virtues, she never learned to wear buskins. He confessed as much when he said that his roughest first thoughts for *St. Winefred's Well* were "of a too lyrical and not enough dramatic cast." [37] But then so are the final fragments. The special virtues of *The Echoes* is not its drama but its madrigal quality; when properly performed by a choral group, this poem can be made to yield a powerful and haunting music, with a wider range of modulation, tempo, and chiming effects than we may be aware of. Its affinities are rather with baroque chamber music than with closet drama. It is, really, a prayer played *con rubato*.

[37] *Letters I*, p. 106.

One runs the same risks in writing about Hopkins' humorous verse as in telling someone else's joke: what if it doesn't strike the listener as funny in the telling? Hopkins wrote some humorous verses in October 1880 at Liverpool, but he hesitated half a year before sending them to Bridges. He had good reason to hesitate, for Bridges did not think them funny, and even considered them vulgar. All Hopkins could do was maintain that, just as in serious poetry there is the strictly beautiful, so in comic verse there is the "strictly funny." What these comic verses of 1880 were we do not know, except that one was on the Church of England. Bridges did not keep them.

So when, in March 1883, Hopkins had "A Trio of Triolets" published in *The Stonyhurst Magazine,* he hesitated to send them to Bridges because they had "the taint of jest." [38] But a year later, and separated from him by the Irish Sea, Hopkins found the courage to send him two of them. Bridges printed only *The Child is Father to the Man* and refused to publish *Cockle's Antibilious Pills.* Abbott printed *No news in the Times to-day* at the end of *Letters I,* but he also felt that *Cockle's Antibilious Pills* was "best served by its present decent obscurity." [39] Nor did Gardner print these two until the Fourth Edition, and even there he relegates them to the Notes.[40] The reader who catches himself laughing at the cleverness expressed in these comic triolets, then, almost finds himself looking around to see if he is being stared at.

But if we do not expect too much from them, they are comic in a light way. Hopkins, of course, is having fun with the triolet form, which, like the rondel and villanelle, he thought too artificial for serious poetry. The triolet works on a principle of delicate repetition. The first line is repeated as the fourth and seventh lines; the second is repeated as

---

[38] Letter of March 26, 1883, *ibid.,* p. 178.
[39] *Letters I,* pp. 317–318.   [40] Poems, pp. 312–313.

the eighth (and last) line. There are only two end-rhymes throughout.

No news in the Times to-day is generated on the day-to-day search for something of value, some worthwhile news in the papers. Hopkins catches the circular tedium of the useless search in the circular movement of the triolet. The form seems to rise to a point of expectancy, of breakthrough in the sixth line, with its medial stop, but then the final lines settle back into repetition. T. S. Eliot, too, sensed the meaninglessness of the daily tabloid-reading ritual in his early *The Boston Evening Transcript* with its dead-end cyclical movement. For Hopkins the good news is not in *The Times*.

Cockle's Antibilious Pills captures the repetitive, exaggerated jargon of Victorian puffing, or advertising. Cockle's Pills were actually advertised in the British dailies. The following puff, for example, appeared in *The Tablet* for January 1, 1881 (p. 27), where it is given as the testimony of one Captain Fred Burnaby: "In fact, the marvellous effects produced upon the mind and body of an Arab Sheik, who was impervious to all native medicines when I administered to him five COCKLE'S PILLS will never fade from my memory." It is obvious what Hopkins' reaction to such claims would have been, he who had spent his life in the cause of the only one who could "heal the nations." The triolet form allows the puffing to condemn itself by its own claims and its own saccharine emotions. We laugh, and the high style evaporates. What would Hopkins have done in an age which sings plainsong to its own products, displayed prominently where executives may see and offer thanks? But then, Ruskin had already foreseen this in his portrayal of the "Goddess of Getting-on," the symbol of the Victorians' "practical and earnest religion." [41] And even earlier, Carlyle had, in *Sartor Resartus,* reduced puffing to the absurd with his anecdote of the mock hat.

[41] "Traffic," in *The Crown of Wild Olive* (1866).

The Child is Father to the Man is from the close of Wordsworth's little lyric, *My Heart Leaps Up*, which also serves as part of the headnote to his *Ode: Intimations of Immortality*, which Hopkins thought very highly of. What Hopkins does here is to create a literal-minded persona who cannot grasp the wisdom of such a paradox as Wordsworth's and who insists on reversing it to fit his own mode of logicality. It is Hopkins at his most playful, fencing with the kind of mentality to which poetry is a closed door. And the sense of confusion, of trying to nail down the meaning, is humorously caught in the repetitions of the triolet. Certainly these pieces are too light to have been handled so roughly by his editors.

The Blessed Virgin compared to the Air we Breathe is the finest and most poetically ambitious of Hopkins' Marian poems. Its length (126 lines) was perhaps justified in Hopkins' eyes by his having been asked in May 1883, probably by his superior at Stonyhurst, "to write something in honour of the Blessed Virgin, it being the custom [during May, Mary's month] to hang up verse-compositions 'in the tongues.' " [42] Written in three-foot couplets (in imitation of a poem in that form by Dixon), the poem, Hopkins admitted, was "partly a compromise with popular taste," and he warded off any of Bridges' forthcoming criticism with the truism "that the highest subjects are not those on which it is easy to reach one's highest." [43] (Bridges, somewhat perversely, told Canon Dixon that the Marian poem was admirable! [44])

The Blessed Virgin (originally titled *Mary Mother of Divine Grace Compared to the Air we Breathe*) is shaped on an extended comparison of Mary, in her role as mediatrix of

[42] Letter to Dixon of June 25, 1883, *Letters II*, p. 108.
[43] Letter of May 11, 1883, *Letters I*, p. 179.
[44] Letter from Dixon to Hopkins, *Letters II*, p. 110. Patmore, who for the most part couldn't understand what Hopkins' poetry was about, also admired the fragment of it Hopkins sent him. See *Letters I*, p. 192, and *Letters III*, p. 355.

God's life-giving graces, to the life-giving air itself. The poem begins by saluting the "Wild air, world-mothering air" which is to be found everywhere, between each hair, between the smallest spaces of the finest snowflake. Even in singing this song of praise to the air, the poet must rely on that air. Air's all-pervasiveness, plenitude ("never spent"), and essentiality for all life act as counters pointing toward a profound truth in the religious sphere. For, as Mary bestowed her humanity on God, dwindling "God's infinity . . . to infancy" and thus mediating between God and man, so she continues her role by letting "all God's glory through" to man. As the air encircles the globe, so too does Mary, in her constant bestowing of her son's (sun's) infinite graces. Further, as men all share the bountiful air, so they are meant to share Mary's very life, which is grace, which is Christ. Extending the analogy until it begins to become as heady as a Crashaw conceit, the poet says that we are Nazareths, Bethlehems, living temples, where Mary, whom we harbor when we harbor life-giving grace, perpetually conceives and brings Christ forth. Men become, by telescoping the process here, new Marys growing into new Christs, insofar as Christian acts make us Christ. This breath (grace) can "baffle death."

The metaphor in Hopkins' masterly hands is amazingly pliable. Lifting our hand up in a blue sky, Hopkins says, we note the light is lambent, fluid, and seems to lap around the spaces between the extended, stretched fingers. Still, for all its deep blue (Mary's color), the light is not stained, it does not interfere with the quality or intensity of light itself, which is colorless. Perhaps on objects apart and some distance away ("aloof, aloft"), as, say, on the outline of a tree, it may give the impression of a light tinting, but this enhances the scene and makes "Earth . . . fairer for" it. Hopkins has some lines in an early sermon which serve as a fine gloss on these last thoughts:

All grace [is] given through Mary: this [is] a mystery. Like [a] blue sky, which for all its richness of colour does not stain the sunlight, though smoke and red clouds do, so God's graces come to us unchanged but all through her. Moreover she gladdens the Catholic's heaven and when she is brightest so is the sun her son.[45]

How does Mary gladden heaven? If it were not for our sea of air, Hopkins reminds us, the sun's light and heat would be unbearable. As science has since confirmed, the sun seen nakedly is terrifying, surrounded by the multitude of stars, all flashing in the blackness of an infinite "grimy vasty vault." But the "world-mothering air" intercedes. Hopkins draws out the analogy. The God of the Hebrews was like this: dazzling in his glory, but terrifying, apart, beyond human comprehension. But the Incarnation has made "our daystar"—the sun-Son—"Much dearer to mankind." Mary's giving God flesh allows us to "see him / Made sweeter" without being "made dim." God has been accommodated to man's limited sight.

In the last verse paragraph, Hopkins asks a boon of his "dear / Mother," that she be his "atmosphere," his "happier world," keeping his sky "sweet and scarless." Reversing Matthew Arnold's metaphor for man's isolation as seen in the islands forever isolated by the "unplumbed, salt, estranging sea," Hopkins prays to be "isled" in Mary's "world-mothering air," which, far from being indifferent, can "fast fold thy child."

It is a good poem and, in its extended conceit, one of Hopkins' most metaphysical. But its doctrinal elements, or more specifically, its Marianism, have militated against its inclusion in the anthologies. Hopkins, of course, would not have been surprised. He hesitated before sending the poem to Bridges probably because he did not think Bridges would care for it.[46] There was a large public in his time (and a far larger one in ours) who, Hopkins regretted, "can no longer

---

[45] Sermon for October 5, 1879, *Sermons,* p. 29.

[46] "I do not suppose I shall find it either convenient or desirable to send you a copy" (*Letters I,* p. 179) .

be trusted to bear, to stomach, the clear expression of or the taking for granted even very elementary Christian doctrines." [47] And even for those more amenable to it, the doctrine of Mary as mediatrix was far from being elementary doctrine.[48]

"I am always jaded," he told Bridges in late March 1883. "I cannot tell why, and my vein shews no signs of ever flowing again." [49] And two months later he voices a similar complaint to Dixon: "I see no grounded prospect of my ever doing much not only in poetry but in anything at all. At times I do feel this sadly and bitterly, but it is God's will and though no change that I can foresee will happen yet perhaps some may that I do not foresee." [50] Although not yet forty, Hopkins felt that his poetic vein was thinning out. But when, removed from Stonyhurst to Dublin and isolated from friends, family, and countrymen, he was coaxed by his muse to write again, there is a radical transformation in Hopkins' poetic voice which touches on the darkness of Lear in its confrontation, not with the world without, but with the self within. It is a confrontation with a darkness so profound and so terrifying that it leaves the shadows of the Ribblesdale landscape far behind and far above.

[47] *Ibid.*, p. 186.

[48] Gardner, sympathetic as he seems to be to an intellectual understanding of this doctrine, appears to chafe at Boyle's razor-fine distinctions and to be puzzled that Boyle will not meet him halfway but demands, in Gardner's words, "a nicer theological adjustment." Cf. *Poems*, p. 283, and Boyle, ch. 3.

[49] *Letters I*, p. 178.   [50] *Letters II*, pp. 108–109.

6.∽ The Dark Night
of the Soul: 1885

Sometime in the bleak twilight days of October 1884, Hopkins conceived and began *Spelt from Sibyl's Leaves,* for early drafts of the poem exist in his unpublished Dublin Notebook for this period. There is an appropriate shadowiness around the inception of this poem which stands at the threshold of the splendid series of sonnets of desolation written most probably between January and midsummer of 1885. Whatever lacunae may exist in our reconstruction of the composition of the 1877 or 1879 sonnets, the beginnings of Hopkins' renewed creativity are heralded by him in letters to his mother or to Bridges written at times when spring was not far off.

But Hopkins' world now was darker and wintry, and almost two years elapsed before he told Bridges about his sonnet. Even then he remarks only on its rhythm. "I have at last completed but not quite finished the longest sonnet ever made and no doubt the longest making," he wrote Bridges on November 26, 1886, from St. Stephen's, Dublin. "It is in eight-foot lines and essays effects almost musical." [1] And two weeks later he finally sends off the sonnet to Bridges with the almost fond remark that this is indeed an exceptional child of which to be proud:

I mean to enclose my long sonnet, the longest, I still say, ever made; longest by its own proper length, namely by the length of

[1] *Letters I,* p. 245.

its lines; for anything can be made long by eking, by tacking, by trains, tails, and flounces. I shd. be glad however if you wd. explain what a *coda* is and how employed.[2] Perhaps I shall enclose other sonnets.[3] Of this long sonnet above all remember what applies to all my verse, that it is, as living art should be, made for performance and that its performance is not reading with the eye but loud, leisurely, poetical (not rhetorical) recitation, with long rests, long dwells on the rhyme and other marked syllables, and so on. This sonnet shd. be almost sung: it is most carefully timed in tempo rubato. . . . I send tonight only one sonnet.[4]

The music of the sprung eight-stress lines of this extraordinarily heavy sonnet is quite a departure from anything Hopkins had created before. The rhythm here is more percussive and owes something of its grounding to traditional Gregorian chant and the older classical heptachord, both of which allow for a wide range of modulation in the chanting voice. The accompaniment remains throughout a steady eight-stress line, marked by a strong caesura after the fourth foot. But the fluctuation of speed between lines is surprisingly great, and Hopkins has here rid himself of the metrical equivalence of the musical "tyranny of the bar." For example, there is the difference between the slow, stately, echoing bass of

Earnest, earthless, equal, attuneable, | vaulty, voluminous, . . .
stupendous

---

[2] As early as December 1886 Hopkins is haunted by the rhythm of a caudated sonnet. But it is not until the following September that he actually writes *Harry Ploughman*, the first of his three sonnets to employ a coda (of sorts).

[3] From September 1885 until shortly before his death nearly four years later, Hopkins again and again promises to send Bridges the sonnets of desolation. But he never does. On November 2, 1887, for example, he writes: "I hope soon to enter a batch of sonnets in my book and when I do that I can send you copies. They are the thin gleanings of a long weary while, but singly good" (*Letters I*, p. 264).

[4] *Ibid.*, p. 246.

of line 1, and the muffled drum-beat finality of the second
half of line 8,

$$\overset{\prime}{\text{whelms, }} \overset{\prime}{\text{whelms, }} \overset{\prime}{\text{and will }} \overset{\prime}{\text{end us,}}$$

whose six syllables receive (at least conceptually) the same
metronomic time as either half of line 1, with ten and nine
syllables respectively. The rhythm of the sonnet was given
Hopkins' careful attention and, in fact, is indispensable to
the understanding of the poem, as we shall see.

The lines may be very long, but they are not monotonous.
And certainly the serious subject matter demands a solemn,
meditative, almost chanting line. In Caradoc's soliloquy
from *St. Winefred's Well,* Hopkins uses a basic Alexandrine
line, which he sometimes expands to seven or eight feet.
Spelt from Sibyl's Leaves is his only sonnet to employ an
eight-stress line, but the rhythmical experiment is a success
because the thought demands such a line. After this sonnet
Hopkins reverted to the Alexandrine line, perhaps because
of the tendency of the eight-stress line with its pronounced
caesura to break into two parts.

Spelt from Sibyl's Leaves has received close attention from
several perceptive critics of Hopkins, including Leavis, Gardner, and Boyle. It has also received several quite different
interpretations and some fine glosses. But that it is first of all
an Ignatian meditation on the state of hell has not, to my
knowledge, been adequately stated. Nevertheless, there are
several notes made for a meditation on hell among Hopkins'
spiritual writings which together offer a prose paraphrase of
the sonnet.

The poem opens with a vivid Ignatian composition of
place. Evening is overtaking day, straining to blend inexorably and irreversibly into night.[5] This blending of evening

[5] See F. R. Leavis' perceptive comment on the opening lines of the
sonnet in *New Bearings in English Poetry* (Ann Arbor, 1960), p. 183:
"This poem opens with evening deepening into night. We are not
merely told that evening 'strains,' we feel evening straining, to become

into night is mimetically captured in the digraph and vowel chiming and smooth blending of word into word in "*Ear*nest, *ear*thless, *e*qual, attune*a*ble." But the dental stops work against a too-easy blending. There is a pause and then a chiming at the other end of the alphabet with "*v*aulty, *v*olumin*ous*, . . . stupend*ous*." Hopkins uses seven epithets to inscape "Evening." Evening is radically different from the "dapple" of day, and the gay, pied complexity of the world of light gives way to somber, undifferentiated uniformity. The colorful mask of the world, which before seemed to be morally neutral, is peeled away to reveal its essentially "earnest" nature. Evening becomes strange and dark and must be judged by quite other than diurnal standards; it is attuneable, able to be harmonized, to be blended into one indistinguishable mass, like matter returning to its primal chaotic state, like the waters of Genesis.

Evening "strains" to become the nighttime as well as the night, the end, of all time. Hopkins stresses that sense of vast interstellar emptiness with the last three epithets of evening and the description of night as "tíme's vást, womb-of-all, home-of-all, hearse-of-all night." All returns to its primordial home, to its original state (its "womb") , to its hearse. Everything moves inexorably toward its end, and the end is like the beginning. For we come from darkness, and we return to darkness. There is in the adjective "voluminous," besides the meaning of volume, the equally relevant meaning of foldings, coilings, and windings (*volumen*) as evening unrolls into night, like parchment leaves on which are inscribed the record of our life. The sense of awe and of terrifying isolation in a strange world where nothing of what we knew remains is captured in the muffled drum-beats of the first two lines. We are under the cavernous "vaulty" dome of evening, in the burial chamber of our life. And we are at the entrance to Virgil's hell in Book Six of the *Aeneid*:

---

night, enveloping everything, in the movement, the progression of alliteration, assonance and rime."

Dimly through the shadows and dark solitudes they wended,
Through the void domiciles of Dis, the bodiless regions:
Just as, through fitful moonbeams, under the moon's thin light,
A path lies in a forest, when Jove has palled the sky
With gloom, and the night's blackness has bled the world of
   colour   [VI, 268–272].[6]

Those commentators who see this sonnet as dealing only
with a pre-Christian world are partially correct in that hell
for Hopkins means experiencing eternal separation from
God, regardless of religion. But the *Dies Irae,* which is a
traditional part of the Roman Catholic Burial Mass, also
joins the pagan Sibyl's prophecies with those of the Bible. In
the first tercet, David is linked with the Cumaean prophetess:

> Dies irae, dies illa,
> Solvet saeclum in favilla:
> Teste David cum Sibylla.

> (Day of wrath, that day
> Will unwind time into ashes:
> Both David and Sybil are witness.) [7]

The receding "hornlight" of the sun, that opaque,
horn-colored, serene twilight which is so pervasive after the
sun has sunk below the horizon, continues to fade in the
west. Above, the cold, flickering white points of the first stars
begin to appear, showing their light but not altering the
disposition of blackness on earth.[8] The "fire-folk" of *The*

[6] Translated by the poet C. Day Lewis, who was himself influenced by
Hopkins, in *The Aeneid of Virgil* (Garden City, N.Y., 1952).

[7] My translation. Hopkins insists that the heathen is forewarned, in
his meditation on hell: "All will be punished according to their guilt,
according to their knowledge and their power . . . the heathen un-
warned by faith, warned indeed but dimly warned by reason, may suffer
little in that flame" (*Sermons,* pp. 243–244).

[8] Speaking of Christ's promise of happiness hereafter, Hopkins commented in his retreat notes only five months before his death that it "is

Starlight Night now seem to sit in judgment, as they "over-bend us" and show us God's anger in the "Fíre-féaturing heaven." The stars reveal themselves as having always been behind the dappled sky, and their progressive unfolding etched against the darkening heavens is caught in the un-folding of the words. "Earliest stars" elides into the more sharply focused "earl-stars," and is then more forcefully stressed in "stárs principal." One phrase literally unravels from the one before, as our life itself ravels off onto "twó spools." The heavens appear in all their terrifying vastness now that earth resolves herself into a world of shadows. There is a similar image of God's awesomeness in the heav-ens, eternally there, beyond the bright dapple of day, in *The Blessed Virgin compared to the Air we Breathe* (May 1883).

As evening becomes night and the light wanes, the com-plexity and variety which all things showed in the light now fade, and shapes (scapes) are forced to blend together, to lose all distinctiveness and selfhood. Only the most elemen-tary outlines breaking against the dark skyline can be made out, and the skeletal selves seem "self ín self steepèd." Left to themselves, without the external light of the sun, the beauty of the trees fades and only the grotesque, frightening, gnarled outline remains. What is true of the trees is true of all things. Earth's unbinding is rapidly and "qúite / Disre-membering, dísmémbering áll now." There has been no signaled shifting from the vividly pictured natural scene of the falling night to the spiritual vision of the Armageddon of the world and of the Last Judgment; the spiritual reality resides as by a sign in the natural, and any allegorical

---

as if one were dazzled by a spark or star in the dark, seeing it but not seeing by it: we want a light shed on our way and a happiness spread over our life" (*ibid.*, p. 262). The hoarlight of the stars seems far away and hollow, and the sparkling presence of God which was so near in *The Starlight Night* of seven years before is removed, for we are entering hell.

transition between the two would only water down the reality of both for Hopkins. The progression of the first six and one-half lines has been from evening to night, from the evening of a man's life to death itself, from judgment to hell.

The speaker turns inward now to make the logical application to himself, and addresses his innermost self, his heart:

> Heart, you round me right
> With: Our evening is over us; our night | whelms, whelms, and
> will end us.

There is a sense of drugged pain in the chiming of the diphthongs—in the *ow* of "round" and "our," which is repeated, in the Greek *aie* of "right," and in the repetition of the short *e* which ceases only in the finality of "end" and is percussively repeated on four stressed words within six syllables: "whélms, whélms, ánd will end us."

In line 9 the speaker, continuing to address his heart, remarks that in the dark night only the blacker outline of the leaves is etched against the sky:

> Only the beakleaved boughs dragonish | damask the tool-smooth
>   bleak light; black,
> Ever so black on it.

"Damask" is a rich and complex verb. It suggests, together with "beakleaved" and "tool-smooth," the streaked metallic hardness of damascene steel. But it also suggests the weaving of damascene cloth in the images of two spools of thread, one black, one white, which follow. One type of damascene cloth is woven with a uniformly dark thread against a uniformly lighter background so that the contrast between the two is all the sharper and more distinctive, and the "twó tell, each off the óther." Both images are there in the straining and grinding of adamantine steel strands (permanence), and in the heightening of one color against the other, with no smooth transition between.[9]

Hopkins insists on the centrality of this dark tree, for the speaker again turns to his heart with "Óur tale, O óur oracle!" Now he applies to himself what he has learned from the leaves by which the Sibyl, the ancient prophetess of Cumae, foretold the future. Life wanes as surely as does the day; it too winds to its west, and all of its multiplicity and multicolor, its "once skéined stained véined varíety" resolve into two final and eternal opposites for each of us. The scapes—the essential, moral meaning of all of our past actions—are like a mixed flock of sheep and goats which is to be separated into "twó flocks, twó folds—black, white; right, wrong." The biblical allusion is to Christ's coming to judge the world: "When the Son of Man comes in his glory, and all the angels with him, he will sit down upon the throne of his glory, and all nations will be gathered in his presence, where he will divide men one from the other, as the shepherd divides the sheep from the goats; he will set the sheep on his right, and the goats on his left" (Matthew 25:31–33). But here the application is rather to the multiplicity of our thoughts and our actions during our lifetime, which will be sorted out according to their underlying moral worth.

In line 12, the speaker makes the resolution to be more aware, to be more wary, of this final moral judgment. He must realize more fully that in the final reckoning only the moral nature of his life will count, that it is this which he must heed ("reck"). He must "mind," that is, regard this

[9] We are in a different world from the aesthetic world of Hopkins' journals of nearly two decades earlier where he could delineate the beauties of night. "Beautiful blackness and definition of elm tree branches in evening twilight (from behind)," he remarks on May 20, 1866 (*Journals*, p. 137). And on June 19, "Aspens blackened against the last light seem to throw their scarcer leaves into barbs or arrowheads of mackerel patterns" (*ibid.*, p. 141). This last observation seems to have especially gestated in Hopkins' imagination and borne fruit in *Spelt from Sibyl's Leaves.*

simple but difficult moral lesson; but the verb focuses on that total awareness to which he must turn his total mind. That world he must be "ware of" is hell, in which for all eternity he will be confronted with the scapes, the patterns, of his past actions. Now their real nature as displeasing to God will be revealed. Here in this inner hell, until the Final Judgment, the disembodied spirit will have to suffer the torture of tasting itself; here, what might have been and what is act on the consciousness like a "rack / Where, selfwrung, selfstrung, sheathe- and shelterless, thóughts agaínst thoughts ín groans grínd."

"The fall from heaven was for the rebel angels what death is for man," Hopkins writes in his meditation on hell. With death, the soul loses all extension and activity outward and is confined in upon itself.

[In] man all that energy or instress with which the soul animates and otherwise acts in the body is by death thrown back upon the soul itself. . . . This throwing back or confinement of their energy is a dreadful constraint or imprisonment and, as intellectual action is spoken of under the figure of sight, it will in this case be an imprisonment in darkness, a being in the dark; for darkness is the phenomenon of foiled action in the sense of sight.[10]

[10] *Sermons,* p. 137. In his remarks by way of prologue to his meditation on hell, Hopkins makes a distinction which some unsympathetic critics have either missed or chosen to overlook. He places stress on the intellectual imagination (the whole passage is most enlightening in clarifying the Ignatian rhetoric of the fire and brimstone sermon which Joyce, "the fearful jesuit," so subtly parodies in *The Portrait*): "[Ignatius] speaks only of the pain of sense: the reason is the end proposed in this meditation [on hell], which is by sensible considerations to deter us from sin. . . . [Ignatius] speaks of the present condition of the lost, who are disembodied; therefore it is, I suppose, that he mingles without reserve or remark physical and figurative things, like brimstone and tears (which the disembodied soul cannot shed) and the worm of conscience. And as it is by the imagination that we are to realize these things so *I suppose it to be by the imagination that the lost*

The world of *Spelt from Sibyl's Leaves* is this world of darkness and frustration.

It is within this dark world that we are confronted with our past actions, which leave "in our minds scapes or species, the extreme 'intention' or instressing of which would be painful and the pain would be that of fire, supposing fire to be the condition of a body . . . *texturally at stress.*" [11] It is these dark scapes of a man's past life which are outlined against the blackness of hell and which Hopkins figures in the "beakleaved boughs dragonish" etched against the night. For "the understanding open wide like an eye, towards truth in God, towards light, is confronted by that scape, that act of its own, which blotted out God and so put blackness in the place of light." [12] The dark background which highlights an even darker "self ín self steepèd" scape is a poetic rendition of St. Theresa's vision of hell, paraphrased by Hopkins: " 'I know not how it is, but in spite of the darkness the eye sees there all that to see is most afflicting.' Against these acts of its own the lost spirit dashes itself like a caged bear and is in prison, violently instresses them and burns, stares into them and is the deeper darkened." [13]

In hell, then, we are our thoughts, and the disparity between what *is* and what might have been is made absolutely and finally clear to us. And the two spools of right and wrong become a rack where our very self wrings against itself, where our thoughts, disembodied and unprotected scapes, are forced to grind against each other. This fiery friction of the two opposing threads rubbing against each other discharges its strain in groaning. And this violent action between what was expected and what is, is marvelously caught in the extreme muscular tension of Hopkins' tortuous

---

suffer them and that as intensely as by the senses or it may be more so. This simple explanation will never strike our scholastics [as opposed to the great medieval tradition of scholastics] *because they do not see that there is an intellectual imagination*" (Sermons, p. 136, italics mine) .

[11] *Ibid.*   [12] *Ibid.*, p. 138.   [13] *Ibid.*

rhythmic stressing of "thóughts agaínst thoughts ín groans grínd." [14]

Of the underlying moral quality of all our actions, Hopkins stresses unequivocally that

God is good[,] and the stamp, seal, or instress he sets on each scape is of *right, good,* or of *bad, wrong.* Now the sinner who has preferred his own good . . . to God's good, true good, and God, has that evil between him and God, by his attachment to which and God's rejection of it he is carried and swept away to an infinite distance from God; and the stress and strain of his removal is his eternity of punishment.

For with death, as he had remarked just before, "the soul is left to its own resources, with only the scapes and *species* [the instressed disembodied thoughts] of its past life; which being unsupplemented or undisplaced by a fresh continual current of experience, absorb and press upon its consciousness ['self ín self steepèd']." [15] That a morally wrong but pleasurable act is repulsive in hell Hopkins insists upon. In hell, the awareness of a scape's repulsiveness is instressed upon us, continually burning itself into our consciousness or, in other terms, into our very self. [16] Hell-fire, then, is explained by

[14] Yvor Winters comments on the rhythm of the last lines of *Spelt from Sibyl's Leaves* that Hopkins "does not provide us with many accent marks until he is about half-way through the poem; from there on he provides marks in abundance, frequently with strange results. . . . We have here [in the last two lines] a kind of bad writing which is purely the result of bad reading; and even the best reading, if superimposed upon what the poet offers, can salvage the poem but very imperfectly" ("The Audible Reading of Poetry," reprinted in *The Structure of Verse,* ed. Harvey Gross [Greenwich, Conn., 1964], p. 136). But as I have suggested, the violent cacophony is functional in instressing the strain or pressure of the soul which is forever frustrated from achieving its proper harmony and resolution of being with God.

[15] *Sermons,* p. 139.

[16] "It would seem that there must be some revelation of himself by God to the soul to awake the strain or *nisus* [pressure] which is either to be gratified or denied. This revelation takes place through the

Hopkins as that terrible counterstress of the self as it is and as it might have been. And if there is a lack of brimstone in Hopkins' sonnet, it is replaced by a suffering all the more terrible because all the more philosophically and logically viable.[17]

The "beakleaved boughs dragonish" means the essential evil of the scapes of the speaker's past actions; the dragon, as we saw earlier, is for Hopkins the devil, a "coil or spiral," a "thrower of things off the track." That the boughs are beak-leaved inscapes the terror and insidiousness of the speaker's past actions; the beak belongs to the devil because he gathers "up the attributes of many creatures. . . . And therefore I suppose the dragon as a type of the Devil to express the universality of his powers . . . and the horror which the whole inspires. . . . [It] symbolizes one who aiming at every perfection ends by being a monster, a 'fright.' "[18]

By meditating on the nature of judgment and hell, it is stressed in upon Hopkins that he must constantly be aware and be wary of a moral world, in which the beautiful dapple of creation is to be used for God's glory by giving it all back to Him. The sharpened agony of this realization of what essentially matters—right, wrong—evokes that bitter self-taste in himself, the frightening realization of his own un-

---

species of a past life [the moral nature of our actions presented to our understanding], by means of which, by instress of which, God testifies that he is pleased or displeased and varies in its intensity with them. But it is one of attraction or repulsion, of yes or no, in any case" (*ibid.*).

[17] See John Henry Newman's *The Dream of Gerontius* (1865) which Hopkins must certainly have known. In the first separation of his soul from the body in death, Gerontius' soul experiences the strangeness of not being able to act within its habitual physical extension:

For it [the severance] drives back my thoughts upon their spring
By a strange introversion, and perforce
I now begin to feed upon myself,
Because I have nought else to feed upon   [ll. 213–216].

[18] *Sermons*, p. 199.

worthiness before the Judge of the Universe, and the pain of mastering himself. His meditation on hell evokes the hell within.

There is no consolation or hope to be found in this sonnet; it has been constructed carefully on Ignatian principles. David Downes comments that "the poetic colloquy ends with the admonishment to avoid trying to live a life, as it were, between right and wrong, for this is to be put on a frightful rack of suffering." [19] But the poem does not say to give over contemplating a strictly moral universe. And the only resolution of the sonnet is the summoning of the speaker's will and understanding to be more aware that only right and wrong finally count. The sonnet is a sonnet of desolation, and in his comments on making the fifth exercise, the meditation on hell, St. Ignatius writes, "here it will be to ask for a deep awareness of the pain suffered by the damned, so that if I should forget the love of the Eternal Lord, at least the fear of punishment will help me to avoid falling into sin." [20] In meditating on a desolate subject, the exercitant is not to summon up images of consolation. And Hopkins does not.

The bitter fruit which Hopkins gleans from the meditation is the "spelt," the hard-grained wheat derived from the Sibyl's leaves. For in the grinding of thought against thought, in the excruciating self-scrutiny of the particular examen, Hopkins hoped, as he wrote some months later in *Carrion Comfort*, that "my chaff might fly; my grain lie, sheer and clear." "Make haste then," Hopkins urged in a sermon on death delivered sometime after his Liverpool ordeal, "work while it is day, and despair of any other chance than this: *the night is coming*, says your master, *when no man can work*." [21]

---

[19] *Gerard Manley Hopkins: A Study of His Ignatian Spirit* (New York, 1959), p. 154.

[20] *The Spiritual Exercises of St. Ignatius*, trans. Anthony Mattola (Garden City, N.Y., 1964), p. 59.

[21] *Sermons*, pp. 245–246. The date is unknown. Internal evidence dates it after his stay at Liverpool.

None of the other six sonnets of desolation were ever sent to either Bridges or Dixon; all were found among Hopkins' literary remains after his death. We cannot be sure of the order in which they were written, but all appear to have been composed sometime between January and August of 1885. For on September 1 of that year Hopkins writes to Bridges, "I shall shortly have some sonnets to send you, five or more. Four of these came like inspirations unbidden and against my will. And in the life I lead now, which is one of a continually jaded and harassed mind, if in any leisure I try to do anything I make no way—nor with my work, alas! but so it must be." [22] But by September, the "war within" was at least temporarily over, and six "terrible" sonnets remain as fragments of a logbook charting those tempest-tossed waters within.

There are a few other pieces of literary flotsam which will help in piecing together what was happening to Hopkins. "I am in a low way of health," he complains to Bridges toward the end of Lent. "The delightful French Father who teaches Logic here [Rev. Jacques Mallac, S.J.] . . . will have it that I am dying—of anaemia. I am not, except at the rate that we all are." On Wednesday of Holy Week, Hopkins proposes "to compose my own requiem," and complains of "that coffin of weakness and dejection in which I live." And in mid-May he complains of "work, worry, and languishment," and more seriously, of "fits of sadness [which] . . . resemble madness." [23]

In this same letter he cries out for rain, for encouragement and inspiration: "There is a point with me in matters of any size when I must absolutely have encouragement as much as crops rain; afterwards I am independent." And yet in his spiritual sterility he has still managed to create two sonnets. "I have after long silence written two sonnets, which I am

[22] *Letters I*, p. 221.

[23] Letters of March 24, April 1, and May 17, 1885, *ibid.*, pp. 210, 214–215, and 216.

touching: if ever anything was written in blood one of these was." [24]

Obviously Hopkins was deeply troubled during this period. Writing to Baillie at about the same time that he told Bridges of his two sonnets, he apologizes for taking nearly a month to write a relatively short letter:

You will wonder I have been so long over it. This is part of my disease, so to call it. The melancholy I have all my life been subject to has become of late years not indeed more intense in its fits but rather more distributed, constant, and crippling. One, the lightest but a very inconvenient form of it, is daily anxiety about work to be done. . . . It is useless to write more on this: when I am at the worst, though my judgment is never affected, my state is much like madness. I see no ground for thinking I shall ever get over it or ever succeed in doing anything that is not forced on me to do of any consequence.[25]

After spending early August at Hampstead and Midhurst with his parents and a few days in Hastings at the home of Coventry Patmore, Hopkins' spirits revived, and he wrote two and possibly three sonnets which show a new, if somewhat restrained, ebullience: *To what serves Mortal Beauty, The Soldier,* and perhaps his third curtal sonnet, *Ashboughs.* But in his letter to Bridges of September 1 he is keenly aware that after he has "had a holiday though not strong I have some buoyancy; soon I am afraid I shall be ground down to a state like this last spring's and summer's, when my spirits

[24] *Letters I,* pp. 218–219. Although he may have been referring to *Spelt from Sibyl's Leaves,* that seems to have been left unfinished four months before. In any event, *Sibyl's Leaves* should be seen as inaugurating the sonnets of desolation, with its meditation on the nature of hell and the depressing sense of God's removal.

[25] Letter of April 24–May 17, 1885, *Letters III,* p. 256. This passage was written at the earliest on May 8 and probably later. In his meditation notes for March 19, 1885, the Feast of St. Joseph, Hopkins writes, "[St. Joseph] is the patron of the hidden life; of those, I should think, suffering in mind and as I do. Therefore I will ask his help" (*Sermons,* p. 260).

were so crushed that madness seemed to be making approaches—and nobody was to blame, except myself partly
for not managing myself better and contriving a change." [26]

Even if we could determine the chronological development of the six sonnets of desolation with certainty—which
we cannot—Hopkins himself has given us a series working
from deepening desolation toward consolation.[27] In analyzing the sonnets, then, I will use the order which Jean-
Georges Ritz gives as the logical order of the poems, without
suggesting that this is the order of their composition.[28] *To
seem the stranger, I wake and feel the fell of dark,* and *No
worst, there is none:* each descends deeper into the emptiness
within. Then there is the beginning of the upswing in *Carrion Comfort,* which continues in *Patience, hard thing,* and
My own heart. Of course the sonnets can be read in and for
themselves, but the series provides an added dimension
which follows too closely the classical descent and ascent of
the Ignatian Exercises to be fortuitous. Thus, while the
following analysis will concentrate on the sonnets as individual and self-sufficient creations, their interrelationships will
also be examined. In fact, the very order of explication will
help explain the larger conception inherent in the sonnets.

To seem the stranger is a cry from Hopkins' deepest self at
a "thírd / Remove" in Ireland. It is a triple lament for an
ever deepening isolation from those objects which were so

---

[26] *Letters I,* p. 222.

[27] St. Ignatius defines desolation in the "Rules for the Discernment of
Spirits," the appendix to his *Spiritual Exercises,* in the following
manner: "I call desolation all that is contrary to the third rule
[spiritual consolation], as darkness of the soul, turmoil of the mind,
inclination to low and earthly things, restlessness resulting from many
disturbances and temptations which lead to loss of faith, loss of hope,
and loss of love. It is also desolation when a soul finds itself completely
apathetic, tepid, sad, and separated as it were, from its Creator and
Lord" (Mattola [trans.], *op. cit.,* p. 130).

[28] It is not necessary to insist on Ritz's as the order of composition,
but it does seem to make the best logical arrangement; see Ritz, p. 250.

dear to him. The first line and a half announce the theme of the sonnet: "To seem the stranger lies my lot, my life / Among strangers." The key word, "stranger[s]," appears near the beginning and is repeated at the critical close of the statement. Hopkins seems a stranger to those around him and those around him are strangers to him. Although it is the expected portion of the missionary priest, the separation is nevertheless difficult and even bitter. In the first quatrain Hopkins echoes the stern words of Christ, that in following him he would be expected to separate himself from his family:

Do not imagine that I have come to bring peace to the earth; I have come to bring a sword, not peace. I have come to set a man at variance with his father, and the daughter with her mother, and the daughter-in-law with the mother-in-law; a man's enemies will be the people of his own house [Matthew 10:34–36].[29]

Hopkins always had a profound love for his native England; by his own admission he was a very great patriot who earnestly desired to forward the honor of his country whenever and in whatever way he could.[30] He firmly believed, as did Carlyle and Ruskin especially, that there was a definite cause-and-effect relationship between the strength of a nation and the moral fiber of its people. But for Hopkins, this also meant the conversion of England back to traditional Catholicism. This wish had been made strongly in both *The*

[29] None of Hopkins' large family followed him into the Church, and his most important interest was a closed matter between him and his family. "Religion, you know," he told Baillie once, "enters very deep; in reality it is the deepest impression I have in speaking to people, that they are or that they are not of my religion" (letter of May 22, 1880, *Letters III*, p. 245).

[30] Cf. Hopkins letter to Bridges (*Letters I*, p. 231), and his comment to Patmore in his letter of June 4, 1886: "Your poems are a good deed done for the Catholic Church and another for England, for the British Empire, which now trembles in the balance held in the hand of unwisdom" (*Letters III*, pp. 366–67); "the hand of unwisdom" refers to Gladstone.

Wreck of the Deutschland and in *The Loss of the Eurydice,* and the wish is there in *In the Valley of the Elwy* and in *Duns Scotus's Oxford.* And now Hopkins, estranged from England by his religion and by his very vocation, loving England as a "wife" but disappointed in her, laments:

> England, whose honour O all my heart woos, wife
> To my creating thought, would neither hear
> Me, were I pleading, plead nor do I: I wear-
> y of idle a being but by where wars are rife.

Victorian Hopkins refuses to "plead" with his wife, although he loves her dearly, for in a very real sense his poems and songs are the offspring of this love. The middle-aged idealist sadly realizes that England will not listen, that she is too set in her ways to change, and that pleading would be useless. He is weary, most obviously, of the constant and seemingly fruitless struggles of the British Empire, specifically in Ireland, to keep its possessions intact. On the theological level, he is weary of the incessant struggle to make England listen to the "word / Wisest," to Christ, the Logos, to whom he was giving his very life. For as the Empire grew, Hopkins was learning, it was also becoming more and more unchristian.

Both the political and theological themes interact in the second quatrain, and there is an illuminating passage in a letter to Patmore which sheds light on Hopkins' Christocentric vision of Empire:

I remark that those Englishmen who wish prosperity to the Empire (which is not all Englishmen or Britons, strange to say) speak of the Empire's mission to extend freedom and civilisation in India and elsewhere. The greater the scale of politics the weightier the influence of a great name and a high ideal. It is a terrible element of weakness that now we are not well provided with the name and ideal which would recommend and justify our Empire. . . . Then there is [the Empire's gift of] civilisation. It shd. have been Catholic truth. That is the end of Empires before God, to be Catholic and draw nations into their Catholicism. But our Empire is less and less Christian as it grows. . . . It is good to be in Ireland to hear how enemies, and those rhetoricians, can treat the things that are unquestioned at home.[31]

But at least Hopkins had been in England, at Roehampton, in Wales, in London, at Stonyhurst; even in the industrial midlands near Manchester or in the North, at Liverpool and Glasgow, he was on his native soil. Then, in January 1884, he was elected to a fellowship at the Royal University of Ireland in Dublin; his duties were to examine students from all over Ireland in the classics for the B.A. degree. Simultaneously he was placed on the faculty of University College, Dublin, to teach Latin and Greek. And this separation from his homeland, which meant intimate contact with a growingly nationalistic and anti-British people, added a new loneliness to the limbo of his existence. "I am in Ireland now; now I am at a third / Remove."

"We have enemies here—indeed what is Ireland but an open or secret war of fierce enmities of every sort?—and our College is really struggling for existence with difficulties within and without," he complains to his mother. And a little over three months later he sighs that "the grief of mind I go through over politics, over what I read and hear and see in Ireland and about England, is such that I can neither express it nor bear to speak of it. . . . They are crying some bad news in the streets. All news is bad."[32] What particu-

---

[31] *Letters III*, p. 367.

[32] Letters to his mother of November 26, 1884, and March 2, 1885, *ibid.*, pp. 163 and 170. Hopkins' sense of honesty and justice eventually made him realize that if Ireland was a state of smoldering rebellion, England's arrogant aloofness was largely to blame. "[It] was felt with reason that to the royal family Ireland owes little gratitude," Hopkins told his mother on May 17, 1885, about Queen Victoria's recently concluded visit. "The Queen, who spends months every year in Scotland, does she not? or did once, has only thrice in all her reign visited Ireland and never lived there. But do not let us talk politics, it kills me, especially under the present Prime Minister [Gladstone]" (*ibid.*, p.

larly galled Hopkins was that in his position there was nothing he could do, for many of his coreligionists and his students were Irish nationalists. All that was left for him was to pray for Ireland and for himself as a professor of classics in Dublin. "Ask his help," he writes in his meditation notes for March 17, 1885, the Feast of St. Patrick. "Ask his help for Ireland in all its needs and for yourself in your position." [33]

In line ten the delayed *volta* appears: "Not but in all removes I can / Kind love both give and get." Hopkins is never whining; he can, in the deepest gloom, keep his judgment clear. There are always those of his "kind" who will give him "kind" love. And the one who really matters, Christ, is with him no matter where he goes. The ability to get and receive love is not what troubles Hopkins so much. The source of his own inner life is felt here in this sonnet. The trouble is without, in his relations to those around him:

> Only what word
>
>   Wisest my heart breeds dark heaven's baffling ban
>   Bars or hell's spell thwarts. This to hoard unheard,
>   Heard unheeded, leaves me a lonely began.

This is the cry of a priest whose life seems outwardly to have been spent in vain. There may be a reference here to his poetry or to his many "beginnings of things, ever so many, which it seems to me might well have been done, ruins and wrecks." [34] But the "word / Wisest" is the Word of God, the Christian message. He has tried to give freely and without stint to others what had been the transforming experience of his life, the "word / Wisest." Christ—who, one would have thought, would benefit by the spread of his Kingdom—has

171). Hopkins more and more came to believe in home rule for Ireland as the only realistic solution to the growing clamor by the nationalists for freedom. But for Hopkins it was a solution based on a weariness with an intolerable situation.   [33] *Sermons*, p. 260.

[34] Letter to Baillie of April 24–May 17, 1885, *Letters III*, p. 255. This reference is almost certainly contemporary with the sonnet.

apparently checked the priest. And the frustration is not so much that *he* has been checked as that Christ's work does not go forward. His own family, for whom he must have prayed constantly, did not hear his "word," nor did his friends Bridges or Dixon or Baillie or, years earlier, Urquhart. In fact, there is no hard evidence that Hopkins ever felt he had been the triggering action for even one convert. Yet conversions are what he wished for all his life.

Hopkins sees himself as one "hoarding" up treasures which he would gladly share with others, but he remains unheard.[35] And when he is heard his words go unheeded, for men are turned to their own self-bent. "My Liverpool and Glasgow experience laid upon my mind a conviction . . . of the degradation even of our race, of the hollowness of this century's civilisation: it made even life a burden to me to have daily thrust upon me the things I saw." [36] In the last line Hopkins does not, as Bridges suggests, mean "leaves me a lonely [one who only] began." [37] Hopkins has not omitted a relative pronoun. He is here making "began" a substantive and thus inscaping his whole sacerdotal life as one who *is* a "lonely began." He is not simply a beginner; the curve of his action is relegated to the past, to what had seemed such a brilliant prologue in his years in Wales. But the intermittent years of service in the field, as he himself deepened in his understanding and love of Christ, do not seem to have resulted in any spiritual fruit in those he had been sent to work with. He is caught in a self-imprisoned past action ("a lonely began"), like a cob of ripe corn imprisoned in its own

[35] Hopkins had a passion for explaining, as he himself said. And in those few letters where Bridges or Dixon asked him to gloss a difficult passage from the Gospels or to explain the meaning of the tertianship, for example, his genius for clarity, intellectual precision, earnestness, and charity is readily apparent. In a way it is sad that so many of his finest religious insights were directed to loose sheets of paper and left scattered among his "wrecks" of things.

[36] Letter to Dixon of December 1, 1881, *Letters II*, p. 97.

[37] *Poems*, p. 289.

husk, unable to spread its own seeds and steadily losing its own vitality.

The stark, bare, straightforward style of this poem, together with the delayed *volta* in the tenth line, shows the influence of Milton and, according to Hopkins himself, of Dryden. "My style tends always more towards Dryden," he tells Bridges in late 1887. "What is there in Dryden? Much, but above all this: he is the most masculine of our poets; his style and his rhythms lay the strongest stress of all our literature on the naked thew and sinew of the English language." [38] There are few poetic experiments in this and the following sonnets. Besides the verbal substantive of line fourteen, there is the break of "wear- / y" in lines 7 and 8, which acts to draw out the word and to imitate the speaker's weariness in getting the word out. What helps make the word-break successful, however, is that Hopkins duplicates the chime of "hear / Me" in "wear- / y," carrying the rhyme into the following line and thus making a double rhyme. "I am sure I have gone far enough in oddities and running rhymes (as even in some late sonnets you have not seen) into the next line," [39] he tells Bridges in February 1887. But it is an oddity only in relation to the starkness of the sonnet as a whole.

The style fits the stark, somber colloquy between Hopkins and Christ. Christ is not once mentioned in the poem, but the very tone of the entire sonnet group becomes increasingly personal: it is the voice of one speaking to a very dear, close, and sympathetic listener. The sonnet in fact becomes more and more a prayer form, a personal talk between the priest and his God.

In *I wake and feel the fell of dark,* the shadows have deepened and the loneliness of the speaker has intensified to exclude Christ, who "lives alas! away." The rhythm of *To seem the stranger* is counterpointed, but here the rhythm is

[38] *Letters I,* pp. 267–268.   [39] *Ibid.,* p. 250.

freer and sprung in places. There is a greater sense of anxiety and even that sense of fear experienced by a lost child. The speaker awakens from his broken sleep with a start to feel the palpable presence of darkness on him: "I wake and feel the fell of dark, not day." Several meanings of "fell" are operative here. First, it is the past tense of fall used substantively. Night has already fallen; the process is complete. That night of the soul which Hopkins accepted but feared in *Spelt from Sibyl's Leaves,* that night which "whélms, whélms, ánd will end us" has come. Second, night is seen as a fell, or desolate moor, similar to Dante's *selva oscura* in the opening of the *Inferno.* Again, night smothers him like the skin of some animal. And finally, the adjectival meaning of "fell" as fierce, cruel, or deadly, used substantively here, is probably also implied and certainly fits. It is that "intense darkness which one can feel" (Exodus 10:21) which was the ninth visitation of God's wrath upon the Egyptians.

The speaker addresses his inmost self, his heart:

> What hours, O what black hoürs we have spent
> This night! what sights you, heart, saw; ways you went!
> And more must, in yet longer light's delay.

The blackness and terror of the seemingly unending night have revealed to the speaker a new and nameless night within. And the worst is not yet over, for although the speaker knows that light *must* come, that light seems purposely to linger. The images here are fundamental and basic: light and darkness, day and night. They represent God's disappearance and the terror of the soul that realizes its complete dependence upon Him. But they also represent God's eventual return in His own good time.

"There are three principal reasons why we are in desolation," St. Ignatius writes:

The first is because we are tepid, slothful, or negligent in our Spiritual Exercises, and so through our own fault spiritual consolation is withdrawn from us. The second is that God may try us to test our worth, and the progress that we have made in His service and praise when we are without such generous rewards of consolation and special graces. The third is that He may wish to give us a true knowledge and understanding, so that we may truly perceive that it is not within our power to acquire or retain great devotion, ardent love, tears, or any other spiritual consolation, but that all of this is a gift and grace of God our Lord. Nor does God wish us to claim as our own what belongs to another, allowing our intellect to rise up in a spirit of pride or vainglory, attributing to ourselves the devotion or other aspects of spiritual consolation.[40]

It is this last point which most concerns Hopkins because it deals with his essential self and his growing realization that apart from God he was nothing, a mere "Jackself," a "scaffold of score brittle bones," as he wrote in his powerful sonnet *The shepherd's brow* only two months before he died.

Hopkins insists, as he had in *The Wreck of the Deutschland,* that what he is saying is autobiographical and absolutely true: "With witness I speak this." But what happened on one particular night happened, with varying degrees of intensity, over a much longer period. On the other hand, that one night seemed to last for years. Time itself becomes warped and plastic here; the subjective stress on the speaker and not the external regularity of any chronometer counts for the experience of time.

> But where I say
> Hours I mean years, mean life. And my lament
> Is cries countless, cries like dead letters sent
> To dearest him that lives alas! away.

The image of "dead letters" is a nightmarish simile which is unsettlingly modern; the speaker pictures himself as a lover sending love letters to his beloved who has left no forwarding address. The lines of communication are cut, and the countless letters pile up unread to gather dust in

[40] Mattola (trans.), *op. cit.,* p. 131.

some dead-letter bin. It is up to "dearest him" to send the speaker news of his whereabouts; in the meantime all the speaker can do is wait. This sense of frustration in being totally unable to act leads logically to the *volta* at the beginning of line 9. Metaphor replaces simile, as the speaker *becomes* what he is conscious of feeling within him; he is a bitter taste, a burning.

> I am gall, I am heartburn. God's most deep decree
> Bitter would have me taste: my taste was me;
> Bones built in me, flesh filled, blood brimmed the curse.
>
> Selfyeast of spirit a dull dough sours. I see
> The lost are like this, and their scourge to be
> As I am mine, their sweating selves; but worse.

God's seeming withdrawal has left the speaker with himself, his innermost being. The paeans which Hopkins had so often sung to the selves of a sprawling, diverse creation dwindle into stark, groaning pains when he looks at his own poor self apart from the sustaining force of God.

"Searching nature," he writes during his retreat in late August 1880, "I taste self but at one tankard, that of my own being." That awareness of oneself, of "my selfbeing, my consciousness and feeling of myself, that taste of myself, of I and me above and in all things, . . . is more distinctive than the taste of ale or alum, more distinctive than the smell of walnutleaf or camphor, and is incommunicable by any means to another man." And a few pages later in his retreat notes he stresses the bitterness of his self-taste: "I have and every other has, as said above, my own knowledge and powers, pleasures, pains, merit, guilt, shame, dangers, fortunes, fates: we are not chargeable for one another. But these things and above all my shame, my guilt, my fate are the very things in feeling, in tasting, which . . . nothing in the world can match." [41]

Hopkins had first written "my self-stuff" for "Selfyeast of

[41] *Sermons*, pp. 123, 125.

spirit." The new phrase is more felicitous, but the earlier also tells. Yeast pressed into kneaded dough raises the whole loaf, making it lighter and tastier. But selfyeast only puffs up and sours. The image of preparing bread is used several times in both the Gospels and in the Pauline Epistles. For example, there is this from I Corinthians 5:7–8, used in the Epistle for Easter Day: "Purge out the old leaven, that you may be a new paste, as you are unleavened. For Christ our pasch is sacrificed. Therefore let us feast, not with the old leaven, nor with the leaven of malice and wickedness, but with the unleavened bread of sincerity and truth." St. Paul bids us to become the unleavened bread, the matzo of the Feast of Passover, made without yeast, and to purge ourselves of our self-yeast which sours the whole being. But Hopkins can do nothing by himself except realize the curse of self-loathing which brims up within.

This self-imprisonment, Hopkins says, is what hell must be like, for hell is only incidentally, as he explains in *Spelt from Sibyl's Leaves,* the stress of fire. Hell is essentially a living with what one has really chosen in place of one's Creator, to live chained for all time to one's self. As the choice of Dante's Paolo and Francesca for one another over God ends in their being intertwined forever, so the fate of the lost for Hopkins is to have to taste at one tankard forever their sweating selves. "Sweating" is Hopkins' inscape for the self deprived of God. There is the acute, pungent odor of living with one's own sweat, generated by one's own uncomfortable heat. God is He whom Hopkins asks in *Thou art indeed just, Lord* to "send my roots rain," and He is, in *The Wreck of the Deutschland,* "A released shower." And when God is removed, the only waters which the self can of itself produce are the stinking, salt-bitter drops of sweat.

Hopkins is intensely aware of the hell of isolation within. But he is also intensely honest; as bad as he feels his condition to be, it is limited by what a man can suffer before his very body short-circuits itself. But the bodiless souls of the lost do not admit this limitation; their suffering is forever.

The theological dimension of this melancholy desolation was better understood by the forty-year-old Jesuit, but the attacks of melancholy themselves were a habitual recurrence. "I had a nightmare that night . . . ," the twenty-nine-year-old Hopkins wrote in his journal.

The feeling is terrible: the body no longer swayed as a piece by the nervous and muscular instress seems to fall in and hang like a dead weight on the chest. . . . It made me think that this was how the souls in hell would be imprisoned in their bodies as in prisons and of what St. Theresa says of the 'little press in the wall' where she felt herself to be in her vision.[42]

Earlier in that same month, completely depressed and fagged, he complained that "nature in all her parcels and faculties gaped and fell apart, *fatiscebat,* like a clod cleaving and holding only by strings of root. But," he noted with resignation, "this must often be." [43]

And again, in the notes Hopkins kept of his eight-day retreat in January 1889, there is the following echo of the sestet of the sonnet: "Jan. 2—This morning I made the meditation on the Three Sins, with nothing to enter but loathing of my life and a barren submission to God's will. The body cannot rest when it is in pain nor the mind be at peace as long as something bitter distills in it and it aches. This may be at any time and is at many." [44]

The lowest pit of desolation and inner torment is touched

[42] Journal entry for September 18, 1873, *Journals,* p. 238. The passage which St. Theresa wrote in her *Autobiography* to describe her vision of hell etched itself upon Hopkins' consciousness like acid, for he recalls another passage from this section during his long retreat in 1881. The lost soul sees the moral scapes of its actions, although it is in the blackness of utter confusion. This gives a meaning to "something I remember in St. Theresa's vision of hell, to this effect: 'I know not how it is, but in spite of the darkness the eye sees there all that to see is most afflicting' " (*Sermons,* p. 138) .   [43] *Journals,* p. 236.

[44] *Sermons,* p. 262. See also Hopkins' comment in his somewhat Joycean meditation on hell about "the worm of conscience, which is the mind gnawing and feeding on its own most miserable self" (*ibid.,* p. 243) .

in *No worst, there is none.* Here there is no relief, no escape except to wish for escape in death or in the temporary truce afforded by sleep. Here Hopkins, with the awareness of his own unworthiness before God and tortured beyond his endurance, comes closest to accepting the comfort of despair. He wishes for a cessation to his torments, although not, I think, for annihilation. God here seems to have forsaken Hopkins and Hopkins can do nothing but cling to the walls of the steep cliff. The poem is intensely honest and intensely painful. And while Bridges thought that *Carrion Comfort* was probably the sonnet Hopkins told him in May was "written in blood," *No worst, there is none* was probably meant.[45] For in this sonnet alone there is no hope, no underlying comfort for the speaker in knowing that he is suffering with a purpose, as he realizes in *Carrion Comfort*. The poem is all darkness.

The poet startles us with the intensity of his unnamed experience: "No worst, there is none." Hopkins employs the superlative "worst" rather than the comparative. He has touched bottom: "Pitched past pitch of grief, / More pangs will, schooled at forepangs, wilder wring." Hopkins, like a violin string, is strung tighter to play at the higher, more piercing and metallic tone of grief. "Pitch" for Hopkins is the distinctive self, and in man this pitch is the most distinctive, most highly strung or stressed of everything in the world. "Nothing else in nature comes near this unspeakable stress of pitch, distinctiveness, and selving, this self-being of my own."[46] The pitching of the speaker, then, racks the whole being, hurling him even beyond grief.

[45] Boyle argues "that No. 65 is the poem 'written in blood.' . . . [Certainly] the octet of No. 64 deals with ultimate spiritual desolation and trial, when Hopkins, like St. Alphonsus, is left with nothing but the refusal of his consent. . . . But in the sestet . . . the light breaks. . . . There is no such relief in No. 65. Here . . . the only comfort that appears is that the pain can't last forever because the weak wretch who suffers must both sleep and die" (Boyle, p. 152).

[46] *Sermons*, p. 123. Furthermore, God is also a Self of an infinitely higher pitch than man, who shapes man toward his own particular

But what grief? The grief itself is unstated, and Yvor Winters sees this outpouring of intense emotion over the nameless as a major flaw in the poem. Not that the grief need be stated, for the pain has the unmistakable ring of authenticity. Nevertheless, the affliction is "a chief- / Woe, world-sorrow"; it is Hopkins' terrifying realization that man, rebellious creature, is unworthy of God's concern. In strict justice, the spiritual syphilis passed on from generation to generation, the "world-sorrow" of sin in both the first parents and in Hopkins, is enough to separate him forever from God. The "cliffs of fall / Frightful" may also refer to man's original Fall and severance from God.

There is no comfort or relief now; the Spirit does not come as a gentle dove, but as the terrible blasting Pentecostal wind which cleanses away the dross of the soul. In two sprung lines the speaker almost admonishes the Blessed Virgin and the Comforter, who is Christ as well as the Holy Spirit, for not coming to his aid:

> Comforter, where, where is your comforting?
> Mary, mother of us, where is your relief?

> My cries heave, herds-long; huddle in a main, a chief-
> woe, world-sorrow; on an age-old anvil wince and sing—
> Then lull, then leave off. Fury had shrieked "No ling-
> ering! Let me be fell: force I must be brief."

All of Hopkins' anguished and "countless" cries coalesce around "a chief- / woe" like frightened sheep gathering closer together, so that their individual cries blend into one general confused woe. His cries are like the shrill metallic ring of searing metal being molded on an anvil, only the

---

pitch or stress of self: "For human nature, being more highly pitched, selved, and distinctive than anything in the world, can have been developed, evolved, condensed, from the vastness of the world not anyhow or by the working of common powers but only by one of finer or higher pitch and determination than itself and certainly than any that elsewhere we see, for this power had to force forward the starting or stubborn elements to the one pitch required" (*ibid.*, pp. 122–123).

heated metal is the speaker himself instressed with the transforming fire of God, whose hammer pounds the kinks from
the twisted shape. "With an anvil-ding / And with fire in
him forge thy will," Hopkins had asked of God almost
ten years before in *The Wreck of the Deutschland*. Now the
reality of that metaphor comes home to the poet.

The pain has its duration, and the curve of pain drops
away sharply, leaving a dull, throbbing sensation. Fury realizes that its attacks must be swift and intense. And the curve
of its attack and withdrawal is wonderfully caught in the
hyphenation of "ling- / ering." The sharpness of the first
syllable catches up the reserve of pain associated with the
other chime words, "wring" and "sing." In "ling- / ering"
itself, the chime of the third syllable echoes the pain of the
first, but the lack of a stress on the last syllable gives the
impression of a dying away. "Fell" in line 8 has, of course,
the same complexity of meanings which that word had in *I
wake and feel the fell of dark*. But in its verbal connotations
it seems to join with the preceding "be" to become "Let me
befell." Fury does not say "Let me befall," for as soon as we
are aware that the pain has come, its intensity has already
passed by. The terrible thing, however, is that Fury's drive is
recurrent and insistent. "And worse I may be yet," Edgar
says in *King Lear;* "the worst is not / So long as we can say
'This is the worst' " (IV, i, 27–28) .[47]

[47] Gardner (I, 178 ff.) holds that the underthought of the entire
sonnet comes from *King Lear*. The dark horror and madness of Lear
make an appropriate mirror image for the desolate, self-tormented
speaker of this sonnet. Sr. Mary Humiliata, in her "Hopkins and the
Prometheus Myth" (*PMLA*, LXX [1955], 58–68) says that "the Prometheus myth constitutes a source for the total body of images in Sonnet
65," and points to Hopkins' careful reading of Bridges' *Prometheus the
Firegiver* at the same time that the sonnet was probably composed. No
doubt there are echoes of the Prometheus figure in the sonnet, but
Gardner's reading seems to hit closer to the mark. Ritz balances the
relative weight of these two literary influences this way: "If, as is likely,
Hopkins was thinking more about the fate of Prometheus than about

In the sestet there is no turn in the argument. Rather, the speaker meditates on the bitter fruit of his ordeal: no man has plumbed the depths and heights of his own interior world. Those who have never experienced the terror within will dismiss this anguish as histrionics; those who have experienced the anguish need no explanation:

> O the mind, mind has mountains; cliffs of fall
> Frightful, sheer, no-man-fathomed. Hold them cheap
> May who ne'er hung there. Nor does long our small
> Durance deal with that steep or deep. . . .

The self is likened to a mountain climber clinging desperately to a steep mountainside, unable to see either to the top above or to the bottom below. He is powerless to move while the strong "whirlwind" threatens to unhinge him. Hopkins is left with only the barren submission of his will to God's will, with the will to keep on clinging, for to let go would be despair.

He can only take whatever small comfort is available and despise his weakness for doing so:

> Here! creep,
> Wretch, under a comfort serves in a whirlwind: all
> Life death does end and each day dies with sleep.

Like the terrified mountain climber who crawls into a mountain crevice as the winds blast against him, Hopkins can only crawl under his bedsheets and hope for a dreamless sleep and temporary cessation from pain. The only comfort lies in the realization that all life comes to an end in death, and so must his. And every day "dies with sleep." The "all" of line 13 seems ambiguous, and yet it is crucial to a correct understanding of the sestet. Since it receives a stress, it seems to mean that with death there is total annihilation:

Lear's when he wrote the poem, the tone and the style nevertheless recall Shakespeare, because both have the same density, the same starkness" (Ritz, p. 603).

> ´
> . . . all
> ´   ´
> Life death does end . . . .

But while an argument might be made for such an interpretation, it does not square with what we know of Hopkins. The line more likely means that since death is a part of every life, then the speaker cannot suffer forever. Hopkins became increasingly weary of life, even at times to wishing for death, but he never seems to have surrendered himself to despairing of God's mercy, as the speaker does not let go and fall into despair here. "I do not feel then that outwardly I do much good," Hopkins admitted near the end of his life, "much that I care to do or can much wish to prosper; and this is a mournful life to lead. In thought I can of course divide the good from the evil and live for the one, not the other: this justifies me but it does not alter the facts. . . . I wish then for death." [48]

The whirlwind or tempest is a rich symbol for the activity of God upon man. Suffering Job answers Baldad the Sueite's taunting about why he, Job, remains patient before God:

If I appealed to him and he answered my call,
I could not believe that he would hearken to my words;
With a tempest he might overwhelm me, and multiply my
     wounds without cause   [Job 9:16–18].

But it is also the whirlwind (*spiritus,* spirit, wind) which preceded the tongues of fire that rested besides the disciples of Christ, the fire of the Comforter at Pentecost: "And suddenly there came a sound from heaven, as of a violent wind [*spiritus*] blowing, and it filled the whole house where they were sitting" (Acts 2:2–3). And while God is One and his powers complementary, the speaker is aware of only the first manifestation of God's power, the terrifying whirlwind. The speaker manifests only incomprehensibility and terror

[48] *Sermons,* p. 262.

at the Holy Spirit's intimate workings on him. The terrible irony, of course, is that the speaker tries to hide from his Comforter and to seek out a more cowardly comfort, but one, at least, which his animal fear can understand.

The sonnet implies a cyclical repetition of Fury's assault. The first quatrain describes the impending attack of Fury and the absence of any spiritual relief. The second quatrain presents the last attack of Fury so vividly that something of its pain is recreated. Finally, in the sestet, in place of any spiritual relief, which must come from without as a gift of God, the speaker ("Wretch") settles for the comforting thought that even these pangs cannot last forever, as he tries to hide from the "Fury" of God. Nevertheless, there is the hypertensive expectation of still another onslaught of the storm.

Carrion Comfort shows Hopkins' pertinacity in willing at least not to despair and to weld his free will to the will of God. Here, finally, light begins to shine through, and God's handling of the speaker at last becomes more readily discernible both to the speaker and to us, as the age-old pattern of desolation followed by consolation and illumination crystallizes. The speaker has maintained his desire to do God's will; however weak and sterile that fiat might seem, it is all he has managed to salvage from "the war within."

Defying the "carrion comfort" of despair which has been proffered him, the speaker resists the powerful temptation to go slack, to fall apart, and to cease to care any longer. The emphatic downbeat on the first syllable and the three repetitions of this "not" in the first eleven words stress the will's refusal to capitulate to the enemy. The roping imagery of "untwist," "slack," and "strands" makes it quite possible that there is a pun on "not." This is quite striking when the poem is read aloud, as Hopkins' poetry should be. He will not untwist; he will *knot* the strands which keep him a man, no matter how tired he is. "Can," which occurs three times, is here the effective reversal of "not," and the quatrain ends with an emphatic yet humble double negative which stresses the final negation of "not":

> Not, I'll not, carrion comfort, Despair, not feast on thee;
> Not untwist—slack they may be—these last strands of man
> In me ór, most weary, cry *I can no more.* I can;
> Can something, hope, wish day come, not choose not to be.

The rhyme words of the first quatrain are particularly important, for "thee" (despair) is essentially the choice of "not to be"; and what assures the continuation of the speaker as a "man" is his ability as a free agent and his choice of continuing to say he "can."

As one critic has pointed out recently, Hopkins' first quatrain may be consciously repudiating Newman's *The Dream of Gerontius.*[49] Gerontius, the "old man," is in his death agony, lying in bed and surrounded by those praying for his soul. As the tide of death overwhelms him, Gerontius can only gasp,

> I can no more; for now it comes again,
> That sense of ruin, which is worse than pain,
> That masterful negation and collapse
> Of all that makes me man; as though I bent
> Over the dizzy brink
> Of some sheer infinite descent   [ll. 107–112].

Hopkins refuses to untwist "these last strands," for as long as he is man he can at least refuse to give his consent to annihilation; Newman's position seems to suggest a more passive state in which the soul dissolves with a whimper before the oncoming flood of darkness. But Hopkins' will is more stubborn. The responsibility to "not choose not to be" cannot be surrendered; death is the surrender of the body only, not of the self.

[49] Brian Vickers, "Hopkins and Newman," *Times Literary Supplement,* March 3, 1966, p. 178.

The second quatrain opens with the speaker abruptly directing a string of four questions to a second addressee who is called only "terrible" and who combines the power and terror of the lion and the tempest. The questions at once show the anger of someone deeply frightened, something of the erotic admiration for a champion (especially in the triple sighs), and a pervading tone of respectful awe. God is a herculean contender who rudely rocks the speaker, a contender powerful enough to wring the entire universe and keep it under his sway. Like a victorious lion over its prey, he seems to rock his still-living victim contemptuously back and forth with his foot. There is no rebellion now, no movement that would bring the foot crashing down. The verbal action of rocking back and forth is continued in the sifting action of fanning the wheat, as the hot summer wind burns through the speaker who lies now completely passive to the Winnower.

"I will reign over you with a strong hand," Yahweh tells his people, "and with a stretched out arm, and with fury poured out. . . . And I will bring you into the wilderness of people, and there will I plead with you face to face" (Ezechiel 20:33, 35). But it is God's foot which rolls the supine wrestler back and forth in that ring-world ("wring-world") of the wrestlers. The "darksome devouring eyes" of God have the qualities of a terrible, awesome power, but they are also the eyes of a passionate lover. For God's single love manifests itself to man as man can best cope with it.[50] Hopkins admits his terror in feeling God's searing love; rebel and coward that he is, he would "avoid thee and flee."

The *volta* comes in line 9 with the one-syllable question so simply asked yet so profoundly answered: "Why? That my chaff might fly; my grain lie, sheer and clear." Using one of the metaphors which Christ himself frequently employed, Hopkins realizes that his ordeal has been fraught with mean-

[50] See *The Wreck of the Deutschland*, I, 9.

ing, a meaning that is glimpsed only when his will has submitted to that ordeal.[51] Hopkins' nonessential concerns have been burned away and the essential self remains purged, "sheer and clear"; the *arbitrium,* the will of the self, is coiled more intimately with the self of God.

Speaking of Christ under the figure of the Winnower, Hopkins wrote in his last retreat in January 1889 that Christ

baptises with breath and fire, as wheat is winnowed in the wind and sun [tempest and fire], and uses . . . a fan that thoroughly and forever parts the wheat from the chaff. . . . The grain is either scooped into this or thrown in by another, then tossed out against the wind, and this vehement action St. John compares to his own repeated 'dousing' or affusion [in his baptism of water]. The separation it makes is very visible too: the grain lies heaped on one side, the chaff blows away the other, between them the winnower stands; after that nothing is more combustible than the chaff, and yet the fire he [Christ] calls unquenchable.[52]

But Almighty God is seen as other figures: besides the lion and the wind, he is the wrestler, the hero, the giant; he is a python, strength-giving water, the rod, and the hand of a master which Hopkins, like a thankful servant, kisses. The ambivalence of the speaker's feeling, oscillating between terror and fawning, is admirably caught in the nervous, staccato alternating exclamations and questionings. Both the Adversary and the mortal speaker dissolve and crystallize into protean shapes on the wrestling-threshing floor; this metamorphosis approximates the speaker's attempt to present the dynamic, blurred violence within:

Nay in all that toil, that coil, since (seems) I kissed the rod,
Hand rather, my heart lo! lapped strength, stole joy, would laugh, chéer.

[51] See *ibid.,* II, 31: "is the shipwrack then a harvest, does tempest carry the grain for thee?" Also cf. *The Starlight Night:* "These are indeed the barn; withindoors house / The shocks."
[52] *Sermons,* p. 267–268.

Cheer whom though? The hero whose heaven-handling flung me,
    fóot tród
Me? or me that fought him? O which one? is it each one? That
    night, that year
Of now done darkness I wretch lay wrestling with (my God!)
    my God.

It is the paradoxical nature of the religious struggle that
the speaker, in spite of (and yet because of) his sound
thumping, has also been victorious, for in finally bending to
God's will he has found himself. In kissing the rod—a sign of
capitulation—he realizes that his freedom is to be found in
becoming God's servant. As he kisses the hand, his heart
drinks in strength and joy and would "laugh, cheer" for the
match in which both God and he are winners.

As the sonnet rounds to an end, the syntax and the
rhythms become surer and more regular, although the metrical outrides give a sense of astonishment and breathlessness.
Furthermore, as the meaning of the struggle assumes its final
shape in the last line, the real nature of the two contenders
becomes clear and fixed: Hopkins, the "wretch," has been
fighting with God, who is only now named.

In his illumination of whom he has been fighting in "That
night, that year / Of now done darkness," he sees that his has
been the privilege of being crucified with Christ, and he
echoes the agonized words of the dying Christ in his "(my
God!) my God." But there is also something of a startled,
shrill whisper as he realizes Who was wrestling in the darkness with him. With the second "my God" there is a sense of
resolution, of fulfillment in submission. "Our hearts will not
rest, O God, until they rest in thee" is the prayer of Hopkins
as well as of St. Augustine.

"One who is in desolation," St. Ignatius tells us in the
eighth of his "Rules for the Discernment of Spirits," "must
strive to persevere in patience, which is contrary to the
vexations that have come upon him. He should consider,
also, that consolation will soon return, and strive diligently

against the desolation." [53] Patience is the virtue which the hypersensitive and fastidious Hopkins had constantly to work hard for. His will, he knew, was imperfectly aligned to God's will. Nearly six years earlier, he had lamented the loss of peace in his curtal sonnet *Peace*. In its place his Lord had left behind "Patience exquisite." But Hopkins had struggled too hard with himself in the interim to use any such delicate epithet now. Patience is now in the terrible sonnet that "hard thing"; in place of the cooing of the wood dove, we now "hear our hearts grate on themselves."

Hopkins realizes wearily what it means even to pray for patience, and in the threefold use of the word in the opening two lines of *Patience, hard thing* there is the sense of endearment, but also the gritty ache as if he were biting on a cinder:

> Patience, hard thing! the hard thing but to pray,
> But bid for, Patience is! Patience who asks
> Wants war, wants wounds; weary his times, his tasks;
> To do without, take tosses, and obey.

Not only is patience a difficult acquisition, but it is extremely difficult even to ask for it. Those who ask are asking for a bitter conflict and suffering within. They are asking for weariness and drudgery for Christ's sake, as Hopkins was constantly harried in having to "examine a nation." One must learn self-abnegation, be buffeted about, and, what seems to become increasingly more difficult, one must learn to give perfect obedience. No wonder, then, that the virtue of patience is not widely understood, is rarely sought, and even more rarely attained.

But unless one has actively sought patience (for it is the paradox of patience that it is a virtue not for the weak but for the heroic and iron-willed) in these things, it cannot be bought. This is the currency with which patience is "bid for"

[53] Mattola (trans.), *op. cit.*, p. 130.

and purchased. In the second quatrain, we see the fruit of patience:

> Rare patience roots in these, and, these away,
> Nowhere. Natural heart's ivy, Patience masks
> Our ruins of wrecked past purpose. There she basks
> Purple eyes and seas of liquid leaves all day.

The difference in tone between the first and second quatrains is distinctive and is meant to be so. One notices in the first quatrain the frequent harsh dentals and full stops, the exclamations, monosyllables, end-stop punctuation, and the sprung lines. These are countered in the second quatrain by the many liquid *l*'s and *r*'s, frequent sibilants, more frequent polysyllables, the relative scarcity of punctuation, and the approximation of a stately prose rhythm reminiscent of Newman.

Patience, like ivy, grows slowly, but it covers over the ruins of our past plans and projects which we had hoped to see realized. Patience, writes Boyle commenting on these lines, "is rooted in pain and endurance; it stays with the suffering heart, wrecked so often in its past high endeavors, and masks the scars." [54] While all one's past lies like a ruined edifice, the lowly ivy dresses up the ruins and imparts to them a serenity and hallowedness. The picture of the purple berries surrounded by the multishaded green ivy, which from a distance look like a rippling sea, is almost Virgilian in its bucolic evocativeness. Hopkins also suggests here the sea change which patience can effect in the tempest-tossed shipwreck of the self.

The two themes of the severity and serenity of patience, so admirably caught in the rhythms of the octet, are repeated in the sestet. The tone of harshness and severity in the first tercet catches the emotional strain the speaker feels in learning that hard thing, patience. But the tone of the final tercet is muted and serene. The argument of the sonnet is starkly

[54] Boyle, p. 114.

clear; each word is a mark of acceptance etched on the speaker's heart. In *Spelt from Sibyl's Leaves* the speaker, painfully confronted with the moral value of his every action, laments that the self-stress working against God's stress creates a terrible friction so that his "thóughts agaínst thoughts ín groans grínd." Here, too, the desire to go against his own natural bent is to hear his very heart grate against itself. To continue the siege upon his heart is to bruise himself more seriously. Yet even so, we do "bid" God to straighten the heart's ways. Hopkins, continuing the auctioneering diction of the opening lines, will bid the dear price necessary to buy patience.

In the final tercet Hopkins uses another bucolic image. The speaker likens the patient man to the prepared crisp honeycombs which the bee, Patience, slowly fills with the honey of "Delicious kindness." This is the increased kindness of God bestowed on the patient man, as well as the growing kindness of the patient man toward others. But unless the walls of the combs are securely firm, "crisp," the honeybee Patience will not fill them. And the way to make them crisp, Hopkins sighs, with a possible pun on "combs" as a verb, "comes those ways we know." Those ways have been mentioned in the first quatrain. There is no other way to gain patience (*patiens* = suffering, and also the Passion of Christ) but by bending (crisp = *crispus* = *curvus* = curved) the stubborn, grotesquely twisted heart to God. Patience, like every other grace, is a gift from God. And written in his Dublin Notebook as a meditation note for the Feast of the Annunciation, March 25, 1885, Hopkins speaks of grace in terms metaphorically similar to those of the final lines of the sonnet. The Blessed Virgin, he notes, "was full of grace, that is / she had received and stored up in her every grace offered and now overflowed in the Son / Christ. So the preparation for grace is grace corresponded with." [55] For Hopkins this

---

[55] *Sermons*, p. 260.

last sentence, like the sonnet on patience, was more than an imaginative exercise in thought. It was a means for transforming himself into the likeness of his Lord.

My own heart let me more have pity on is the last of Hopkins' desolate sonnets of 1885 and it signals Hopkins' awareness that he has been too hard upon his "poor Jackself." [56] The opening quatrain is in the form of a triple imperative to his will to lift the siege on his all-too-human heart. The "let me" formula is repeated and then implied in the third elliptical clause:

> My own heart let me more have pity on; let
> Me live to my sad self hereafter kind,
> Charitable; not live this tormented mind
> With this tormented mind tormenting yet.

The "me" of line 1 is used to signify Hopkins' *arbitrium,* his free will, aspiring at whatever cost toward complete harmony with God. "My own heart," on the other hand, is the natural bent of the self into its own curve of interests. Still, there are not two selves but one with two contrary stresses, and that self which would force itself beyond its endurance ends by simply being a "sad self."

Among the insights of the final lines of the previous sonnet was the realization that kindness would come to the man

---

[56] "There is a way of thinking of past sin," Hopkins had written while making the Third Exercise of the First Week during his retreat at Beaumont Lodge in September 1883, "such that the thought numbs and kills the heart, as all this Week of the Exercises will do if care is not taken in giving it. It does not seem that we are to pray for this, but for that feeling towards past sin which our lady felt or would feel when sins were presented to her and shrunk from them instantaneously and which our Lord . . . , who means us to copy His nature and character as well as we can and put on His mind according to our measure. For they turn from sin by nature (or our Lady as if by nature) and finding it embodied with a thing they love find it infinitely piteous: 'O the pity of it!' and why should it ever have been?—these are the sort of words that express it. So that we may pity ourselves in the same way, that such a thing as sin should ever have got hold of us" (*ibid.,* pp. 134–135).

who was patient. In this sonnet Hopkins literally takes this insight to heart; he is to be more patient with himself, more kind and charitable to himself, and to pity himself for his past sins and imperfections.

"Pray not to be tormented," Hopkins writes in a meditation on the demoniac in St. Matthew.[57] The note is contemporary with his composing of *Spelt from Sibyl's Leaves*. By summer, when Hopkins wrote *My own heart*, the fury of the attack had at last temporarily subsided. But the speaker recalls here that so all-pervasive is his torment that he not only possesses a tormented mind, he lives it. The mind begets torments which yet beget further torments in a cyclical frenzy caught in the triple verbal repetition: "tormented," "tormented," "tormenting."

In the second quatrain the speaker realizes that he is utterly incapable of being the author of his own comfort:

> I cast for comfort I can no more get
> By groping round my comfortless, than blind
> Eyes in their dark can day or thirst can find
> Thirst's all-in-all in all a world of wet.

"Cast" is a key word here;[58] it has the meaning of directing one's eyes in search of something. But it also means that the speaker sends out his thoughts like a pack of hunting dogs in search of a trail. To look within oneself for comfort is an empty task, for the speaker himself is "comfortless," and the epithet has a substantival force. His thoughts can only feel about blindly as they stumble in the interior darkness.

The search is as fruitless, the speaker laments, as blind

---

[57] Entry for January 19, 1885, in meditation notes in *ibid.*, p. 259.

[58] See Boyle's remarks on the imagery of this sonnet in ch. 7, "The Valley of the Shadow," pp. 147–161, but particularly the lucid and exciting opening paragraphs on the "casting" imagery and the substantive force of "comfortless," "blind eyes," and "thirst." Boyle's is certainly a most responsive reading of this sonnet (despite some scholarly meanderings), and of necessity I have had to cover some of my ground in his tracks.

eyes groping around in the darkness within for the day which is without. Or the search is as impossible as thirst's ever being satisfied, although there is a whole world of water which remains exterior to it. There is a pronounced sense of panic in the metaphors Hopkins has chosen to present the futility of the self to comfort oneself. Only the comfort of the Comforter, who is directly addressed in *No worst, there is none*, can bring the speaker what he casts for. For God is as pervasive as the daylight, although the blind man cannot see it. He is as omnipresent as the waters themselves, although thirst can be present in the midst of plenty.

The tone of the hortatory sestet is remarkably tender and kindly cajoling; the speaker addresses his "Jackself," much as St. Francis affectionately referred to his body as his jackass. He "advises" himself to stop probing the darker recesses of his soul and to stop tormenting himself. He has let his thoughts, like a pack of vicious hunting dogs, snipe too long at his poor Jackself, tormenting the poor beast to near madness. There may be here an intentional sardonic parallel between Actaeon turned into a hart and torn apart by his own hunting dogs and the poor, jaded Jackself of Hopkins being internally torn apart by his own tormenting thoughts.

Unless the thoughts which dog the speaker are called off, comfort or consolation will never be able to take hold within. Like the slow, steady growth of patience imaged in the fledgling and the ivy, comfort will not take root unless the soul prepares itself for its reception.[59] "Consolation

---

[59] Ignatius defines spiritual consolation as follows: "I call it consolation when the soul is aroused by an interior movement which causes it to be inflamed with love of its Creator and Lord, and consequently can love no created thing on the face of the earth for its own sake, but only in the creator of all things. It is likewise consolation when one sheds tears inspired by love of the Lord, whether it be sorrow for sins or because of the Passion of Christ our Lord, or for any other reason that is directly connected to His service and praise. Finally, I call consolation any increase of faith, hope, and charity and any interior joy that calls and attracts to heavenly things, and to the salvation of one's soul,

should be our normal state and . . . when God withdraws it he wishes us to strive to recover it/. Cf. 'da nobis in eodem Spiritu recta sapere et *de ejus semper consolatione gaudere*'" (Grant us through the same Spirit a right judgment and help us to rejoice always in his consolation), Hopkins wrote during his tertianship.[60] The priest must prepare himself for the graces of consolation, which will come from without in God's own time and in God's own place and meted out with God's own measure ("size"). The colloquial phrasing emphasizes the intimacy between the speaker and his self, which almost touches on good-natured swearing in "God knows what."

The consolation ("smile") of God is likened to the sudden appearance of the pied, dappled skies breaking through the overcast heavens between two mountains like a pie wedge, lighting up a "lovely mile" on the pilgrim's journey. The largeness and bountifulness of God's consolation are reflected in the macrocosmic terms of the simile—"skies," "mountains," "mile"—and are contrasted with the smallness, darkness, and thirst of the self. The wedge of light between the mountains also suggests God's enormous smile, which, when it comes, is completely disproportionate to what was reasonably expected. "[We] want a light shed on our way and a happiness spread over our life," [61] Hopkins wrote near the beginning of his last retreat. And that light, which is the consolation of God, when it breaks through the gloom, shines without stinting:

Even natural "consolation" or good spirits come and go without any discoverable reason and certainly God *could* make us most happy without our knowing what we were happy about, though of course the mind would then turn with pleasure to any, the first pious thought that came, as its object. . . . But the greater

inspiring it with peace and quiet in Christ our Lord" (Mattola [trans.], *op. cit.*, pp. 129–130).

[60] *Sermons*, p. 205. As Devlin notes, the Latin is from the Collect for Whitsunday. [61] *Ibid.*, p. 262.

the disproportion [between what is expected and what is given]
the greater the likelihood of the consolation being from God.[62]

Significantly, to find in Hopkins' sonnets a cousin to this
sacramental image of God's smile flashing between the
mountains in the valley of the shadows, we must go back
almost eight years to *Hurrahing in Harvest* of September
1877, with its vision of God's shoulder wedged between the
hills, upholding his world. For while some of the sonnets of
1879 and 1880 inscape the distinctive selves of places and
men, the vision of God in nature belongs uniquely to the
sonnets written in the springtime world of Wales, just as
much as the terrible sonnets are a product of the "winter-
world" of Dublin. And even the image of light breaking
through the mountains recalls "dark Maenefa the mountain" of northern Wales rather than the terrain of Dublin.

The sonnets of desolation, conceived and written in an
appropriate secretive darkness, are the literary remains of a
time of intense mental anguish which most of us can only
imagine, in which there are few lights and even the lettering
on the road signs is in a different language. Road maps
usually make poor literature because their purposes are utilitarian rather than aesthetic. But the seven sonnets of desolation, admired by so many readers for so many different
reasons, are most clearly read by following the map of St.
Ignatius' *Spiritual Exercises*. With this guide for the way, it
is clear that Hopkins, like Dante before him, was going
down profound depths only to go upward toward God.

During that same first fall and early winter which he spent
in Dublin and which formed the setting for his dark *Spelt
from Sibyl's Leaves,* Hopkins was again busy on his projected tragedy, *St. Winefred's Well.* In the so-called Dublin
Notebook there are a number of rough drafts of the opening
of Caradoc's soliloquy, dating from October and November

[62] *Ibid.,* p. 207, from notes made in the long retreat.

1884. Exactly five years before, Hopkins had been inspired by the idea of writing a short verse drama in two or three acts about the martyrdom of the Welsh virgin St. Winefred at the hands of the chieftain Caradoc and of her miraculous restoration to life through the intercession of her uncle, St. Beuno.[63] But even though he told Bridges in 1879 that he hoped to be able to send him the murder scene and some others in a short time, it appears that he was not equal to the task of generating the necessary dark passion for Caradoc's pure evil. Lack of firsthand experience with the profound darknesses in man was the reason why the central portion of the play could not go forward.

And lack of dramatic experience was the reason why the drama itself could not get on, for only in the first ten lines of the opening scene does Hopkins bring two characters together on the stage; the rest of the fragments are dramatic soliloquies. *The Leaden Echo and the Golden Echo* is a choral lyric; there is here what amounts to a ritualistic strophe and antistrophe, statement and counterstatement, without any dramatic interaction. He wrote to Bridges:

I seem to find myself, after some experiment, equal to the more stirring and critical parts of the action, which are in themselves the more important, but about the filling in and minor parts I am not sure how far my powers will go. I have for one thing so little varied experience. In reading Shakespeare one feels with despair the scope and richness of his gifts, equal to everything; he had besides sufficient experience of life and, of course, practical knowledge of the theatre.[64]

Practical knowledge of the theater never came, but his years spent in the confessional and in visiting the sick, dying, and dead in Liverpool and Manchester, together with the nervous exhaustion from which he was more and more suffering and the spiritual dryness which came with the twilight months of his first autumn in Dublin, registered a profound

---

[63] See *Letters I,* p. 92.   [64] *Ibid.,* pp. 92–93.

impact upon him. They gave him that "sufficient experience of life" and an insight into the nature of evil which he was able to translate into the powerful soliloquy of Caradoc. Like Browning, however, Hopkins is a lyric poet. And Hopkins' own tensions and frustrations are the materials out of which the soliloquy is generated. During this time Hopkins was uttering frequent cries of not being able to do anything creative, of being time's eunuch; but at the same time he realized that this acidity was God's will. "Providentiae nostrae incertae et non est in homine via ejus" (What Providence holds for us is uncertain, for God's ways are not open to man), he wrote Bridges in May 1885.[65] With what brilliant but painful insight Hopkins could write about that perverse ecstasy of being endlessly frustrated:

To hunger and not have, yét | hope ón for, to storm and strive and
Be at every assault fresh foiled, | worse flung, deeper disappointed,
The turmoil and the torment, | it has, I swear, a sweetness,
Keeps a kind of joy in it, | a zest, an ecstasy,
Next after sweet success. |

Hopkins plumbs here as deeply as ever Milton did into the psychogenesis of the satanic mind's masochistic refusal to submit. The intellect is fascinated with its ability to contemplate perversion for its own sake.

Apart from the choruses of *The Echoes*, there are three extant fragments of *St. Winefred's Well*, which total 124 lines. Hopkins designated them A, B, and C when he sent them to Bridges in April 1885.[66] Fragment A is the opening scene; it is a scene of advent and expectation. The dialogue

[65] *Ibid.*, p. 216.

[66] See *Letters I*, p. 211. Hopkins was working on his tragedy again when he was on holiday in North Wales in September–October 1886, as he told both Bridges and Dixon. He had written a little, and thought he might be able to finish it. These fragments have disappeared. See *Letters I*, p. 227, and *Letters II*, p. 143.

is crisp and even curt; all here is lean. In the first ten lines
Teryth tells his daughter Winefred, who is eagerly awaiting
her uncle, Lord Beuno, to expect Beuno and his deacon,
Dirvan. Teryth possesses that kind of masculinity which
Hopkins so admired. He is gruff, matter-of-fact, a man who
wastes no words, who gives orders and expects to be obeyed.
But he also loves his daughter dearly, to the point of doting
upon her. Already, however, by line 14 we learn from Teryth's soliloquy that he is tormented by the thought that he
will lose Winefred. He tries to dismiss these premonitions as
a sign of weakness. Fragment A is early and probably dates
back to 1879.

Fragment C seems to have been written soon after *The
Echoes* was completed, for Hopkins alludes to it in December 1882.[67] Fragment C is Beuno's monologue, a joyful hymn
of praise to God for restoring Winefred and for the boon of
the fountain of water which miraculously arises from the dry
dene where Winefred's severed head fell. To this holy well
pilgrims will flock, not only from Wales but from "elmy
England," and from "Erin, France and Flanders."

Hopkins often sings the praises of "moist and musical"
water: he sketched running brooks in his youth and in middle age; only weeks before he died he sketched a picture of
"wild rash and reeling water." The *raison d'être* of his beautiful *Epithalamion* fragment is only incidentally his youngest brother's marriage, for line after line describes some
"Southern dean or Lancashire clough or Devon cleave."
Wild, fresh streams were signs for Hopkins of God's own
eternal freshness. Winefred's fountain, Holywell, near the
theologate of St. Beuno's in North Wales, seems always to
have filled Hopkins with a reverent awe. Six weeks after he
arrived in Wales he wrote in his journal that he and another
seminarian

walked over to Holywell [about seven miles east of St. Beuno's]
and bathed at the well and returned very joyously. The sight of

the water in the well as clear as glass, greenish like beryl or aqua-marine, trembling at the surface with the force of the springs, and shaping out the five foils of the well quite drew and held my eyes to it. . . . The strong unfailing flow of the water and the chain of cures from year to year all these centuries took hold of my mind with wonder at the bounty of God in one of His saints, the sensible thing so naturally and gracefully uttering the spirit-ual reason of its being (which is all in true keeping with the story of St. Winefred's death and recovery) and the spring in place leading back the thoughts by its spring in time to its spring in eternity.[68]

St. Winefred's Well, Hopkins told Bridges in April 1877, "fills me with devotion every time I see it and wd. fill anyone that has eyes with admiration, the flow of ἀγλαὸν ὕδωρ is so lavish and so beautiful." [69]

The tour de force of the *Winefred* fragments is, of course, Caradoc's soliloquy, the longest fragment, B. There is noth-ing else quite like it in Hopkins' poetry. If the sonnets of desolation touch on black depths, still the poet calls after his God, although distant and seemingly unresponsive. And *Spelt from Sibyl's Leaves* is a glimpse of the condition of hell. But in Caradoc's speech we touch on a "deep insight" into evil without any admixture of repentance. The solilo-quy is a study of a soul which has despaired of ever calling on God's grace—the unforgivable sin. It is not often that we

[68] Entry for October 8, 1874, *Journals*, p. 261. His companion was C. W. Barraud, S.J., who published two plays on two saints, *St. Thomas of Canterbury* and *St. Elizabeth of Hungary* (both 1892). Perhaps Bar-raud and Hopkins discussed the possibility of writing a play on St. Winefred.

[69] *Letters I*, p. 40. See also Hopkins' little lyric *On St. Winefred* (no. 139) and a Latin version of this (no. 175), both probably written in 1877. *St. Winefred's Well* was for Hopkins a dramatizing of an extraor-dinary religious event. For most people, as for Bridges, the story of St. Winefred would be treated as a myth or, as Hopkins said, "a fable, as no doubt you [treat] the Gospels" (*ibid.*). Bridges, holding only to myth, could go to the other extreme in his dramas, addressing mytho-logical figures in all earnestness within the context of the play. Such an approach made Hopkins physically ill.

find such a study. There is something like it in Marlowe's figure of Dr. Faustus or in Dostoevsky's Svidrigailov. Lady Macbeth tells her husband, who has just murdered the king, "Consider it not so deeply." This is just what Caradoc does. He is an intelligent person who sees the full evil of his act but sticks by it, "Loyal to his own soul." Unlike the typical murderer (if one can use such a phrase) as we see him in the cow-eyed, unthinking henchmen in Jean Anouilh's *Becket*, Caradoc's act fills him "With dreadful distillation of thoughts sour as blood," for he "Must all day long taste murder."

It is interesting to follow the steps by which Caradoc comes to realize just what he has done and then to see how he damns himself out of his own mouth. Caradoc enters with a bloody sword in his right hand. His first reaction is disbelief; like Raskolnikov, he cannot realize there has been a murder. Caradoc's first impulse is to place the blame on Winefred. Her attempt to flee to her uncle Beuno to save herself from being violated becomes in Caradoc's eyes the act of a rebel who is then killed in revenge. He vacillates back to disbelief, but his bloody sword, that "workman [who] from his day's task sweats," tells him otherwise. Like Macbeth's dagger, Caradoc's sword will not stay clean. But worse is his irrevocable act: Winefred is dead. He recalls the murder scene and helplessly dwells on her eyes, for "In all her body, I say, no place was like her eyes." The heavens darken at the heinous deed; God is angry.

But Caradoc will not repent; there is "no law nor / Lord" to check him. Virtue becomes synonymous with valor, right becomes resolution in the egocentric world of Caradoc. But this steeling of the will demands an impossible strain on the flesh. Weariness is inevitable, but what comfort is there? Ironically, Caradoc has quenched the world's light, dashed down its "one rich rose," in slaying Winefred. Earth is now "a winter withering." And so Caradoc has caught himself in a dilemma by destroying what he valued most. He has hacked himself in hacking Winefred, and "choice of better or worse way" is now all in the past. He can only taste the fruits of that act and "all day long taste murder." The options are closed by his own self-will. He will "not yield, / Not hope, not pray." He chooses what Hopkins calls in a sonnet contemporary with this soliloquy that "carrion comfort, Despair." In intensity and fierceness of will, Caradoc's decision is not very different from Hopkins' own harsh and glittering resolution: "I can; / Can something, hope, wish day come, not choose not to be."

Analyzing his poetic idiosyncrasy and his need for an audience in a letter to Bridges, Hopkins commented, "I think the fragments I wrote of *St. Winefred,* which was meant to be played, were not hard to understand." [70] This is true; the language is clear, or as clear as the complexity of the thoughts will allow. And the prosodic vehicle for the drama is also adequate. Where Yeats was to arrive at a four-stress line and Eliot at a variable-stress line that continues to return to a line of six stresses, Hopkins devised an eight-stress sprung line with a strong caesura and with the final stress in each half-line frequently silent. Many of the lines, then, have six pronounced stresses, but the pause must be considered, and Hopkins does have the extra two stresses available when he needs them, especially when the speech draws to an emotional crescendo. So, for example, Caradoc's soliloquy begins with the six-stress line:

My heart, where have we been? | What have we seen, my mind?

But the high point of that speech is expanded to eight stresses:

Deed-bound I am; one deed treads all down here | cramps all doing. What do? Not yield.

[70] Letter of September 25, 1888, *Letters I,* p. 291.

I find the metre difficult, but very flexible and full of capacity.
. . . [Ideally] every line has 8 feet, 8 stresses; but not equal—4
dimeters or bars of 2 feet each. Then at the pause in the middle
of the line and at the end one of these 8 feet may be and commonly is suppressed, so that 6 are left. This gives boundless
variety, all of which is needed however to control the deep
natural monotony of the measure, with its middle pause and
equal division.[71]

It is an exciting prosodic development, and the soliloquies of
Caradoc and of Beuno (what we have of it) are as good
verse drama as any passage of equal length in either Eliot's
Murder in the Cathedral or in Yeats's *Purgatory*. Hopkins'
drama, like these, would probably have had the tightness
and classical economy of a Greek drama. As it is, however,
St. Winefred's Well must be consigned to the limbo of Hopkins' mature fragments.

[71] Letter to Coventry Patmore of April 4, 1885, *Letters III,* p. 360.

7⨯ Retreat and Recovery: 1885

The yearly retreat which Hopkins made at Clongowes Wood College in mid-August of 1885 may stand as a symbol for his retreat from the dense inner night chronicled in the desolate poems. There are some sonnets and a few fragments which were also composed in 1885, but they are so different in subject, treatment, and intensity that they require a separate chapter. In the remaining poems there is an uplifting, or at least a truce, in the speaker's voice, but there is also a weariness, a contraction of the spirit, which followed after the long night's skirmish. While, therefore, *Ashboughs, To what serves Mortal Beauty,* and *The Soldier* are clearly good poems, they do reveal a decline in intensity and finish.

Ashboughs, like the "terrible" sonnets, was never sent to Bridges or Dixon but was found in draft form in two versions among Hopkins' posthumous papers. The earlier draft, Bridges tells us in his notes to the poem, is a curtal sonnet on the "same sheet with the four sonnets 66–69, and preceding them: second, an apparently later version in the same metre on a page by itself; with expanded variation from seventh line, making thirteen lines for eleven." [1] Both Bridges and Gardner have relegated Hopkins' third and final curtal sonnet to the section entitled "Unfinished Poems, Fragments, Light Verse, &c. (1862–89)" because, as Ritz says, it "is accompanied by an unfinished variant." Nevertheless, "the

---

[1] *Poems,* p. 313.

first version written on the model of *Pied Beauty* has the necessary eleven lines. It is a completely finished 'caudated' sonnet." [2]

Any exact dating is impossible, but manuscript evidence points to a period contemporary with the terrible sonnets, probably sometime in the summer of 1885. Both Gardner and Ritz are aware that *Ashboughs* harks back to that earlier time in Wales. [3] For aesthetic reasons then, it seems fitting to place the poem after *My own heart,* which also ends with a backward glance at Wales.

The poem was first written as a curtal sonnet, in a light, sprightly, five-stress sprung rhythm with many hurried feet. Nothing, the poet sings, nurtures the mind or has in it such deep poetry as a tree whose boughs seem to explode against the heavens. Indeed, the organic unity of the tree seems to have had, as we can gather from scattered remarks of Hopkins', the same Coleridgean esemplastic unity as a well-wrought poem. "I looked at some delicate flying shafted ashes—there was one especially of single sonnet-like inscape," he had written in his journal years before. [4]

And, indeed, the meticulously natural description of the ash boughs in lines 4–6 is unlike anything Hopkins had written in his poetry for years. They too seem to belong to the young Hopkins at Oxford and at Roehampton and at Mt. Manresa. In his fragment *Richard,* written in mid-July 1865, almost twenty years before, Hopkins had described a "brush of trees" as

> thinning skywards by degrees,
> With parallel shafts,—as upward-parted ashes,—
> Their highest sprays were drawn as fine as lashes,
> With centres duly touch'd and nestlike spots.

The precision of observation and the obvious relish which he took in observing are still with the jaded, prematurely aging

[2] Ritz, p. 548 n.   [3] Gardner, II, 348, and Ritz, p. 549.
[4] *Journals,* p. 259.

priest of forty. Gardner thinks there is a greater, more primitive gusto here.[5]

> They touch heaven, tabour on it; how their talons sweep
> The smouldering enormous winter welkin! May
> Mells blue and snowwhite through them, a fringe and fray
> Of greenery: it is old earth's groping towards the steep
>   Heaven whom she childs us by.

The only difficulty is in reading the final two lines. Does "it" of line 10 refer to an object—the ash tree? Or does it refer to an activity—the groping of the tree toward heaven? What do "whom" and "she" refer to? Heaven or earth? And, finally, how are we to interpret the verbal force of "childs"? Does it mean "begets" or "makes as a child again"?

The sonnet demands a good deal of attention before it reveals its meaning, but reveal it it does.[6] The most satisfactory reading seems to be this: this stretching of the boughs of the tree toward heaven *is* "old earth's groping towards the steep / Heaven" by whom earth (she) [7] childs us (my eyes [l. 1] and myself, as well as those who are perceptive to a sacramental vision of nature). That is, we are impregnated with inspiration when we see how mute nature itself literally stretches out its gnarled hands toward heaven, how all things —but more noticeably trees—cry their dumb hosannahs to God. The gnarled hands are called "talons" to suggest that nature's unconscious praise is less perfect than the conscious,

---

[5] Gardner, II, 350–351.

[6] This relatively little-known sonnet is a classic example of the Russian formalist Viktor Shklovsky's theory of *defamiliarization;* that is, making objects strange to make them new for us. The sonnet moves at a fairly rapid pace until the last two lines, when the fruit drawn from the meditation on nature forces us to stop and slowly retrace our steps to see anew the significance of the ash boughs.

[7] In line 7 ("They touch heaven, tabour on it") Hopkins uses the indefinite pronoun "it" to refer to heaven. He is much too careful a poet to have "she" refer to heaven four lines later.

self-willed praise that man alone of all earthly things can give, as gnarled branches in their groping only approximate human hands outstretched in supplication.

But a second meaning of "childs" is also there: seeing the old twisted trees groping toward heaven gives us another hint of that Edenic world when man and nature were in their radically innocent state, like little children. For a few moments, this sacramental glimpse of heaven "childs" us and makes us children again.[8] It is difficult not to see the jaded priest in the image of the ash tree, with hands upstretched in praise in all seasons, in his "winter-world" as well as in his spring world, but grateful now for his breaking forth again into blossom after the freezing, numbing cold of his desolation.

To what serves Mortal Beauty? and *The Soldier* were most likely written within a week of each other. The first is dated August 23, 1885. Hopkins was making his annual eight-day retreat at Clongowes Wood College in County Kildare, where he went on August 21.[9] *The Soldier,* dated "Clongowes, Aug. 1885," would then have been written between August 21 and the end of the month. In fact, the sonnets

---

[8] Gardner's reading of the final line of the variant is unfortunately misleading. He thinks that Hopkins probably changed "Heaven whom she childs us by" to "Heaven with it whom she childs things by" because "it seems Hopkins may have feared the monistic or pantheistic implications of 'us.' His very first thought had been, 'Heaven once Earth childed by' [*sic*], which could refer equally to the creation of Adam and ash-boughs; so that his second [first?] thought, 'us,' is more authentic than the ugly and timid 'things'; for in a physical sense human beings are indeed children of Earth" (Gardner, II, 351–352). But Hopkins' concern is not with decorum but with an angle of perception. The emendation probably means (and it is certainly less satisfying than the first version) that when we see this groping of the old trees toward heaven, we are inspired to see how all *things* praise their Creator. And we see also how all *things* seem to recover their pristine innocence. This is true in all seasons, but, as Hopkins says, it is especially so in May. See *Spring* (May 1877) and *Ribblesdale.*

[9] See *Letters III,* p. 172.

form a pair, for both are poetic commentaries on the Ignatian *Spiritual Exercises*. *To what serves Mortal Beauty?* is a
commentary on "Principle and Foundation," which begins
the exercises for the first week, as *The Soldier* is a commentary on "The Kingdom of Christ," which serves as prologue
to the exercises of the second week. Both sonnets are also
written in the same meter, sprung Alexandrines, and both
use the strong medial caesura to help break up the monotony
to which the even-stressed Alexandrine line is vulnerable, as
Hopkins well knew.

To what serves Mortal Beauty? was sent to Canon Dixon
sometime, it seems, near August 23. But a slightly altered
version was not sent to Bridges until three years later. "I
enclose by the same hand a sonnet of some standing which
Canon Dixon has had and you have not," he writes Bridges
on September 7, 1888.[10]

The sonnet is didactic, a subtle and balanced judgment of
the meaning of human beauty. It is Hopkins' particular
poetic understanding of the Ignatian "Principle and Foundation" which reads in part:

Man is created to praise, reverence, and serve God our Lord, and
by this means to save his soul. All other things on the face of the
earth are created for man to help him fulfill the end for which
he is created. From this it follows that man is to use these things
to the extent that they will help him to attain his end. Likewise,
he must rid himself of them in so far as they prevent him from
attaining it.[11]

Hopkins would have read and pondered this text at the
beginning of his annual retreat. The sonnet begins with the
statement of a question in the first two and one-half lines; it
is answered in general terms in the next two and one-half
lines. A particular example is given in lines 6–8. The tradi-

[10] *Letters I,* p. 283.
[11] *The Spiritual Exercises of St. Ignatius,* trans. Anthony Mattola
(Garden City, N.Y., 1964), p. 47.

tional division of the Petrarchan octet, then, is not followed except in rhyme scheme.

What purpose does the beauty of a particular person serve, asks Hopkins. That proud but fleeting form which the artist tries to capture forever ("the O-seal-that-so feature") is dangerous because it can set the blood dancing more wildly and heatedly, Hopkins is aware, than even Henry Purcell's stirring rhythms can. In Christian-Platonic terms Hopkins explains that physical beauty keeps us aware of the absolute, eternal good of God. For God has created beautiful people to give us some inkling of what His goodness and beauty must be. A quick glimpse of physical beauty can give us a spiritual insight into the goodness of God as well as into the spark of divinity in man. In this sense beauty has an effect of serenity and stasis. But too long a gaze at beauty can be disturbing, can arouse the erotic impulse and become a self-absorbing end in itself. This awareness of the charm and yet potential danger of physical beauty is a constant theme in Hopkins' letters, sermons, and poetry—for example, in *Spring* (1877). "I think . . . no one can admire beauty of the body more than I do, and it is of course a comfort to find beauty in a friend or a friend in beauty. But this kind of beauty is dangerous," he once told Bridges.[12] And a Jesuit who knew Hopkins remembered this about him:

What struck me most of all in him was his childlike guilelessness and simplicity, his gentleness, tender-heartedness, and his loving compassion for the young, the weak, the poor, and for all who were in any trouble or distress. Joined to this and closely connected with it, was his purity of heart and shrinking dread of anything that tended to endanger, especially in the young, the angelic virtue.[13]

The angelic virtue is chastity. This traditional identification of chaste innocence with angelic virtue gives special force

[12] Letter of October 22, 1879, *Letters I*, p. 95.

[13] Quoted in G. F. Lahey, S.J., *Gerard Manley Hopkins* (London, 1930) , p. 132.

to the example in the poem of the boys' angelic beauty: their beauty shows the power of physical beauty to act for spiritual good. Pope Gregory, walking through crowded Rome about the year 600 and seeing some recently arrived young prisoners, golden-haired, blue-eyed Angles from far-off Britain, quipped his famous pun, "Non Angli sed angeli." This chance encounter prompted Gregory to send the first Christian missionaries, led by St. Augustine, to convert Britain. And had it not been for their physical beauty, Hopkins suggests, Gregory might never have noticed these British lads. Father Gregory was struck by their physical beauty, which led him to turn to the far more valuable beauty of their souls.[14]

The sestet marks not so much a turn in the argument as a mildly hortatory insistence on maintaining a proper hierarchy of values. All men find the need to worship and love something, some image of beauty, even if it be only an idol, and Hopkins also takes an oblique glance at those who would worship art, the "block or barren stone." Christianity says, however, to love that which is most worthy of our love, the "selves" or souls of men, and the soul is reflected in the mold of the body and particularly in the face.[15] It is, then,

[14] As Devlin suggests, the germ for this sonnet may perhaps be found in some meditation notes Hopkins jotted down for the Feast of St. Gregory, March 12, 1885. Notice how even here natural beauty is linked in Hopkins' mind with the fear that that beauty may be pock-marked by sin:

St. Gregory the Great— (I) His meeting with the boys in the market place[.]

Angeli—natural endowments; De ira—state of sin; Alleluia—employment in God's service. Consider under the first point [of the Ignatian meditation] the best you know of England, under the second the worst, under the third the hopes of its conversion and pray for that (Sermons, p. 259).

[15] Hopkins believed that the beauty of the soul manifests itself in the beauty of the body: "For though even bodily beauty, even the beauty of blooming health, is from the soul, in the sense, as we Aristotelian Catholics say, that the soul is the form of the body, yet the soul may

perfectly in accord with Christianity to admire physical beauty, the first tercet explains. Yet, the second tercet tacitly admits, this kind of beauty is dangerous, so how are we to "meet" it?

> Merely meet it; own,
> Home at heart, heaven's sweet gift; then leave, let that alone.
> Yea, wish that though, wish all, God's better beauty, grace.

We are to acknowledge within ourselves that mortal beauty is "heaven's sweet gift." For it is meant to be a pointer toward "God's better beauty, grace." Wish for grace and you wish for "all," since it is spiritual beauty which informs physical beauty and gives to physical beauty its value within an absolute hierarchy of values.[16]

Unlike *To what serves Mortal Beauty?,* Hopkins' other poem of this period, *The Soldier,* was never sent to either Bridges or Dixon and, like the greater number of the sonnets of 1885, was found after his death among his papers. The reason it was probably not sent, if we exclude for a moment Hopkins' admitted growing indifference toward his poems, lies in the tone of the sonnet, which comes close to being chauvinistic. "[It is] a task of great delicacy and hazard to write a patriotic song that shall breathe true feeling without spoon or brag," he explains to Bridges, speaking of his musical score for his *What shall I do for the land that bred me.* "How I hate both! and yet feel myself half blundering or sinking into them in several of my pieces, a thought that makes me not greatly regret their likelihood of perishing."[17]

The tone of the sonnet does need some explanation. Hop-

---

have no other beauty, so to speak, than that which it expresses in the symmetry of the body—barring those blurs in the cast which wd. not be found in the die or the mould" (*Letters I,* p. 95). For Hopkins a favorite corollary to the idea of the beauty of the soul is that in commending and sacrificing himself entirely to God, the physical beauty of the individual is kept and will shine forth in greater splendor in the resurrection.

[16] See Ritz, p. 532, for a different emphasis.   [17] *Letters I,* p. 283.

kins was proud of his love for the British Empire, and yet he was not blind to its faults. *The Soldier* is based on the military simile of the soldier Christ, and it evokes the sense of manliness we feel is, or at least should be, present in the military profession. The tone is ambivalent because Hopkins realizes that many redcoats and tars fall sadly short in the qualities of courage, sacrifice, obedience, and willingness to lay down one's life in defense of a just cause; nevertheless, the very wearing of the smart uniform—a symbol of manliness and pride in one's country—may help to make the soldier himself manly and patriotic.

Still, while Hopkins qualifies his remarks, there is a sense of slight discomfort in the octet, an uneasy sense of patriotism which seems to have been shared by many Victorian writers, for many of those who signed up for voluntary duty in Her Majesty's service signed up for quite other reasons than honor and sacrifice, as Hopkins very well knew.[18] We cannot blame Hopkins alone for the apparent tone of an inbred British middle-class superiority; the distinction between soldierly ideal and soldierly reality is clear in the writings of Thomas Carlyle, a product of the Scottish peasant class, and especially in *Past and Present,* written forty-two years before *The Soldier:*

Who can despair of Governments that passes a Soldier's Guardhouse, or meets a redcoated man on the streets! . . . Often, in these painfully decadent and painfully nascent Times, with their distresses, inarticulate gaspings and "impossibilities"; meeting a tall Lifeguardsman in his snow-white trousers, or seeing those two statuesque Lifeguardsmen in their frowning bearskins, pipeclayed buckskins, on their coal-black sleek-fiery quadrupeds, rid-

[18] See Hopkins' letter to Baillie of May 1, 1888, *Letters III,* p. 293. Hopkins is rankling there at the military disgrace suffered by the British soldiers at the hands of the Boers on Majuba Hill in South Africa (February 26–27, 1881). He attributes the cowardice of the British soldiers to their poverty and general misery, brought about by poor urban living conditions.

ing sentry at the Horse-Guards,—it strikes one with a kind of mournful interest, how, in such universal down-rushing and wrecked impotence of almost all old institutions, this oldest Fighting Institution is still so young! Fresh-complexioned, firm-limbed, six feet by the standard, this fighting man has verily been got up, and can fight. . . . He of the red coat, I say, is a success and no failure! . . . Multiform ragged losels, runaway apprentices, starved weavers, thievish valets; an entirely broken population, fast tending towards the treadmill. But the persuasive sergeant came; by tap of drum enlisted, or formed lists of them, took heartily to drilling them. . . . Let no man despair of Governments who looks on these two sentries at the Horse-Guards.[19]

Hopkins, by his very nature, had a deep-seated admiration and love for the military ideal. His ambivalence in tone, however, derives from his lofty spiritual application. For his analogy is between the propagation of the British Empire's aims, which he found unspiritual and therefore partly unjustifiable, and the propagation of the heavenly kingdom of his commander-in-chief, Jesus Christ. The analogy is self-consciously strained and almost blunders into "spooning."

Clearly, Hopkins saw himself as a knight or soldier of Christ, a metaphor which had the sound approval of the Spanish knight-turned-priest who had founded the Order of Jesus.[20] "There is something of the soldier about Hopkins,"

---

[19] Book IV, Chapter 3 ("The One Institution") in Everyman's Library edition (London, 1962), pp. 250–252.

[20] Cf. the metaphor of the king-knight relationship which opens the second week of the Ignatian *Spiritual Exercises*, "The Kingdom of Christ" (Mattola [trans.], *op. cit.*, p. 67). Continuing the military metaphor, Hopkins made the following comments during his long retreat: "But what of those who refused to come not from dislike of [Christ] the king's terms, the particular hardships of this campaign, but from dislike of soldiering altogether, from complete cowardice, and yet able-bodied men?—Not only they would be despised for cowardice but in the general movement of the commonwealth towards the great war this would be held disaffection and they would be disfranchised [*sic*] in the hour of triumph. . . . The point is that we are in duty and loyalty

Ritz explains. "For him as for St. Ignatius, the myth of the military is essential. Life is one 'tough campaign.' "[21]

The operation of the Incarnation in the man who bravely serves his "soldiering through" recalls the theme of *As kingfishers catch fire* where "Christ plays in ten thousand places" in the activities of the virtuous man. Hopkins identifies the operation of the Incarnation in men not with the distinctive personality, the particular self of a man, but with the nature of the activity of a person. A man becomes Christ insofar as he imitates the activity of Christ, especially by doing his part in imitating the great sacrifice of Christ by participating in the great life-campaign of the *De Processo* in which all creation follows Christ in returning to God.[22]

"But our lives and in particular those of religious, as mine, are in their whole direction, not only inwardly but most visibly and outwardly, shaped by Christ's," Hopkins wrote near the end of his life.[23] For the rope which Christ reeves or fastens is the life of the Christian (cf. *The Deutschland*, I, 4). And Christ will reeve the soldier in his service to the long and arduous campaign, as he gave the first example. Christ "led the way," he told a Liverpool congregation, "went before his troops, was himself the vanguard, was the forlorn hope, bore the brunt of battle alone, died upon the field, on Calvary hill, and bought the victory by his blood."[24]

There remain to be discussed only three sonnet fragments

---

bound to follow Him ('Regis,' 'Christum Dominum nostrum, Regem aeternum') and it is for Him to choose what or where" (*Sermons*, pp. 163–164).   [21] Ritz, p. 143.

[22] For the central importance of the procession, see Hopkins' letter to Bridges, *Letters I*, p. 149, and also *Sermons*, p. 197.

[23] "Without that even outwardly the world could be so different that we cannot even guess it. And my life is determined by the Incarnation down to most of the details of the day" (*Sermons*, p. 263).

[24] Sermon of April 25, 1880, *ibid.*, p. 70. Hopkins remarked in his sermon for December 14, 1879: "If we do well he [Christ] smiles, he claps his hands over us" (*ibid.*, p. 49).

of 1885, numbers 150, 153, and 154 in the Fourth Edition,[25] and a lyrical fragment (155). *Strike, churl; hurl, cheerless wind* (154) is apparently the first quatrain of an unfinished Petrarchan sonnet in sprung rhythm. The speaker addresses the unseasonable wind and hail which destroy the May blossoms and which affect the speaker himself by holding joy back and keeping "Hope pale." Spring brings with it the promise of good things which the "churl" winter destroys. "May 17, and still winter," Hopkins complained in a postscript to a letter to Baillie written at about the same time as the fragment.[26]

The fragment is similar to the lines of a younger contemporary of Hopkins, A. E. Housman, written eleven years later, *The chestnut casts his flambeaux*. But whereas the speaker in Housman's poem blames the Creator for nature's caprice, Hopkins' evil is a counterforce to fulfillment. As Ritz says, Hopkins "sees in the wind and hail which massacre the beauty of May the evil which chases joy away, lays low the harvests, and is forever frightening hope." [27]

The times are nightfall (150) is akin in imagery to *Spelt from Sibyl's Leaves* and in theme is close to *To seem the stranger*.[28] The times—and Hopkins undoubtedly is refer-

---

[25] Ritz calls the fragment *Moonrise* (June 19, 1876) an unfinished sonnet also (Ritz, p. 34 n); but the seven seven-stress lines show no discernible rhyme scheme.

[26] Letter of April 24–May 17, 1885, *Letters III*, p. 257.

[27] Ritz, p. 247.

[28] Ritz dates this fragment January 1885, which would make it contemporary with *Spelt from Sibyl's Leaves*. This or the previous month would fit in well with the season and time mentioned in the fragment. The "one" of line 6 may refer to the attempt of the Liberals to save Gladstone's failing reputation, since his foreign policy had snagged in Ireland and in Egypt, where he failed to end the siege of Khartoum, and which ended in a British defeat. In a passage from his Dublin Notebook quoted in *Sermons*, Hopkins notes, "Khartoum fell Jan. 26 [1885]." Seven weeks later he writes in his meditation notes the

ring to the political unrest in Ireland—are nightfall, are
winter; the light fades and will soon be gone. Hopkins laments in the second quatrain that he can do nothing in this
commonweal:

> And I not help. Nor word now of success:
> All is from wreck, here, there, to rescue one—
> Work which to see scarce so much as begun
> Makes welcome death, does dear forgetfulness.

There is, then, little that the speaker can do to change the
worsening condition around him. But, with the *volta* in line
9, the speaker turns within, for at least here his "will is law
in that small commonweal." There is no final resolution to
the poem, however, and the fragment ends with this phrase.

It is almost the same with *To his Watch*. This fragment
unintentionally offers an ironic answer to the speaker's question to his watch, "shall I / Earlier or you fail at our force,"
by admitting a third alternative, for the inspiration for the
sonnet fails before either. The speaker's watch is, like himself, subject to cessation. The tick-tock regularity of his heart
beats like his watch; both are works of intricate, delicate art,
but both will one day lie in ruins. The duty of both is
"telling time"; the watch tells time with metronomic fidelity,
the speaker must make time "tell" or count, for what a man
does with his time is what God will judge him by. Our one
spell of life ends either in "comfort's carol of all or woe's
worst smart."

Day succeeds day and there is no way that we can hold
back time and call it our own. The fact that "that last and
shortest" day of our death is coming is one of the few things
of which we can be certain. There is a great uneasiness in the
tone of the poem, as though if the speaker were to be

---

following: "Let him that is without sin etc—Pray to keep to this spirit
and as far as possible rule in speaking of Mr. Gladstone for instance"
(*Sermons*, pp. 318 and 260).

weighed he would be found wanting. "[If] I died now," Hopkins confessed despondently five months before his death, "I should die imperfect, no master of myself, and that is the worst failure of all. O my God, look down on me." [29]

The Soldier is probably the last sonnet Hopkins wrote in 1885. Hopkins' muse had forced him to utter things about which he was usually reticent, partially because he did not like to "make capital" of his religious insights, as he had expressed it in 1879. He had been forced almost against his will to compose his desolate sonnets, poems of a very high order. The poetic aftermath, however, was a temporary cessation from the *via purgativa* and a return to earlier themes: the value of mortal beauty, and the presence of Christ in the just man. There is in the last few poems of 1885 a certain flatness after the strain of the desolate sonnets. And that sense of beauty and freshness and innocence so present in the sonnets of 1877 had been tempered in *To what serves Mortal Beauty?* Hopkins could hardly have suffered the aridity described in the desolate sonnets without a deepened awareness that life is hardly a matter of burning always with a "hard, gemlike flame" or being "present always at the focus where the greatest number of vital forces unite in their purest energy," as his Oxford tutor and friend, Walter Pater, had urged.

Thee, God, I come from, to thee go is on the same sheet as a first draft of *To what serves Mortal Beauty?* and may also have been written during Hopkins' retreat at Clongowes Wood College in mid-August 1885. It is written in four-line stanzas with four-stress sprung lines rhyming aaba; in the

---

[29] *Ibid.*, p. 262. See Devlin's comment on this passage: "There may be a symptomatic confusion of thought here. The state of perfection which the profession of a religious enjoins is a constant *striving* for perfection; the complete attainment of it is not possible in this life. . . . Further, self-mastery is a means to closer union with Christ; it is not an end in itself. *Perfect* self-mastery is an academic rather than a religious ideal" (*ibid.*, p. 319).

third line, the medial-stressed word rhymes with the terminal word. It reads as though it were to be a public prayer, and sounds like nothing Hopkins had written since his undergraduate days, although there is a firmer rhythmic control here. There are echoes of certain other pieces of Hopkins'; there is the "sir" of *Thou art indeed just, Lord* in "Help me, sir, and so I will." And stanza 2,

> What I know of thee I bless
> As acknowledging thy stress
> On my being and as seeing
> Something of thy holiness,

recalls stanza 5 of *The Wreck of the Deutschland,* especially "For I greet him the days I meet him, and bless when I understand." And the "I see / With thy might that thou art mild" of stanza 4 recalls the image of God's paradoxical nature in stanza 9 of the great ode. It seems almost unbelievable that the poet who wrote "Bad I am, but yet thy child" could have composed the terrible sonnets just a few months before. But then he did not write these lines in blood.

8 "Summertime Joys" and "Winter World": 1886–1889

Hopkins wrote his impressive fragment *On the Portrait of Two Beautiful Young People* on a well-earned holiday at Monasterevan, some forty miles southwest of Dublin. Hopkins was a frequent guest here, at the large, roomy house of the Cassidys, prosperous distillers and brewers. It was here that he spent his last three Christmases, watched the brown waters of the River Barrow, saw the quaint country churchyard, and distributed Communion at a nearby church built during the height of the Great Famine of the forties. And it was here, at Christmas 1886, that he saw the portrait which inspired his poem, "an elegy in Gray's metre,"[1] a poem "severe" and with "no experiments."[2] Hopkins worked on the elegy between Christmas and January 2, but Dublin proved "museless" and he never finished it. What we have, then, are nine four-line stanzas which Hopkins sent to Bridges, and three stanzas (and some lines) apparently rejected by Hopkins which exist among his early drafts.[3]

Because there is no internal necessity determining the length of the poem, it is difficult to say just how much of it the thirty-six lines represent. Gray's *Elegy* itself is 128 lines.

[1] Letter to Dixon of January 27, 1887, *Letters II*, p. 150.
[2] Letter to Bridges of January 2, 1887, *Letters I*, pp. 248–249. The stanzas rhyme abab and the lines each have five stresses.
[3] In the Fourth Edition the editors print the discarded Fairlop Fair stanza, but Norman White has pointed out two overlooked stanzas in his letter in the *Times Literary Supplement*, August 22, 1968, p. 905.

The outline of the poem remains incomplete and can only be guessed at. It would seem to have thematic affinities with *The Bugler's First Communion* and with *The Leaden Echo and the Golden Echo*: time plays havoc with all physical beauty and can do worse to spiritual beauty. In fact, mortal beauty is dangerous and lends itself to frequent incursions of vanity and self-will. Put yourselves, therefore, in God's keeping.

If we may see one of the rejected stanzas as a stone in the arch, it would appear that the resolution of this fragment would have been parallel with the resolution of *That Nature is a Heraclitean Fire* written nineteen months later. Here is the stanza, as printed by Norman White:

> See where a lighthouse lifts above the world,
> Across this millionny, this mouthing foam
> Its bright eye broke but now, my heart, and hurled
> The deep, not dark nor Delphic, rede of Rome.[4]

"Severe," Hopkins says of the language; certainly it is clipped. There is a tightness here which is really too constricting, and while the general meaning of the elegy reveals itself easily enough, a number of phrases have been compressed beyond the point of their resiliency. Still, what is gained is a nervousness, a crackling in the lines, which gives evidence of the syntactical compression possible in Gray's metrical form. Slow, somber melancholy gives way to an electric quality made up of such opposite impulses as nostalgia, vatic anger, sorrow for lost innocence, and priestly advice. The elegy for the dead gives way to an elegy for lost beauty, both mortal and moral. What is uncharacteristic about this poem is the level, steady gaze of the middle-aged Hopkins which undercuts any doting or sentimentality in the portrait of the young girl leaning contentedly against her

---

[4] *Ibid.* "Broke," in the third line, is Hopkins' variant for "breaks"; I have used it to avoid an unnecessary mixing of tenses.

brother, both effusing a light of grace and innocence. Hopkins did not know the children personally when he saw the portrait, although they still lived at Monasterevan. But he did see them later (in fact they are almost the last people mentioned in Hopkins' final letter to Bridges, although characteristically not by name) .[5] The point is, however, that his not knowing them when he wrote the lines lends to the poem a detachment and objectivity missing in, for example, *The Bugler's First Communion.*

Hopkins begins with his eye upon the picture, which serves as a ready-made composition of place. Since we do not know what portrait is involved here (it is not a picture of the Cassidy family, it would appear), we can only surmise that Hopkins is drawing a parallel between the dewy bluebells in the background of the portrait, whose veins are overrunning with tears of sap, and the vein of tears we all have for beauty's fleetness. Like Aristotle, Hopkins muses that happiness can only be counted when we look backwards. True, the parents have been blessed in "one fair fall"—their children. But the future holds the door open to ambition, "hope, hazard, interest." These youths are not now as they appear here in their "young delightful hour," which dissolved like a daydream or like the momentary ringlets on the River Barrow. The first image recalls Prospero's "We are such stuff as dreams are made on" as the second recalls Heraclitus' flux.

The young man looks out intently from the picture onto life. But what, the poet wonders, is that gaze fixed on? There is only one adequate good, the poet insists, and that is God. All else, riches included, must serve that good. And none can know just where that deepest bent of the heart is pointed; whether it is "all foredrawn to No or Yes." The trouble with the beauty of youth and the earnest look which the poet so admires in the painting is that that earnestness can be employed in the service of sin, for the best (the most sensi-

---

[5] *Letters I,* p. 306.

tive) are also potentially capable to will the worst. And then all that freshness meant for heaven is like a tree in bloom destroyed by worms, "havoc-pocked."

Such corruption is as old as the Fall, and certainly the poet does not know the inner dispositions of these beautiful young people. But he does know by wracking experience that the young are sooner or later corrupted, perhaps by themselves, most probably by others. There is in the last two lines of the fragment a frustration and helpless sorrow that such corruption should be the rule. Hopkins faces this un-flinchingly, but he will shout out against it, however useless such a gesture might be. One thing is certainly clear here: Hopkins' esthetic perspective has narrowed considerably; he cannot look upon the portrait for long without moral concerns edging insistently into the forefront. Years in the confessional had made of Hopkins a "burning witness."

On September 28, 1887, Hopkins wrote to Bridges from The Mourne Hotel, Rostrevor, County Down, in Northern Ireland. He had just spent several days vacationing near the market town of Dromore, about seventeen miles southwest of Belfast, in a house where Bishop Percy, the famous editor of *Reliques of Ancient English Poetry,* had once lived.

With other things I have not got on, but I have been touching up some old sonnets you have never seen [probably the "desolate sonnets"] and have within a few days done the whole of one, I hope, very good one and most of another; the one finished is a direct picture of a ploughman without afterthought. But when you read it let me know if there is anything like it in Walt Whitman, as perhaps there may be, and I should be sorry for that.[6]

Nevertheless, Hopkins did not send *Harry Ploughman* to Bridges until his next letter two weeks later, when he was back at St. Stephen's Green. On October 11 he writes:

I will enclose the sonnet on Harry Ploughman, in which burden-lines (they might be recited by a chorus) are freely used: there

[6] *Ibid.,* p. 262.

is in this very heavily loaded sprung rhythm a call for their employment. The rhythm of this sonnet, which is altogether for recital, not for perusal (as by nature verse should be) is very highly studied. From much considering it I can no longer gather any impression of it: perhaps it will strike you as intolerably violent and artificial.[7]

Apparently Bridges had some strong reservations about the sonnet, for Hopkins goes to some length to defend the plasticity of its syntax and musical rhythms. But Hopkins insisted that his experiments functioned to present more immediately the dynamic activity of the ploughman. "I want Harry Ploughman to be a vivid figure before the mind's eye; if he is not that the sonnet fails." [8] Hopkins was aware of the strangeness of his syntax to an English ear, especially to one trained in the conventional metrical patterns and rhetoric of Victorian poetry. And even Hopkins wavers before his own "wind- lilylocks -laced." "The difficulties are of syntax no doubt. Dividing a compound word by a clause sandwiched into it was a desperate deed, I feel, and I do not feel that it was an unquestionable success." [9]

If Hopkins must remold language and increase the modulation of stresses to present the dynamic figure of Harry Ploughman, and if this means sacrificing immediate comprehension, then so be it. For a poem is the hard crystal which presents experience in a fresh and compressed manner, so that the total experience of the poem explodes against the brain. The poet will defend any amount of prose glossing on the poem, for there are many tensions working simultaneously within it to present the experience which in prose is only described. But all such explanation should be exterior to the poem itself.

Harry Ploughman is unlike any other poem of Hopkins'. Indeed, in phonal and tonal patterns it is very highly

[7] *Ibid.*, p. 263.   [8] *Ibid.*, p. 265.   [9] *Ibid.*

pitched, even for Hopkins. The Petrarchan sonnet supplies the basic formal structure for the poem, but the poem does not really work as a sonnet, primarily because there is no "afterthought," as Hopkins himself said, no significant *volta* in the argument, for the poem does not develop any argument. Where the normal *volta* would occur there is a turn but it is only to a greater dynamic intensity; there is no logical or emotional shift.

Nor is the poem quite a perfect caudated sonnet, for it does not follow the formal pattern of the one famous caudated sonnet in English literature prior to Hopkins: Milton's *On the New Forcers of Conscience*. In fact Hopkins was not sure how to construct a formal caudated sonnet when he wrote *Harry Ploughman*. "I shd. be glad . . . if you wd. explain what a *coda* is and how employed," he mentioned in a letter to Bridges of December 11, 1886.[10] And on November 2, 1887, three weeks after he had sent Bridges *Harry Ploughman*, he asks him to "please tell me how correctly to make codas to sonnets; with the most approved order of rhymes and so on. And do not say that I know and that I can find for myself and that there is one in Milton (that one is not enough), but do what I ask you."[11] Bridges in his generous way responded immediately, for four days later Hopkins replies: "I am thankful to you for the account of the coda, over which you gave yourself even unnecessary trouble. . . . It seems they are formed on an invariable plan and that Milton's sonnet gives an example. Of course one example was enough if there is but one type; but you should have said so."[12]

Hopkins himself calls the five half-lines "burden-lines" suitable for a "chorus." There seems to have been a very strong rhythm haunting the poet's mind, a rhythm which had to break out of the conventional 4–4-turn-3–3 sonnet

---

[10] *Ibid.*, p. 246.   [11] *Ibid.*, p. 263.   [12] *Ibid.*, p. 264–265.

pattern, and the choric chiming of the burdens served Hopkins' need. Despite the idiosyncratic mode of the poem, however, the sonnet is justified by Hopkins' achievement.[13]

Gardner perceptively demonstrates that the two chief qualities of the ploughman around which the sonnet is constructed are caught in the repetition of the hard *br,* or *b . . . r . . . ,* and the liquid *l* sounds

to signalize the two chief characteristics of Harry's physique and action—strength and grace. The keywords of the first *motif* are *broth . . . , barrelled, barrowy, brawn, beechbole, broad,* and *bluff* (hide). At the beginning of the sestet, the two *motifs* are delicately interlaced. . . . The whole poem comes as near to "the condition of music" as language may.[14]

The first eleven lines, that is, the octet and three burden lines, present Harry Ploughman rather statically, in architectural terms, almost as if he were a sculptured figure. The muscular knotting and slack of the well-coordinated body is particularly stressed, for the individual parts are subservient to one organic whole and form "one crew." There is a muscularity and restricting force in the consonantal clusters and many stops, as though the potential energy were straining slowly and then with increasing rapidity; the pace accelerates, breaking through the constricting elements themselves as the plougher begins slowly to plough through the sillion and then picks up speed.

Harry is partially defined in terms of the structure of a Gothic cathedral, which also combines strength with grace and movement; his anatomy includes "rack of ribs," "flank," "nave," and "barrelled [vault]," and the whole "Stand[s] at

---

[13] Ritz, along with Gardner, has treated *Harry Ploughman* as if it were a caudated sonnet, and for purposes of general classification this will do. The *Epithalamion* fragment will be considered after *That Nature is a Heraclitean Fire,* which it precedes chronologically, in order that Hopkins' development of the caudated sonnet may be more easily examined.   [14] Gardner, II, 142–143.

stress." Harry's "Churlsgrace" is a result of all his members in complete harmony.

In the second part of the sonnet, lines 12–19, the movement of the lines mimetically gathers momentum with the plougher, and with speed the muscular strain of the movement increases. There is the sense of a forward glide faltering because of the number of stops in the last two lines. We have the upward curve of the action described: a slow movement as the plough grips the soil, and then an increased movement as the plough wallows through the stubborn earth. The furrow is formed and the dirt sprays up in the wind or falls behind, while the ploughman's locks whirl out or hang, intermittently caught in the same wind, with earth and hair furling like the shining spray of water from a fountain. Stress and slack, Hopkins realizes, are necessary to any movement.

The rhythm of line 9 is forceful and excited, like the opening of *The Starlight Night;* the fluid movement becomes more noticeable, along with the dragging tension on the straining ploughman, whose "cheek crimsons." His curls are thrown out as if interlaced with the wind. But it is also the man's strength, his "Churlsgrace," which hurls out his locks. And as the "frowning feet" lash to the work, the locks furl out gracefully, as do the cold furls of earth. There is generated a harmony of action between the man and his work well done, an interaction imaged in the final simile of gracefully spraying water which simultaneously describes the action of the flowing locks and liquid soil.

Harry Ploughman has not received much attention from the critics, but those who have dealt with it seem to hold that there is either no central theological significance to the poem or that, if there is, it is only by implication. Some of these implications, however, should be examined.[15] The figure of the ploughman was particularly important for Hopkins be-

[15] One of these implications may be found in the passage from *Sermons* which is quoted on p. 145.

cause of Christ's admonition to the man who had put his hands to the plough not to look back. The priest links "the disgrace of putting the hand to the plough and looking back in the kingdom of heaven" with the "recreant knight" of the third point of the Ignatian exercise on "The Kingdom of Christ." [16] Again, the figure of the active ploughman, hair and soil furled out in the wind, recalls Hopkins' comments on the body as the living temple of God: when the "member" of Christ (the allusion to the Mystical Body is important) "is in all things conformed to Christ . . . , [this] best brings out the nature of the man himself, as the lettering on a sail or device upon a flag are best seen when it fills." [17] So the dynamic energy and inherent dignity in the ploughman doing his work well manifest the living temple, or living cathedral, of the Holy Spirit. The wind which can "cross-bridle" the ploughman (rein him in by the cross, while allowing him ease in movement) is the Holy Spirit inspiring (breathing into) the ploughman. He on his side cooperates with his own strength and "Churlsgrace," so that the whole scene presents the intimate interaction of God, man, and the earth in grace-giving work.

"For there is a perennial nobleness, and even sacredness, in Work," Carlyle had pronounced in *Past and Present.*

Were he never so benighted, forgetful of his high calling, there is always hope in a man that actually and earnestly works. . . . The latest Gospel in this world is, Know thy work and do it. "Know thyself": long enough has that poor "self" of thine tormented thee; thou wilt never get to "know" it, I believe! . . . Consider how, even in the meanest sorts of Labour, the whole soul of a man is composed into a kind of real harmony, the instant he sets himself to work! [18]

[16] *Sermons,* p. 163. See also *Letters II,* p. 88, where Hopkins confesses to Dixon that he is afraid of "a severe judgment from God . . . for the backward glances I have given with my hand upon the plough."

[17] *Sermons,* p. 195.

[18] *Past and Present,* Book III, Chapter 11 ("Labour"), p. 189.

Despite the difference of the tone and the anti-intellectual appeal of Carlyle to leave off examining the inner spaces— "Think it not thy business, this of knowing thyself; thou art an unknowable individual" [19]—Hopkins' presuppositions about the dignity of work are as much a part of Victorian England as they are of the Gospels.[20]

In an early letter to Bridges (August 2, 1871), the young seminarian Hopkins, deeply troubled by the news of a revolutionary government in Paris, evoked a coming apocalypse, tragic but necessary: "Horrible to say, in a manner I am a Communist. Their ideal bating some things is nobler than that professed by any secular statesman I know of (I must own I live in batlight and shoot at a venture). Besides it is just.—I do not mean the means of getting it are." He suggests that the old tradition and civilization are justifiably in the line of fire because modern English society itself is founded on such upheavals as the dissolution of the extensive medieval monasteries by Henry VIII, as well as on the great industrial revolution. Therefore England "is itself in great measure founded on wrecking. But [the working classes] got none of the spoils, they came in for nothing but harm from it then and thereafter. England has grown hugely wealthy but this wealth has not reached the working classes; I expect it has made their condition worse." Furthermore, he continues in the same letter, the old traditions are unfortunately linked to the "iniquitous order" of society in the eyes of the masses. "But as the working classes have not been educated they know next to nothing of all this and cannot be expected to care if they destroy it. The more I look the more black and deservedly black the future looks, so I will write no more." [21]

[19] *Ibid.*

[20] For a discussion of the relation between this sonnet and an 1870 painting which also portrays stasis and energy see Paul L. Mariani, "Hopkins' 'Harry Ploughman' and Frederick Walker's 'The Plough'" in *The Month,* n.s. XL (1968), 37–45. This article includes a reproduction of "The Plough."   [21] *Letters I,* pp. 27–28.

For all of its radical sentiments, there remains something about this early letter which suggests the young man. It is earnest and impassioned, but its tone is that of someone who has not had much firsthand experience with the working classes. Subsequent contact with them and with the Liberals tempered his enthusiasm; a growing sense of man's moral intransigence had made the priest skeptical of the claims of "revolutionaries." One is so "fagged," he complained to Bridges after hearing the confessions of the day laborers living in the Liverpool slums, "one is so fagged, so harried and gallied up and down. And the drunkards go on drinking, the filthy, as the scripture says, are filthy still; human nature is so inveterate. Would I had seen the last of it." [22]

Hopkins was, if we must label him, a social idealist, a Tory, who in broad outline accepted the political and social ideas of Disraeli. If he does not describe any particular member of the English laboring class, it is because his poetry is concerned primarily with other things. But he was painfully aware of the severe economic difficulties of the workers in the eighties due to widespread unemployment. He knew too what the lack of bread on the table could do to a man's moral constitution. The tragic unemployment of thousands of able-bodied workmen in the eighties and probably the march of the unemployed on "Bloody Sunday" in 1886 no doubt served as the immediate stimuli for Hopkins' writing *Tom's Garland: upon the Unemployed.*

This is the only one of Hopkins' three caudated sonnets actually modeled on Milton's sonnet. Hopkins wanted the coda for its repetitive force and emphasis, "for a sonnet. . . in some sort 'nello stilo satirico o bernesco' " (in a satiric or bernesque style) .[23] The rhyme scheme of *On the New Forcers of Conscience* is as follows (the first line of each tercet is

[22] *Ibid.,* p. 110.

[23] Letter of November 6, 1887, *Letters I,* p. 266. Francesco Berni (1498[9]–1535), a satiric poet who frequently mocked the Petrarchan style, often appended very long codas to his sonnets for satiric effects. He raised satirical poetry to a literary genre called after him *bernesco.*

a half-line): abba abba cdedec cee eff. *Tom's Garland* has the following rhyme scheme (the first line of each tercet is a half-line): abba abba ccdccd dee eff. Both sonnets have twenty lines. The only difference between the two occurs in the Petrarchan sestet of each, and this sestet traditionally allows for variation.

Tom's Garland begins as a rollicking, carefree poem which pokes some good fun at thick-skinned Tom and Dick. Tom is garlanded not with a crown of flowers or gold upon his head but with "squat and surly steel." The string of epithets works like a transcribed Greek adjectival construction which affectionately inscapes Tom; a strong caesura after the first half-foot of the second line brings us full circle: "Tom—garlanded with squat and surly steel / Tom; . . . ." Tom is king of his domain, the earth, an idea implied in "garlanded," "squat[ter]" (ownership of domain by right of possession and working of the earth), and "surly" (from the Middle English *sirly,* meaning lordly or imperious). But the epithets work simultaneously in an opposite and satiric manner. For a squatting position is certainly comic in connection with a king, "surly" has changed from its meaning of imperious to its meaning in Hopkins' time of simply "harsh" or "rude" and even "threatening." And finally Tom's proper garland is a pair of hobnail boots.

"Sturdy Dick" is likewise inscaped in terms of footwear. It is the end of the day's work and "Tom's fallowbootfellow piles pick / By him and rips out rockfire homeforth." Dick's heavy hobnail workman's boots scrape out sparks on the stones in a lively manner while he goes home to his meal. Here is that sense of friendship and community, of being part of the commonweal.[24]

Hopkins dwells fondly on the figure of Tom, whose name

---

[24] On the nature of justice and the commonweal, see Hopkins' sermon for Sunday evening, January 11, 1880, delivered at St. Francis Xavier's, Liverpool, in *Sermons,* pp. 53–58. The whole sermon is important in connection with Hopkins' ideas on the duties and responsibilities of the head to its members and vice versa.

he repeats six times in the first six lines: what are the things that really concern Tom? Hopkins, who had worked among the Toms in Bedford Leigh, Glasgow, London, and Liverpool, where he labored largely with the Irish, answers, incorporating the Irish speech pattern: "Tom Heart-at-ease, Tom Navvy: he is all for his meal / Sure, 's bed now." There is an extra poetic yield as Hopkins works across the fifth line; the line means "and sure he has his meal and his bed." But also Tom's heart can be at ease as long as he can be sure of food and bedding for himself and his family ("sure of his bed now").

The poet puts his and Tom's blessing on this lowly but secure and carefree way of life as "So be it" (Amen) becomes "Low be it." Tom can swing his low lot lustily and heartily, though. And the reason for it is given simultaneously with the statement of his ability to do so in a hyperbaton which extends from the end of line 5 to the middle of line 8. Using the same freedom of syntax as in the first line—a string of epithets leading up to and ending in Tom and then reversing itself and leading away from Tom—the rhythms swing and rollick through the suspended parenthesis in the same carefree way as "sturdy Dick" swings home.

> Low be it: lustily he his low lot (feel
> That ne'er need hunger, Tom; Tom seldom sick,
> Seldomer heartsore; that treads through, prickproof, thick
> Thousands of thorns, thoughts) swings though.

Hopkins gives us a linguistic jawbreaker in the play on "through," "thoughts," and "though." (The mind almost balks before "swings though" and tends no substitute "swings through.") The alliteration of "thick / Thousands of thorns" adds to the complexity. It is as if Hopkins were intentionally teasing his navvy, who couldn't be bothered with such linguistic subtleties, much less with complex thoughts. There is no insult or haughtiness intended. The attitude that the intellectual complexities of life are for others and not for Tom is simply and honestly the attitude of many of the working class. Hopkins lets Tom speak for himself; there is a strong stress on the "I" as Tom gives his own opinion:

> Commonweal
> Little I reck ho! lacklevel in, if all had bread:
> Country is honour enough in all us.

And what is country? It is the body politic, the forty-three-year-old traditionalist and conservative tells us. It is

> lordly head,
> With heaven's lights high hung round, or, mother-ground
> That mammocks, mighty foot.

Here the commonwealth is seen in the age-old metaphor of the human body, each part of which has a purpose and all of whose parts are organically subordinated to the head for the common good of all. The commonweal is both the head, with its crown of stars ("quickgold" stars Hopkins had called them in *The Starlight Night*), and the "mighty foot" which breaks up, "rips out," and thus gains sustenance for the body ("mammocks" mimics "mama") from "mother-ground." The macrocosmic figure of the mighty foot digging up the earth echoes the similar but microcosmic figure of sturdy Dick ripping out rockfire.

The *volta* occurs only now, in the second half of line 12. Tom is satisfied with his low lot; he is the lower part of the body politic, but he has freedom from want and freedom from care. But what if he cannot speed on either road? He is not adequately equipped for those professions which demand a good deal of intellectual activity. Besides, he knows that such ways are perilous, thought-wearying, disheartening. Most Toms are not overly ambitious in this direction. But if the way that Tom would normally go is closed to him so that he cannot do his work safely and his needs are not provided for in return for his labor ("nor yet plod safe shod

sound"), then no way is open to him. Big, good-natured
Tom cannot nor does he care to rule, and if he cannot work
with his hands and his feet and gain a just wage for himself
and his family, then he is without so much as a *place* among
men:

> Undenizened, beyond bound
> Of earth's glory, earth's ease, all; no one, nowhere,
> In wide the world's weal; . . . .

In the whole circumference (there is probably a homophonic pun here on weal-wheel) of the world's wealth, there
is no place for the unemployed, who now become "no one."

The force of "undenizened" inscapes graphically and emotionally the nameless and now dehumanized unemployed
masses who are out of their natural environment, like fish
out of water. There is that sense of suffocation, that terror of
gasping for oxygen, that becomes the new lot of the nameless
Toms when economic constrictions overwhelm them and
threaten to end them. It is being bare of both "gold" and
"steel" which brutalizes the "seldom sick, / Seldomer heart-
sore" Tom, for Tom now has the cares that go with having
possessions without having any of those possessions. The
unemployed are bare of wealth and share the cares of both
the rich and the poor. But the clause can also be read as an
imperative demanding that the entire commonweal "care,
but share care."

The failure to care for the unemployed transforms them
in the eyes of those safely within the commonweal from
nameless masses with no place in the body politic into a
subhuman species, feeding like werewolves on the body itself:

> This, by Despair, bred Hangdog dull; by Rage,
> Manwolf, worse; and their packs infest the age.

Hopkins does not mitigate the potential brutality of the
unemployed, but he does emphasize that Tom is an abnor-

mal character "bred" by an abnormal situation. "Bare" of bread, he bares his fangs. The sympathy and charity of the portrait of Tom are qualities, however, which came of Hopkins' own growing humility and charity in his capacity as a slum priest who had come to know the dignity as well as the potential danger of the working masses.[25]

This emotional and intellectual complexity is necessary to understand the assumptions underlined in the sonnet, for Hopkins knew the shortcomings of the navvy as well as the dignity—the grace—he acquired through work. This Victorian belief in the dignity of the worker, which was preached in an oversimplified manner by Carlyle and was expressed in a more balanced way in the social writings of Ruskin and Morris and Leo XIII, was accepted wholeheartedly by Hopkins.

"I laughed outright and often, but very sardonically, to think you and the Canon could not construe my last sonnet; that he had to write to you for a crib," Hopkins told Bridges a month after he had sent *Tom's Garland*. "It is plain I must go no farther on this road: if you and he cannot understand me who will?"[26] With Bridges' bewildered reception of *Tom's Garland*, Hopkins' brief excursion into the poetry of social criticism ended. But if this road was now closed to

[25] The harsh language that Hopkins uses toward the unemployed mobs was echoed by many thinkers in the mid-eighties. See, for example, the concluding paragraphs of Thomas Hardy's "The Dorsetshire Labourer" which first appeared in *Longman's Magazine* in 1883 and which Irving Howe calls "a careful and realistic study of English agricultural workers." Speaking of the depopulation of the villages and the exodus of the workers to the industrial centers, Hardy laments that they "are nobody's care." Every undenizened villager "imbibes a sworn enmity to the existing order of things, and not a few of them, far from becoming merely honest Radicals, degenerate into Anarchists, waiters on chance, to whom danger to the State, the town—nay, the street they live in, is a welcomed opportunity" (*The Selected Writings of Thomas Hardy*, ed. Irving Howe [New York, 1966], pp. 136–137).

[26] Letter of February 10, 1888, *Letters I*, p. 272.

Hopkins, the way was open to further experiment with the coda itself.

At the close of his last letter to the Reverend Canon Dixon, written on July 29, 1888, from St. Stephen's Green, Hopkins noted that he was nearing the end of yet another batch of examination papers and was beginning to see light.[27] He also complained about the cloudy days and rainy weather. "What a preposterous summer! It is raining now: when it is not? However there was one windy bright day between floods last week: fearing for my eyes, with my other rain of papers, I put work aside and went out for the day, and conceived a sonnet. Otherwise," he lamented, realizing that his literary energies had for so long been spent on reading and grading student themes, "my muse has long put down her carriage and now for years 'takes in washing[.]' The laundry is driving a great trade now."[28]

Hopkins did not send Dixon this new sonnet and he does not mention it by name. But there is no doubt that he was referring to *That Nature is a Heraclitean Fire and of the comfort of the Resurrection,* for the autograph copy carries the information "July 26, 1888. Co. Dublin." Not only did he not send the poem to Dixon, he apparently did not even keep a copy for himself, for the only copy is the one he sent to Bridges from Monzie Villa, Fort William, on Saturday, August 18, 1888. Fort William was the touring center for the Scottish West Highlands, over one hundred miles north-northwest of Glasgow, and the starting point for the ascent of Ben Nevis. It was here that Hopkins had come for his summer vacation soon after writing to Dixon. "Six weeks of

[27] Gardner is mistaken in assuming that the "two Dromore sonnets and *That Nature is a Heraclitean Fire* (the only finished poem of the year 1888) were all begun when the poet was away from Dublin on vacation, at times when he felt justified in forgetting his lectures and examination papers" (Gardner, II, 360). *St. Alphonsus Rodriguez* was composed in October 1888.   [28] *Letters II,* p. 157.

examination are lately over," he wrote Bridges, "and I am now bringing a fortnight's holiday to an end.

I have leave to prolong it, but it is not very convenient to do so and I scarcely care. It appears I want not scenery but friends. . . . I am feeling very old and looking very wrinkled. . . . I will now go to bed, the more so as I am going to preach tomorrow and put plainly to a Highland congregation of MacDonalds, MacIntoshes, MacKillops, and the rest what I am putting not at all so plainly to the rest of the world, or rather to you and Canon Dixon, in a sonnet in sprung rhythm with two [sic] codas.[29]

There is one further mention of the poem in a letter to Bridges written five weeks later from St. Stephen's Green. "I am sorry to hear of our differing so much in taste," Hopkins wrote.

I was hardly aware of it. (It is not nearly so sad as differing in religion.) I feel how great the loss is of not reading, as you say; but if I did read I do not much think the effect of it would be what you seem to expect, on either my compositions or my judgments.

I *must* read something of Greek and Latin letters and lately I sent you a sonnet, on the Heraclitean Fire, in which a great deal of early Greek philosophical thought was distilled; but the liquor of the distillation did not taste very Greek, did it? The effect of studying masterpieces is to make me admire and do otherwise. So it must be on every original artist to some degree, on me to a marked degree.[30]

Structurally *That Nature is a Heraclitean Fire* is a further experiment in the caudated sonnet form. It has twenty-four lines eked out by three codas and a final refrain or echo line, and has the following rhyme scheme (the first line of each tercet and the last line are half-lines) : abba abba cdcdcd dee eff fgg g. The final burden line of *That Nature is a Heracli-*

[29] *Letters I*, pp. 278–279.
[30] Letter of September 25, 1888, *ibid.*, pp. 290–291.

tean Fire links this sonnet with *Harry Ploughman,* which ends with a similarly short line. But it is clear from a comparison of the pattern of the rhyme scheme of Milton's caudated sonnet with *That Nature is a Heraclitean Fire* that Hopkins has firmly grounded his sonnet on Milton's and has gone on his own road from there. Another extension of the caudated sonnet form is Hopkins' employment of an Alexandrine sprung line with a heavy medial pause which creates a marked percussive tempo—in fact, a vigorous chant. The rhythms mirror the widely modulated activities presented in the poem, from the nuances of subtle, rapid change to a grave, heavy flatness, and finally to the stark, emphatic monosyllabic beat of the closing lines.

That Nature is a Heraclitean Fire opens with a vivid composition of place. The speaker is out walking, apparently alone with his thoughts, observing the storm scape of still-turbulent clouds ("yestertempest") racing over the countryside. Sensitive to and perceptive of his surroundings, his imagination catches fire and responds joyfully and playfully to the protean cloud formations. The storm clouds are unsubstantial, and their shapes change as rapidly as they move. The speaker watches the light through the trees and observes the kaleidoscopic effect of light, altering between "roughcast" and "dazzling whitewash," fleck and change as the clouds pass behind the elm branches. Light and shadow shift patterns constantly.

Turning his eyes earthward, he sees how the strong warm wind seems, like a giant, to wrestle the earth and dry up all the standing pools from the recent storm. He checks off the steps by which the sun and wind transform watery mud into dust, literally pulverizing the soft footprints of the men who preceded him down the dirt road:

Delightfully the bright wind boisterous | ropes, wrestles, beats earth bare
Of yestertempest's creases; | in pool and rutpeel parches

Squandering ooze to squeezed | dough, crust, dust; stanches,
    starches
Squadroned masks and manmarks | treadmire toil there
Footfretted in it. . . .

The mood of the speaker, who humanizes the activity of
the clouds and the wind, becomes more sober as he is made
more aware that nature itself is indifferent to the cyclic
processes that it generates, and that the process is always
toward change and annihilation of the scape of a particular
object. The carefree wind and heat obliterate all traces of
the storm. But they obliterate too all signs of man's signature
in the earth, here scaped in the lowly image of footprints—
those "Squadroned masks and manmarks"—"Footfretted" in
the soft mud, which crumble away to dust. In fact, the
beauty of nature is kinetic; it depends upon a continuing
process of destruction and generation; the old is peeled away
to reveal the new. And this process of the new springing from
the funeral pyre of the old continues, seemingly, for its own
sake: "million-fuelèd, nature's bonfire burns on." The clouds
moving across the heavens now assume an uncanny resemblance to the smoke from a huge conflagration, the bonfire
of the whole world.

The speaker's reflection continues to spiral downward and
inward, toward the inevitable chaos and strife at the center
of a materialistic and atomistic universe: the dark cold waters at one pole of the Heraclitean flux. At this point the
eternal process simply reverses itself and all is caught up in
an equally indifferent fire, but Hopkins dwells on the nadir,
since the Heraclitean upswing offers no comfort to man. For
even man, nature's "bonniest, dearest to her, her clearest-
selvèd spark," [31] is part of nature's vast bonfire and is eventually "quench[ed]" in the black waters of personal extinction.
And what is more, even the most individuating marks of

[31] See *Sermons*, p. 122. Human nature is "more highly pitched, selved,
and distinctive than anything in the world."

collective humanity—the fame of man's greatest exploits ("firedint"), as well as the genius of man's ideas ("mark on mind"), to say nothing of the vast, anonymous majority of mankind—all are soon erased from the fluctuating and unsteady consciousness of the mind. From the long-range viewpoint, the flux ultimately "beats level" man and all his works:

But quench her bonniest, dearest | to her, her clearest-selvèd spark
Man, how fast his firedint, | his mark on mind, is gone!
Both are in an unfathomable, all is in an enormous dark
Drowned.

    The speaker has plumbed as far into chaos as the mind can go. Following this desolate meditation to its inexorable conclusion, he has come to a modernistic vision of man's utter insignificance and impermanence. Despite his apparent worth, in a world thus conceived (and Heraclitus speaks for many) man seems to have no more intrinsic or lasting value than the four elements—air, earth, fire and water—of which he is composed. Nature's bonfire scoffs at man's claims to any special dignity or permanence:

       O pity and indig | nation! Manshape, that shone
Sheer off, disseveral, a star, | death blots black out; nor mark
         Is any of him at all so stark
But vastness blurs and time | beats level. . . .

The speaker's mood has shifted from gaiety and playfulness in the opening lines to a growing depression from line 10 to the middle of line 16. Now the second *volta* in the speaker's meditation occurs. And it occurs immediately:

                          Enough! the Resurrection,
A heart's-clarion! Away grief's gasping, | joyless days, dejection.

This is a summons to the heart, a clear, shrill, unmistakable trumpet blast. The dark waters of chaos and despair which had threatened to swamp the poor wreck who is the speaker are suddenly dispersed. The strong, steady, eternal beacon of the risen Christ beckons. It had always been there had the speaker but looked upward; it was there for the nuns in the terrible night on the deck of the wrecked "Deutschland," and it is there for the fagged and harried wreck of a priest. There is a significant poetic yield in declaiming the preposition "Across" slowly so that what is suggested is "a cross" shining in the dark to the speaker: "Across my foundering deck shone / A beacon, an eternal beam."

Having received this assurance of the theandric nature of man—and therefore a guarantee of the intrinsic worth of all that he does, however trivial or apparently meaningless—the speaker can afford to flaunt death with an outrageous impunity. Let the body "fade" out like a light waning, he orders:

> Flesh fade, and mortal trash
> Fall to the residuary worm; | world's wildfire, leave but ash.

The "residuary" worm, the inheritor of man's physical estate, will receive the "mortal trash," what Hopkins had elsewhere called his "bone-house, mean house." The "world's wildfire," which is the seemingly eternal flux of nature, will burn up all substances (wildfire was an inflammable mixture used by the Greeks which would burn on any material). But in the Christian revelation, too, the bonfire will end in the final consummation of the world and will leave but ash. The classical Greek world view is thereby imaginatively reduced from a self-perpetuating alpha and omega to a mere instrument of God.

Hopkins blends several biblical images of man's sudden metamorphosis into a unified visual and auditory image.[32] We are given a superb catalogue of worthless fragments which have in common their accidental being. But the catalogue ends with a substance—a self—which is as permanent

[32] See II Peter 3:10, I Corinthians 15:52–54, and Matthew 24:29–32.

and immutable as any we know.[33] There is no doubt that
man changes constantly, but the essential self abides within
the trash:

In a flash, at a trumpet crash,
I am all at once what Christ is, | since he was what I am, and
This Jack, joke, poor potsherd, | patch, matchwood, immortal
diamond,
Is immortal diamond.[34]

The final coda is a masterpiece which will repay close
study. A "Jack" is a generic and pejorative name for a
common fellow, but it also denotes that which is without any
specific or definitive self. A "joke" of a man is a laughing-
stock, but he is also something lacking substance or genuine-
ness. The "poor potsherd" recalls the shard with which poor
Job scraped his oozing sores.[35] But it is also a fragmentary

[33] Hopkins made the following distinction between intrinsic and
accidental being: "Self is the intrinsic oneness of a thing, which is prior
to its being and does not result from it *ipso facto,* does not result, I
mean, from its having independent being; for accidental being, such as
that of the broken fragments of things or things purely artificial or
chance 'installs,' has no true and intrinsic oneness or true self: they
have independent existence, that is / they exist distinct from other
things and by or in themselves, but the independence, the distinctness,
the self is brought about artificially" (*Sermons,* p. 146).

[34] Hopkins' following observations may have crystallized into the
images of the final lines: "The winter [of 1871–1872] was long and
hard. I made many observations on freezing. For instance the crystals in
mud.—Hailstones are shaped like the cut of diamonds called brilliants.
—I found one morning the ground in one corner of the garden full of
small pieces of potsherd from which there rose up . . . long icicles"
(*Journals,* p. 201).

[35] W. A. M. Peters, S.J., points out how the words themselves change
from the Jack to the immortal diamond, especially if we mentally
supply "Job's" before "poor." Then we have Jack→joke→ (Job's) poor
potsherd→patch→matchwood→immortal diamond. This is convincing
except for the final element, which is as radically altered as the self is.
*Gerard Manley Hopkins: A Critical Essay toward the Understanding of
his Poetry* (London, 1948), p. 47.

object with only accidental being. A "patch" is a ninny or dolt (from the Italian *paccio*), but it is also a scrap or odd leftover used to mend something, a superfluity. "Matchwood" is wood splinters which burn away quickly to ash; wood shavings, too, have no more than accidental being. But within this list of insignificant, comical objects, there abides the immortal diamond, which has both an intrinsic as well as a transcendent self. What had always been there is suddenly purified and raised to a new level of being.

Diamond, which of itself is merely a hard, imperishable substance, a fragment of crystallized coal buried in the earth, is suddenly ("In a flash") made a precious, beautiful object by reflecting the light of the beacon (Christ), which gives the diamond its especial value and without which it is merely a cold, hard stone. For it is of the nature of the Incarnation and of its corollary, the Resurrection, that God communicates His divine life to man, and the human vessel reflects this life while maintaining its distinctive self.[36]

It is interesting to note how Hopkins has caught the dynamism of flux and the dynamism of theandric permanence.

---

[36] Despite his remarkable presentation of much of Hopkins' philosophical and theological thought, J. Hillis Miller's evaluation of Hopkins' insight into the immediacy and personal significance of the Resurrection is less convincing than the earlier sections of his long essay. He does not see that for Hopkins the self is transformed without being obliterated. And he underplays the all-importance of the Resurrection in a theology of Incarnation: "[Hopkins] is sustained by nothing but the comfort of the Resurrection, the hope of that miracle of transubstantiation which will . . . change him from one allotropic form of himself to another so different that if there is any secret continuity between the two it is only that the same neutral possibility of being is, in each case, made real by God, made real in forms which are as far apart as the whole distance from hell to heaven" (*The Disappearance of God: Five Nineteenth-Century Writers* [Cambridge, Mass., 1963], p. 358). Hopkins' whole point, of course, is that as a particular human self, the "neutral possibility" has already been negated by God's choice, and man's essential being needs only to be purified and perfected.

As the poem rounds to an end, we sense a spatial and temporal contraction in the images and corresponding intensification of emotion. The syntax is forced forward by the catalogue, but the copulative verb "Is" holds the last movement in the permanent moment of self-identity.

The rich flurry of dynamic verbs in the opening section reflects and imitates the continual process of the Heraclitean flux itself: "chevy," "throng," "glitter," "arches," "lace, lance, and pair," "ropes, wrestles, beats," "parches," "stanches, starches," and "burns." The first movement of the sonnet, including the first *volta*, is marked by transitive verbs, shading off in the second part into verbs reflecting processes which are reversible in the Heraclitean flux but which are final in man: "quench," "drowned," and finally "beats" man level.

But in the second turn, the copulative verb, which seems so colorless and thus assiduously to be avoided in poetry, is made at once not only the most affirmative but also the most dynamic verb of the sonnet. It is the perfect verbal equivalent for the supraspatial and supratemporal shift from dynamic flux to transcendent permanence. The transmutation from dust to risen god will happen, Hopkins implies, as swiftly as the poem here turns from dejection to joy.[37]

God's assumption of human nature strikes Hopkins as the strongest argument for the resurrection of man. For if Christ condescended to suffer for man, then the value of men is infinitely more than we may suspect. This is the argument Hopkins hammers home in the pounding monosyllables of

I am all at once what Christ is, | since he was what I am.

The percussive rhyming of the last two codas also intensifies and clarifies the emotional import of the thought. In the

[37] Hopkins himself has written on the force of "is": "I have often felt . . . [about] the depth of an instress or how fast the inscape holds a thing that nothing is so pregnant and straight forward to the truth as simple *yes* and *is*" (*Journals*, p. 127). Hopkins' spiritual notes on the Resurrection are in *Sermons*, p. 194.

grouping of "trash," "ash," "flash," and "crash," the sharp, shrill rhymes suggest that sudden transformation which will burn away man's trash, revealing the glorified body. Again, the "[wha]t I am, and" is ingeniously rhymed with "diamond" to show the identity between the essential self and its divine spark. And these are rhymed with the second "diamond" to reinforce and make final the identity.

Images of light and sound recur throughout the poem, and these constitute one of Hopkins' most subtle effects. The bright lights are reflected off the whitewashed clouds, forever changing in intensity and creating an image of strong but diffused and blurred light. Man is nature's "clearest-selvèd spark," a star shining apart and above; his mark or impression on mind is "firedint." But both man and his works are "quench[ed]," "blur[red]" and blotted "black out" in the primordial chaotic flood, fire's opposite. The images of sound parallel the images of light, and the boisterous and mindless moan of the wind is a correlative of the eternal flux which pervades the first two parts of the sonnet.

But the blurred and muffled quality of the sound and light images, like the involved and congested syntax, gives way to the sharpness and clarity of "flash," "heart's clarion," and "trumpet crash," just as amorphous, ever-changing clouds give way in the poem to the permanence of diamond. Suffocating with the terrible darkness of formless flux without and within, the wreck of the poet suddenly sees the strong, clear, steady beam of the Light shine forth.

That Nature is a Heraclitean Fire is clearly a masterpiece. The amount of sheer intelligence at work in fusing so many elements of sound and sense into an organic experience is both surprising and exciting. And although the conclusion rests on Christian doctrine, it has an integrated and esemplastic harmony with the rest of the poem. Those critics like Claude C. Abbott who suggest that the conclusion of the sonnet jumps out of the pattern like a pious afterthought have not adequately understood what Hopkins is doing.

The three caudated sonnets represent a new direction, a further stretching of the traditionally rigid limits of the Petrarchan sonnet. There is an opulence, a joy in creativity, a new plumbing of the dynamic potentialities of language and melodic rhythm which constitute no less than a chant to the risen Christ.[38] Hopkins had just over ten months to live when he created his optimistic carol to the permanence of man in the Resurrection. His last sonnets, however, cease to be hymns and become more like personal colloquies whispered by Hopkins to his God.

Sometime in March or April of 1888, probably while administering or proctoring examinations in classics at University College, Dublin, Hopkins found some time to begin a marriage ode in honor of his youngest brother and his wife.[39] The *Epithalamion* fragment is mentioned only once, in a letter to Bridges in May 1888,[40] but it was never sent and was found among Hopkins' papers after his death a year later. What we have are five sides of a first draft and some rough sketches on Royal University of Ireland examination paper.

The fragment is a jubilant celebration of boys swimming and diving and laughing in a river lined by a "bushybow-

[38] That Hopkins was consciously working toward a chanting voice in his caudated sonnets, culminating in *That Nature is a Heraclitean Fire,* may be gathered from the absence of counterpoint, which pitches a melodic line against a line approximating the speaking voice. What is substituted is a line "with long dwells on the rhythm," a chanting voice, in fact, the next step beyond recitation. Speaking of music, which for Hopkins had many correspondences to poetic recitation, the poet told Bridges in the same letter in which he sent his last caudated sonnet that the "only good and truly beautiful recitative is that of plain chant; which indeed culminates in that. It is a natural development of the speaking, reading, or declaiming voice, and has the richness of nature" (*Letters I,* p. 280).

[39] See Robert Bridges' note to *Epithalamion, Poems,* p. 317. Everard Hopkins (1860–1928) married Amy Sichel in April 1888. There are two extant unpublished letters to Everard owned by the University of Texas.   [40] See *Letters I,* p. 277.

ered wood." A stranger traveling by is attracted by the happy shouts, finds a pool nearby, strips, and frolics too in the "kindcold element." Hopkins established the composition of place, "summer's sovereign good," but broke off at the interpretation of this natural setting. While, therefore, we can make some guesses as to the outline of the whole, there is not enough information to unravel the entire symbolic significance of the physical scene. But perhaps we can hazard a guess. Hopkins gives us a few clues. The "Southern dean or Lancashire clough or Devon cleave"—that is, the leafy hood which opens onto the water—is "wedlock," entrance to the condition of "Spousal love." The "listless stranger" walking in the summer's heat is the bachelor (like Hopkins' brother, Everard) who witnesses "unseen" what others are already enjoying and opts to enter into marriage also. Stripping himself to taste that joy, he enters those waters with their "heavenfallen freshness," while all about his bower are ranked his family and friends, who contribute to the coolness and sweetness of the scene and who in turn are refreshed by those waters, by spousal love in their midst.

Hopkins had a high regard for marriage; in fact, he admitted that he was sometimes "spoony" over a married couple. What is remarkable about the *Epithalamion* piece is its freshness and spontaneity. It stresses the coolness which marriage offers after the feverishness and listlessness of the solitary journey. It can be a partial recapturing of Eden, a freedom from restraint, as imaged in the clothes and especially the heavy walking shoes, in which the heat and burden of concupiscence gives way to the playful innocence and fecundity of the bower. Hopkins' chastity is rewarded in the insight that the highest moments of marital love which we recall are not the heat of sexuality but its joy and unrestrained freedom. He has found an image for this sense of marriage's "sovereign good" in the inviting shout from the carefree boys enjoying the refreshing river's fullness.

But if we were to remove the title and end the poem with

line 42 we would have an exuberant picture of summer. Nor is there any hint of an allegorical reading in the lines themselves, so intently has Hopkins focused on the natural beauty of the pastoral scene. And while he places the scene in the England familiar to his family, what he says of the river fits the "burling Barrow Brown" as seen from the estate of Lord Drogheda at Monasterevan:

> a candycoloured, where a gluegold-brown
> Marbled river, boisterously beautiful, between
> Roots and rocks is danced and dandled, all in froth and water-
> blowballs, down.

What a joy and spontaneity in the language is here, in this "gambolling and echoing-of-earth note." It is tempting to see in the listless stranger the figure of Hopkins himself, that stranger among strangers, the English Jesuit administering to Irish students, breaking away in his rich imagination from the drudgery of "examining a nation" to swim naked, alone, in some pool somewhere with "flake leaves light" above him "as the stars or as the angels there."

In the midst of the drudgery of preparing examinations in early October 1888, Hopkins rushed a short, hurried letter off to Bridges. He had been asked to write a poem in honor of a recently canonized member of the Society of Jesus, St. Alphonsus Rodriguez.

I ask your opinion of a sonnet written to order on the occasion of the first feast since his canonisation proper of St. Alphonsus Rodriguez, a laybrother of our Order, who for 40 years acted as hall-porter to the College of Palma in Majorca: he was, it is believed, much favoured by God with heavenly lights and much persecuted by evil spirits. The sonnet (I say it snorting) aims at being intelligible.

Hopkins enclosed an early version of the sonnet along with variants.[41]

[41] *Ibid.*, pp. 292–293. The version with variants sent to Bridges is printed in the body of this letter.

But Bridges objected to the epithets Hopkins applied to God—"mountain-mason, continent- / Quarrier, earthwright"—as "cheeky." And he had apparently disliked what he thought was a confusion of thought on Hopkins' part in setting next to the "trickling increment" of growing things the different activity of God's hewing mountains. Hopkins defends the verbal exactness of the two opposing forces by which God shapes nature and insists that "exploit" is the right word. He insists on broad boundaries for a poetic language: if the proper word "has nothing flat or poor about it it is the best word to use in poetry as in prose." Finally, he maintains that he does not use verbal filler:

By "regular indoors work" I understand you to mean a drawing finished at home with the eye no longer on the object, something poorly thrown in to fill up a blank the right filling of which is forgotten. But "so we say" is just what I have to say and want to say (it was made out of doors in the Phoenix Park with my mind's eye on the first presentment of the thought): I mean "This is what we commonly say, but we are wrong." [42]

What Hopkins says of the sestet, that it is "both pregnant and exact," is true of the entire sonnet.[43] The poem has two turns; the first occurs at the beginning of line 6 ("But"), the second at the standard ninth line ("Yet"). There are also two kinds of activity portrayed which are operative in two relatively opposing quantities. Swift, short-lived action in the magnanimous spirit—the grand heroic gesture of Christ and the martyrs—is the most easily understood type of glorious conquest because it can be readily perceived. But, Hopkins insists, it is not the only kind of heroic exploit. There is another kind of battle: the long, agonizingly drawn-out holding action within. But such actions are smaller only in that they occupy the inner spaces. Otherwise the heroism is as great. And despite the seeming lack of external events, the

[42] *Ibid.*, p. 297.   [43] *Ibid.*

world within is crowded with the contenders of that inner war.

Although we cannot see this long inner conflict and ultimate conquest, Hopkins argues that what earth does not witness it nevertheless manifests. The second *volta* demonstrates the unseen activity of God within by the demonstrable activity of God operating in and through external nature. God operates in sundry and even opposing ways, for He is both "a winter and warm" Who works on St. Paul in one way and on St. Augustine in another. He can shape in the large scale, hewing out mountains and whole continents, but He is also the power Who with indiscernible slowness delicately veins flowers and gives length to the tall trees. The entire sestet is a loose sentence constructed in two parts. The three-line parenthesis describes God's differing activities in nature; the final three lines describe the growth of St. Alphonsus Rodriguez by the second manner of God's activity —by "trickling increment":

> Yet God (that hews mountain and continent,
> Earth, all, out; who, with trickling increment,
> Veins violets and tall trees makes more and more)
> Could crowd career with conquest while there went
> Those years and years by of world without event
> That in Majorca Alfonso watched the door.

We have presented in the sonnet, then, a pattern of progressive actions which may be expressed in the following way. Hopkins focuses first on the "glorious day" of martyrdom for giants like Christ and the hero-martyrs (ll. 1–5). But the inner spiritual struggle is silent and unseen (ll. 6–8). Nevertheless, God also works in another way: in giant things (mountains and continents and tall trees) as in small (violets). In all of these he works slowly, where time is told in months and years and centuries (ll. 9–11). And this is how God worked sainthood in St. Alphonsus: by the Brother's obedience in small things (watching the door) over many seemingly uneventful years. The action, then, moves from the large, swift manifestation—the flash—to the small, slow, hidden drama within.

The progression of the verbs precisely conveys this line of development. The terrible, shaping "strokes," which have "gashed" flesh and "galled" shield, now "tongue" and "trumpet" the victory and "forge" the martyr's day. God shapes, literally "hews . . . out" conquest from the very flesh of Christ and the martyrs. And God "hews . . . out" the great mountains and the continents, natural figures of greatness and largeness. But just as He "Veins violets" and "makes trees more and more," He could, in the silent world within (and the emphasis on silence is important), "crowd career with conquest" during all those outwardly eventless years that Alphonsus, in strict obedience to his calling as porter, seemed simply to have "watched the door."

"Crowd," here, suggests "crown." But the choice of "crowd" is the perfect stroke, for it suggests that the inner world was so thronged with events that the victory itself had to be squeezed in as the sweet culmination. The phrase is also a good example of what Kenneth Burke has called the poetic analogue to musical augmentation. For the *cr* consonants which first appear in juxtaposition are then repeated in the same order but with a vowel interceding. "Could crowd career with conquest" may be transcribed as follows: *c-d cr-d c-r-r* with *c-nq-st*. (There is also alliteration in the *c*'s and consonantal repetition in the voiced *d*'s and unvoiced *t*.) [44]

Pick, Gardner, and Ritz have all pointed to the relation of this sonnet to *The Windhover* of eleven years before.[45] And certainly the lowly figures of the galled clods of earth and the

---

[44] See all of Burke's "On Musicality in Verse" (1940) in *Perspectives in Incongruity,* ed. Stanley Edgar Hyman (Bloomington, Ind., 1964), pp. 110–118.

[45] Cf. Pick, *Gerard Manley Hopkins: Priest and Poet* (New York, 1966), pp. 153–154; Gardner, I, 184; and Ritz, p. 533.

gashed embers flashing forth into light are a symbol of the reward which crowns the menial tasks of Alphonsus. There is also here an echo, probably, of a stanza of Hopkins' patriotic military poem, of which he had sent Bridges an improved musical score in late September, about the time he wrote this sonnet. The fourth stanza of *What shall I do for the land that bred me* says that honor is gained by sticking to one's duty until death:

> Where is the field I must play the man on?
> O welcome there their steel and cannon.
> Immortal beauty is death with duty,
> If under her banner I fall for her honour.

If in his previous sonnet, *That Nature is a Heraclitean Fire*, Hopkins had stressed the anticipation of the final utter transformation, here he dwells on the long process, "years and years by of world without event," which leads finally to spiritual victory. And what Hopkins has done in the last line of this sonnet is to stress the apparent insignificance and triviality of Alphonsus' position at the same time that the music of that line seems to sigh after his mastery of means in achieving the final victory. We recall that final, tender, almost swooning exclamation at the close of *The Windhover*, with its modulation of "ah" and "awe" sounds: "blue-bleak embers, *a*h my dear, / F*a*ll, g*a*ll themselves, *a*nd g*a*sh gold-vermilion." There the color and activity were complemented by the exclamations. In the final line of *St. Alphonsus Rodriguez*, Hopkins himself understands the significance of the victory of this saint who heroically prepared himself to receive the transforming mastery of God. For, if the poem ends on an apparent anticlimax, it exults in the serene victory behind these undramatic appearances.

Alphonsus' saintliness was a protracted affair, won by a perfect obedience to and patience before God's will. In his exegesis of the fifth and sixth chapters of St. Paul's Epistle to the Galatians, an exegesis undertaken at Bridges' request,

Hopkins had written that it is useless for any man to compare his moral actions with another's. Each man has different strengths and weaknesses, so that exulting in one's strengths is simply pride, since of themselves men can do nothing. "If they once did the works of the flesh," he continued, "and now do those of the spirit or if they once did a little of these good works and now do a great deal, then there is a positive gain, an advantage *of themselves over themselves,* and of this [they] may be proud, that is they may exult at it; but always within the world of their own beings." [46]

This is what Hopkins was looking for in his own life: the patient, gradual metamorphosis of the gray dray horse into the noble steed. It is what he had asked of God in that important retreat at Beaumont in September 1883: "During this retreat I have much and earnestly prayed that God will lift me above myself to a higher state of grace, in which I may have more union with him, be more zealous to do his will, and freer from sin." [47]

Hopkins was clearly aware that God would work in him with a "lingering-out sweet skill," that his own holiness would come in the "well performance" of the duties sent his way. Just before he had asked God's help he had recalled that in his covenant of obedience with God he had to perform his share as well as he could:

For thus it behoves us to fulfil all justice: I remembered Fr. Whitty's [Hopkins' Master of Tertians during his long retreat] teaching how a great part of life to the holiest of men consists in the well performance, the performance, one may say, of ordinary duties[.] And this comforted [me] against the thought of the little I do in the way of hard penances; for if I am not now called to those it is better not to bewail my cowardice or nonperformance in the matter but to say thus, in such and such an appointed way, it behoves me to fulfil all justice[.]

[46] Letter of September 10, 1888, *Letters I,* p. 288. About three weeks later he composed his sonnet in honor of the saint.

[47] *Sermons,* p. 253.

Also since God gives me at present no great humiliations and I am not worthy of them and did not accept them well when they came [it behoves me] to welcome the small ones whenever such shall occur[.] [48]

The work which had been given Hopkins was to prove a grinding, eventless existence, the galling, fatiguing work of "examining a nation." In his last retreat, he closely examined himself. The conclusions are not histrionic or blown up so that he can pity himself. In real humility and honesty he passes judgment on his five years spent in Dublin lecturing and grading innumerable essays ("fallen leaves of my poor life between all the leaves of it") .[49] It is not his work he is hard on; he had done this well enough. It is the self-bent will which chafes and will not rest under the dry, fruitless work assigned, fruitless because Hopkins had fears that the whole structure of the University itself would collapse of dry rot at any time. Simply as a scholar, Hopkins needed the sense of permanence and stability. It is no wonder that he was so taken by the patience and final peace which Alphonsus had won.

From mid-October until mid-March 1889, a period of five months, Hopkins seems to have written no poetry. The only documents which reveal something of the man himself during this period are the letters he writes to Bridges. And it may seem intolerable and frustrating that two of these should have been destroyed by Bridges.

Up through the end of April, 1889, by which time his final three sonnets were finished, Hopkins still possessed his sharp wit and imaginative edge, despite the deep-rooted weariness and fatigue he was experiencing. In the last months of his life, there emerges in the letters a note of irony and humor which is dark but crystalline, deflating without being morose. This is important in giving us a clue to Hopkins' frame of mind during the little more than five weeks between the

[48] *Ibid.*   [49] *Letters I,* p. 296.

writing of the first and the third of the last sonnets. There is little doubt in my own mind that Bridges destroyed two letters written between March 24 and April 29 because in them Hopkins continued to poke unusually strong fun at Bridges' habit of publishing in very small quantities at the same time that he clearly wanted a poet's fame. In his last letter, on April 29, he tells Bridges to stop pouting:

And I want you too to "buck up," as we used to say at school, about those jokes over which you write in so dudgeonous a spirit. I have it now down in my tablets that a man may joke and joke and be offensive; I have had several warnings lately leading me to make the entry, tho' goodness knows the joke that gave most offence was harmless enough and even kind. You I treated to the same sort of irony as I do myself; but it is true it makes all the world of difference whose hand administers.[50]

All three final sonnets treat the speaker with self-deflating irony and even dark comedy; there is no self-pity in them that is not exploded by the speaker himself. The speaker finds it harder and harder to take seriously either himself or others in the face of a growing awareness of God's all-pervasive presence. While the awareness of man's smallness before God is only obliquely shadowed in Hopkins' last letters, it informs the core of all three of his last sonnets.

Finally, there emerges in these last sonnets a sense of patience and of waiting which is more deep-rooted than in the poems of desolation written four years before. In those there had been a sense of anxiety, presented most vividly in the image of the speaker's wrestling with God as with a contender. But that sense of rebellion against God, which is perhaps what Devlin meant when he called the image "somehow alien to Catholic spirituality," is gone from the last sonnets.[51] True, there is in 1889 an aridity, a spiritual dryness of the soul, but what is present is a significant realignment of the will, a fuller dependence upon God, the Lord of

[50] *Ibid.*, p. 303.   [51] *Sermons*, p. 118.

all life. There is no doubt that Hopkins is again undergoing a period of desolation, but he seems even more aware of the nature of the dark night and waits patiently for God's consolation.

"In time of desolation," writes Ignatius in the "Rules for the Discernment of Spirits," "one should never make a change, but stand firm and constant in the resolutions and decision which guided him the day before the desolation, or to the decision which he observed in the preceding consolation." And again: "One who is in desolation must strive to persevere in patience, which is contrary to the vexations that have come upon him." [52]

Along with this greater patience—a radical change in a man who by temperament was so hypersensitive and self-exacting—there is a growing feeling of his own littleness before his Lord, a feeling of complete dependence and trust. This new sense of his own unimportance does not give rise to self-loathing and disgust, however, as it does in his notes to his last retreat. Rather, it expresses itself in a quiet, sophisticated humor at his own expense. In the war waged within, this transformation was certainly no small victory for a man as aware of the self as Hopkins. In one sense God has disappeared, but it is only to draw Hopkins after Him.

For some critics of Hopkins, looking for other signs, there is in the priest's last poems a bitterness, a collapse, a giving-in to despair. J. Hillis Miller, for example, sees Hopkins at the end as back where he began, with a hidden God, undergoing something close to a crisis of faith. And James Reeves holds, even more untenably, that it "is doubtful if any great poet has ended his poetic life on a note of deeper hopelessness and desolation." [53] There is, rather, a very real spiritual gain at the end of Hopkins' life if we can read the

[52] *The Spiritual Exercises of St. Ignatius,* trans. Anthony Mattola (Garden City, N.Y., 1964) p. 130.

[53] *Selected Poems of Gerard Manley Hopkins* (London, 1964), p. 98.

signs. He seems to have entered into the vestibule of orthodox contemplation, or something very like it.[54]

On the second Sunday in Lent, after five months of poetic silence, Hopkins composed his next sonnet, *Thou art indeed just, Lord*. At the heading of the copy sent to Bridges he wrote "Justus es, &c. Jer. xii. I (for title), March 17, '89." The first quatrain is a powerful translation of Jeremias, and the entire sonnet continues the images of fruitful vegetation in contrast to the sterile speaker. In its context, the opening verses of the twelfth chapter of Jeremias concern the just man's lament that his ways fail while the wicked man's ways prosper. But the Lord promises to restore the balance. What we have in the sonnet, however, is only the just man's lament. Here are the relevant verses from Jeremias:

Thou indeed, O Lord, art just, if I plead with thee, but yet I will speak what is just to thee: why doth the way of the wicked prosper: why is it well with all them that transgress, and do wickedly? Thou has planted them, and they have taken root: they prosper and bring forth fruit: thou are near in their mouth, and far from their reins. And thou, O Lord, hast known me, thou hast seen me, and proved my heart with thee   [Jeremias 12:1–3].

But there is another passage from Jeremias which also echoes the images of fertility and sterility in the sestet of the sonnet. In the Epistle for the Mass of the previous Thursday, March 14, taken from Jeremias 17:5–10, Hopkins would have read the following:

Thus saith the Lord: Cursed be the man that trusteth in man, and maketh flesh his arm, and whose heart departeth from the Lord. For he shall be like tamaric in the desert, and he shall not see when good shall come: but he shall dwell in dryness in the desert in a salt land, and not inhabited. Blessed be the man that

[54] To understand Hopkins' spiritual condition see, for example, Père Ludovic de Besse, *La Science de la Prière* (Paris, 1903), translated as *The Science of Prayer* (London, 1925), quoted in Dom Cuthbert Butler's *Western Mysticism* (Dublin, 1960), pp. 12–13.

trusteth in the Lord, and the Lord shall be his confidence. And he shall be as a tree that is planted by the waters, that spreadeth out its roots towards moisture: and it shall not fear when the heat cometh. And the leaf thereof shall be green, and in the time of drought it shall not be solicitous, neither shall it cease at any time to bring forth fruit. The heart is perverse above all things, and unsearchable, who can know it? I *am* the Lord who search the heart, and prove the reins: who give to every one according to his way, and according to the fruit of his devices.

These verses from Jeremias form the background against which the speaker of the sonnet presents his case. God has promised greenness and fruition to the just man, so the speaker has a just cause which he pleads in the role of a skillful *advocatus* before the *dominus*. He begins by stressing the justice of his Lord and then the justness of his cause. The speaker is a just man (although he does not say this bluntly) but his ways are disappointed, defeated, thwarted, while the ways of the sinner prosper. He has presented his grievances formally, but he is a friend of the *dominus* and he says so. The tone is ambiguous and even confused. He will plead his cause in justice, but he pleads like a rejected lover. There is no "O thou my friend" in the passages from Jeremiah.

The double "sir," the respectful "thou," and the tender, almost heartbreaking "friend" create both distancing objectivity and intimacy. And the emphatic placing of the second "sir" where the *volta* would normally come further emphasizes the formal yet chiding address. To make the speaker's situation all the more unbearable, there appear all around him the first signs of green spring. Even the common cow parsley—"fretty chervil"—laces the banks and is shaken by the wind. But the speaker is not moved by the wind. In a literal sense, he is not sensibly moved by inspiration, is not breathed into by the "lord of life." The appeal now is to God's universal bestowal of life and energy upon all nature. Then, in the final, one-sentence line the advocate-friend makes his plea for inspiration, for growth: "Mine, O thou lord of life, send my roots rain." The force of "mine" is twofold: it refers both to the "lord of life" and to the speaker's "roots." The final plea is a request, but it is a request made as much to a friend as to the Almighty.

Hopkins has precisely caught the nervous rhythms of unfolding, budding vegetation in "fretty" (fretted like lacework, but also nervous), and in "wakes," which derives originally from the Latin *vegere,* to rouse or excite. This new spring is precisely what Hopkins himself desires; he needs the keen nervous energy which allows for productive work.

Hopkins has crystallized here several recurring complaints made in his letters and in his retreat notes. "There is a point with me in matters of any size," he wrote Bridges in mid-May 1885 when he was in the grip of his earlier desolation, "when I must absolutely have encouragement as much as crops rain." [55] And on the following September 1 he wrote again to Bridges. The passage is quite similar to the opening lines of his last poem, *To R. B.:*

[It] is widely true, the fine pleasure ["fine delight"] is not to do a thing but to feel that you could and the mortification that goes to the heart is to feel it is the power that fails you: *qui occidere nolunt Posse volunt* [those who won't kill want to feel they can]: it is the refusal of a thing that we like to have. So with me, if I could but get on, if I could but produce work I should not mind its being buried, silenced, and going no further; but it kills me to be time's eunuch and never to beget.[56]

And finally, there is this entry in his private notes during his last retreat on New Year's Day, 1889:

I began to enter on that course of loathing and hopelessness which I have so often felt before, which made me fear madness and led me to give up the practice of meditation except, as now, in retreat and here it is again. I could therefore do no more than repeat *Justus es, Domine, et rectum judicium tuum* and the like,

[55] *Letters I,* pp. 218–219.   [56] *Ibid.,* pp. 221–222.

and then being tired I nodded and woke with a start. Five wasted years almost have passed in Ireland. I am ashamed of the little I have done, of my waste of time. . . . [But] what is life without aim, without spur, without help? All my undertakings miscarry: I am like a straining eunuch.[57]

There is, however, far less anxiety and fretfulness and far more waiting on the Lord in the tone of the sonnet than there is in these prose selections. Still, in his contention with God Hopkins is wasting his energies in not being fully content to remain peacefully in this dry state. He is still chafing at the rein. Only in his next sonnet, *The shepherd's brow*, can he finally laugh at himself for even contending with his Lord—he whose final self-evaluation is to see himself as a finicky perfectionist who in strict justice can demand nothing of God.

The shepherd's brow bears the autograph date April 3, 1889. It was never sent to Bridges, and Hopkins did not paste a copy into his own manuscript volume. Five full drafts, however, were found on the same sheet as a complete draft of *To R. B.* That it was not sent, however, does not prove that it was not finished. "I believe I enclose a new sonnet," Hopkins wrote on April 29, in his last letter to Bridges. "But we greatly differ in feeling about copying one's verses out: I find it repulsive, and let them lie months and years in rough copy untransferred to my book. Still I hope to send you my accumulation." [58]

Despite Hopkins' own comment on his personal manuscript methodology, Bridges insisted that *The shepherd's brow*, a "cynical" sonnet, was not worthy of inclusion among Hopkins' "last serious poems." [59] But in the last half dozen years or so, this sonnet has found strong and able defenders for admitting it into the canon of Hopkins' finished and considered poems between *Thou art indeed just, Lord* and *To R. B.* And in their revised editions of Hopkins' poetry,

---

[57] *Sermons*, p. 262.   [58] *Letters I*, p. 304.   [59] See *Poems*, p. 296.

Pick and Gardner have both so placed the sonnet. Again, what is especially important is the tone of the speaker, and this can be most reasonably ascertained by examining the meaning, diction, and rhythms of the poem itself, as well as Hopkins' other writings for whatever light they can shed.

The shepherd's brow is primarily based on a strong contrast between truly heroic figures and man's essentially comic littleness. The Gradual for Wednesday of the fourth week of Lent—the day the sonnet was composed—serves as an ironic contrast to the opening of the poem: "Come, children, hearken to Me: I will teach you the fear of the Lord. Come ye to Him and be enlightened: and your faces shall not be confounded" (Psalm 33:12, 6). The sonnet is also in one sense an expansion of a gloss Hopkins had written for Bridges on a difficult Pauline passage: "The man who thinks he is of some worth, when in truth he is worth nothing at all, is merely deluding himself" (Galatians 6:3). Only six weeks after he had written *That Nature is a Heraclitean Fire*, Hopkins interpreted this passage as follows: "However men may deceive themselves, of themselves they are nothing and nothing they do has any moral goodness from their doing it." [60]

Hopkins, as we have seen, is not guilty of a facile optimism. He was fully aware that God's gifts were freely and bountifully given, and that man of his own merit was not worthy of these gifts, nor in strict justice were they due him. It is the especial beauty of *The shepherd's brow* that the priest who had given his all to his Friend can turn the lesson of Job to his own account and wryly smile at his own temperamental fussiness.

The opening sentence of the poem may refer to the Good Shepherd Christ, transfigured on Mt. Sinai and visited with the terrible storm at his crucifixion, which havoc and glory he "owns" up to (acknowledges) but also "owns" in the sense of authorship. Or it may refer to Moses as described in

---

[60] Letter of September 10, 1888, *Letters I*, p. 288.

Paradise Lost. Allusions to this epic which Hopkins so deeply admired and which so markedly influenced his own poetic diction and rhythms are many, and the angels falling from heaven are certainly a distinct pointer to Milton's epic.[61] Milton calls Moses "That Shepherd, who first taught the chosen Seed" (I, 8). In Book XII God appears before Moses on Mount Sinai "In Thunder, Lightning and Loud Trumpet's sound" (l. 229), as mediator for the rest of the chosen people, who are too terrified to confront "the voice of God" which is "To mortal ear . . . dreadful (XII, 235–236). Or the shepherd may be St. Peter, transformed with the other disciples by the Paraclete appearing in the form of tongues of fire on Pentecost Sunday. There is both horror and glory felt in the presence of God.[62] In the Old and New Testaments there are evidences of God's working through nature and uplifting man.

In the second sentence of the sonnet, by contrast, Hopkins vividly etches the still-heroic figures of the fallen angels in epic rebellion against God. This, too, echoes *Paradise Lost.* The fallen Satan

> above the rest
> In shape and gesture proudly eminent
> Stood like a Tow'r   [I, 589–591].

Between the "Arch Angel ruin'd" and Moses' confrontation with God's terrifying and glorious presence in the form of lightning there is a further implied comparison. Satan's visage is described by Milton in this manner:

> his face
> Deep scars of Thunder had intrencht, and care
> Sat on his faded cheek, . . . under Brows

[61] Devlin notices several Miltonic references in Hopkins' treatment of Satan. See especially *Sermons,* p. 309.

[62] See Hopkins' sermon for Sunday, April 25, 1880, at Liverpool, *ibid.,* pp. 74–75. This passage is also important for an understanding of the theological nature of inspiration in *To R. B.*

> Of dauntless courage, and considerate Pride
> Waiting revenge   [I, 600–605].

Hopkins underlines the heroic majesty of God's mediator and God's rebel and the epic tragedy of the latter. It is around this contrast that the first quatrain is generated:

> The shepherd's brow, fronting forked lightning, owns
> The horror and the havoc and the glory
> Of it. Angels fall, they are towers, from heaven—a story
> Of just, majestical, and giant groans.

But against this dramatic and heroic setting the poet contrasts man simply as man in language which may perhaps be best described as astringent and darkly comic. In the second quatrain Hopkins includes himself—"we"—in his description of man as no "tower" but merely a "scaffold":

> But man—we, scaffold of score brittle bones;
> Who breathe, from groundlong babyhood to hoary
> Age gasp; whose breath is our *memento mori*.

Man is a pathetically dependent creature whose very existence depends upon his ability to draw in his next gulp of air, and who, with every breath, may be reminded of his own mortality. Seen in the light of his frail ground of being, man's pretensions to any semblance of heroic or tragic stature are presumptuous and comic. And the speaker, recalling Isaias' rebuke to Satan, "Thy pomp is brought down to the grave and the noise of thy viols" (Isaias 14:11), ironically deflates the stormy pretensions of man in the double pun on bass (base) and viol (vile): "What bass is *our* viol for tragic tones?"

Hopkins had already chronicled, in his meditation notes written during his long retreat, his admiration for the epic heroism of the fallen angels with their "giant groans," in spite of his abhorrence of their rebellion:

This song of Lucifer's was a dwelling on his own beauty, an instressing of his own inscape, and like a performance on the organ and instrument of his own being; it was a sounding, as they say, of his own trumpet and a hymn in his own praise. Moreover it became an incantation: others were drawn in; it became a concert of voices, a concerting of selfpraise. . . . They would not listen to the note which summoned each to his own place (Jude 6) . . . they gathered rather closer and closer home under Lucifer's lead and drowned it, raising . . . a counterpoint of dissonance and not of harmony.[63]

Against these angelic groans Hopkins contrasts man's meager gasps for breath, and perhaps the groans of man who "voids" in shame. Angelic beauty has some pretensions to "a grasp of godhead," as Hopkins remarks a few lines later in the same meditation. But this is not true for "Man Jack," whose ground of being, whose essential self is "just" (i.e., only, if a "just" account were to be given) air and gas. Apart from God's uplifting power man is a sorry thing.

The first half of the sestet is a further emphasis and concentration of "Man Jack," in language which recalls the starker mood of Shakespeare. Boyle has accurately defined Hopkins' meaning of "Jack" as a "male representative of the nature of something, . . . the individual *supposit* or person with reference to his nature merely, without speaking of his individual good or bad qualities." [64] Man Jack has high pretensions about himself, but his acts are tediously cyclical and basically undifferentiated from the animal: breathing, eating, voiding (there may be a pun here on the Elizabethan Jack-jake), mating, and death. Here is T. S. Eliot's descriptive triad of "birth, copulation, and death."

Furthermore, pride and vanity in a woman, which lead her to blazon forth her name, can also make of her a hussy. For this connection between vanity and sexual promiscuity, Victorian Hopkins has supplied his own lengthy gloss in a letter of September 24, 1883, to Coventry Patmore, strongly criticizing that poet's line, "Women *should* be vain":

---

[63] *Sermons*, pp. 200–201.   [64] Boyle, pp. 156–157.

In particular how can anyone admire or (except in charity, as the greatest of sins, but in judgment and approval) tolerate vanity in women? Is it not the beginning of their saddest and most characteristic fall? What but vanity makes them first publish, then prostitute their charms? In Leonardo's famous picture "Modesty and *Vanity*" is it not almost taken for granted that the one figure is that of a virgin, the other that of a courtezan? If modesty in women means two things at once, purity and humility, must not the pair of opposites be no great way apart, vanity from impurity? Who can think of the Blessed Virgin and of vanity? . . . Nothing in good women is more beautiful than just the absence of vanity and an earnestness of look and character which is better than beauty. . . . It is the same in literature as in life: the vain women in Shakspere are the impure minded too, like Beatrice.[65]

"Hussy," if strong, is again the exact word for Hopkins in a poem exposing the ludicrousness of man's (and woman's) pride.

When Hopkins writes that man blazons his name boldly, the implied comparison is again with God's lightning on the brow of Moses; it is a light from without informing Moses, not his own small light. The comparison is also with Satan's fallen but still visible glory, manifested by Milton in images of dimly majestic light:

> his form had yet not lost
> All her Original brightness, nor appear'd
> Less than Arch Angel ruin'd, and th' excess
> Of Glory obscur'd: As . . . the Sun new ris'n
> Shorn of his Beams [I, 591–596].

But Hopkins, who identifies himself with man in lines 5 ("we") and 8 ("our"), in line 9 contemptuously disassociates himself from man Jack with an emphatic "He!" The speaker has set up a comparison between man Jack, undistinguished by his generically undifferentiated "manmarks," and the distinctively individuated selves of the shepherd

[65] *Letters III*, pp. 308–309.

with God's lightning on his brow and the heroic figures of the fallen angels. In line 12, the speaker isolates himself above the Jacks to plead his own particular case, his own self, and his intensely personal agony. It is a rhetorical and, I think, an intentionally histrionic line which, for one who had spent life itself upon God's "cause," is also seriously meant. In its pounding parallel structure the line gathers to a final crescendo: "And I that die these deaths, that feed this flame, / That . . . ."

The delayed *volta* of the sonnet—the real turn—comes with the aposiopesis at the beginning of line 13. In effect, the last two lines act much like the final summary in the tag-couplet of a Shakespearian sonnet. Throughout the poem there have been two implied comparisons: visual images of light are compared to light's particular reflections, and audio images of heroic angelic groaning are set against unheroic human gasping. In the final two lines the speaker effectively diminishes both of these comparisons in humbly and wryly estimating his own small stature. First the speaker, "fronting" his own tiny reflection in the concave mirror of a polished spoon, sees his own upside-down, grotesque, and comical "masque" there. The implied comparison with the glory of the visages of Moses and Satan completely and effectively deflates his own contentious and presumptuous pleading. The speaker catches himself up short—the sudden catch in his voice is mirrored in the break in the thought—and ends his meditation with a prayer of humility, chiding himself for having thought that his "tempests" counted for much more than the "fire and fever fussy" of a precisionist. "Fussy" is Hopkins' own particular inscape for himself, and it is both comic and unflattering.

Secondly, not only do Hopkins' tempests find their effective diminuendo in "fire and fever fussy," but the large number of *s*'s and *m*'s, together with the many long vowels in the last two lines, seem to imitate the speaker's own breath quietly but unmistakably escaping from him like air and gas sputtering through a leaky blow pipe (an image used in *To R. B.*). The rhythm, temporarily reinforced by the *t* and *f* sounds of Hopkins' prayer, undergoes a further but delicately humorous deflation in the *s*'s of the final "fussy":

That . . . in smooth spoons spy life's masque mirrored: tame
My tempests there, my fire and fever fussy.

The very real suffering has been deflated by the speaker himself to fussiness, but there is a deeply instressed heroic patience in this self-chiding which should not escape the reader. The jaded poet who almost four years before had felt the agony of *Carrion Comfort* has not suffered less in *The shepherd's brow,* but he has mastered himself more completely. Here is the Pauline paradox of finding the strength of God in recognizing one's own weakness.

The sonnet, with its quiet but powerful ending, is an important chapter in the journal of Hopkins' struggle for self-mastery, for a more complete humility and patience through remaining fully receptive to God's will. There is a buckling under, a refusal to "contend" even ironically with his Lord as he had in *Thou art indeed just, Lord.* Bent more completely out of himself in the unrelenting forge of Christ, tempered under terrible pressures, Hopkins has stubbornly retained his poised and subtle humor. It is one of the most noble and endearing qualities of his character, this private joke between himself and his Lord who knows him better than he knows himself. This same patient humor is seen again in the sestet of *To R. B.,* where the breath of divine and poetic inspiration (the inbreathing of the Holy Spirit) seems also to be unavoidably escaping from a broken Hopkins.[66]

To R. B. was enclosed in Hopkins' last letter to Bridges. The theme of the poem is an *ave atque vale* for Bridges, as if

[66] For a comparison of *The shepherd's brow* with a passage from *Middlemarch* see Paul L. Mariani, "The Artistic and Tonal Integrity of Hopkins' 'The Shepherd's Brow,'" *Victorian Poetry,* VI (1968), 63–68.

the poet were standing over the grave of his dead creativity and explaining why he cannot write anymore. But the poem itself tells us otherwise, for there is no flagging in execution, no decline in poetic excellence. The poet is in masterful control of his central images of gestation and the "blowpipe flame," as well as of his melodic line and his tonal shifts. As Gardner tellingly remarks, "We should hardly expect the really moribund writer to give us such a perfect description of incipient life." [67]

The sonnet opens with a sentence which in length exactly coincides with the first quatrain. Inspiration, or insight, that "fine delight," Hopkins says, impregnates the receptive mind with the seed, the nucleus of "immortal song." Speaking of the inspiration he had for a tune, Hopkins had written Dixon three years before that the "disproportion is wonderful between the momentary conception of an air and the long long gestation of its setting." [68] The moment of inspiration, which literally means in Latin a breathing into, burns into the mind; there is an explosion of ecstasy and then the long period of quiet activity fructifying in the work of art. The concentration of the inspiration is stressed explicitly in the image of the blowpipe, which concentrates a flow of air and gas to create a more intense flame in a particular direction (the "aim" of line 7).

Once the inspiration has been given—and it is given from without, not from within the receptive mind—the mind, like the mother, can "now" (and the word is twice repeated in the poem) alone bring the seed of inspiration to fruition. The period of poetic gestation, however, is not the mother's nine months but rather Horace's nine years. The mind can "comb" her song, that is, rid it of any snags, but also, like the bees, strengthen the structured parts of the poems (the combs) to produce a sweeter honey. Direction ("aim") and

[67] Gardner, II, 366.   [68] Letter of June 30, 1886, *Letters II*, p. 135.

intensity given, the rest is largely a matter of good craftsmanship.

The octet has presented a precise and stimulating classical account of the nature of inspiration as prime mover. In the sestet, Hopkins offers his explanation for his own relative scarcity of poetic output:

> Sweet fire the sire of muse, my soul needs this;
> I want the one rapture of an inspiration.
> O then if in my lagging lines you miss
>
> The roll, the rise, the carol, the creation,
> My winter world, that scarcely breathes that bliss
> Now, yields you, with some sighs, our explanation.

This is a superb closing for several reasons. First, there is the syntactical reason. We are given a direct statement in lines 9 and 10 for Hopkins' creative decline: he lacks the "Sweet fire." The long final periodic sentence then strains upwards in the drum-roll crescendo culminating in the magnificent twelfth line. This line is another good example of Hopkins' musicality. "Roll" and "rise" are alliterated, and "carol" is a chime of "roll." The fourth term is related to the third by augmentation: *"c-r-l,* the *cr-t-n."* The long *o* of "roll" suggests a low bass, which shifts to the upward long *i* of "rise." This is followed by the downward short *a* and *o* of "carol," and followed by the two long, ascending vowels, *e* and *a,* of "creation." The overall effect is a surging upward, like a long drum roll, which just begins to falter in the last unaccented syllable of line 12.

But having reached this height, the rhythms begin to fall back, breaking up finally into the gasping last line which threatens, like a cranky blowpipe, to expire before the end of the thought. Secondly, the feminine rhyme endings are a master stroke, for the weak, unstressed final syllables seem to be barely hissed out. And in the final line the frequent pauses and the large proportion of unstressed syllables in the last phrase compared to the other phrases creates a purposely flat ending:

$$\times \quad / \quad \times \quad / \quad \times \quad / \quad \cdot \quad \times \quad / \quad \times / \quad \times$$

Now, | yields you, | with some sighs, | our explanation.

There is "scarcely" any inbreathing or inspiring now. Left almost entirely to himself, the poet can only emit "sighs," small gasps of breath. With inspiration sputtering irregularly, Hopkins for many years had been able to produce only a few sonnets at long intervals. "It is now years that I have had no inspiration of longer jet than makes a sonnet," he had mentioned to Bridges in early 1888.[69]

The metaphor of the blowpipe goes back even earlier. In his meditation on hell during the long retreat of 1881, Hopkins had made the following relevant comments:

How then is the soul so set at stress? As I suppose by some main stress from without, and that this is expressed by "ingentes illos ignes" [those huge fires] St. Ignatius speaks of, as the current of air in the blowpipe casts or addresses a jet of flame this way or that. The seven gifts of the Holy Spirit are spoken of as seven spirits, seven jets or currents of breath.[70]

The inspiration whose scarcity Hopkins laments is the gift of the Holy Spirit. God hardly ever moves him to write now; the longest poem he can create is a sonnet.

The complaint is an old one. More than ten years before he had made a similar lament to Bridges:

I cannot in conscience spend time on poetry, neither have I the inducements and inspirations that make others compose. Feeling, love in particular, is the great moving power and spring of verse and the only person that I am in love with seldom, especially now, stirs my heart sensibly and when he does I cannot always "make capital" of it, it would be a sacrilege to do so.[71]

Hopkins' ideas on the nature of poetic inspiration had undergone a profound religious metamorphosis since his Ox-

[69] *Letters I*, p. 270.   [70] *Sermons*, p. 137.
[71] Letter of February 15, 1879, *Letters I*, p. 66.

ford days. At twenty he had propounded, in a somewhat magisterial tone, the theory that inspiration was grounded largely in a poet's physical constitution:

The first and highest [kind of poetry] is poetry proper, the language of inspiration. The word inspiration need cause no difficulty. I mean by it a mood of great, abnormal in fact, mental acuteness, either energetic or receptive, according as the thoughts which arise in it seem generated by a stress and action of the brain, or to strike into it unasked. This mood arises from various causes, physical generally, as good health or state of the air or, prosaic as it is, length of time after a meal. But I need not go into this; all that is needful to mark is, that the poetry of inspiration can only be written in this mood of mind, even if it only lasts a minute, by poets themselves.[72]

As Devlin remarks, "It is interesting to compare this youthfully sophisticated theory of atmospherics and mealtimes with the more primitive belief of twenty years later: that natural inspiration comes direct from God." [73] It should be stressed that Hopkins was as aware as Housman or any other poet of the artist as craftsman. But he came to realize that rhetoric and inspiration (or insight) were qualitatively different things. "The strictly poetical insight and inspiration of our poetry seems to me to be of the very finest, finer perhaps than the Greek," he wrote to Dixon in August 1886, "but its rhetoric is inadequate—seldom firstrate, mostly only just sufficient, sometimes even below par. By rhetoric I mean all the common and teachable element in literature, what grammar is to speech, what thoroughbass is to music, what theatrical experience gives to playwrights." [74]

In his last year Hopkins again took to sketching, a pastime he had practiced during his Oxford years. He actually did very few pictures in that final year, but the last one, a rough,

---

[72] Letter to Baillie of September 10, 1864, *Letters III*, p. 216. Cf. the very similar remarks of the seventy-four-year-old Housman in the conclusion of his Leslie Stephen Lecture, *The Name and Nature of Poetry* (n.p., 1933). [73] *Sermons*, p. 311.   [74] *Letters II*, p. 141.

energetic line sketch of water,[75] can be reasonably interpreted as a pictorial counterpart of the subject of Hopkins'
last poem: the twofold flow of inspiration. In the lower
right-hand corner of the sketch Hopkins has written "Lord
Massey's domain, Co. Dublin April 22, 1889." April 22 is
also the day that he composed *To R. B.* The sketch must be
studied for a while before we realize we are looking down
from above into a rather dark, swirling, deep-pocketed
brook. What is most powerful about the sketch is the con-
striction of water squeezed through the pressure of jutting
rocks and then flowing outwardly in fanlike lines. It seems to
have been the compression of water into a jet followed by its
easeful release which caught Hopkins' attention. And this
same compression is found in the first twelve lines followed
by the release in the final two lines of *To R. B.* (as well as of
The shepherd's brow).

In this poem on the nature of poetic inspiration, however,
Hopkins' account falls somewhat short. His has caught the
second phase of inspiration but not the primary movement:
the silent brooding of the Spirit over the dark waters within.

In the years when he was most lamenting the loss of his
muse—the Dublin years—he was creating his finest poetry.
Whether in the lavish experimental style of *That Nature is a
Heraclitean Fire* or in the plain style of the desolations of
Jeremiah in *Thou art indeed just, Lord,* Hopkins' poems do
not demonstrate any lapse of poetic utterance. And if there is
a quantitative loss in the creation of only a handful of poems
for these years, there is toward the end a positive gain in the
flowering of a poetic voice with the authentic ring of spiritual humility and acceptance. In the last poems there has
been, to paraphrase Hopkins' own words on the nature of
grace, an advantage of himself over himself.

Read correctly, these last sonnets amount to a new direction in lyrical poetry. Just as those last unfinished statues of

[75] Published in *Journals* as drawing no. 33 of Appendix I.

Michelangelo mark a radical departure from the familiar terrain of classical sculpture in probing the little-known spiritual regions within and beyond death, so too do Hopkins' last sonnets mark a similar break with tradition. For there is little in the whole of English lyrical poetry which touches so convincingly that darkness preceding dissolution, when the soul, stripped to its essential self, must finally confront its Creator. There has been no loss of inspiration here. Rather, a vision of a rarely visited, dark, spiritual plateau has been translated into religious poetry of a very high order. In the story of his poems the last sonnets mark the final struggle—without exultation—of Hopkins to solder his will more firmly to God.

Appendix A

Hopkins and the Sonnet

English poets have always felt both at home and uncomfortable with the sonnet. They have admired its continental gravity and dignity, while wishing to adapt the form to their own idiom. But just how far the form can be stretched without breaking is more than a matter of whim. Furthermore, there seems never to have been a shortage of sonnet purists —and this is especially true of the period from about 1885 to 1920—who have questioned every departure from the Italian form, whether organic or not. It must be confessed that some sonnets, as good as they may be on other levels, such as a number by Wordsworth, have not always utilized the particular potentialities of the sonnet form.[1]

[1] Wordsworth has, of course, many first-rate sonnets. He stands like the Colossus of Rhodes as leader of the modern practitioners of the sonnet form. Furthermore, so serious a student of Milton as Wordsworth would hardly have misunderstood the structure of the Italian sonnet. It is clear that Wordsworth purposely altered the rhyme schemes and worked against the emotional crescendo toward which the Italian sonnet builds. But the deliberate use of anticlimax and the accordion compression which results from running the rhymes of the octet into the sestet work against the potentialities of the sonnet form itself, whether done consciously or unconsciously.

In choosing not to exploit the potentialities of the Italian model, Wordsworth seems at times to have ruptured the delicate tension between freedom of expression and the traditional mold. This is what Hopkins was probably objecting to in some of Wordsworth's sonnets. Many of them have the curve of a fireworks display: an emotional discharge somewhere near the traditional *volta* and then a soft anticli-

By his own testimony we know that Hopkins himself was not a close student of sonnet literature. He did know the sonnets of Petrarch, Surrey, Shakespeare, Herbert, Milton, Wordsworth, and Keats. In all likelihood, he knew Donne's work in the form. He admired Gray's one sonnet, *On the Death of Richard West*, probably through his reading of the "Preface" to the *Lyrical Ballads*. He had read Coleridge's sonnets, for there seems to be a distinct echo of one of them in his *Thou art indeed just, Lord*. As an undergraduate he had read Charles Tennyson Turner's sonnets and had been influenced by George Meredith's sequence of sixteen-line sonnets, *Modern Love*. No doubt he knew the sonnet literature of Elizabeth Barrett Browning and of Christina and Dante Gabriel Rossetti. And of course he knew Bridges' work in the form.

But most of his reading of sonnet literature had been done in the mid-sixties at Oxford. He admitted to Dixon in 1881 that he had not read much literature in the years after graduating from Oxford because he had been so busy with his priestly duties. "On the Sonnet and its history," he told Dixon, "a learned book or two learned books have been published of late and all is known about it—but not by me." [2] The Jesuit Hopkins had few literary texts near him. Because of his vow of poverty, which he scrupulously observed, he could take no personal property—and this included books—from assignment to assignment. Often he

---

max in the last five or six lines like sparks wafting softly back to earth. Seldom is there any steady crescendo building up and exploding only in the final lines, as in Hopkins' sonnets.

There are, however, two sonnets in which Hopkins seems to have followed Wordsworth's parabolic structure. Both *The shepherd's brow* and *To R. B.* reach their drum-roll crescendo at the end of the twelfth or beginning of the thirteenth lines, and then fall away to a deflated whisper. But here Hopkins is manipulating the form so that it organically follows the curve of his own emotional weariness.

[2] Letter of October 29, 1881, *Letters II*, p. 85.

asked Bridges to send him new copies of his poems because he had been forced to leave his friend's old volumes behind at Stonyhurst or Liverpool. He read novels and critical essays from time to time, but they were found at random at the places where he was staying. He admitted to not having read Dixon's *History* because he had been too busy at Liverpool and could not get to the library.

Nowhere, perhaps, is Hopkins' lack of knowledge about contemporary scholarship on the sonnet clearer than when he comments on Surrey. When he censured Dixon's sonnets for their departure from the Italian or Shakespearian norm, Dixon mildly remonstrated with him. There were, Dixon held, great temptations to abandon the Italian form. Hopkins' demonstration of the beauty of this form, however, had been forcible and Dixon promised that he would attempt in the future to follow it. Yes, "hernia," or overlapping, in the rhyme pattern was especially to be avoided. But what of the practice of Surrey and Spenser, the Canon asked. He may have been thinking of Surrey's adaptation of Petrarch's *The Soote Season (Sonnetto in Morte* 42), which has only two rhymes throughout. Or he may have recalled the same poet's *Alas so all things nowe do hold their peace,* in which the rhymes of the octet are continued in the sestet. And the rhyme scheme of Spenser's *Amoretti* also mingles the rhymes of the octet with the sestet (abab-bcbc-cdcd-ee). Spenser even translated some sonnets of Joachim du Bellay into fourteen-line poems in blank verse. Dixon knew that the Elizabethan sonneteers, who established the genre in England, had experimented freely with the form, "doing in English what it did in Italian, but yet not the same. They were the men, I suppose, who brought the sonnet into England: but, so far as I know, they did not write in the regular sonnet way, any of them. Was not Milton the first who did?" [3]

[3] Letter to Hopkins of October 26, 1881, in *Letters II,* p. 80.

"Surrey's sonnets are fine," Hopkins answered three days later, "but so far as I remember them they are strict in form. I look upon Surrey as a great writer and of the purest style." Still, it had been long since he had studied Surrey, and there were few literary works at Manresa House where his tertianship was about to begin in earnest. So Hopkins added, "But he was an experimentalist, as you say, and all his experiments are not successful. I feel ashamed however to talk of English or any literature, of which I was always very ignorant and which I have ceased to read." [4]

This is the point. In the final analysis, he did not really care what English poets in an earlier age had done with the form. He had hit upon the intrinsic potentialities and beauties of the Italian form. And it was the form itself rather than the work of earlier sonneteers that most interested him. In effect, what he did was to inject his own life into the tight, beautifully carved, formally perfect Italian mold. "The strength of the genie," Richard Wilbur has remarked, "comes of his being confined in a bottle." [5] Hopkins' mature sonnets manifest the truth of this statement thirty-six-fold.

Hopkins had some strong ideas about what a sonnet is and is not. He had an acute sense of the musical and lexical potentialities of the sonnet, and with those things which he recognized as distinctive to the form—proportion and rhyme scheme—he never tampered. When he did alter the sonnet form, he gave it a new name; it became a subspecies, as it were, of the genus sonnet. This alternation occurs only six times: with his three "curtal" (short or bobbed) sonnets, which maintain the same proportions between octet and sestet but in an abbreviated form, and the three sonnets with codas (or burdens) which had the sanction of a whole host of Renaissance Italian poets and of the venerable Milton himself.

[4] *Letters II*, p. 87.
[5] *Mid-Century American Poets,* ed. John Ciardi (New York, 1950), p. 7.

Proportion and rhyme scheme both pertain to the intrinsic form of the sonnet. Hopkins invariably employs the Italian sonnet with its fourteen lines and four rhymes, two rhymes each for the octet and sestet with no crossing of boundaries. Of his forty completed sonnets of fourteen lines, all are written in the Italian mode. All have the necessary octet rhyme scheme: abbaabba. Thirty, including all of his sonnets of 1865, end in the most accepted order of rhymes for the sestet: cdcdcd. The other ten end with the order ccdccd.[6]

What Hopkins insists upon in theory, he does in practice. He maintained, as strongly as critics of the sonnet like William Sharp and T. W. H. Crosland did, the organic necessity of proportion and rhyme. There is only one "sonnet proper": the Italian form. There are stricter and looser forms, and the Shakespearian form is "a very beautiful and effective species" of sonnet, although simpler and less powerful than the Italian. It is valid because it maintains the necessary bipartite division of eight and six. On this Hopkins is firm:

Now it seems to me that this division is the real characteristic of the sonnet and that what is not so marked off and moreover has not the octet again divided into quatrains is not to be called a sonnet at all. For in the cipher 14 is no mystery and if one does not know nor avail oneself of the opportunities which it affords it is a pedantic encumbrance and not an advantage. The equation of the best sonnet is

$$(4 + 4) + (3 + 3) = 2 \cdot 4 + 2 \cdot 3 = 2 (4 + 3) = 2 \cdot 7 = 14.$$

From this mathematical equation Hopkins draws three conclusions. First, that the sonnet is asymmetrical according to the simple ratio of 4 to 3. He cites several examples of the playing of unequal parts off against one another. He calls to mind St. Augustine's example from the *De Musica* of the hexameter and the ionic trimeter divided by their caesura, and he recalls the major and minor 5:4 scales. Hopkins also

[6] See Ritz, pp. 478–479.

suggests that the 4:3 ratio is perfect; higher ratios would be impracticable, lower ratios too simple.

Second, the ratio is doubled ("as all effects in time tend to be, and all very regular musical composition is"): $2(4 + 3) = 14$. Third, even parts are paired against even, uneven against uneven: $(4 + 4)$, $(3 + 3)$. The rhymes too "are founded on a principle of nature and cannot be altered without loss of effect." Since the octet and sestet are distinctive parts which allow for a musical balance, their rhymes must be kept separate. Otherwise "a downright prolapsus or hernia takes place and the sonnet is crippled for life." [7]

With the intralineal proportions of the English sonnet, however, Hopkins was dissatisfied. The length of the English iambic pentameter line was, in most cases, absolutely shorter than the "equivalent" Italian *endecasillabo*. "The reason why the sonnet has never been so effective or successful in England as in Italy," Hopkins told Dixon at the end of October 1881, "I believe to be this: it is not so long as the Italian sonnet; it is not long enough." While the proportion of part to part and part to whole is most important, Hopkins asserted, nevertheless so is size as an absolute. Using the architectural analogy of the Parthenon, Hopkins correctly noted that if it had been built on a markedly larger scale, its intrinsic proportions would no longer have served. Either "the proportions must be changed or the Order abandoned." [8]

The same held true of the English sonnet. The difference in vowel quantity between Italian and English was a real difference, not merely a relative one—a difference which made the English model, in comparison, "light, tripping, and trifling." The Italian sonnet, like the Parthenon, had long been admired for the perfection of its internal and

[7] All of the above relevant quotations are from Hopkins' letter to Dixon of October 12, 1881, *Letters II*, pp. 71–72.

[8] All of the quotations from Hopkins in this paragraph are from his letter to Dixon of October 29, 1881, *Letters II*, pp. 85–87.

external proportions. And since the external proportions of the English sonnet ("14 lines, 5 feet to the line, and the rhymes") *could* be strictly modeled on the Italian model, the shortcomings were to be found in the shorter English decasyllabic line itself.

Taking two lines from an Italian sonnet, Hopkins illustrated their absolutely greater length. First, the Italian *endecasillabo* line has more syllables, although the final light syllable and elided syllables do not count in the scansion:

> Non ha l'ottimo artista alcun concetto
> Che un marmor solo in se non circonscriva.

The Italian line with its thirteen syllables to the English ten is nearly a quarter again as long.

And, secondly, the Italian syllables themselves carry more weight and, properly read, take longer to read. "We have seldom such a delay in the voice as is given to the syllable by doubled letters (as *o*ttimo and conce*tt*o) or even by two or more consonants (as art*is*ta and *c*irconscriva) of any sort, read as Italians read. Perhaps then the proportions are nearer 4:3 or 3:2." [9] The Italian sonnet was actually from a quarter to as much as a third longer than the English.

There were various devices, however, used in the best English sonnets to counteract this intrinsic shortcoming. Hopkins lists seven, all of which he himself employed in his own sonnets.[10]

First, there is "gravity of the thought, which compels a longer dwelling on the words." The opening, meditative lines of *God's Grandeur, Peace, Ribblesdale, Thou art indeed just, Lord,* and *To R. B.* readily illustrate this device.

Second, there are "inversions and a periodic construction." The opening lines of *Peace* illustrate both perfectly:

> When will you ever, Peace, wild wooddove, shy wings shut,
> Your round me roaming end, and under be my boughs?

[9] *Ibid.,* p. 86.   [10] All of these devices are listed in *ibid.,* pp. 86–87.

Again, there is *To what serves Mortal Beauty?* with its cate-
chetical question-and-answer form which withholds the answer until the final phrase of line 14. And four inversions in
the first five lines force the thought to keep to the line of
argument without speeding up the movement.

Third, the poet can employ "breaks and pauses." The
second quatrain and final tercet of *Carrion Comfort,* with
their manifold questions, is perhaps the most famous use
Hopkins made of this device. But in the final lines of all
three of Hopkins' last sonnets this retarding device is used to
great effect. In *Thou art indeed just, Lord,* for example, we
have fifteen stops of varying degrees in the last five and one
half lines:

> See, banks and brakes
> Now, leavèd how thick! lacèd they are again
> With fretty chervil, look, and fresh wind shakes
>
> Them; birds build—but not I build; no, but strain,
> Time's eunuch, and not breed one work that wakes.
> Mine, O thou lord of life, send my roots rain.

And there is the strong break in the thirteenth line of *The
shepherd's brow* which acts like the final turn in a Shakespearian sonnet.

Fourth, the poet can increase the gravity of a line or
section "by many monosyllables." Almost any sonnet of Hopkins' will reveal how much he favored a strong monosyllabic
line. Lines 4, 6, 7, 8, 11, and 14 of *God's Grandeur* are
entirely monosyllabic. So is the excited opening of *The Starlight Night,* and the fifth and last lines of *Hurrahing in
Harvest.* Here are some lines randomly selected:

> Why? That my chaff might fly; my grain lie, sheer and clear.
> Nay in all that toil, that coil, since (seems) I kissed the rod
> > [*Carrion Comfort*].
> No worst, there is none. Pitched past pitch of grief
> > [*No worst, there is none*].

In wide the world's weal; rare gold, bold steel, bare
                    In both; care, but share care—
                                        [*Tom's Garland*].
Nine months she then, nay years, nine years she long
Within her wears, bears, cares and combs the same
                                        [*To R. B.*].

The last example has only one polysyllable in two lines. But
there are whole quatrains or tercets which contain almost
nothing but monosyllables. *I wake and feel the fell of dark,
not day*, for example, contains only thirteen polysyllables—
all dissyllables—in its fourteen lines.[11]

Fifth, the line may be retarded "by the weight of the
syllables themselves, strong or circumflexed and so on, as
may be remarked in Gray's sonnet, an exquisite piece of art,
whatever Wordsworth may say, 'In vain to me the smiling
mornings shine . . . .' " Hopkins has employed this lesson
well, for example, in the strong vocalic opening of no. 68:
"To seem the stranger lies my lot, my life." If we transcribe
the vowels in Gray's opening we have six full vowels (or
diphthongs). Hopkins goes one better. The full vowel
sounds of both add dignity to the line and give the sense of
both poets' sighing.

In the sixth and largely in the seventh instances, Hopkins
was breaking new ground, or better, exploring and fixing as
principles what earlier poets had experimented with. The
sixth device, " 'outriding' feet," Hopkins calls a "mechanical
remedy" for a "mechanical difficulty." By outriding feet he
meant extra syllables added to a line of sprung feet, which
he grafted gradually to his sonnets of 1877 until he had
achieved in them a fully sprung rhythm. Gardner and Ritz
have dealt with sprung rhythm in all of its manifestations,
and in Chapter 3 (and in part in Appendix B) I have dealt

---

[11] Unless "hours," which occurs three times, is to be counted as a
dissyllable. In a poem as taut and as delicately balanced as this, the ear
does tend to dwell on the word until it begins to sound like a cry of
pain.

at some length with the probable development of this dynamic accentual rhythm as it evolves from the standard rhythm of *God's Grandeur* to the fully sprung lines of *Hurrahing in Harvest*. The accentual conception allowed Hopkins to go from a line like the counterpointed

> / x / x   x   /   x   /   x   /
> Generations have trod, have trod, have trod

to the flexibility of these sprung lines composed just six months later:

> /   /   /   /   /
> The heart rears wings bold and bolder
> /   /   /   /   /
> And hurls for him, O half hurls earth for him off under his feet.

There are four accents running together in the first line and they seem to coil up to spring into the final "bolder." The second line has two outriding feet, following the first and third rising feet. The rhetorical emphasis thus supplied by the metrical rhythm is of itself one of the most exciting developments in the history of nineteenth century verse. But Ritz is right when he holds that while these sprung devices add a dimension of flexibility and grace to the line, it is the potentialities of Hopkins' seventh instance, the use of the Alexandrine (and the line of eight accents used in *Spelt from Sibyl's Leaves*) which gave him a line of the highest gravity and dignity.[12] Hopkins had the prior example of the French sonnet in Alexandrines, a measure used to approximate the Italian line in French. With *Henry Purcell* in the spring of 1879, Hopkins began to employ the longer Alexandrine in his sonnets. Over the next nine years he used it six more times,[13] perhaps to greatest effect in the poignant *Felix Randal* and in the percussive plain chant of *That Nature is a Heraclitean Fire*. The logical development

[12] See Ritz, p. 486.

[13] These are the curtal sonnet *Peace* (1879), *Felix Randal* (1880), *Carrion Comfort*, *To what serves Mortal Beauty?*, *The Soldier* (all 1885), and *That Nature is a Heraclitean Fire* (1888).

of the Alexandrine led to the seven- and eight-stress line of Caradoc's soliloquy (late 1884) and to the eight-stress line of *Spelt from Sibyl's Leaves* (October 1884–January 1885), which Hopkins called the longest sonnet ever written. Here he comes close to straining the integrity of his line, which is saved almost solely by his subject.

Within the restrictions which he set for himself by employing the difficult Italian form, Hopkins was able to find a remarkable freedom and an authentic and individual voice, a voice with tremendous range. It is worth watching the gradual shift in emphasis in that voice. We hear the youthful enthusiasm of the poet at the discovery of God's presence in the world around him in the sonnets of 1877. For example, there is the powerful and ecstatic final tercet of *God's Grandeur*, the exclamatory openings of *The Starlight Night* and *The Windhover*, or the intoxicated headiness of *Hurrahing in Harvest:*

> I walk, I lift up, I lift up heart, eyes,
> Down all that glory in the heavens to glean our Saviour.

Later there is the tender, sensitive, manly, and, above all, distinctively individual voice of the priest reminiscing on the dead farrier: "Felix Randal the farrier, O is he dead then? my duty all ended . . . ?" Five years later, there is the straining, agonized voice of the speaker in *Spelt from Sibyl's Leaves*, with his new and terrifying realization of what it means to be confronted with the constant, wearying demands of a moral world. Or there is the gentle, self-deprecatory tone of *My own heart:* "Soul, self; come, poor Jackself, I do advise / You, jaded, let be." Or again, there is the more sardonic self-scorn of the very late *The shepherd's brow*, where the speaker, catching a glimpse of himself, perhaps in one of J. Alfred Prufrock's coffee spoons, can only beg his Lord to tame his fussy fevers.

I have tried to catch the correct tone of the sonnets. Those who know the body of sonnet literature are aware how difficult it is for a poet to create a distinctive voice in a mold as imitative and tradition-encrusted as the form had become by Hopkins' time. The sonnets of 1877, studded with exclamation marks, are easy to read as hyperbole, and Hopkins seems often in them to be shouting out the good news of the Incarnation with just a breath of quaintness. But it is the special value of the late sonnets, as we saw in Chapters 6, 7, and 8, to have captured an older, storm-weathered voice, to offer the full spectrum of emotions with all their subtle nuances, from contentious irony to loving supplication.

Hopkins complimented Dixon on possessing a "true humanity of spirit, neither mawkish on the one hand nor blustering on the other." It was one of "the most precious of all qualities in style, and this I prize in your poems, as I do in Bridges'. After all it is the breadth of his human nature that we admire in Shakespeare." [14] More than either of his friends, both of whom had this quality to a high degree, Hopkins attained a poetic voice at once distinctive and filled with a broad, deep caritas. It is perhaps this fine humanity of spirit which endears him, finally, to so many.

[14] *Letters II*, p. 74.

Appendix B✍

A Note on Hopkins' Prosody

Perhaps the first thing that comes to the mind of most readers when they think of Hopkins is his experimentation with a new rhythm, what he called "sprung rhythm." Hopkins himself stressed the rhythmic aspect of his poetry. When he broke his seven-year self-imposed silence to write *The Wreck of the Deutschland* at his rector's "request," it was not an idea which needed utterance, but a "new rhythm" which had been long "haunting" his ear.[1] Explaining the essence of sprung rhythm to Dixon, he emphasized that *"one stress makes one foot,* no matter how many or few the syllables." Sprung rhythm meant "something like *abrupt* [rhythm] and applies to rights only where one stress follows another running, without syllable between."[2]

This packing of stresses was not a characteristic of what Hopkins called "Standard" or "Common Rhythm," that is, syllabic verse, where the line of poetry consists of a fixed number of feet. There are essentially four kinds of feet in accentual verse, each of which contains one accented and one or two unaccented syllables. These are the iamb ($^{×\prime}$) and the anapest ($^{××\prime}$), and their mirror opposites, the trochee ($^{\prime×}$) and the dactyl ($^{\prime××}$). The first two Hopkins called "rising" feet because the syllables move toward the stress in each foot, the last two "falling" feet because the syllables fall away from the stress. Packing of stresses can normally

[1] Letter to Dixon of October 5, 1878, *Letters II*, p. 14.
[2] *Letters II*, p. 23.

occur (if we except the spondee, as Hopkins would) only when a foot is reversed, so that its stress comes in contact with the stress of the adjacent foot, as when an iamb and a trochee or dactyl are juxtaposed.

But sprung rhythm, which lays heavier stress *on* the stress than common rhythm does, allows for greater rhythmic freedom. In sprung rhythm, a foot consists of a stress (which Hopkins first conceived of as coming last, but later settled on as coming first in the foot—either movement will do) following (or followed by) three, two, one, or no stresses. For sprung rhythm consisted "in scanning by accents or stresses alone, without any account of the number of syllables, so that a foot may be one strong syllable or it may be many light and one strong." [3]

Hopkins insisted that sprung rhythm was "the nearest to the rhythm of prose, that is the native and natural rhythm of speech, the least forced, the most rhetorical and emphatic of all possible rhythms, combining . . . opposite and, one wd. have thought, incompatible excellences, markedness of rhythm—that is rhythm's self—and naturalness of expression." [4] His rhythms were a musical refinement, a cultivation, of the very rhythms of English speech. For, as he explained, there were sprung rhythms "in music, in nursery rhymes, and popular jingles, in the poets themselves." He cited the nursery rhyme

> "Ding, dong, bell; Pussy's in the well;
> Who put her in? Little Johnny Thin.
> Who pulled her out? Little Johnny Stout."

Here Hopkins himself underscored the positions in which sprung rhythm occurred. "For if each line has three stresses or three feet it follows that some of the feet are of one syllable only." [5] An excellent example of sprung rhythm is to

---

[3] *Ibid.*, p. 14.   [4] *Ibid.*, p. 46.   [5] *Ibid.*, p. 14.

be found in the last two lines of *Hurrahing in Harvest* (1877) :

The héart réars wíngs bóld and bólder

And húrls for him, O hálf hurls éarth for him óff under his féet.

Both lines receive five stresses each. The first has but eight syllables, the second fifteen. As an aid in softening the abruptness of the rhythm, Hopkins employed a number of devices, the most important here being the hanger or "outride," indicated by the loop beneath the line. In his "Preface" to his poems (1883) , he defined "outrides" as "one, two, or three slack syllables added to a foot and not counting in the nominal scanning. They are so called because they seem to hang below the line or ride forward or backward from it in another dimension than the line itself." [6] And in his note to *Hurrahing in Harvest,* Hopkins explains that the "strong syllable in an outriding foot has always a great stress and after the outrider follows a short pause." [7]

A foot in sprung rhythm normally consists of from one to four feet, but "for particular rhythmic effects it is allowed . . . to use any number of slack syllables, limited only by ear." Hopkins actually uses slack syllables sparingly. In stanza 31 of *The Wreck of the Deutschland* (1876) , for example, we get this five-stress line with twenty-one syllables:

Fínger of a ténder of, Ó of a féathery delicacy, the bréast of the. . . .

The slack syllables are as light as the "feathery delicacy" Hopkins speaks of here. In scansion, however, the lyrical unit is not the line, but the stanza or the entire lyric, and the rhythm is what Hopkins calls over-rove, that is, extra unstressed or slack syllables at the end of one line are part of

[6] *Poems,* pp. 48, 269.   [7] *Letters II,* p. 39.

the first foot of the next line, a grace which makes the verse "flow in one long strain to the end of the stanza." [8]

Together with overreaving of syllables Hopkins used spill-over, or "running," rhymes. Hopkins' rhymes are often virtuoso performances in themselves. That Bridges disliked them is clear from his "Preface to the Notes"; Hopkins once told him in a letter that he too regretted some of them. They were "past changing, grubs in amber: there are only a few of these; others are unassailable; some others again there are which *malignity may munch at* but the muses love." [9] Bridges had been objecting to the *a* rhymes of stanza 14 of *The Deutschland:* "leeward," "drew her / D——," and "endured." Part of Hopkins' answer is missing, but his argument is clear. The *h* in "drew her," when "rightly read," is evanescent; and "endured" is meant to be read with a marked circumflex, so that it is three, not two, syllables, "something like en-dew-ered." "Leeward" is not "le-wurd," but "lü-wurd." When they are read aloud, these rhymes will approximate each other. But it is an effect, as Hopkins said about the rhyming of "electric" with "wrecked her? he / C——" in *The Loss of the Eurydice,* and "must have been prepared, as many things must." [10] Sometimes he even breaks a word for the end rhyme. In *The Windhover,* "king- / [dom]" rhymes with "wing" and "swing" and "thing"; in *Spelt from Sybil's Leaves* "——bend us" is made to rhyme with "end, as- / [stray]." Even in the stark sonnets of desolation, "hear / Me" is rhymed with "wear- / y" and "sing" with "ling- / [ering]." In running rhymes, Hopkins always places the rhythmic stresses in the same parallel position, so that the manner in which a multiple rhyme is to be pronounced is made clear.

Besides terminal rhyme, Hopkins also frequently used techniques he mastered from the Welsh *cynghanedd,* or chime music: rhyme, assonance, consonance, and allitera-

[8] *Letters I,* p. 86. See also what Hopkins says in his "Author's Preface" in *Poems,* p. 48.   [9] *Letters I,* p. 180.   [10] *Poems,* p. 243.

tion, often linked together with compound epithets. Nor were these devices used only for ornamentation; such chimes manifested the variety and underlying unity of things themselves as reflected in the words for those things. His large word groupings clustering around a single etymological root reveal the same tendency to find singleness within variety, unity beneath sprawling diversity. Hopkins' sharp chiming of words against each other finds its equivalent in the nature of the stress of his sprung rhythms. In *That Nature is a Heraclitean Fire,* for example, Hopkins moves toward the realization that the distinctiveness of man may be swallowed up by death. His language precisely captures this loss of distinctiveness, this shading off of man into an indistinguishable mass, in his grouping of vowels and a soft *n* sound, which move down a scale until the words become all slack, without any pitch or sharpness. (The large number of slack syllables reinforces this concept.) None of the words but "dark" have an end-stop, and all melt into an indistinguishable mass:

Both are in an unfathomable, all is in an enormous dark
Drowned. . . .

Against this line he places the percussive sharpness of

. . . world's wildfire, leave but ash:
In a flash, at a trumpet crash,

where the rhyming at short intervals and the many dentals reinforce the percussive stress of the lines. The markedness of the rhythm, the inscape of the sound, echoes the markedness of that part of the human inscape ("Manshape") which resists slack, and which cannot be lost or swallowed up.

Hopkins uses compound epithets to inscape, that is, capture the particular energy and stress of, a thing in the stress of the poetic line itself. His epithets combine alliteration, assonance, and consonance to add to the unity and compactness of the thing's distinctiveness. So, for example, Hopkins talks in *The Starlight Night* of the "Wind-beat whitebeam" and of "mealed-with-yellow sallows." This phrasing captures the dynamism of the things, a dynamism which would be lost in the conventional phrasing of "whitebeam beaten by the wind," or "sallows mealed with yellow." Compound epithets recur frequently; here are some of them: "dapple-dawn-drawn Falcon," "Fresh-firecoal chestnut-falls," "wilful-wavier / Meal-drift," "champ-white water-in-a-wallow," "brown-as-dawning-skinned," "skies / Betweenpie mountains," "fallowbootfellow," "echoing-of-earth note," "wind- lilylocks -laced," and "With-a-fountain's shining-shot furls." Compound epithets are sometimes hyphenated, sometimes not, as in the overwhelming crescendo of possessives in the close of *The Wreck of the Deutschland:* "Our hearts' charity's hearth's fire, our thoughts' chivalry's throng's Lord."

Even a brief inspection of Hopkins' prosody reveals the dynamism that is characteristic of everything he wrote. A typical poem of Hopkins' is always an act of participation which permits us to experience for ourselves the "doing-be" of a rising sun, or a gliding falcon, or a powerful blacksmith, or at times to behold the man "acting" out himself.

ᴎ Bibliography

WORKS BY GERARD MANLEY HOPKINS

STANDARD EDITIONS

The Poems of Gerard Manley Hopkins. First edition edited by Robert Bridges (London: Oxford University Press, 1918). Second edition edited by Charles Williams (London: Oxford University Press, 1930). Third edition edited by W. H. Gardner (London: Oxford University Press, 1948); revised, with additional poems (London: Oxford University Press, 1956). Fourth edition edited by W. H. Gardner and N. H. MacKenzie (London: Oxford University Press, 1967). *Hopkins* (variorum edition), Oxford English Texts series, edited by N. H. MacKenzie (London: Oxford University Press, forthcoming).

The Note-Books and Papers of Gerard Manley Hopkins. Ed. Humphrey House. London: Oxford University Press, 1937.

The Letters of Gerard Manley Hopkins to Robert Bridges. Ed. Claude Colleer Abbott. London: Oxford University Press, 1935. Second edition, 1955.

The Correspondence of Gerard Manley Hopkins and Richard Watson Dixon. Ed. Claude Colleer Abbott. London: Oxford University Press, 1935. Second edition, 1955.

Further Letters of Gerard Manley Hopkins: Including His Correspondence with Coventry Patmore. Ed. Claude Colleer Abbott. London: Oxford University Press, 1938. Second edition, 1956.

The Journals and Papers of Gerard Manley Hopkins. Ed. Humphry House, completed by Graham Storey. London: Oxford University Press, 1959.

*The Sermons and Devotional Writings of Gerard Manley Hop-
kins.* Ed. Christopher Devlin, S.J. London: Oxford University
Press, 1959.

SELECTIONS

A Hopkins Reader. Ed. John Pick. London: Oxford University
Press, 1953. Revised and enlarged, with poems annotated; Gar-
den City, N.Y.: Image Books, 1966. Contains a substantial
selection of Hopkins' prose.
Poems and Prose of Gerard Manley Hopkins. Ed. W. H. Gardner.
Baltimore: Penguin Books, 1953. Revised, 1963. Full glosses
on the poems, on the images, diction, and prosody.
Selected Poems of Gerard Manley Hopkins. Ed. James Reeves.
London: Heinemann, 1953.
Hopkins Selections. Ed. Graham Storey. London: Oxford Uni-
versity Press, 1967.

MANUSCRIPTS

There are, besides the works listed above, a number of unpublished manuscripts and perhaps twenty other letters. Six
of these are collected in an article by Graham Storey, "Six Letters
of Gerard Manley Hopkins," *The Month,* n.s., XIX (1958), 263–
270. Another letter, which originally appeared in the November
1888 issue of the *Stonyhurst Magazine,* was reprinted with notes
in *Dublin Review,* no. 505 (1965), 289–292. The Reverend Anthony Bischoff, S.J., of Georgetown University, who has been
writing what will be the definitive biography of Hopkins and
who probably owns more Hopkinsiana than anyone else, has at
least ten unpublished letters. Hopkins' manuscripts are carefully
collated and examined in Bischoff's "The Manuscripts of Gerard
Manley Hopkins," *Thought,* XXVI (1951), 551–580. A few fragments which are omitted in *Poems* are supplied by Norman
White in his letter in the *Times Literary Supplement,* August 22,
1968, p. 905.

WORKS ABOUT GERARD MANLEY HOPKINS

BOOKS

These studies represent a wide range of critical approaches and
levels of scholarship. Those which contain what I feel to touch
most pertinently on the central core of Hopkins' poetics and

poetry are marked with an asterisk. All, of course, add to our knowledge of Hopkins. Professor Gardner's work, like Pick's, was a pioneer endeavor and in one sense can never be superseded. Still, in the light of subsequent scholarship, it had best be read with the caveat in mind that much has been learned since the forties about Hopkins. Hartman's Twentieth Century Views volume (1966), like the earlier Kenyon Critics (1945) and *Immortal Diamond* (1949) collections, is uneven in quality. Eleanor Ruggles' book is a popular, semifictional account of Hopkins' life. W. Stacy Johnson's study is really not so much about the poet as Victorian as it is a reading of a number of Hopkins' mature poems, with special emphasis given to certain recurring images (such as light) and themes (such as the landscape of the mind and the self). Hopkins as Victorian is a difficult topic, and while Bender, Downes, Johnson, Hillis Miller, Mizener and others have shed some light on this subject, there is still a book to be written on it. (See also Gerhard Müller's "G. M. Hopkins: der Victorianer.")

Bender, Todd. *Gerard Manley Hopkins: The Classical Background and Critical Reception of His Work.* Baltimore: The Johns Hopkins Press, 1966.

*Boyle, Robert, S.J. *Metaphor in Hopkins.* Chapel Hill: University of North Carolina Press, 1961.

Downes, David. *Gerard Manley Hopkins: A Study of His Ignatian Spirit.* New York: Bookman Associates, 1959.

*———. *Victorian Portraits: Hopkins and Pater.* New York: Bookman Associates, 1965.

Gardner, W. H. *Gerard Manley Hopkins (1844–1889): A Study of Poetic Idiosyncrasy in Relation to Poetic Tradition.* 2 vols. London and New York: Oxford University Press, 1958.

Grigson, Geoffrey. *Gerard Manley Hopkins.* Writers and their Work, no. 59. London: Longmans, Green, 1955.

*Hartman, Geoffrey, ed. *Hopkins: A Collection of Critical Essays.* Twentieth Century Views. Englewood Cliffs, N.J.: Prentice-Hall, 1966. Essays by Geoffrey H. Hartman, F. R. Leavis, Yvor Winters, John Wain, Robert Bridges, Romano Guardini, H. M. McLuhan, J. Hillis Miller, Giorgio Melchiori, F. O. Matthiessen, Walter J. Ong, Sigurd Burkhardt, and Austin Warren.

*Heuser, Alan. *The Shaping Vision of Gerard Manley Hopkins.* London: Oxford University Press, 1958.

Hunter, Jim. *Gerard Manley Hopkins*. Literature in Perspective. London: Evans Brothers, 1966.

Johnson, Wendell Stacy. *Gerard Manley Hopkins: The Poet as Victorian*. Ithaca, N.Y.: Cornell University Press, 1968.

*Keating, J. E. *The Wreck of the Deutschland: An Essay and Commentary*. Kent State University Bulletin, January 1963.

*The Kenyon Critics. *Gerard Manley Hopkins*. Norfolk, Conn.: New Directions, 1945. Essays by Austin Warren, H. M. McLuhan, Harold Whitehall, Josephine Miles, Robert Lowell, Arthur Mizener, and F. R. Leavis.

Lahey, G. F., S.J. *Gerard Manley Hopkins*. London: Oxford University Press, 1930.

Lees, Francis N. *Gerard Manley Hopkins*. Columbia Essays on Modern Writers, no. 21. New York: Columbia University Press, 1966.

McChesney, Donald. *A Hopkins Commentary: An Explanatory Commentary on the Main Poems, 1876–89*. London: University of London Press, 1968.

MacKenzie, N. H. *Hopkins*. Writers and Critics. Edinburgh and London: Oliver and Boyd, 1968.

Peters, W. A. M., S.J. *Gerard Manley Hopkins: A Critical Essay toward the Understanding of his Poetry*. London: Oxford University Press, 1948.

Phare, E. E. *The Poetry of Gerard Manley Hopkins: A Survey and Commentary*. Cambridge: Cambridge University Press, 1933.

*Pick, John. *Gerard Manley Hopkins: Priest and Poet*. London: Oxford University Press, 1942. Second edition, 1966.

——, ed. *Gerard Manley Hopkins: The Windhover*. The Merrill Literary Casebook Series, no. 9560. Columbus, Ohio: Charles E. Merrill, 1969.

*Ritz, Jean-Georges. *Le Poète Gérard Manley Hopkins, S.J.: L'homme et l'œuvre*. Paris: Didier, 1963.

——. *Robert Bridges and Gerard Hopkins, 1863–1889: A Literary Friendship*. London: Oxford University Press, 1960.

Ruggles, Eleanor. *Gerard Manley Hopkins*. London and New York: W. W. Norton, 1947.

*Schneider, Elizabeth W. *The Dragon in the Gate: Studies in the Poetry of G. M. Hopkins*. Perspectives in Criticism, no. 20.

Berkeley and Los Angeles: University of California Press, 1968.

Weyand, Norman, S.J., ed. *Immortal Diamond: Studies in Gerard Manley Hopkins.* London: Sheed & Ward, 1949. Essays by members of the Society of Jesus with a foreword by John Pick and an "Interpretive Glossary of Difficult Words" in Hopkins' poems by R. V. Schoder, S.J.

SELECTED ESSAYS

Allison, Alexander W. "Hopkins' 'I Wake and Feel the Fell of Dark,'" *The Explicator,* XVII (1959), Item 54.

Andreach, Robert J. "Gerard Manley Hopkins" in *Studies in Structure: The Stages of the Spiritual Life in Four Modern Authors* (New York: Fordham University Press, 1964). The book deals with Hopkins, Joyce, T. S. Eliot, and Hart Crane.

———. "Hopkins' 'The Windhover,'" *Tulane Studies in English,* XI (1961), 87–95.

Assad, Thomas J. "A Closer Look at Hopkins' '(Carrion Comfort)'". *Tulane Studies in English,* IX (1959), 91–102.

Auden, W. H. "The Knight of the Infinite," *New Republic,* August 21, 1944, pp. 223–224.

August, Eugene R. "The Growth of 'The Windhover,'" *PMLA,* LXXXII (1967), 465–468.

———. "Hopkins' Dangerous Fire," *Victorian Poetry,* I (1963), 72–74.

Ayers, Robert W. "Hopkins' The Windhover: A Further Simplification," *MLN,* LXXI (1956), 577–584.

Baker, William E. "The Strange and the Familiar," in *Syntax in English Poetry, 1870–1930,* Perspectives in Criticism, no. 18 (Berkeley and Los Angeles: University of California Press, 1967), pp. 84–94.

Bates, Ronald. "Downdolphinry," *University of Toronto Quarterly,* XXXVI (1967), 229–236.

———. "Hopkins' Ember Poems: A Liturgical Source," *Renascence,* XVII (1964), 32–37.

———. "The Windhover," *Victorian Poetry,* II (1964), 63–64.

Baum, Paull F. "Sprung Rhythm," *PMLA,* LXXIV (1959), 418–425.

Bender, Todd K. "Hopkins' 'God's Grandeur,'" *The Explicator,* XXI (1962), Item 55.

Bernad, M. A. "Hopkins' 'Pied Beauty': A Note on its Ignatian Inspiration," *Essays in Criticism,* XII (1964), 217–220.

Bischoff, A. "Gerard Manley Hopkins," *Victorian Notes,* no. 13 (1958), pp. 23–24.

Blackmur, R. P. "Text and Texture," *Virginia Quarterly Review,* XIII (1937), 449–453.

Boyle, Robert. "A Footnote on 'The Windhover,'" *America,* LXXXII (1949), 129–130.

———. "Hopkins' Imagery: The Thread for the Maze," *Thought,* XXXV (1960), 57–90.

Britton, John. "'Pied Beauty' and the Glory of God," *Renascence,* XI (1958), 72–75.

Burkhardt, Sigurd. "The Poet as Fool and Priest," *ELH,* XXIII (1956), 279–298.

Busby, Christopher. "Time's Andromeda," *Dublin Review,* no. 480 (1959), pp. 183–190.

Campbell, Sister M. Mary Hugh, S.C.M.M. "The Silent Sonnet: Hopkins' 'Shepherd's Brow,'" *Renascence,* XV (1963), 133–142.

Chard, Leslie. "Once More into *The Windhover,*" *English Language Notes,* II (1965), 282–285.

Chevigny, Bell Gale. "Instress and Devotion in the Poetry of Gerard Manley Hopkins," *Victorian Studies,* IX (1965), 141–153.

Clarke, Robert Boykin, S.J. "Hopkins's 'The Shepherd's Brow,'" *Victorian Newsletter,* no. 28 (1965), pp. 16–18.

Cohen, Selma J. "Hopkins' 'As Kingfishers Catch Fire,'" *Modern Language Quarterly,* XI (1950), 197–204.

Daiches, David. "The Victorian Poets," in *A Critical History of English Literature* (New York: Ronald Press, 1960), II, 1042–1048.

Davie, Donald. "Hopkins as a Decadent Critic," in *Purity of Diction in English Verse* (London: Routledge and Kegan Paul, 1967), pp. 160–182.

Deutsch, Babette. "The Forgèd Feature," in *Poetry in Our Time,* 2d ed. rev. and enl. (Garden City, N.Y.: Anchor Books, 1963), pp. 321–348.

Devlin, Christopher, S.J. "An Essay on Scotus," *The Month,* CLXXXII (1946), 456–466.

——. "The Image and the Word," *The Month,* n.s. III (1950), 114–127, 191–202.

——. "Time's Eunuch," *The Month,* n.s. I (1949), 303–312.

Doherty, F. "A Note on 'Spelt from Sibyl's Leaves,' " *Essays in Criticism,* XIV (1964), 428–432.

Donoghue, Denis. "The Bird as Symbol: Hopkins's Windhover," *Irish Studies,* XLIV (1955), 291–299.

——. "Technique in Hopkins," *Irish Studies,* XLIV (1955), 446–456.

Downes, David A. "Hopkins and Thomism," *Victorian Poetry,* II (1965), 270–272.

——. "The Hopkins Enigma," *Thought,* XXXVI (1961), 573–594.

Driscoll, John P., S.J. "Hopkins' 'Spring,' Line 2, and 'Spring and Fall,' Line 2," *The Explicator,* XXIV (1965), Item 26.

Driskell, Leon V. "The Progressive Structure of 'The Windhover,' " *Renascence,* XIX (1966), 30–36.

Duncan, J. E. "The Catholic Revival and the Metaphysicals," in *The Revival of Metaphysical Poetry: The History of a Style 1800 to the Present* (Minneapolis: University of Minnesota Press, 1959), pp. 91–102.

Durr, Robert A. "No Worst There is None," *The Explicator,* XI (1952), Item 11.

Eleanor, Mother Mary. "Hopkins' 'The Windhover' and Southwell's Hawk," *Renascence,* XI (1961), 21–27.

Empson, William. *Seven Types of Ambiguity* (New York: New Directions; 1947), pp. 285–286. (Originally published in 1930 by Chatto & Windus, London).

Fiore, Amadeus, O.F.M. "Hopkins' Relation to the *Deutschland* Nuns," *Renascence,* XVIII (1965), 45–48.

Fussell, Paul, Jr. "A Note on *The Windhover,*" *MLN,* LXIX (1949), 271.

Gardner, W. H. "Anvil-Ding and Tongue That Told: The Early Journals and Papers of Gerard Manley Hopkins," *The Month,* n.s. XXV (1961), 34–47, 82–95.

——. "Hopkins and Newman," *Times Literary Supplement,* September 15, 1966, p. 868.

——. "The Windhover," *Times Literary Supplement,* June 24, 1955, p. 349.

Gavin, Sr. Rosemarie Julie. "Hopkins' 'The Candle Indoors,'"
The Explicator, XX (1962), Item 50.

Gibson, Frances. "The Influence of Welsh Prosody on the Poetry
of Hopkins," *Xavier University Studies,* VI (1967), 21–28.

Gibson, Walker. "Sound and Sense in G. M. Hopkins," *MLN,*
LXXIII (1958), 95–100.

Gibson, William M. "To R. B.," *The Explicator,* VI (1947),
Item 12.

Giovannini, Margaret. "The Caged Skylark," *The Explicator,*
XIV (1956), Item 35.

——. "Hopkins' 'God's Grandeur,'" *The Explicator,* XXIV
(1965), Item 36.

Gomme, A. "A Note on Two Hopkins Sonnets," *Essays in Criticism,* XIV (1964), 327–331.

Goodin, George. "Man and Nature in Hopkins' 'Ribblesdale,'"
Notes and Queries, VI (1959), 453–454.

Greiner, Francis J. "Hopkins' 'The Habit of Perfection,'" *The
Explicator,* XXI (1962), Item 19.

——. "Hopkins' 'The Windhover' Viewed as a Nature Poem,"
Renascence, XV (1963), 68–75, 95.

Grennan, Joseph E. "Grammar as Thaumaturgy: Hopkins'
'Heraclitean Fire,'" *Renascence,* XV (1964), 208–211.

Hafley, James. "Hopkins: 'A Little Sickness in the Air,'" *Arizona Quarterly,* XX (1964), 215–222.

Hallgarth, Susan A. "A Study of Hopkins' Use of Nature,"
Victorian Poetry, V (1967), 79–92.

Harrison, Thomas P. "The Birds of Gerard Manley Hopkins,"
Studies in Philology, LIV (1957), 448–463.

Hartman, Geoffrey H. "Hopkins," in *The Unmediated Vision:
An Interpretation of Wordsworth, Hopkins, Rilke and Valéry*
(New Haven: Yale University Press, 1954). Hopkins section revised for inclusion in the Twentieth Century Views
series.

Haskell, Ann Sullivan. "An Image of 'The Windhover,'" *Victorian Poetry,* VI (1968), 75–77.

Hill, Archibald A. "An Analysis of *The Windhover:* An Experiment in Structural Method," *PMLA,* LXX (1955), 968–978.

——. "'The Windhover' Revisited: Linguistic Analysis Reassessed," *Texas Studies in Literature and Language,* VII (1966),
349–359.

Hines, Leo. "Pindaric Imagery in G. M. Hopkins," *The Month,* n.s. XXIX (1963), 294–307.

Holloway, Sr. Marcella M. "No Worst, There is None," *The Explicator,* XIV (1956), Item 51.

Hufstader, Anselm. "The Experience of Nature in Hopkins' Journal and Poems," *Downside Review,* LXXXIV (1966), 127–149.

Humiliata, Sr. Mary. "Hopkins and the Prometheus Myth," *PMLA,* LXX (1955), 58–68.

Huntley, J. F. "Hopkins' 'The Windhover' as a Prayer of Request," *Renascence,* XVI (1964), 154–162.

Jankowsky, Kurt R. "Gerard Manley Hopkins," in *Die Versauffassung bei Gerard Manley Hopkins, den Imagisten und T. S. Eliot: Renaissance altgermanischen Formgestaltens in der Dichtung des 20. Jahrhunderts* (Munich: Hulber, 1967), pp. 19–134.

Jennings, Elizabeth. "The Unity of Incarnation: A Study of Gerard Manley Hopkins," *Dublin Review,* no. 484 (1960), pp. 170–184.

Johnson, Wendell Stacy. "The Imagery of Gerard Manley Hopkins: Fire, Light, and the Incarnation," *Victorian Newsletter,* no. 16 (1959), pp. 18–23.

Keating, Joseph, S.J. "Impressions of Father Gerard Manley Hopkins, S.J.," *The Month,* CXIV (1909), 59–68, 151–160, 246–258.

Kelly, Hugh. "The Windhover—and Christ," *Irish Studies,* XLV (1956), 188–193.

Kilmer, Joyce. "The Poetry of G. M. Hopkins," *Poetry,* IV (1914), 241–245.

King, Donald R. "The Vision of 'Being' in Hopkins' Poetry and Ruskin's *Modern Painters," Discourse,* IX (1966), 316–324.

Kissane, James. "Classical Echoes in Hopkins' 'Heaven-Haven,' " *MLN,* LXXIII (1958), 491–492.

Kopper, Edward A., Jr. "The Windhover," *The Explicator,* XXII (1963), Item 54.

Leavis, F. R. "Gerard Manley Hopkins," in *New Bearings in English Poetry* (Ann Arbor: University of Michigan Press, 1960), pp. 159–193. (Originally published in 1932 by Chatto & Windus, London.)

Lees, Francis Noel. "Gerard Manley Hopkins," in *The Pelican*

Guide to English Literature, vol. VI, *From Dickens to Hardy,* ed. Boris Ford (Baltimore: Penguin Books, 1958), pp. 371–384.

——. "The Windhover," *Scrutiny,* XVII (Spring 1950), 32–37.

Lewis, C. Day. *A Hope for Poetry* (Oxford: B. Blackwell, 1934), pp. 6–13.

Litzinger, Boyd. "The Genesis of Hopkins' 'Heaven-Haven.'" *Victorian Notes,* no. 17 (1960), pp. 31–33.

——. "Once More, 'The Windhover,'" *Victorian Poetry,* V (1967), 228–230.

——. "The Pattern of Ascent in Hopkins," *Victorian Poetry,* II (1964), 43–47.

McDonnell, Thomas P. "Hopkins as a Sacramental Poet: A Reply to Yvor Winters," *Renascence,* XIV (1961), 25–33, 41.

MacKenzie, Norman H. "Gerard and Grace Hopkins: Some New Links," *The Month,* n.s. XXXIII (1965), 347–350.

——. "Hopkins MSS: Old Losses and New Finds," *Times Literary Supplement,* March 18, 1965, p. 220.

McQueen, William A. "'The Windhover' and 'St. Alphonsus Rodriguez,'" *Victorian Newsletter,* no. 23 (1963), 25–26.

Mariani, Paul L. "The Artistic and Tonal Integrity of Hopkins' 'The Shepherd's Brow,'" *Victorian Poetry,* VI (1968), 63–68.

——. "Hopkins' 'Felix Randal' as Sacramental Vision," *Renascence,* XIX (1967), 217–220.

——. "Hopkins' 'Harry Ploughman' and Frederick Walker's 'The Plough,'" *The Month,* n.s. XL (1968), 37–45.

Martin, Philip M. *"The Wreck of the Deutschland* by G. M. Hopkins," in *Mastery and Mercy: A Study of Two Religious Poems* (London and New York: Oxford University Press, 1957), pp. 1–72.

Martz, L. L. *The Poetry of Meditation* (New Haven: Yale University Press, 1954), pp. 321–326.

Miller, Bruce E. "On 'The Windhover,'" *Victorian Poetry,* II (1964), 115–119.

Miller, J. Hillis. "Gerard Manley Hopkins," in *The Disappearance of God: Five Nineteenth-Century Writers* (Cambridge, Mass.: Harvard University Press, 1963), pp. 270–359. This essay is reprinted in part in the Twentieth Century Views volume.

Milward, Peter, S.J. "The Underthought of Shakespeare in Hopkins," *Studies in English Literature* (University of Tokyo), XXXIX (1963), 1–9.

Montag, George E. "Hopkins' 'God's Grandeur' and 'the Ooze of Oil Crushed,' " *Victorian Poetry*, I (1964), 302–303.

——. " 'The Windhover': Crucifixion and Redemption," *Victorian Poetry*, III (1965), 109–118.

Morati, Luciano. "Spiritualità e ispirazione nella poesia di Gerard Manley Hopkins," *Letture*, XV (1960), 563–570.

Müller, Gerhard. "G. M. Hopkins: Der Victorianer," in *Festschrift zum 75 Geburtstag von Theodor Spira*, eds. Helmut Viebrock and Willi Erzgräber (Heidelberg, 1961), pp. 233–239.

Myers, John A., Jr. "Intimations of Mortality: An Analysis of Hopkins' 'Spring and Fall,' " *English Journal*, LI (1962), 585–587.

Nassar, Eugene Paul. "Hopkins, Figura, and Grace: God's Better Beauty," *Renascence*, XVII (1965), 128–130.

Noel, Sr. M., S.C. "Gathering to a Greatness: A Study of 'God's Grandeur,' " *English Journal*, LII (1964), 285–287.

Noon, William T., S.J. "Gerard Manley Hopkins," in *Poetry and Prayer* (New Brunswick, N.J.: Rutgers University Press, 1967), pp. 107–127.

O'Brien, A. P. "Structure Complex of Hopkins's Words," *Indian Journal of English Studies*, I (1960), 48–56.

Ochshorn, Myron G. "Hopkins the Critic," *Yale Review*, LIV (1965), 346–367.

O'Dea, Richard J. " 'The Loss of the Eurydice': A Possible Key to the Reading of Hopkins," *Victorian Poetry*, IV (1966), 291–293.

Onesta, P. A. "The Self in Hopkins," *English Studies in Africa*, IV (1961), 174–181.

Pace, George B. "On the Octave Rhymes of 'The Windhover,' " *English Language Notes*, II (1965), 285–286.

Payne, Michael. "Syntactical Analysis and 'The Windhover,' " *Renascence*, XIX (1967), 88–92.

Pendexter, Hugh, III. "Hopkins' 'God's Grandeur,' " *The Explicator*, XXIII (1964), Item 2.

Phillipson, Dom Wulstan. "More Light on Hopkins," *Downside Review*, LXXVI (1958), 402–410.

Pitchford, Lois W. "The Curtal Sonnets of Gerard Manley Hopkins," *MLN*, LXVII (1952), 165–169.

Pitts, Arthur W., Jr. "Hopkins' 'The Wreck of the Deutschland,' Stanza 29," *The Explicator*, XXIV (1965), Item 7.

Rader, Louis. "Hopkins' Dark Sonnets: Another New Expression," *Victorian Poetry*, V (1967), 13–20.

Rathmell, J. C. A. "Explorations and Recoveries—I. Hopkins, Ruskin, and the *Sidney Psalter*," *London Magazine*, VI (1959), 51–66.

Ratliff, John D. "Hopkins' 'The May Magnificat,' 19–22," *The Explicator*, XVI (1957), Item 17.

Reiman, Donald H. "Hopkins' 'Ooze of Oil' Rises Again," *Victorian Poetry*, III (1966), 39–42.

Richards, I. A. "Gerard Hopkins," *The Dial*, LXXXI (1926), 195–203.

——. "Poem VI ['Spring and Fall']," in *Practical Criticism* (New York: Harvest Books, 1929), pp. 80–90.

Ritz, Jean-Georges. "The Windhover de G. M. Hopkins." *Études Anglaises*, IX (1956), 14–22.

Sambrook, James. "Hayton and *Mano*," in *A Poet Hidden: The Life of Richard Watson Dixon, 1833–1900* (London: 1962), pp. 61–68, and elsewhere.

Scheve, Brother Adelbert, F.S.C. "The Wreck of the Deutschland, Stanza 33," *The Explicator*, XVII (1959), Item 60.

Schneider, Elisabeth. "My Own Heart Let Me More Have Pity On," *The Explicator*, V (1947), Item 51.

——. "My Own Heart Let Me More Have Pity On," *The Explicator*, VII (1949), Item 49.

——. "Sprung Rhythm: A Chapter in the Evolution of Nineteenth-Century Verse," *PMLA*, LXXX (1965), 237–253.

——. "The Windhover," *The Explicator*, XVIII (1960), Item 22.

——. "*The Wreck of the Deutschland*: A New Reading," *PMLA*, LXXXI (1966), 110–122.

Schoeck, R. J. "Influence and Originality in the Poetry of Hopkins," *Renascence*, IX (1956), 77–84.

——. "*Peine forte et dure* and Hopkins' 'Margaret Clitheroe,'" *MLN*, LXXIV (1959), 220–224.

Sharples, Sister Marian. "Conjecturing a Date for Hopkins' 'St. Thecla,'" *Victorian Poetry*, IV (1966), 204–209.

Shea, F. X., S.J. "Another Look at 'The Windhover,'" *Victorian Poetry*, II (1964), 219–239.

Sherwood, H. C. "Spelt from Sibyl's Leaves," *The Explicator*, XV (1956), Item 5.

Smith, Grover. "A Source for Hopkins' 'Spring and Fall' in *The Mill on the Floss?*" *English Language Notes*, I (1964), 43–46.

Sonstroem, David. "Making Earnest of Game: G. M. Hopkins and Nonsense Poetry," *Modern Language Quarterly*, XXVIII (1967), 192–206.

Spira, Theodor. "Gerard Manley Hopkins: Zu einer deutschen Neuerscheinung," *Anglia*, LXXIV (1956), 333–344.

Stevens, Sr. Mary Dominic, O.P. "That Nature is a Heraclitean Fire," *The Explicator*, XXII (1963), Item 18.

Stillinger, Jack. "Hopkins's 'Skates Heel' in 'The Windhover,'" *Notes and Queries*, VI (1959), 215–216.

Sutherland, Donald. "Hopkins Again," *Prairie Schooner*, XXXV (1961), 197–242.

Templeman, William D. "Hopkins and Whitman: Evidence of Influence and Echoes," *Philological Quarterly*, XXXIII (1954), 48–65.

———. "Ruskin's Ploughshare and Hopkins' 'The Windhover,'" *English Studies*, LXIII (1962), 103–106.

Thomas, A., S.J. "Gerard Manley Hopkins: 'Doomed to Succeed by Failure,'" *Dublin Review*, no. 508 (1966), pp. 161–175.

———. "G. M. Hopkins and the Silver Jubilee Album," *The Library*, XX (1965), 148–152.

———. "G. M. Hopkins and 'Tones,'" *Notes and Queries*, XII (1965), 429–430.

———. "G. M. Hopkins: An Unpublished Triolet," *Modern Language Review*, LXI (1966), 183–187.

Thomas, J. D. "The Windhover," *The Explicator*, XX (1961), Item 31.

Vickers, Brian. "Hopkins and Newman," *Times Literary Supplement*, March 3, 1966, p. 178.

Ward, Dennis. "The Windhover," in *Interpretations: Essays on Twelve English Poems*, ed. John Wain (London: Routledge and Kegan Paul, 1955), pp. 138–152.

Watson, Thomas L. "Hopkins' 'God's Grandeur,'" *The Explicator*, XXII (1964), Item 47.

Weatherhead, A. Kingsley. "G. M. Hopkins: 'The Windhover,' " *Notes and Queries,* III (1956), 354.

White, Gertrude M. "Hopkins' 'God's Grandeur': A Poetic Statement of Christian Doctrine," *Victorian Poetry,* IV (1966), 284–287.

Winters, Yvor. "The Audible Reading of Poetry," in *The Structure of Verse,* ed. Harvey Gross (Greenwich, Conn.: Fawcett Publications, 1964), pp. 131–149.

——. "The Poetry of Gerard Manley Hopkins," *Hudson Review,* I (1949), 455–476, and II (1949), 61–89. Reprinted in *The Function of Criticism,* ed. Alan Swallow (Denver: The Swallow Press, 1957), and in *On Modern Poets* (New York: Meridian Books, 1959).

Wolfe, Patricia A. "The Paradox of Self: A Study of Hopkins' Spiritual Conflict in the 'Terrible Sonnets,' " *Victorian Poetry,* VI (1968), 85–103.

Wooton, Carl. "The Terrible Fire of G. M. H.," *Texas Studies in Literature and Language,* IV (1963), 367–375.

Wright, Brooks. "God's Grandeur," *The Explicator,* X (1951), Item 5.

Yeats, W. B. "Introduction," in *The Oxford Book of Modern Verse, 1892–1935.* (Oxford: Clarendon, 1936), pp. xxxix–lxi.

Zelocchi, Rosanna. "La 'barbarica bellezza' di Gerard Manley Hopkins," *Convivium,* XXIX (1961), 461–471.

BIBLIOGRAPHICAL STUDIES

There is no up-to-date bibliography of Hopkins. The two best critical survey-essays are M. A. Charney's "A Bibliographical Study of Hopkins Criticism, 1918–1949," *Thought,* XXV (1950), 297–326; and John Pick's essay in *The Victorian Poets: A Guide to Research,* ed. F. E. Faverty (Cambridge, Mass.: Harvard University Press, 1956), pp. 196–227. They are thorough and critical, but the first goes only through 1949; the second is complete only to the early fifties. There is also a short but thorough bibliography which covers the fifty-five years before Charney's study: Edward H. Cohen. "A Comprehensive Hopkins Bibliography: 1863–1918," *Bulletin of Bibliography,* XXV (1967), 79–81. Three good bibliographies are: Norman Weyand's "A Chronological Hopkins Bibliography," in *Immortal Diamond: Studies in*

Gerard Manley Hopkins (London: Sheed and Ward, 1949), pp. 395–436, which is thorough through the mid-forties; Jean-Georges Ritz's "Bibliographie," in his *Le Poète Gérard Manley Hopkins, S.J.: L'homme et l'œuvre* (Paris: Didier, 1963), pp. 673–709, which lists virtually everything, but only up through the early fifties; and W. H. Gardner's short listings in the *CBEL*, V (1957), pp. 600–604. There are, besides, Professor R. C. Tobias's sketchy remarks on Hopkins in his annual "The Year's Work in Victorian Poetry," which appears in the summer issue of *Victorian Poetry*, and the annual bibliographic listing (incomplete) in the June issue of *PMLA*. See also Elgin W. Mellown's two essays, "Gerard Manley Hopkins and His Public, 1889–1918," in *Modern Philology*, LVII (1959), 94–99; and the follow-up, "The Reception of Gerard Manley Hopkins' Poems, 1918–30," in *Modern Philology*, LXIII (1965), 38–51, which deals with the first and second editions; and Derek Stanford's "Christian Humanist: Recent Works on Hopkins" in *The Month*, n.s. XXIV (1960), 158–164.

✣ Index

A Commentary on the Complete Poems of
Gerard Manley Hopkins

Designed by R. E. Rosenbaum.
Composed by Kingsport Press, Inc.,
in 11 point linotype Baskerville, 2 points leaded,
with display lines in monotype Baskerville.
Printed from type by Kingsport Press, Inc.,
on Warren's 1854 Text, 60 pound basis,
with the Cornell University Press watermark.
Bound by Kingsport Press, Inc.,
in Holliston Roxite B Linen Finish
and stamped in black foil.